To VE-Day Through German Eyes

To VE-Day Through German Eyes

The Final Defeat of Nazi Germany

Jonathan Trigg

AMBERLEY

Half-title page: Along with local collaborators, on their surrender many hundreds of Antwerp's German garrison were temporarily held in the cages of the city's zoo. (Author's collection)

Title page: German POWs march through Aachen after their surrender. Charlemagne's former capital was the first major German city to fall into Allied hands. (Author's collection)

First published 2020
This edition published 2022

Amberley Publishing
The Hill, Stroud
Gloucestershire, GL5 4EP

www.amberley-books.com

Copyright © Jonathan Trigg, 2020, 2022

The right of Jonathan Trigg to be identified as the Author
of this work has been asserted in accordance with the
Copyrights, Designs and Patents Act 1988.

All rights reserved. No part of this book may be reprinted
or reproduced or utilised in any form or by any electronic,
mechanical or other means, now known or hereafter invented,
including photocopying and recording, or in any information
storage or retrieval system, without the permission in writing
from the Publishers.

British Library Cataloguing in Publication Data.
A catalogue record for this book is available from the British Library.

ISBN 978 1 3981 1236 0 (paperback)
ISBN 978 1 4456 9945 5 (ebook)

1 2 3 4 5 6 7 8 9 10

Typeset in 10.5pt on 13pt Sabon.
Typesetting by Aura Technology and Software Services, India.
Printed in the UK.

Contents

About the Author

Having passed out from the Royal Military Academy Sandhurst, Jonathan Trigg served as an infantry officer in the Royal Anglian Regiment, completing tours in Northern Ireland and Bosnia, as well as in the Gulf. After working in the City, he now has his own business training the long-term unemployed to get them into work. His books have been translated into Norwegian, Swedish, Finnish, Danish, Polish, French, Czech and Dutch editions. His title *Death on the Don: The Destruction of Germany's Allies on the Eastern Front* was nominated for the 2014 Pushkin Prize for History. He is the author of the best-selling *D-Day Through German Eyes*.

Dedication

New Year's Day 1945 in England was grim: cold, grey, rationing, the war, but human beings have an extraordinary way of dealing with such situations that sometimes involves new life. On that day in the solid working-class village of Dursley, Gloucestershire, Robert Keith Trigg made his first appearance. Skinny, small, the fourth of five children born to Kath, who worked in the local Listers factory, and Jack, who made Spitfire wings in nearby Filton. He was destined to attend the local school, get a job in the local factory, meet a local girl, and live out his life close to the house he was born in. Instead he chose a different path – hard work, determination and sheer bloody-mindedness took him to the top of his profession, saw him travel the world, meet a girl from hundreds of miles away, and raise a brood of unruly boys. He's a restless soul, forever looking for something to do, and then determined to do whatever that something is, and do it well. Sometimes impatient – always caring – he has taught me how to be a man, a husband and a father, and wherever I walk in life I know he walks beside me – a strong hand on my shoulder, sometimes pushing, forever guiding – so thank you Dad, for everything, and a happy seventy-fifth birthday; this book is for you.

Acknowledgements

This book has been written to coincide with the 75th anniversary of VE-Day and the end of the costliest war in Europe's long history of costly wars. It follows on from the first book in the *Through German Eyes* series, *D-Day Through German Eyes – How the Wehrmacht Lost France*, published last year as part of the 75th D-Day commemorations. This second volume picks up from the Allied victory at Falaise and the resultant headlong German retreat, and covers the last period of the war where Nazi Germany, caught in a vice between the forces of the western Allies and the Soviets, was finally defeated in a maelstrom of violence that left the Continent traumatised. Hardly an acre of land or a single home in Europe was left untouched by the war, with hundreds of millions of people suffering extraordinary hardship and grief; none more so than in the Balkans and the east – what the historian Tim Snyder calls the 'bloodlands' – where the conflict was fought out with a brutality that even today defies comprehension. Having said that, this book seeks not to try and cover what is an almost limitless subject, but focuses largely on what was the Western Front, where the Anglo-Americans and their allies from Canada, France, Poland and various other nations, fought it out against Hitler and the Wehrmacht. This is not to demean in any way the importance of the Eastern Front and the indelible contribution of the Soviet Union to the defeat of Hitler and the Nazis, rather it is a choice of what story to focus on – and it's a choice I've made.

Many of the same Caesars who faced each other in Normandy in the summer of 1944 would continue their struggle to the very end; the likes of von Rundstedt, Dietrich and Model on the German side, and Eisenhower, Montgomery, Bradley and Patton on the other, but as with the previous volume, this book is emphatically *not* about them – though they figure prominently – but about the view from the foxhole and the soldier sitting in it, often up to his knees in mud and water as he froze and suffered through what seemed interminable months before it was all finally over. It is those men (and sometimes women) whose stories inspired this book, and their words fill its pages. Unfortunately, many have passed away before this book could be published, but to one and all I say thank you.

A thank you as well to Jimmy McLeod for sharing his picture collection, and to my amazing wife Rachel and our wonderful children; Maddy and Jack.

A Note on Nomenclature

During the war, most Germans used the term 'Russians' to cover everyone in the now-extinct Soviet Union's Red Army, despite the multitude of nationalities and ethnic groups within it, and for ease, I've left it like that. On place names many of these have changed since the war; most notably in the former Soviet Union and regions that have since changed in 'national ownership', for example, those parts of what was the Third Reich that are now Poland. I have given the place name at the time and then in brackets afterwards given the modern name; e.g. Breslau (modern day Wrocław in Poland). On country names I have given them as they are now, so Belarus and not Byelorussia. I have tended to use the German nomenclature for their own military units e.g. the 88th Infantry Division is written as *88. ID*, short for *88. Infanterie-Division*, and for German ranks, Captain is *Hauptmann* etc. The exception is where the holders are Waffen-SS, and there I've used that organisation's own designation of *SS-Hauptsturmführer* and so on. There is a table of comparative ranks in the appendix.

As ever in any such work there are bound to be errors, my apologies, but where they have been made they are all my own and I ask the readers forbearance.

Introduction

Adolf Hitler was dead. The war in Europe had finished. The old saying, 'It'll all be over by Christmas' had come true. From the Courland peninsula in Latvia, down through central Germany all the way to Vienna and the Po Valley in northern Italy, millions of dejected German soldiers were trudging into captivity, even as a greater number of former forced labourers and POWs were walking in the opposite direction as they began their footsore journeys home. The Soviet Red Army sat camped on the east bank of the mighty Vistula river, its senior commanders angered at not having won the race to Berlin, but its rank and file still happily toasting victory with vats of vodka, while already expelling German civilians at gunpoint from the lands it now occupied and claimed as its own. The discovery of Hitler's concentration camps, and the horrors of the Holocaust, were showing the world the true nature of Nazism, and the hunt was now on for the men and women who had perpetrated what would become known as 'genocide' and other 'crimes against humanity'. The cost of victory had been high, but the dash across Europe by the Western Allies from Normandy, through Belgium, over the Rhine and into the Third Reich's very heart in the autumn of 1944 had dealt the death blow to Hitler's regime. Winter had come, but not in time to save the Nazis. Stalin's decision to secure the Balkans and eastern Europe for his new communist empire had, paradoxically, saved Germany from a vengeful Soviet army, and allowed the Americans, British and Canadians to mop up the last pockets of Nazi diehards in Saxony and Silesia.

After more than five years of fighting, this new year of 1945 would surely begin with peace – except it didn't, and it wouldn't.

The utter brilliance of the D-Day invasion on 6 June had been followed by a ten-week campaign of attrition in Normandy that had burnt away the very core of the Wehrmacht in the west, so that when the collapse came, it was spectacular. A fighting army and an occupation infrastructure that had inserted itself into every facet of life on continental Europe became just so much flotsam and jetsam almost overnight. *Oberst* Fritz Fullriede – a vastly experienced officer who had served in the First World War and had just been posted to the West that autumn, saw it for himself: 'The whole west front has collapsed. The other side is marching about at will … the enemy is already in Belgium and on the German frontier. Romania, Bulgaria, Slovakia and Finland are pleading for peace. It is exactly like 1918.'

The comparison was a pretty good one. Back then, the month of August had heralded a crushing defeat for the Imperial German Army in France at Amiens – just as it had twenty-six years later at Falaise – and warlord Erich Ludendorff had christened the 8th day of that month in the first war 'the black day of the German Army'. He was right, and less than four months later it was all over; Germany had capitulated. Could the same have been true second time round in 1944? Ludendorff's 'black day' had seen fifty thousand German soldiers surrender, about the same number as were captured in the Falaise Pocket, and on both occasions, as the Germans retreated so the Allies advanced. Only now – in 1944 – the Western Allies weren't limited to the speed of a marching man or a horse-drawn gun, their armies were the most mechanized forces the world had ever seen. The replacement of the hoof and boot by the wheel and internal combustion engine made for an advance that could cover in an hour what had previously taken a day in the last war and could – should – have meant the end of the war before Christmas 1944. After all, back in 1918, the German August defeat at Amiens was followed by peace in November.

The fact that the conflict dragged on through the winter of 1944, then spring and almost into summer of the following year, was the culmination of a whole series of decisions taken by both sides – many of which turned out to be mistakes; some fairly minor, others monumentally huge, and all tragic. Tragic, because they condemned untold thousands to a misery that could have been avoided.

As it was, in the summer of 1944 the Wehrmacht suffered two of the greatest defeats ever inflicted in the history of arms; in Normandy in the West, and in Belarus in the East. Two entire German army groups more or less ceased to exist – losses roughly equivalent to all the armed forces of the western Allies on the Continent at the time. It wasn't just men either, it was the equipment they needed to fight – panzers, assault guns, artillery, mortars, transport, ammunition, fuel, supplies – all gone, along with vast swathes of territory that meant the Wehrmacht would very soon be defending its own borders. No other military force in the world – save perhaps the Red Army – could have sustained those calamities and survived, but the Wehrmacht did, and not only survived but fought on for the best part of another year. How? How was this possible for an army that was described at the time by the best-informed intelligence service in the world as '...no longer a cohesive force, but a number of fugitive battle groups, disorganized and even demoralised, short of equipment and arms'.[1]

That same intelligence service confidently predicted that 'the enemy in the West has had it' and that 'two and a half months of bitter fighting have brought the end of the war in Europe within sight, almost within reach.' Major-General John Kennedy, the Assistant Chief of the British Imperial General Staff, wrote in September, 'If we go at the same pace as of late, we should be in Berlin by the 28th.'

Hubris? Well, not according to Bernard Montgomery's original plan for the invasion, which predicted that the Allies would only reach the Seine River on D+90, when in fact they reached it on D+81. Eisenhower's combative, red-haired Chief of Staff, Walter 'Beetle' Smith, was confident enough to publicly announce: 'militarily the war is won.' The facts backed Smith up; almost an entire year's production of panzers and guns lay smashed or abandoned across France, the Luftwaffe had been shot out of the sky, and four German armies were little more than remnants, scurrying east as fast as they could drive or run, as the Allies liberated France behind them. Belgium was reached and its capital freed, the weather was still fine, and there was at least two months left of the summer campaigning season. Hitler, still recovering from the July Bomb plot, and plagued by headaches and stomach cramps, collapsed in exhaustion, and had to undergo surgery to remove a polyp from his vocal cords. For the best part of three weeks the dictator was confined to his bed, leaving the country's leadership in limbo.

At this point of maximum opportunity, the Allies dropped the ball, and the Germans picked it up.

The fumble began at the very top of Allied high command. Dwight D. Eisenhower, whose genius lay in commanding a multi-national coalition and not in military strategy, decided to ignore the Clausewitzian maxim of concentration of force and, to paraphrase Frederick the Great, 'decided to attack everything, and ended up attacking nothing'. Not that Eisenhower was solely culpable. Bernard Montgomery – Great Britain's best field commander of the war, but also a distinctly vinegary personality – chose this exact moment to make a series of military blunders. With the Allied army's logistical needs at their zenith, his surprise capture of Antwerp and its priceless port was a godsend, but one he squandered by his blasé refusal to prioritise the capture of the estuary that ran from the sea to the quaysides. With German guns and mines blocking the way, it would be an unbelievable eighty-five days before the first supplies were unloaded on Antwerp's wharves. In the meantime, Monty found himself with a whole airborne army, as one historian memorably described, 'burning a hole in his pocket.' So was born *Operation Market Garden* and the disaster at Arnhem.

The timing couldn't have been worse, given that this was the moment when the Anglo-Canadians began to run out of men, and the Americans began to run out of patience with their old-world comrades.

In the East, the Red Army's headlong charge across Belarus and Poland came to a halt at the Vistula River. Stalin had no coalition to worry about, only a ruthless strategy to begin shaping the post-war world to the advantage of Soviet Russia. That meant holding the line in Poland, while securing the Balkans and eastern Europe for Moscow and its murderous brand of communism.

The Nazi empire now had its most defensible borders since D-Day, based on two mighty rivers; the Vistula in the east, and the Rhine in the west. Crossing these barriers was definitely not beyond the capabilities of the Soviets and Anglo-Americans respectively, but neither was it a simple task. With the Allies stalled in the west from lack of logistics, and the Red Army focused elsewhere, Berlin could seize the moment. The Wehrmacht now had what it needed most that autumn – time. With the sort of urgency that, frankly, had eluded the Third Reich for almost its entire existence, Germany's military-industrial muscle finally got itself into gear. Under Albert Speer's guidance, Germany's factories, mines and workshops churned out more of pretty much everything than ever before – and quality wasn't sacrificed for quantity – in fact, German industry was now manufacturing some of the most advanced weapons of the age; jet and rocket fighters such as the Messerschmitt Me 262 and 163 Komets, megalith panzers such as the Tiger II (more commonly known as the *Königstiger*), the *StG 44* – the world's first true assault rifle, and even a new generation of U-boats that were almost undetectable by Allied aircraft. The men who would use this equipment were the last reserves of manpower the country could furnish, the majority of them formed into a new type of unit, the *volks-grenadier* division (*VGD*), smaller than all the formations that had preceded it, but bristling with more modern, automatic weaponry than ever before. Most of the *VGD*s would be sent west to fight an Allied army in a state of flux, as it shifted from being a force more or less balanced between Britain and the United States to one where America very much held the whip hand.

That shift caused it to lose focus as it slogged away fighting a series of battles along Germany's western border that were as bloody as they were pointless. Those battles ate up men and resources, but most importantly they ate up time, so when Aachen, Metz and especially the Hürtgen forest were all finally in Allied hands it was too late to end the war in 1944.

Providence then took a hand, and as so often before came to the aid of the Allies in the figure of Adolf Hitler. Having carefully husbanded a strategic reserve worthy of the name, he proceeded to throw it at objectives he could never reach and were pointless to attain; in the West at Antwerp, and in the East at Budapest. By his actions Hitler denuded the Eastern Front of any hope it had of holding Moscow's main offensive in the north, and all too predictably the Soviets took full advantage. Their January assault took them from the Vistula to the banks of the Oder River – just forty-five miles from the heart of Berlin. It was true that by this time Nazi Germany had lost the war, and even if Hitler hadn't sent his armies into the Ardennes and the Hungarian plain, that verdict would not change – but equally, a mass of fifty-plus divisions that included the bulk of the *panzerwaffe* (the Wehrmacht's panzer arm), crashing into the Red Army on the Polish prairie, could have done untold damage – another Kiev, another Cannae? A Soviet Union forced onto the defensive could have then been forced to sit and watch as the western Allies leapt the Rhine and took Berlin as their prize.

In reality, it was the western powers that ended up sitting and watching.

Finally, in late March, the Americans and British crossed into the heart of Germany, encircled the Ruhr and the Wehrmacht's last field army of any note, and then headed northeast to the capital – only they didn't, not really. In yet another almost inexplicable blunder, Eisenhower decided to allow the Soviets to take Berlin, while swallowing the chimera of a last-ditch Nazi stronghold in the south – the so-called 'Alpine Redoubt'. By now, organised German resistance had more or less collapsed, and the western and eastern allies met each other in a flurry of greetings and celebrations, only to soon discover they neither trusted nor liked each other overly much.

As the fighting began to die away, the flow of refugees clogged the roads, railways and sea-lanes, and mushroomed into the greatest shifts in population that Europe had ever experienced – shifts that today would be called 'ethnic cleansing'. This was suffering on a truly monumental scale, even as crowds gathered in London, Washington and Paris to celebrate the day that so many thought might never come: Victory in Europe day – VE-Day.

There were no such celebrations in Germany. The country's armed forces had lost a world war, for the second time in less than thirty years; this book is the story of that failure, told by the losers.

1

Summer 1944: The German Defeat

'I saw the SS destroy a village in Russia ... just because the partisans had shot a German soldier. The village wasn't to blame in any way, but they burned down the village, root and branch, and shot the women and children.'[1]

This was Russia in 1944.

'...our soldiers simply entered a village and if there was anything they didn't like, they just shot a few people, just like that.'[2]

This was Italy in 1944.

'*Oberjäger* Müller was a sniper from Berlin, he shot women who went to greet the English soldiers with bunches of flowers...'
    'Did you shoot women too?'
    'Only from a distance. They didn't know where the shots came from.'[3]

And this was northern France in 1944, as the Wehrmacht retreated in chaos after the disaster at Falaise.

Back in the UK, British intelligence had set up illicit recording devices in a number of prisoner-of-war detention facilities – most notably Trent Park in north London – and occasionally used *agents provocateurs* to encourage inmates to indiscretion. It worked.

What the intelligence service really wanted was military secrets, such as confirmation of the existence of German V-1 and V-2 rocket development, provided when *General der Panzertruppe* Wilhelm von Thoma discussed with another general the details of his visit to Kummersdorf[4] earlier in the war, and a plethora of information on the capabilities of German aircraft from downed Luftwaffe pilots.

But these nuggets were hidden away among hours and hours of innocuous conversations between, oftentimes, young men bored by inaction and the tedium of imprisonment. Useless as most of these revelations were, they included snippets of horror such as when *Jäger* Einziel recounted his and *Oberjäger* Müller's cold-blooded murder of women in the act of celebrating their liberation. What lay behind this almost casual savagery was usually two things; firstly, disgust at civilians the perpetrators felt were now somehow *betraying* their recent occupiers, and secondly, anger at the fate of their own vaunted armed forces – the once-almighty, and now humbled, Wehrmacht. What Einziel and Müller were seeing around them was nothing less than the wholesale disintegration of the military structure upon which their whole lives had been built. As the Paris-based German businessman, Hermann Voss, recalled on witnessing the German retreat in France at first-hand: 'The decay was absolute. The retreat of the German armies had turned into a rout ... columns of cars, transports of wounded, panzers, guns and civilians blocked up every road.'[5] His view was echoed by a fellow-countryman who was himself part of that rout: 'I cannot convey what the scene is like, this isn't a retreat, but a flight ... the cars are laden with schnapps, cigarettes, and hundreds of tins and fats and meat.' This was more than a bitter pill to swallow – this was toxic – and the reaction of many like Einziel and Müller was to lash out at the defenceless.

Not that the two *jägers* should have been surprised at the unfolding disaster. The German defeat in Normandy had literally torn the heart out of the *Westheer* (the German army in the West). Exact casualty figures are disputed, but it's generally accepted that the Wehrmacht lost around half a million men in the battle for France, along with fifteen hundred panzers, 3,500 guns and an additional twenty thousand non-armoured vehicles of all types. Before D-Day, Germany was losing an average of 417 panzers per month – after D-Day that figure shot up to 655 for the next six consecutive months. The formations left in the west were mere shadows, as twenty-year-old Wolfgang Dombrowski acknowledged of his own élite 9. *SS-Panzerdivision 'Hohenstaufen'*: 'The division was virtually burnt-out in the Normandy fighting'[6] Armoured divisions, like Dombrowski's own, could only field an average ten panzers each (instead of the almost two hundred on their official establishment), while the mass of infantry divisions were lucky to be at one-quarter strength; in fact so bad was the position of the infantry that eight divisions were officially classified as 'remnants' and a further eight were dissolved, with their survivors shared out amongst the rest.

France wasn't just a disaster for the Army either. The men in Luftwaffe sky blue had earned themselves an undeserved reputation for abandoning the French skies to their Allied foes, when the truth was that they had bled to death fighting an unequal battle. The German air force lost over fourteen hundred aircraft and hundreds of pilots in France, including swathes of irreplaceable aces from the Eastern Front (the so-called *Experten*), as attested by the fifty-two kill *jagdflieger* (fighter pilot) Heinz Knoke when ordered to carry out another mission with his remaining five worn-out aircraft:

> The order is worse than insanity; it is nothing less than murder!... The other squadrons aren't able to leave the ground because their fields are being strafed by enemy jabos [German slang for Allied fighter-bombers] ... Döring [Knoke's wingman] tries to climb too soon and stalls. His left wing drops and he plunges to crash into the trees – he is killed instantly... We encounter more than sixty Thunderbolts and Mustangs – there can be no escape, it's the end. The battle doesn't last more than a few minutes. Unteroffizier Wagner is the first to be shot down; he doesn't escape from his burning aircraft. Then I see another aircraft on fire, and Feldwebel Freigang bales out. His wingman goes down in flames a few moments later. That only leaves myself and my wingman, Feldwebel Ickes ... bullets slam into my aircraft like hailstones.

Bailing out after shooting down a Mustang, Knoke watched the Americans 'continue to thunder, circle and mill around like mad, it's a few minutes before it dawns on them that not a single Messerschmitt is left in the sky... During six missions ... the squadron lost twelve aircraft – we're finished.'[7]

The Kriegsmarine fared little better. Relegated to a tertiary role during the campaign, Germany's sailors had done their best with what little they had. The majority of the few surface ships they possessed in France had been sent to the bottom of the sea, and their U-boats were increasingly under threat from superior Allied might and technology, forcing Nazi Germany's submariners to extremes of underwater endurance, as laid out plainly in the log of *U-480*:

> ...12 Sept 1944. 0511hrs. 300 miles west of Ireland, surfaced for the first time in 40 days. The boat stinks. Everything is covered in phosphorescent particles... The shields of the twin anti-aircraft guns can't be opened; the hinges appear to have rusted up...
> ...1710hrs. ...the whole flak armament is now unserviceable, the gun shields have been torn away from their mountings and are fouling the guns ... everything ... is corroded and covered with growth...[8]

Again and again the U-boats slipped their moorings and stole out into the Bay of Biscay or the English Channel, only to be hunted down and sunk by Allied aircraft or warships; by the end of September the average life expectancy of a U-boat commander was just two patrols. They were still deadly though. Hartmut von Matuschka's *U-482* sank four merchant vessels and the British corvette HMS *Hurst Castle* in the first week of September before safely returning to base. Those same French bases were now almost all German islands in an Allied sea, and the order was given to abandon them and sail for the relative security of Norway. In all, some eighteen U-boats left their Biscay bases and went north, the last being *U-267*, which left St Nazaire on 23 September. Only Rupprecht Fischler's *U-445* was lost in the operation, sunk by HMS *Louis* with all hands. As it turned out, the safety of northern waters proved illusory, as the Royal Air Force began a series of bombing raids on the new U-boat lairs, with *U-228* and *U-993* destroyed in Bergen harbour on 4 October – just two of the 242 U-boats the Kriegsmarine would lose in 1944.[9] By that date the German U-boat arm was in crisis, with only thirty-six boats in total at sea in the north Atlantic, and twenty-eight of those heading back home after completing their patrols.

Incredibly, even as the Allies were driving hell for leather for the German border, some in the Nazis senior leadership still believed that France was a diversion, and that an Anglo-American invasion of Scandinavia was a realistic prospect; and this included some at the headquarters of U-boats West, who made the following entry in their War Diary on 1 October:

...by withdrawing six Schnorchel [the Schnorchel was a German innovation allowing U-boats to remain submerged while still drawing air from above] boats for the Atlantic we are taking a risk, because in the event of an attack on Norway or Jutland [Denmark] it will not be possible to replace them quickly. However, as it is now late in the year for a large-scale landing, the risk must be taken.

Back in the path of the Allied advance, all was chaos. *Leutnant* Richard von Rosen – last seen in Cagny in Normandy, helping to blunt the British *Goodwood* offensive with his Tigers – found himself and his unit caught up in the flight:

High Command had ordered the Abteilung [roughly equivalent to a battalion] to Liège in Belgium, but it had no fuel... I discovered the whereabouts of a petrol dump, I drove there and with much cunning and deception got a chit for five cubic metres... One could sense everywhere the eleventh-hour mood: apparently the enemy wasn't far off.

The requisitioned gasoline only got Rosen and his surviving panzers so far, until they again found themselves with empty tanks. His luck held, and he managed to get his hands on a railway wagon of fuel barrels, only for other hands to try and pilfer his good fortune: 'From all sides vehicles now appeared like moths to the flame to bag some fuel. At first I patrolled around the wagon, believing that my mere presence would keep all undesired visitors away – not so! From now on I sat on my barrels, pistol in hand.' Mobile again, Rosen's unit drove to Maastricht, where they gorged on food and drink from a soon-to-be-blown-up depot, before finally crossing into Germany: 'It was a strange feeling to be back in Germany ... and not wonderful.'[10] Strange indeed. Many saw the rout as something almost medieval, with the fleeing Germans weighed down by the baggage and loot of years of occupation, and accompanied by a horde of camp-followers, as remarked on with distaste by a resident of the Dutch industrial city of Eindhoven: 'Many vehicles had young women sitting in them – the sort that usually fraternised with Germans.'[11] One *landser* (the nickname for Germany's ordinary soldiers, equivalent to the British Tommy), Walter Görlitz, was of the same opinion: 'Naval troops marched northward without weapons, selling their spare uniforms... They told people the war was over and they were going home. Lorries loaded with officers, their mistresses and large quantities of champagne and brandy, contrived to get back as far as the Rhineland.' Heinz Knoke saw it at first hand as he and his squadron retreated towards the Reich:

I am deeply shocked ... by what I've seen with my own eyes during the last two days on the French highways... I am sick with disgust at watching our occupation forces pack up without any thought of resistance ... personal safety seems to be all that matters to them ... the retreat has degenerated into a cowardly, panicky rout ... all conception of military duty is forgotten; baggage clutters up the roads, vehicles are loaded with crates full of food, drink and loot, often their French girlfriends travel with them to share in the spoils.[12]

Thousands of collaborators and their families also went east, by whatever means they could find, to try and escape the retribution they dreaded. One Dutchman saw his local train station filled with these poor wretches: 'The station waiting room looked like a junk store with tramps. Crying faces and hanging heads.' One such 'crying face' was Julien Hertenweg, a fifteen-year-old from Genk in Flanders, and one of nine children in the Hertenweg family:

When the Allies came closer in September 1944 and Belgium threatened to be 'liberated', we fled to Lüneburgerheide in Germany. The resistance and gangs of thieves had become more active in Limburg during the last months of the war and had already killed many innocent relatives of collaborators... As defeat came closer, more and more opportunists joined the resistance.

Hertenweg's brother-in-law, Frans Boven, had been killed in Russia fighting in the Waffen-SS, and two brothers would also serve in the armed SS, while one of his sisters had worked in a Junkers aircraft factory in Germany since 1943. The whole family now found itself 'living in the summer residence of Oberstabs-Ingenieur (senior staff engineer), Helmut Schelp ... my mother and sisters helped in the household of the estate and my father worked in the forge.' Hertenweg saw nothing wrong in his family's relationship with his country's occupiers:

> Nobody thought the Germans would lose the war, so life just went on as normal; children went to school, people went to work, and medical care became free – life was good. We all admired Germany; how well they organized everything, how they always behaved very correctly towards us.[13]

He was far from alone. Over forty thousand Belgians served in the Wehrmacht or Waffen-SS during the war (the majority were Flemish, but thousands of French-speaking Walloons also volunteered), and no fewer than fifty thousand Dutchmen did the same. The number who supported the Germans but didn't go as far as wearing their uniform, was much, much higher. One Dutchman who *did* wear a German uniform was Jan Munk: 'I joined the Waffen-SS in 1942. I wasn't a member of the NSB (the Dutch pro-Nazi party the Nationaal-Socialistische Beweging), but was always arguing in school about the Germans, so one day my schoolmates said to me 'if you like them so much why don't you join them?' so I did.' Munk fought in Russia with the *5. SS-Panzerdivision 'Wiking'*, was badly wounded, and after recovering was on leave at home in Leiden in September 1944.

> At the end of my leave I prepared to return to my unit. My mother packed me some sandwiches, and to my great surprise my brother Gerrit – who was very anti-Nazi – volunteered to give me a lift to where I could hitch a lift with a German column... After the war Gerrit told me he had been a member of the resistance and had given me that lift to make sure I wasn't knifed in the back on the way to the road![14]

The majority of the population of the Low Countries were of the same mind as Gerrit, and not Jan, and were glad to be free of the hated *Moffen* (a Dutch derogatory term for Germans, like the French *Boche* or British *Kraut*), and it all came to a head on *Dolle Dinsdag* – 'Mad Tuesday' – 5 September 1944. Hearing radio broadcasts announcing their imminent liberation, the Dutch population were delirious, thronging the streets, hanging Dutch orange national flags everywhere, and mercilessly mocking the bedraggled *Moffen*. The gun had definitely been jumped though – much of the Netherlands would stay in German hands right up to the end of the war.

That was not the case for Belgium, which was mostly liberated in a few days by the charging Anglo-Canadians. Indeed, the War Diary of the Irish Guards Armoured Regiment for 2 September read thus: 'It was our longest drive, 82 miles in 13 hours.' That same evening, their Corps Commander – the capable, white-haired, Brian Horrocks – gathered his officers in Douai in northern France just sixteen miles from the Belgian border, and briefed them that their objective for the following day was none other than the city of Brussels – almost ninety miles away. The next morning, the armoured cars, Sherman tanks and Bren-gun carriers of the Guards Armoured Division coughed into noisy life and swept into Belgium, where some unwelcome resistance delayed their entry into Brussels until the morning of 4 September. Led by their commanding officer, Allan Adair in his Cromwell tank, the Guards were mobbed by huge crowds of cheering civilians seemingly intent on drowning their liberators in a sea of flowers, kisses and wine. No wonder that Carol Mather – a British officer serving in Monty's headquarters – said: 'We really did believe that if things went according to plan the war could be over by Christmas.'[15] Mather's German opponents felt much the same, with even the diehard Nazi, Kurt '*Panzermeyer*', commander of the *12. SS-Panzerdivision 'Hitlerjugend'* (the *HJ*), believing:

> In truth the Ruhr lay undefended in front of the Allied spearheads and nothing could prevent Montgomery from occupying Germany's weapons forge. One powerful drive by ten to fifteen Allied divisions into the northwest would break the backbone of German resistance and end the war in weeks.[16]

Meyer knew what he was talking about. His division had fought itself close to death in Normandy, and its survivors were now desperately trying to hold a defensive line on the Meuse River. Even this proved pointless though, as one of the *HJ*'s neighbouring units upped sticks and retreated further east without warning, leaving Meyer's flank open and unprotected. The division had little choice but to follow in its neighbour's wake.

The fall of Brussels sent a shock wave through German high command in Berlin that was swiftly eclipsed by the news received a few hours later that the city of Antwerp had fallen to the British 11th Armoured Division. Worse still for the Germans, Belgian *résistants* had managed to secure Antwerp's giant harbour and its dock facilities before they could be destroyed by Wehrmacht demolition teams. Europe's second largest cargo port was still operational, and in Allied hands. With the one thousand acres of wharves, dozens of loading cranes and warehouses secure, the now-free Belgians set about rounding up any Germans left in the city, as well as those locals deemed to have collaborated with them. First to go into the bag was the city's commander, the magnificently named *Generalmajor* Graf Christoph zu Stolberg-Stolberg. He was closely followed by almost six thousand of his original fifteen-thousand-strong garrison, the rest having fled the city as fast as they could. With so many prisoners to accommodate, the municipal zoo was pressed into service as a detention facility, with one large cage used to house captured German soldiers, another for collaborators, and a third for the collaborators' families – last but not least, young women suspected of sleeping with their occupiers were put in a separate pen, prior to the ritual humiliation of having their heads shaved in front of the crowds.

With Brussels and Antwerp freed, one German officer noted in horror, 'The British advance ... had, in effect, encircled General von Zangen's *15. Armee.*' The once-mighty *15. Armee* was now well and truly stranded on the southern side of the Scheldt estuary and seemingly doomed to capture or annihilation, in what would become known to the Allies as the Breskens Pocket. The rest of the *Westheer* in the Low Countries – the remnants of *7. Armee* and *5. Panzerarmee* – were just so much military flotsam, scrabbling to keep ahead of the Allied spearheads. There was nothing else; no defensive line, no strategic reserves, no mass of reinforcements on the way. The gate into the very heart of the Third Reich was open and barely defended. Final defeat was staring the Wehrmacht in the face, as the *Hohenstaufen's* Wolfgang Dombrowski understood only too well: 'When we arrived in Holland the situation was desperate.' One last effort by the Allies would finish the *Westheer* and end the war, as the *landser* Fritz Jeltsch admitted: 'We were finished, there was no hope.'

There would be no help either from the *Ostheer* (the German army on the Eastern Front) for Dombrowski and his comrades. On the third anniversary of Hitler's invasion of the Soviet Union back in June 1941, Moscow had launched *Operation Bagration*, an offensive still little known in the West even today, but undoubtedly one of the most significant campaigns of the war. Everything about *Bagration* was gigantic in scale; over two million Red Army soldiers faced off against fewer than half that number of Germans, their five thousand-plus tanks and assault-guns outnumbered the panzers by more than five to one, and they were supported by over thirty thousand guns and mortars and six thousand aircraft.[17] Even the battlefield itself was huge, as the fighting raged over an area four times the size of East Prussia. Aimed at *Generalfeldmarschall* Ernst Busch's *Heeresgruppe Mitte* (Army Group Centre), the Soviets threw the 166 divisions of four entire Red Army Fronts against the Germans. Largely immobile due to a lack of vehicles and fuel – and ordered by Busch and Hitler to stand their ground regardless – the fate of the *landsers* was sealed. In just five days the frontline was broken in six different places; Minsk fell, and with it all of Belarus. Busch was sacked, but it made no difference. In a calamity even greater than Stalingrad, *Heeresgruppe Mitte* was immolated, losing a truly staggering third of a million men. By August, even as the Western Allies were racing to try and close the Falaise Pocket, the Red Army had advanced some three hundred miles and were within spitting distance of Warsaw and the German province of East Prussia. Werner Block was a panzer driver in the *Ostheer*:

> I was just seventeen when I enlisted – I volunteered for the Waffen-SS, they were the élite you know. My father objected, and as I was so young I needed his permission to join-up, so I said 'Papa, I don't want to join the infantry, I want to join the Waffen-SS and I want to join the panzers'. So, he said yes.

After his training, Block was sent east, where the reality of war soon became apparent:

> I hadn't been in Russia long when we were driving across the steppe – I had my hatch open and my commander was sitting on the deck behind me. Anyway, I couldn't hear much because of the noise of the engine, but then I could feel something dripping on my head, down the side of my neck you know, and it kept on dripping, anyway I tried to wipe it with my hand and it was blood. My commander had been shot and was sitting on the deck bleeding.

By the summer of 1944 Block was a veteran, and he experienced the *Ostheer*'s retreat at first-hand:

> I had my hatch open – I shouldn't have, but it was so hot, the inside of the panzer was like a furnace – anyway, a shell landed close to us, very, very, close, and then my commander's head literally landed on my lap as I was sitting there. It had just been blown clean off – his eyes were still open and looking at me, straight at me - it was horrible, just horrible … but the worst thing was the smell of roasting flesh, and to hear the sounds of men burning to death in their panzers.[18]

So it was for the *Ostheer,* even as the *Westheer* was losing Brussels and Antwerp, *SS-Obersturmführer* Metzger and his men were fighting for their lives in eastern Poland:

> The Kompanie was positioned with three assault-guns one kilometre west of the cemetery at Dzierzenin … a large-scale attack by the enemy

... was finally defeated through massed fires at 1100hrs... I continued to block the north ... and at 1700hrs defeated another strong enemy attack in front of my position. In the process one assault-gun suffered bad track and final drive damage ... we attempted to turn back a new enemy attack at 1745hrs. The enemy – who was vastly superior, gained ground and was soon directly along my left flank. While engaging enemy infantry I caught sight of two T-34s [Soviet tanks] two hundred metres off my right flank ... both were knocked out in twenty seconds with two rounds. The entire attack stopped ... and portions of the attacking forces streamed to the rear.[19]

General der Panzertruppe, Nikolaus von Vormann, was the commander of *9. Armee,* desperately trying to hold some sort of line: 'The enemy's attack has completely broken through 73. Infanterie-Division's front ... during the past several weeks of combat 9.*Armee* has become so decimated that at this point it is only equivalent to a very mediocre fighting force.' The Swedish SS war correspondent, Gösta Borg, reported from the frontline:

The roads on the enemy's side are filled with convoys, every wooded area is bristling with tanks, infantry and heavy formations ... new artillery units bombard road crossings, battery positions and command posts; one battalion reports that a rye field is filled to bursting with stalking enemy infantry ... a car burns – black clumps, the stink of burning flesh, blood, rags, sun, dust, and flies. The first wounded; bloody bandages, open combat-jackets, day-old beard stubble, eyes strangely open... Men, many boys, dig for their lives, aim, load, shoot, scream or crawl away; many of them die before they hit the ground.

Finally, a combination of overlong supply lines and stiffening German resistance halted the Soviets on the banks of the river Vistula. The check to the Red Army's advance gave the *Ostheer* a breathing space but couldn't hide the truth that *Bagration* was probably Nazi Germany's worst defeat of the war.

For the *Westheer,* it meant there would be no help from the East. So, could men instead be stripped from the southern front in Italy – after all there were still some twenty-eight divisions there fighting the Anglo-Americans. Those same Allied troops had first landed on the Italian soil of Sicily back on 9 July 1943, and ever since then had been involved in a campaign of bloody attrition where the weather and the very land itself seemed to be against them. Forced to fight for literally every foot, they ground their way up the peninsula from south to north. Their progress could best be described by the old joke, where a city dweller asks for directions from a farmer leaning on a fence, who replies: 'Well, if I was going there, I wouldn't be starting from here.' The reality is that it is far easier to conquer Italy (or in the Allied case liberate it) from north to south, but as it stood in September 1944 the Wehrmacht's forces in the peninsula were under-strength and worn down, as *SS-Hauptsturmführer* Willfried Segebrecht of the *16. SS-Panzergrenadier-Division 'Reichsführer SS'* knew all too well: 'Until then we'd seen Italy as a land of peaches and sunshine, but now it was different. We couldn't see into the distance, the mountains were somehow oppressive … there were terrible wounds.' In the fighting just south of San Marcello Pistoiese in Tuscany, northwest of Florence, Segebrecht saw one of his most trusted NCOs – *SS-Unterscharführer* Bühler - blown to bits in a shell blast: 'I couldn't believe it, and I crept back into my bunker and was not ashamed of my tears.'[20]

However, the lack of fighting men, panzers and artillery wasn't the greatest threat to the Wehrmacht's ability to fight on; either in the West, the East or the South – that threat was posed by the loss on 30 August of an obscure city of fewer than a hundred thousand people some thirty-five miles north of Bucharest in Romania, that hardly anyone in Europe had ever heard of, let alone visited; Ploieşti. Originally an unassuming centre for handicraft manufacturing, the then-town was revolutionised by the discovery of oil, and the establishment in 1856 by the Mehedinţeanu brothers of the world's first large-scale refinery. Foreign investment – particularly from Great Britain and the United States – transformed the city at the beginning of the twentieth century, and by 1939 Romanian oil was powering the Third Reich's rearmament. Almost a dozen refineries dotted the area in 1944, with the largest – the *Astra Romania* – producing 146,000 metric tonnes of gasoline per month at its peak. In broad terms, the Romanian fields poured twenty-five million tonnes of oh-so-precious oil into the Axis war machine.

Hitler – obsessed with the economics of modern warfare – was often quoted as saying that without Romanian oil and Swedish iron ore, the Wehrmacht would grind to a halt. So it was perhaps surprising that Allied planners hadn't identified oil – and Nazi Germany's lack of it – as an Achilles heel waiting to be exploited right from the beginning of hostilities. It was true that the Americans bombed Ploieşti in '42 and again in '43, but as late as the end of June 1944, oil targets were only third on the heavy bombers' priority list behind aircraft factories and rail links from Germany to Normandy. These 'oil targets' included the Third Reich's synthetic fuel production network as well, where, at great expense, almost half of all German gasoline and two-thirds of her specialist aviation fuel were produced. Nevertheless, the bombing offensive against them steadily ramped up from the end of July with devastating effect. By September barely a single synthetic fuel plant was fully operational, with monthly production down from 175,000 tons to a minuscule twelve thousand. The impact on the Luftwaffe especially was catastrophic, with the supply of high-octane aviation spirit dwindling to next to nothing. Strenuous efforts were made to conserve fuel stocks, including more or less grounding the Luftwaffe's night-fighter arm, with losses among RAF bomber crews consequently dropping from eleven per cent in June to less than two per cent three months later.

By the end of October, the Oil Campaign was top priority for the Allied bomber effort, and on 2 November the combined forces of the United States Eighth and Fifteenth Air Forces launched an all-out attack on the Nazis fuel industry. Losses were heavy, with forty bombers shot down, but the Luftwaffe had fared far worse, losing three times as many aircraft and seventy precious pilots killed or wounded. As supremo for the Third Reich's industrial production, Albert Speer recognised the gravity of the situation:

> In October–November '44 new raids were made on the oil industry, and those raids were so successful that production was almost nil. The stock of gasoline for the Army was running very short; we had no more fuel to train fighter pilots for instance, and panzers were only able to move short distances.[21]

That translated to a general order put out in the autumn of 1944 to the entire Wehrmacht, slashing the daily divisional allocation of fuel from 7,200 gallons to a niggardly 1,200 gallons.[22] To run the war effort, Berlin was now left with the tiny Nagykanizsa oilfield in Hungary,[23] and the odd well in Austria desperately squeezing out a few barrels.

Back in the Netherlands, Wolfgang Dombrowski – unaware of all the goings on in the East, but all too familiar with the might of the Anglo-Americans – didn't hold out much hope for the *Westheer*'s position: 'It seemed impossible that a front could be built out of these disparate fleeing elements... We felt that once we got over the German border it would all be over.'[24]

2

Flight Turns to Fight!

We have lost a battle, but I tell you we will win this war. Despite everything that has happened, do not allow your firm, confident faith in Germany's future to be shaken one bit. Gain the time which the Führer needs to bring into operation new troops and new weapons. They will come.

This was September 1944. The speaker wasn't a senior Nazi *apparatchik* like the head of the SS, Heinrich Himmler, or the Propaganda Minister, Joseph Goebbels, but Walter Model, Germany's top military officer in the West – the *Oberbefehlshaber West*; *OB West* for short. This text is from his Order of the Day – *Tagesbefehl* – a full two days before *Dolle Dinsdag*. Hollow bombast? Or was there something more to Model's bold statement? *Hauptmann* Barthel appeared to agree with his commander: 'It still won't be fatal for us if France falls.'[1] Even the ever-cynical Wolfgang Dombrowski seemed to be adopting more of a glass half-full attitude:

We believed the war was probably over, but you must realise that we lower ranks were only eighteen to nineteen years old, and our officers were only aged between twenty-four and twenty-nine – still all only youngsters! Life's deeper issues didn't concern us too much, so we were prepared to fight on.[2]

Barthel and Dombrowski typified a change in the *Westheer* as it left the bitter fields of France and Belgium behind it, and found itself closing up on the borders of the Reich itself; German resolve was stiffening, and it was stiffening at exactly the wrong time for the Allies.

The wrong time? Everything was going the Allies' way, surely? Well, actually it wasn't, and the problem was at the very top of the Allied military leadership, where politics, missed opportunities and downright mistakes would squander an undeniable chance to end the war by Christmas.

Senior command among the Allies on D-Day, and during the campaign in Normandy, was united and balanced, with clear roles and responsibilities for all concerned – the exact opposite of their German counterparts in fact. Dwight D. Eisenhower was the man in overall charge, acting as the coalition's unifier and the bridge between the political leaders in London and Washington and the military commanders in the field. Montgomery was the battlefield supremo, subordinate to Eisenhower, and responsible for planning and executing a strategy for the Allies to establish a secure landing and then go on to grind the *Westheer* to dust. Then came success at Falaise, and with it conflict and confusion, at the very moment when there should have been neither.

The nub of the issue was simple; what was the best and quickest way finally to defeat Nazi Germany and end the war in Europe? Montgomery – as acting Allied land force commander – was clear in his appraisal of the situation. A single, all-powerful thrust into Germany, aimed at capturing Berlin, was the answer. Resources would be ruthlessly stripped from all other fronts to maximise force at one critical point – and that would be in the north through the Netherlands, over the Rhine and into the Ruhr – Germany's industrial heart – and then on across the north German plain to the capital. Naturally, this thrust would be commanded by Montgomery himself, and spearheaded by his Anglo-Canadian 21st Army Group. This proposal was massively controversial among the Allies.

Controversial, because it seemingly ignored the changing realities in the Allied alliance, and relegated the emergent American behemoth to a subordinate role. Back on D-Day, it had been the Anglo-Canadians who had borne the weight of the landings; three-quarters of the invasion fleet, more than half the air armada, and over half of the assault troops were Anglo-Canadian. This was the high-water mark for Britain and her Empire in terms of military power in the war; from then on, that power leaked inexorably away. The Canadian government's decision that only volunteers would serve overseas – a policy that placated many French Canadians and others opposed to involvement in 'Britain's war'– inevitably starved Harry Crerar's First Canadian Army of the manpower it desperately needed. By August, Canadian divisions were undermanned, and British units were being used to prop them up. Not that Britain was in any better shape – far from it. Indeed, fighting a global war for five years had worn Britain's resources wafer thin. Being an imperial power, with possessions and interests worldwide, Britain's premier armed service had always been its oldest; the magnificent Royal Navy. It had maintained its pre-eminence over the seas ever since it had prevailed at Trafalgar by outbuilding its opponents, and by 1939 was the largest naval force on the planet comprising no fewer than 332 warships (in 2019 the Royal Navy had seventy-five commissioned vessels). Even after the heavy losses of the early war years, including the *Royal Oak*, the *Hood*, *Repulse* and *Prince of Wales*, the Navy grew to over five hundred warships by mid-1944, with manpower quadrupling from two hundred to eight hundred thousand men.[3] The Royal Air Force grew even more rapidly, with just under two hundred thousand aircrew in 1944, kept flying by an additional million men and women in its support services. But it was in Britain's Army where the greatest wartime explosion in strength occurred. Britain has always favoured an all-volunteer army, only resorting to conscription at times of maximum national emergency, such as in early 1939 when the National Service (Armed Forces) Act was rushed through Parliament to counter the growing threat of Nazi Germany. The initial stipulations of the bill created a liability to military service for all fit men between the ages of twenty and twenty-three. This age range was progressively increased as the war dragged on, until it applied to all men between eighteen and forty-one years of age, increasing the size of the Army to a peak of 2.9 million. However, this seemingly rosy picture masked the grim reality of growing shortfalls on the frontline. A British infantry division in north-western Europe in the summer of 1994 had a theoretical establishment of 18,347 men, but this was rarely achieved, particularly amongst the fighting companies at the sharp end, who totalled a little over six thousand of that number. This was the inevitable consequence of an Allied infrastructure with a ratio of combat to support troops of 1:9, and a philosophy that emphasised artillery, intelligence and logistics above the man with the bayonet – and it was the latter that was desperately needed in the late summer of '44. Even as early as D-Day itself, the British War Office estimated that the Army would have one hundred thousand men fewer by December than it had at the end of 1943. By August, as casualties mounted, that grim prediction was fast coming true, with just 2,654 fully trained, combat-ready infantrymen left in the country awaiting deployment to the Continent. To try and fill the gaps a series of measures were introduced; at first these were relatively minor, such as the amalgamation of different battalions within the same regiment – for example the merger of the 2nd and 6th Battalions of the Royal Inniskilling Fusiliers. Then troops were stripped from subsidiary fronts; most British infantry battalions in Italy were reduced from four to three rifle companies, with the surplus men sent to France. Next, formations had some of their subordinate units reduced to cadres; like the 168th Brigade of the 56th (London) Infantry Division – again, the men released went to fill the gaps in France. At the same time, thirty-five thousand men from the Royal Artillery and the RAF Regiment (the RAF's ground security arm) were compulsorily retrained as infantrymen and sent up the line, along with thousands of comb-outs from support and service units. Needless to say, these measures were hugely unpopular among the vast majority of men concerned, who knew just how dangerous the frontline really was. Many of their new comrades weren't too happy about the process either, with one British infantry company commander complaining about the replacements: 'Many men are weak in weapon-handling, I know several who didn't even know that a grenade had to be primed. Some NCOs can't map read, even on roads.'⁴

Not even this proved enough, and all too soon much more drastic steps had to be taken, as Montgomery explained to the Chief of the British Imperial General Staff – Alan Brooke – in a telegram.

> Regret time has come when I must break up one Inf Div. My Inf Divs are so low in effective rifle strength that they can no (repeat no) longer fight effectively in major operations. Request permission to break up 59 Div at once. Montgomery.

The 59th (Staffordshire) Infantry Division – whose shoulder patch was a charming slag heap crowned with a pit winding gear tower to commemorate the coal-mining heritage of its recruitment area – had fought with distinction in Normandy, and its disbandment was no black-mark on its record or the men in it, rather, as the American historian Carlo D'Este explained, it '…had been selected because it was the junior division in 21st Army Group and not as a result of its performance in battle'. The 59th wasn't alone. The British 1st Armoured Division in Italy, having suffered severe losses in the August battles in the peninsula, was also broken up with most of its men sent to other units as replacements.

In contrast to Britain and Canada, the United States was just getting into its stride. Blessed with a large, healthy and well-fed population, it was able to grow its puny 1940 army of 175,000 men into an eight-million-man colossus by late 1944, with a further four million in the Navy, Marines and Airforce. Somewhat disingenuously, President Roosevelt sent a letter to the British Prime Minister Winston Churchill in October '44 where he complained that: 'All of us are now faced with an unanticipated shortage of manpower.' Churchill must have smiled wryly at the generalisation.

What this meant for Allied strategy in Europe in the autumn of 1944 was that there was no way that the Americans were going to acquiesce to Montgomery's single 'thrust in the north' proposal. This was doubly true when implicit in the plan was the subordination to Monty's command of Bill Simpson's Ninth and Courtney Hodges's First US Armies – American public opinion, and the American president, simply wouldn't wear it – and Eisenhower knew it. It wasn't just at home where there was opposition to the idea of playing second fiddle to an imperial

Britain either, but in the highest military circles as well. Omar Bradley commanding the US Twelfth Army Group[5] and so often the epitome of the quiet, laid-back Missourian, had had just about enough of both Montgomery and what he saw as British pretensions to superiority; along with Patton, Bradley furiously lobbied Eisenhower to rebuff the British plan and back a thrust further south, under American command. Faced with squabbling generals, Eisenhower's answer was to be 'Ike', the ultimate consensus builder, and man most capable of squaring any circle – there would be no single thrust, but instead, a 'broad front' along the entire line, to take the Allies into Germany.

As a *political* strategy it was matchless, as a *military* one it was disastrous.

The problem could be summed up by one conversation between George Patton as commander of the US Third Army, and Bradley: 'Damn it Brad, just give me four hundred thousand gallons of gasoline and I'll put you in Germany in two days.' But 'Brad' didn't have four hundred thousand gallons of gas – nothing like it in fact. There were now seven Allied armies facing the *Westheer* – four American and one each from Britain, Canada and France – and while their incredible level of mechanization was a huge boon, it was also a major problem. To illustrate, a single American armoured division typically contained 4,200 vehicles – including 232 x M4 Sherman tanks – and used twenty-five thousand gallons of fuel per day for normal movement, which increased to one hundred thousand for cross-country fighting. Even a lowly American infantry division burnt 6,500 gallons a day; meaning that the four Allied armies in the north alone got through a million gallons each and every day.[6] Factor in ammunition, food, spares, clothing and all the other paraphernalia of war, and the total supply requirement of an average Allied division was six hundred tons per day.

On top of that, was the responsibility of liberation – the Allies had to feed the civilian population too, or risk possible starvation and unrest. This was no simple task when Paris alone swallowed up 2,400 tons of food a day. That is a truly phenomenal rate of consumption – not that the Allies didn't have the fuel (or supplies), they did, in abundance; the issue was how to get it to the troops, and that *how* was the Achilles heel of Eisenhower's broad-front strategy.

One of the many reasons for the extraordinary success of the D-Day plan was that it wrong-footed the Germans by not aiming to capture a major French port on the day itself. Berlin had long considered it impossible to reinforce and supply a landing force without the use of a big harbour, and had planned the defences of *Festung Europa* (Fortress Europe) accordingly. By using the Normandy beaches, the Allies had sidestepped the majority of Wehrmacht defences and greatly improved their chances of success. Brilliant though that decision was for D-Day, by late August it had become a very large chicken coming home to roost! Now, every bullet, every shell, every morsel of food and every single drop of gasoline had to be landed on the sands of Normandy and then shipped over three hundred miles to reach the frontline – and not by train, as the Allies 'Transportation Plan' bombing campaign had trashed the railway network between France and Germany so thoroughly that thirty-one thousand American railcars had to be dismantled and sent to France to be reassembled and put on the tracks to try and make up the numbers; but repairing those same tracks, bridges and cuttings, was going to take some time. So, in the meantime, the only way to move anything was by road, in trucks – this then was the genesis of the famous 'Red Ball Express'. The name – a common American railway term at the time — was something of a misnomer, as it was actually the designation given to the first organised route – there were soon several others such as the *Green Diamond* and *White Lion* – where traffic was ruthlessly organised for the sole purpose of trucking supplies to the front as quickly as possible. Traffic was one-way on the routes, with strict controls on access, speed and breakdowns, and with designated protection battalions to police it.

The trucks themselves were mainly provided by the US Transportation Corps, which, back in 1943, had requested 240 new companies be established for the upcoming landings; they were allowed two-thirds of that number, with the majority equipped with light or medium wagons, and not the biggest type that carried far more freight. African-Americans constituted seventy-five per cent of the crews – US forces were heavily segregated at the time, and African-American combat units were still very few – while the gasoline itself was loaded into good old five-gallon jerrycans, of which a staggering twenty-two million had been shipped to France by the beginning of September.[7] The convoy system began in late August and was soon utilising between six and seven thousand trucks with the aim of delivering anything between five and ten thousand tons of supplies per day.[8] As a logistical operation it was simply extraordinary, and bears comparison to the Berlin Airlift of 1948–1949. It was typical of the can-do attitude of the very best of American military thinking, but it was also its own worst enemy, as one American officer said of it: 'It was the greatest killer of trucks that I could imagine.' Seventy trucks per day was the cost – lost to accidents, mechanical failure or ambushes by German stragglers; with seven thousand lost in all.[9] Trucks weren't the only thing used up; the convoys guzzled a daily total of three hundred thousand gallons of the very same fuel it was created to carry. Magnificent effort it certainly was, but it still wasn't enough.

By the end of August, Patton's Third Army was running dry; on the 30th it received thirty-two thousand gallons – ten per cent of its needs – and when, the following day, a daring thrust was made to capture an intact bridge over the River Meuse at Verdun, fourteen of the seventeen tanks in the assault group ran out of gas before reaching their objective.

The situation was made far worse by the old adage, 'an army marches on its stomach', or to put it another way, man cannot live on gasoline alone – and definitely not a soldier in the Allied armies; in fact, it was calculated that those men needed the grand total of 66.8lbs of supplies *per man, per day*. This included 8lbs of ammunition, 7.2lbs of rations and even 7.3lbs of construction materials. The system just couldn't cope.

It was just as bad for the Anglo-Canadians, where the British government's insistence on purchasing vehicles from civilian manufacturers through a blizzard of separate contracts had led to the madness of a vehicle fleet totalling several hundred different models; with all the problems inherent in such a system for maintenance, spare parts and a lack of interoperability. The War Office also demonstrated its almost uniquely dreadful approach to procurement when it realised – too late – that its just-delivered batch of fourteen hundred brand-new Austin trucks were useless due to faulty engine pistons. A check of the also brand-new replacement engine stocks then found that they had the same defect, leaving the British no option but to press into service abandoned former Wehrmacht horse-drawn wagons. The results were inevitable. In late August an entire Canadian corps was stuck fast for several days due to lack of fuel, and two of the eight divisions in the British Second Army were ordered to hold on the line of the Seine River to allow the other six the fuel to carry on advancing.

The solution to the logistics crisis was clear; the Allies needed ports on their route of advance so the supply strain could be taken by the cavernous holds of ships and not the limited space on the back of a truck. The northern coast of France and Belgium was dotted with some of the finest harbours in Europe, surely at least one could be used? Brest in Brittany for example, was ideal; the most important base for the French fleet on the Atlantic coast, it had deep enough water for the largest vessels, miles of quays and wharves, acres of warehouses and excellent docking facilities – it also had forty thousand German soldiers sitting in it, commanded by *General der Fallschirmtruppe* Hermann-Bernhard Ramcke. A highly-decorated veteran of Crete, Italy, Russia, and most famously North Africa, Ramcke had been ordered to hold Brest to the 'last man and the last bullet' by Hitler himself, and as a dedicated Nazi he was determined to do so.[10] Most of the garrison were second-rate troops at best, being unemployed naval personnel, construction units and the static, fortress regiments of the *343. Infanterie-Division (343. ID)*. However, sprinkled among them were Russian front veterans from the *266. ID* and paras from *2. Fallschirmjäger Division*. The city itself was heavily fortified, the medieval stone walls supplemented by modern pillboxes, concrete bunkers, and all manner of gun emplacements. With ample stocks of ammunition and food, the defenders waited for the inevitable attack.

The American 2nd Infantry Division were the first to reach the city on 7 August, and then began a long, hard fight to break through the defences. Heavy artillery and tanks were brought in, and the beautiful old town was more or less razed. Ramcke led his men from the front, and his fellow *fallschirmjäger* in particular fought tenaciously. August became September, and still the Germans clung on. Specialist British Crocodile flamethrower tanks were brought in to help reduce the forts that girdled the city, and finally the last and most powerful, Fort Montbarey, succumbed. Ramcke surrendered the port and its garrison to Ernest Hemingway's friend, Charles Canham, the deputy commander of the US 8th Infantry Division, on 19 September. Over thirty thousand Germans marched into captivity, but before they did, they demolished the port so completely that it would only become operational again after the war's end. American casualties were high; 9,831 killed or wounded, and with over fifty thousand more Germans trapped in the newly christened *Festungen* up and down the coast, the Allies took the decision not to try and capture any more, but to leave them besieged. This meant Dunkirk, Lorient, La Rochelle and Saint-Nazaire couldn't be used by the Allies, and they were only liberated after hostilities ceased.

So, if not Brest, or any of the other northern French harbours, where? As it happened, a plum had fallen into Allied hands at the beginning of September – Antwerp. Antwerp, with its ten square miles of docks, twenty miles of water-front and no fewer than six hundred cranes, was Europe's second largest cargo port behind Rotterdam, and the answer to the Allies mounting logistical problems with its eighty thousand tons of daily unloading capacity. When it fell – still operational – into British hands on 4 September, it seemed like the answer to Eisenhower's prayers. Convoys could now sail directly up the Scheldt estuary, dock at Antwerp and unload their cargo holds for a short drive forward to the front. Except they couldn't, and they couldn't because a huge mistake was made, and it was none other than Montgomery himself who made it.

Antwerp is connected to the sea by the estuary of the River Scheldt, a forty-mile long waterway bordered to the north by Walcheren Island, inevitably designated *Festung Walcheren* by Hitler. In anticipation of the Allied capture of Antwerp, the Germans had dug in two whole battalions of anti-aircraft and coastal artillery on Walcheren and sown the estuary with mines. Any attempt to clear the mines using Royal Navy minesweepers would see the ships sent to the bottom by the big German guns. To further complicate matters for the Allies, *General der Infanterie* Gustav-Adolf von Zangen's ninety-thousand strong *15. Armee* held the southern bank of the estuary opposite *Festung Walcheren*. Once the most powerful field army in the Wehrmacht, *15. Armee* had been side-lined in the Pas de Calais during the invasion and had seen its best divisions drained away to try and hold the Allies in Normandy.

Now it was retreating up the coast and found itself on the southern bank of the Scheldt – by chance, the perfect place to be to frustrate the enemy. Von Zangen was told by *OB West*: 'Enemy supplies, and therefore his ability to fight, are limited by the stubborn defence of the harbour, as intelligence reports prove. The attempt of the enemy to occupy the Western Scheldt in order to obtain the free use of the harbour of Antwerp must be resisted to the utmost.'

Von Zangen passed on the order to his command, with his own emphasis:

> Therefore, I order all commanders as well as the National Socialist indoctrination officers to instruct the troops in the clearest and most factual manner... After overrunning the SCHELDT fortifications, the English would finally be in a position to land great masses of material in a large and completely protected harbour. With this material they might deliver a death blow at the NORTH GERMAN plain and at BERLIN before the onset of winter... The enemy knows that he must assault the European fortress as speedily as possible before its inner lines of resistance are fully built up and occupied by new divisions. For this, he needs the ANTWERP harbour. And for this reason, we must hold the SCHELDT fortifications to the end. The German people are watching us.

First order of business for von Zangen was to get the bulk of his forces over the Scheldt to Walcheren, and then leave a rearguard to hold the southern bank for as long as possible. The diminutive ex-commander of *344. ID* – *General der Infanterie* Eugen-Felix Schwalbe – was tasked with the move across the river, and set to it with a will.

With no bridges, Schwalbe requisitioned two old Dutch freighters, sixteen river barges, three ferries and a few motorised rafts. This 'fleet' immediately began to take men and equipment on the three-and-a-half mile trip from Breskens to Flushing on Walcheren. Everything had to be done at night due to the ever-present *jabo* threat, so during the day the troops sheltered out of sight of prying eyes, only moving up to their embarkation points as darkness closed in. One of the men ferried across was twenty-three-year-old *Feldwebel* Erich Hensel:

> On the Scheldt an Oberstleutnant arrived with a truck full of booty champagne and two women. 'Give me that boat!' he demanded, but the Unteroffizier skippering the ferry retorted indignantly 'You're staying there!' and off we sailed. Our company commander, a decent man, was ashamed that we had witnessed such a scene.[11]

Attempted hijackings like this were rare, and in the main the operation went off with no panic and remarkable efficiency – hugely aided by the fact that Montgomery seemed unconcerned at what was happening. An entire German Army – admittedly a weakened one, but nevertheless still an Army – was cut-off on the wrong side of an estuary and ripe for destruction; if Montgomery had moved with speed and decisiveness he could have bagged von Zangen and his forces, while at the same time clearing the southern bank of the Scheldt. Instead, Schwalbe was gifted an almost unbelievable sixteen nights to affect the miraculous escape of *15. Armee. Generalleutnant* Erwin Sander's *245. ID* was the first to cross, closely followed by Walter Poppe's *59. ID,* then Erich Diester's *346.* and Josef Reichert's *711. IDs.* Poppe – a Russian front veteran – was amazed the Allied navies didn't intervene to stop them. He expected 'to be blown out of the water'. In the end, no fewer than nine divisions escaped;[12] a total of almost eighty thousand men, well over four hundred guns, several thousand trucks and other vehicles, and even a few thousand horses.[13] These men and their equipment were now available to reinforce Walcheren and form a defensive line in the Netherlands – including garrisoning the towns of Nijmegen, Eindhoven and Arnhem.

Left behind as the rearguard commander in Breskens was *Generalmajor* Kurt Eberding. A Russian front veteran like Poppe, the core of his command was *64. ID,* a scratch formation only created in August that year, whereupon it had been thrown into the fighting in France and suffered heavy casualties. By the time it dug in behind the Leopold Canal, it had been reinforced with every man Eberding could find who hadn't been ferried across the Scheldt. That took its strength to over ten thousand, although only around a quarter were frontline soldiers, the rest were support and service personnel. Centred on the estuary town of Breskens, Eberding and his men now formed what Berlin entitled *Scheldt Festung Süd* – Scheldt Fortress South – better known as the Breskens Pocket. They would prove a thorn in the Allies' side for weeks to come.

With the Scheldt blocked, the Antwerp docks sat idle, and for the first time Allied soldiers began to feel the effects of supply shortfalls. This was especially true in that most vital of military logistics: ammunition. Throughout the war in the west, members of the Wehrmacht always spoke of the Allies' ability to bring to bear a truly vast amount of firepower that they could never match – they would fire an average of two tons of ammunition per minute of the campaign[14] – as part and parcel of the Allied battle philosophy of prioritising the battle of *matériel* versus the Hitlerian ethos of the battle of the man. Now, in Patton's Third Army in particular, Allied guns were increasingly falling silent, with many batteries allocated just four shells per day.

Allied stuttering, caused by Montgomery's misjudgement, came at exactly the moment when German panic began to subside, to be replaced by what can only be described as the Wehrmacht's September miracle.

From a disorganised mass of soldiery, and the almost complete breakdown of authority, the Nazi war machine – for the last time in the conflict – somehow reconstituted itself. Whereas on D-Day, German commanders at all levels failed to show initiative and drive, the beginning of September showcased the very best the Wehrmacht could produce. Rudolf '*Rudi*' von Ribbentrop – son of Nazi Germany's Foreign Minister, Joachim, and himself an *SS-Hauptsturmführer* in the *Hitlerjugend* Division – explained how it achieved this transformation:

> The German Army disposed of the oldest and most efficient management system ... based on the fundamental knowledge that the highest effectiveness of all troops could only be attained if each soldier was capable of acting independently in the 'emptiness of the battlefield'... the basic precepts of the German military code were that German troops of all ranks must be able to act independently and on their own initiative.[15]

This was a far cry from the stereotype of Nazi automatons, incapable of any thoughts of their own, blindly marching into battle. As the Allied pursuit slackened, leadership at small unit level in particular re-asserted itself and order began to be restored. Alfred Ziegler – a motorcycle dispatch rider in the *9. SS-Panzerdivision 'Hohenstaufen'* remembers the turnaround: 'The eight day break we had after the shambles in France and Belgium was decisive. During this time, we regrouped and re-equipped. I managed to get my motorbike repaired. It had received a bullet straight through the engine block from a jabo.' His comrade Wolfgang Dombrowski said: 'There were only seven men left in the battalion who had completed the original year-long training in Dresden, and naturally the replacements weren't as well trained ... but despite the occasional grumbling of artillery fire in the distance, we were happily living in virtual peacetime conditions.'[16]

There was also a change in leadership at the very top of the *Westheer* at that time; in desperation, Hitler turned, once again, to the old Prussian warhorse Gerd von Rundstedt, to try and steady the ship. Having sacked him – for the second time in the war – only a few weeks ago, the Nazi dictator met with the man who openly derided him as 'that Bohemian corporal': 'I would like to place the Western front in your hands again.'

Von Rundstedt could have refused. He could have told Hitler the truth about the military situation – he could have demanded complete freedom of action as the price for his acceptance, but instead he settled for 'My Führer, whatever you order, I shall do to my last breath.'

He then drove to his new headquarters in Aremberg near the city of Koblenz, and received situation reports from his staff, including his *Chef der Führungsabteilung* (Head of Leadership section), *Oberst* Bodo Zimmermann.

Zimmermann told his boss that he had a total of forty-eight infantry and fifteen panzer/motorised divisions at his disposal – but in reality they were all so degraded that the true figure in terms of combat power was more like twenty-seven divisions altogether; the Allies had around sixty. Rundstedt said privately, 'As far as I was concerned the war ended in September.' However, in public, he limited himself to a message to Berlin stating that 'Heeresgruppe B has only about a hundred panzers in working order.' The stuff of revolution it wasn't. Not that the Prussian septuagenarian was the only senior officer whose moral compass went AWOL that September. His new Chief of Staff – and no fan of Hitler – *General der Kavallerie* Siegfried Westphal, recalled: 'I became Chief of Staff (COS) to OB West – *Feldmarschall* von Rundstedt – at the beginning of September. We had three army groups with eight armies but no troops!'[17] Westphal had only just returned to duty after suffering a mental breakdown while serving in Italy, but despite this, and the awful position in the West, he would simply carry on, with no real thought given to the fact that Germany was beaten – even though prolonging the war would simply prolong the agony.

Walter Model – now relieved of the role as *OB West* and limited to command of *Heeresgruppe B* – was another senior commander who might have confronted the leadership in Berlin and demanded a change. A contemporary, Friedrich von Mellenthin, described him as '…an alert, dapper, fiery little man, never separated from his monocle, and although a soldier of great driving power and energy, yet he could hardly be regarded as an adequate substitute for Manstein. In particular, Model was too prone to interfere in matters of detail and to tell his corps and army commanders exactly where they should dispose their troops.' A poor-man's Manstein or not, he was probably the only general officer who made Hitler uneasy, as the dictator himself admitted: 'He is my best field marshal… I trust that man to do it, but have you seen those eyes? I wouldn't want to serve under him.' Model would remain commander of *Heeresgruppe B*, and the Allies' principal foe in the West until almost the end.

Deplorable as this lack of moral fibre in senior headquarters undoubtedly was, the German command hierarchy finally began to take a grip of the military situation at the front, and improvise a defence running through the Netherlands, down the Ardennes/Eifel, past the Vosges, Alsace-Lorraine and southern Germany to the Swiss border.

Kurt Student – architect of Nazi Germany's airborne forces – was hurriedly brought in and told to establish *1. Fallschirm-Armee* and take command in southern Holland with around twenty-thousand ill-trained and hurriedly assembled troops furnished by Hermann Goering himself, of which Friedrich von der Heydte said: 'Those new paratroop divisions are second-rate flak field divisions … it's just pure vanity on Goering's part.' Von der Heydte wasn't impressed by the reinforcements for his own beloved *Fallschirmjäger-Regiment 6 (FJR. 6)* either: 'The young replacements constituted seventy-five per cent of the regiment, and they were barely trained or not at all.' One of his veterans, Albert Sturm, shared his commander's view: 'Many of the boys were just seventeen years old, not even really grown up. They'd received an extra ration of milk during jump school, and on joining us the doctors ordered they continue to receive additional milk to make them stronger.' *Oberleutnant* Siegfried Dietrich of the regimental staff knew the recruits needed help, so he 'made sure that one or two 'old fighters' were in each troop'. Regardless, another *FJR. 6* veteran, Franz Hüttich, saw little to give him much confidence: 'Flying personnel – older members of the Luftwaffe who didn't have any aircraft and could be spared from the logistics and administration offices – they all came to us ... we all knew it wouldn't amount to anything.'

Typical of the new units created was *Fallschirm-Regiment Hoffmann*, named after its commander, *Oberstleutnant* Hoffmann, and mainly filled with youngsters culled from a training depot. Heinz Volz, an experienced officer posted into the regiment, wasn't hopeful: 'The regiment ... had no issue of uniform parachute smocks and practically no weapons.' Two out of the three battalion commanders had no combat experience, neither did the majority of the company commanders and ninety per cent of the NCOs – Hoffman himself had none either. Volz tried to help prepare the regiment for combat: 'Above all we tried to at least get the majority of soldiers equipped with bicycles in order to make the unit more mobile – there was insufficient fuel for the few motorcycles at our disposal.' Unfortunately for the Dutch, those bicycles were stolen from the local civilian populace, and *Fallschirm-Regiment Hoffmann* wasn't the only German unit culpable – a country that before the war had an estimated four million bikes for its eight million people, ended the war with a few hundred thousand at most.

As Student improvised, his fellow Luftwaffe general officer Friedrich Christiansen, already in the Netherlands, threw a screen of fortress battalions and Luftwaffe personnel forward towards the Albert Canal to hold the line. Make do and mend was the order of the day; *Generalleutnant* Kurt Chill – already a Knight's Cross holder – went against orders, and on his own initiative turned around the survivors of his *85. Infanterie-Division*, scooped up the passing remnants of *84* and *89. ID*s and set them up in a defensive position. His fellow general, Karl Sievers, gathered the men of his static *719. ID* and ordered them to dig in on the Albert Canal's northern bank alongside Christiansen's Luftwaffe men. Siever's division – and the middle-aged men who filled its ranks – found themselves defending an impossibly long seventy-five mile stretch of front with an artillery regiment jokingly referred to as the 'Artillery Museum of Europe' given the age and variety of its guns. Elsewhere, '*Schiffstammabteilungen*' – emergency ship cadre battalions – were formed from unemployed Kriegsmarine sailors, and Luftwaffe ground staff were corralled into the '*Fliegerhorst*' units that were their air force equivalent. A battalion of Dutch SS men, the *SS-Wachbattailon 3*,[18] was relieved of its role guarding the Amersfoort concentration camp and sent forward – much to the chagrin of the men involved whose motivation for volunteering was dubious at best, and mainly seemed to be an understandable desire to avoid being sent as forced labour to the Reich. Regardless, these intrepid fighters found themselves advancing to the sound of the guns behind their forty-six-year-old commander *SS-Obersturmbannführer* Paul Helle. Helle himself had no combat experience, being a reserve officer, and relied completely on his young adjutant, *SS-Untersturmführer* Albert Naumann, who was indeed a veteran, but one without the use of his right arm due to a serious wound suffered on the Russian front.

Michael Lippert[19] – an experienced Waffen-SS officer, and now commander of the SS NCO's School at Arnhem – received his orders to stop all training and take his young trainees to the front, seeing for himself the signs of German retreat on the way, 'A torrent of German soldiers dammed up… A shambles of innumerable vehicles, carrying every conceivable load'. Other, perhaps less than first-rate, units followed, such as *Generalleutnant* Berthold Stumm's *176. ID*. Put on 'blitz trains'[20] in Aachen, Stumm's seven thousand men were rushed northwest to take up a place in the line. How useful they would be was a moot point; the division had no battle experience, and its ranks consisted of ex-Luftwaffe men, an 'ear' battalion of men with serious hearing problems, an 'eye' battalion of short or long-sighted soldiers, a 'foot' battalion for those with major podiatry issues, while the rest were 'stomach' cases, men with severe stomach and intestinal disabilities who had hitherto been classed as 'unfit for military service'. The division was disparagingly nicknamed a *kranken* (sick) division by its neighbours.

However, the fact remained that these measures began to work. Allied Intelligence at SHAEF informed Eisenhower that German frontline strength trebled in the six weeks up to mid-October. Wolfgang Dombrowski's commander, *SS-Hauptsturmführer* Hans Möller, saw the effect of the re-building work with his own eyes:

> On 6 September we reached our assembly area north-east of Arnhem … here Scharführer Bicking had already done a lot of work to raise our readiness. Where the crafty old fox had managed to get all the parts to produce two useable lorries and three armoured half-tracks was a mystery to me.[21]

The advancing Allies hit the still-forming German line, and the resultant fighting was savage, as Student's rough and ready forces grappled with their powerful opponents. Heinz Volz described *Fallschirm-Regiment Hoffman's* first taste of combat: 'The battalion suffered its first losses in Luyksgestel. Leutnant Hansbach was killed on 13 or 14 September by a direct artillery strike in his trench. A member of the battalion staff was torn to pieces when a shell splinter set off the grenades he was carrying. At the same time a feldwebel fell by the door of the command post, killed by a mortar burst.' Nevertheless, discipline stayed firm as Volz recalled when the phone rang during an artillery bombardment: 'During a short pause, Major Schacht of the Army staff explained that he wasn't used to being made to wait on the telephone, without at least some information on the immediate situation – as military protocol demanded.'[22] Von der Heydte's *FJR. 6* also made its mark, despite the misgivings of some of its old hands, including that of *Oberjäger* Anton Richter:

> It was only a few valiant men... Everything happened in a matter of seconds. Two panzerfausts roared, flames shot out and in a single detonation two Sherman tanks burst apart. Before the English had even realised what had happened, submachine-guns and hand grenades were booming in the night and the assault troop made their getaway.[23]

Fritz Fullriede, who, just a few days previously had been raging about the collapse, began to notice a change in his men:

> The II Abteilung ... after being inserted in the wrong place and stabbed in the back by its neighbours, was surrounded by strong forces ... and was practically wiped out in a three-day battle, only a few stragglers and panzers returned. Almost all the panzers, self-propelled artillery, anti-tank and flak elements were lost... The I and III Abteilungen ... were sent to Eindhoven ... these orders are sending them all to the devil... It's unbelievable that following the loss of so many men that the soldiers can still laugh and crack jokes.[24]

It's telling that of the eighty or so Waffen-SS officers and two hundred rankers that British Intelligence were secretly recording back in the prisoner-of-war camps in the UK at that time, not one said they believed the war was lost that autumn – or made any disparaging remarks about Hitler.[25] True, the Waffen-SS were not the same as their Army brethren, but it seemed that the mass of the *Westheer* had made a collective – almost unconscious – decision not to give up but to turn and fight, although this feeling was by no means universal, as one soldier admitted: 'We were fifteen men, and we were just sitting there, and no-one dared say 'we'll just sit here and wait to be taken prisoner by the Amis' (German nickname for the Americans) – and then that evening some landsers showed up and said 'right, come with us' and we had to follow them.'[26] The Allies noticed the change too:

> Battle groups were formed from regiments or from stragglers and were named after their commanding officer; they varied in strength from a hundred to three thousand men, and many went into battle so quickly

that the men didn't know the name of their own battle group. Food and ammunition were short, but some of these groups fought with great, and at times fanatical, determination.[27] ... The degree of control exercised over the regrouping and collecting of the apparently scattered remnants of a beaten army was little short of remarkable. Furthermore, the fighting capacity of the new battle-groups ... seems unimpaired.[28]

Despite these views on the Allied side, the truth was that at the beginning of September the *Westheer* was beaten, and just as back in September 1918, Germany's senior military figures had an opportunity to call a halt to the slaughter and end the war – but they didn't. The reasons why they didn't centre on the character of the different regimes at the time, and the personalities of the men involved. In 1918, Kaiser Wilhelm II was not nearly as powerful inside Germany as Hitler was in 1944, and neither did he possess the sort of security infrastructure that the Nazis had – the aftermath of the 20 July Bomb Plot had demonstrated that. As for the generals themselves, the Second World War generation fell back on their oath of loyalty to Hitler, constantly citing it as their excuse as to why they didn't confront the dictator, whereas when the Kaiser had said to his own commanders 'What about the oath?' they replied, 'Today, it is just words.' The von Rundstedts of the Wehrmacht may have despised Hitler and the Nazis – although many like Model did not – but they weren't prepared to overthrow them either, preferring instead to fight on. The result was that the Wehrmacht pulled off one of its great triumphs; a scramble defence that started to solidify a line in front of the main Allied advance in the north, where Montgomery's bungling of the Antwerp situation only made matters worse. One can't help but feel that the description of this period in the US Army's official post-war report of the campaign – *Strategy in North-West Europe* – smacks of post-op rationalisation: '... the need for additional supplies at forward points to sustain the drive, made it apparent that no further large-scale offensive could be launched until additional forces could be concentrated and the logistical situation improved ... a period of relative inactivity was essential.'

That 'period of relative inactivity' was the window of opportunity to end the war. Instead, all the advantages the Allies had so painstakingly won in France would be frittered away in a host of relatively obscure battles that seemed to be more about straightening the line rather than winning the war. These battles would be kicked off by one of the most spectacular, most courageous and most ill-thought-out Allied operations of the war – and altogether they would cost upwards of two hundred thousand Allied casualties before a carol was sung.[29]

Arnhem and the German Miracle

Had the pious, teetotalling Montgomery wobbled into SHAEF with a hangover, I could not have been more astonished than I was by the daring adventure he proposed... I never reconciled myself to the venture, but I nevertheless concede that Montgomery's plan for Arnhem was one of the most imaginative of the war.

This was Omar Bradley's view of the most unMontgomery-like operation the man himself ever launched. It was incredibly innovative and hugely daring – and an unmitigated disaster that sacrificed the lives of thousands of men on a plan that should never have seen the light of day. As the French general Pierre Bosquet said of another British military calamity almost a hundred years earlier: 'C'est magnifique, mais ce n'est pas la guerre: c'est de la folie.' ('It's magnificent, but it isn't war: it's madness').[1]

Arnhem – or more correctly *Operation Market Garden* – has been covered in not one but two Hollywood feature films and innumerable books, and was even the inspiration behind Richard Adams's famous story of courageous rabbits, *Watership Down*.[2] Invariably, these offerings – splendid as they almost all are – tend to focus on the outstanding bravery of the men involved, particularly the British paratroopers, and on the poor decision-making by some senior officers involved. What none of them really challenge is why the operation had to be launched at all; because it didn't, and by mounting it there's a strong argument that the war was actually lengthened, not shortened. The operation swallowed up vast amounts of resources that could have been used far more profitably elsewhere; it also gave the Wehrmacht a huge fillip, and most importantly it squandered a lot of precious time, time that should have been spent breaking into Germany with the all-arms offensive that could have brought the war to a close.

As it was, *Market Garden* was the lovechild of the bickering within high command that bedevilled the Allies from their victory at Falaise onwards. Even as far back as Eisenhower's 'walk across a field of bodies' in Normandy, the Allied supremo had put his *broad front* strategy into motion, confirming with Bradley that his newly created Twelfth Army Group – which included Patton's Third Army – could continue to advance east towards the city of Metz and the German Saarland. At the same time, he promised to support Montgomery's thrust in the north towards the Ruhr. With not enough fuel and ammunition – let alone other supplies – to fully support both, each would be drip-fed enough to maintain operations without enabling either to strike a decisive blow. Antipathy between the Allied generals reached its zenith, as Major Mather on Monty's staff remembered: '...the trouble came, and we knew it would, when the American forces outnumbered the British. We knew Eisenhower might take over then, but we didn't really believe it could happen.' But it did. Eisenhower took over command of land operations from Montgomery at the beginning of September, and in the resulting furore almost sacked the acerbic British general, while at the same time fending off the threatened resignations of Bradley, Patton and a clutch of other American seniors keen to be rid of Montgomery's high-handed arrogance.

In the middle of all this bad blood, Montgomery presented *Market Garden* to Eisenhower, and it isn't too much of a stretch to see Ike giving it the green light as a combined Anglo-American operation to help heal those wounds and placate Britain's fiery general.

In concept, the plan was simple; Brian Horrocks' British XXX Corps would launch a major, lightning offensive through the Netherlands to reach the Rhine at the Dutch town of Arnhem in a total of just sixty hours, where it would cross over the bridge and enter the Reich itself. To achieve that objective, it would have to cross no fewer than six major rivers and canals, and to do that, bridges over those obstacles would be seized intact and held by three entire airborne divisions landing by parachute and glider. It would be the largest operation of its kind of the war – of any war. However, simple though the concept was, it was also deeply flawed, both in principle and practicality. Regarding the latter, an assumption that an armoured corps of some twenty thousand vehicles could advance one hundred kilometres in sixty hours against an enemy fast hardening his defences was sheer folly, especially when that advance could only use a single road. Plus, and contrary to popular myth, the Allies *knew* there was German heavy armour in the target area, and yet still considered a force of lightly armed paratroopers capable of holding them off, while at the same time deciding to negate the only advantage the British paras would have at Arnhem – that of surprise – by landing them miles away from the bridge itself. The list went on; communications would be very poor due to the use of radios with little range and interference from all the conurbations in the area, air support would be patchy, and the whole force couldn't even be landed on one drop and so would only arrive in dribs and drabs.

If *Market Garden* had been presented at the British Army's own Staff College, the student concerned would have got an 'F' in red pen.

Regardless of all the above, the biggest flaw in the plan was that it wasn't even the best route into Germany; as the captured panzer general Heinrich Eberbach told his fellow prisoners: 'The whole point of their main effort is wrong. The traditional gateway is through the Saar.' Eberbach wasn't alone in his view, the *15. Armee*'s commander, von Zangen, explained: 'With obstacles in the form of water courses traversing it from east to west ... the terrain offers good possibilities to hold on to positions.'[3]

To put it mildly, Eisenhower had backed the wrong horse. *Market Garden* had zero chance of success, and in all likelihood would just lead the Allies into a cul-de-sac in northern Holland, having to fight their way from river to canal to river, without being able to achieve the decisive breakthrough that would lead to a rapid advance into the heart of Nazi Germany.

There was an alternative – the American thrust in the south. It was some 320 miles from Arnhem to Berlin (it had been around 240 from Falaise to Brussels) – while only fifty miles more from Metz to the Nazi capital, and the latter route negated the need to drive through the ultra-congested industrial landscape of the Ruhr. Down in the south the country was open and seemingly made for the talents of an attacking general like Patton. His Third Army had already shown what it was capable of in its headlong charge from Brittany all the way to Alsace-Lorraine. Surely this was the horse to bet on? Eisenhower decided it wasn't, and instead *Market Garden* was a go.

'Low-category troops in brigade strength with a few tanks'. This was how the British general 'Boy' Browning described German strength in the Arnhem area to the man selected to lead Britain's 1st Airborne Division into battle; the tall and imposing Scot, Roy Urquhart. One of Urquhart's men – James Sims – recalled how this information filtered down to him and his mates: 'Intelligence told us we had nothing to worry about ... no armour ... and only second-rate line of communications troops and Luftwaffe personnel – a piece of cake.'

Those 'second-rate troops' mainly consisted of the remnants of not one but two Waffen-SS panzer divisions, the *9. Hohenstaufen* and the *10. Frundsberg* of the *II SS-Korps*. Badly gutted in Normandy, they had escaped Falaise and been ordered to a rest and refit area in the Netherlands – Arnhem. There, the idea was to send one division home to fully reconstitute, after having handed over all its remaining heavy equipment and vehicles to the other. That division would then follow in due course. Only having around three thousand men each, and a small number of panzers, they were less than their usual formidable selves, but they had a trick up their sleeves that made them a paratroopers worst nightmare – as the *Frundsberg*'s commander, Heinz Harmel, pointed out:

The whole II SS Panzer Korps had been especially trained .... in countering a landing supported by airborne forces in Normandy. This training benefited us enormously during the Arnhem operation. At the lower end, NCOs and officers were taught to react quickly and make their own decisions. NCOs were taught not to wait until an order came, but to decide for themselves what to do.[4]

SS-Sturmbannführer Sepp Krafft, a highly-decorated Waffen-SS veteran sitting oblivious in Arnhem, was of the same opinion as Harmel: 'We knew from experience that the only way to draw the teeth of an airborne landing with an inferior force is to drive right into it.'[5] Krafft and his men were also lucky to have some reinforcements in the shape of those other Normandy veterans *Oberstleutnant* Ernst Heyna and the men of *352. ID*. It was these men who had almost repulsed the American landing at Omaha beach on D-Day, and who had subsequently proved such a dogged opponent to the Allies as they fought their way inland. Sent to the Arnhem area – just like their SS comrades – to rest and refit, they would immediately join the *Frundsberg* to combat the landings; albeit Heyna only had two hundred men fit for action, the rest having been lost in France.

The point was that Allied intelligence knew they were there but they just didn't rate them very highly, and hugely underestimated how swiftly they would react. Not that every man who would face the British paras was a well-trained veteran though – far from it. Alongside the Waffen-SS tankers and panzer grenadiers were Berthold Stumm's *176. ID*, rushed so quickly from Aachen and now suffering from the nature of many of the invalids in its ranks. This was especially true of the 'ear' battalion, where every man was either deaf, or had one or both ears badly damaged or missing completely. In addition – as if this wasn't enough – to qualify for entry into the 'ear' battalion, a man had to have another minor disability, such as a missing finger or rheumatism. One veteran recalled some of the resulting issues:

Verbal orders could only be given by a frantic series of gestures. Inspecting the guard at night was a nerve-wracking and hazardous task since the men on duty couldn't hear anyone approach, then when suddenly confronted in the dark they fired first and attempted to find out who it was later. In one 'ear' battalion two sergeants of the guard were killed in this way shortly after the unit went into action. Casualties from artillery fire were also inordinately high because the men couldn't hear the sound of approaching shells and therefore took cover much too late.[6]

A replacement in another unit also found the experience of meeting his new comrades harrowing: 'Today I was transferred to the *42. Machine-Gun Fortress Battalion*... This battalion is made up of half-crippled home guard soldiers – I found many among them quite obviously mentally unbalanced, some others had their arms amputated, others were one leg short.'

A feldwebel in a neighbouring division was just as disillusioned:

> A convoy had been shot up by jabos, we bandaged the wounded and sent them back. We had to leave the dead lying in the street, because with jabos overhead any unnecessary movement may be fatal. Some of the dead are so mutilated as to be unrecognizable. One of our comrades commits suicide by hanging ... we are in a hell of a fine place.[7]

In the middle of all this, on the morning of Sunday 17 September, Heinz Volz, the young *leutnant* with *Fallschirm-Regiment Hoffmann* recalled: 'At about midday we suddenly discerned an unearthly droning noise coming from the air. A huge stream of transport aircraft and gliders approached out of the enemy hinterland ... this enormous swarm was escorted by countless fighters.'[8] One of Heinz Harmel's junior NCOs, nineteen-year-old *SS-Rottenführer* Rudolf Trapp, saw it too: 'The sky over us was black with aircraft – an armada – absolutely full with transport aircraft and bombers towing gliders. There was an immediate alarm – no time to eat!'[9]

Kurt Student – a paratrooper himself of course, saw it all from his headquarters at Vught, nine miles west of the American drop-zones. There was '...roaring in the air of such intensity that I left my study and went onto the balcony. Wherever I looked I saw aircraft; troop carriers, and large aircraft towing gliders. An immense stream passed low over the house. I was greatly impressed.'

Leutnant Joseph Enthammer was with a V-2 launching unit near Arnhem when he saw the spectacle: 'That cannot be, it never snows in September, they must be parachutists!' (The observation supplied the title of Robert Kershaw's book on the German view of *Market Garden* and the Battle of Arnhem.)

The Americans of the 82nd and 101st Airborne Divisions dropped between Eindhoven and Nijmegen, while their comrades in the British 1st Airborne headed further north for Arnhem. German reaction was immediate, although it wasn't as slick as some historians have suggested, as Friedrich von der Heydte reported: 'Air landings were reported everywhere ... it appeared that the only defence that had been organised in a short time was against the British paratroopers in Arnhem ... everywhere else where the Allies had landed complete chaos seemed to rule.'[10]

Von der Heydte's description was partially accurate; the American landings were successful, but while the Germans didn't manage to majorly interfere with them, they did manage to blow up the bridge over the Wilhemina Canal at Son before the 101st 'Screaming Eagles' could secure it. They also put a brake on the 82nd, securing the main road bridge over the Waal River at Nijmegen. Both actions created delays the Allied plan couldn't cope with. However, it was at Arnhem where German reaction was both quickest and most successful, as Wolfgang Dombrowski detailed: 'This was just like a wild west shoot-out, there was no front, sections and half-sections fought scattered actions against similar size British groups.' The idiocy of throwing away surprise by landing miles away now came back to bite the British on the backside, as only a single unit, John Frost's 2nd Battalion, managed to find a way along an unguarded road through the German units streaming to the sound of the guns. As James Sims recounted, 'We passed an SS police barracks with several dead men outside. Slumped across a machine-gun were two bodies in Luftwaffe blue – they were a boy and a girl about my age – she was lying beside him with the ammunition belt threaded through her fingers, her blonde hair streaked with blood.' Frost and his men reached Arnhem and captured the north end of the bridge.

Across the area, German units flung themselves into action – one such was the forty-seven-year-old Michael Lippert's SS-NCO School. Lippert, described later by one of his students as 'a father-figure type, admired and respected by the soldiers',[11] first reported to the designated local commander, *Generalleutnant* Hans von Tettau,[12] for orders, but was less than impressed by what he heard: 'Lippert, we're in the shit, we're finished.' He replied, 'Herr General, firstly the British have not got us yet, and secondly, if they have got us then we won't make it easy for them.'[13]

The SS officer's view was the one that prevailed across pretty much all Wehrmacht forces involved, as the Allies quickly realised they had hugely underestimated the strength of German resistance. Nowhere was this more debilitating for *Market Garden* than further south in the path of XXX Corps' advance, as one of von der Heydte's officers recounted:

The front, which had been relatively quiet ... suddenly erupted into hell, as at 1400hrs an unearthly crescendo of artillery fire fell ... for an hour the soil shook time and time again... Hauptmann Brockes was killed by a direct hit from a mortar round on his command post ... a shell fragment from above penetrated his skull.

Determined to strike back, the German paras waited until British tanks advanced on their single, open road – and then struck:

A large number were knocked out by panzerfausts firing from ten to twelve metres away ... we were able to impose a decisive block because the terrain left and right of the road wasn't suitable for tanks, being sandy and boggy ... the fighting was extremely bitter, and a foxhole sheltering a wounded man can easily be collapsed by a waltzing tank.[14]

The hoped-for lightning charge from XXX Corps all too quickly became a bloody slog-fest, with German units fighting bitterly for every yard, as *FJR. 6*'s *Oberjäger* Willy Renner described:

> Our assault team consisted of about fifteen men and was ordered to clear a residential street. Hand grenades were thrown up into the living spaces or down into the cellars ... we came across an English soldier who had suffered a stomach wound... I assume he had been hit from the street and that his comrades had left him lying in the house because they couldn't take him with them. We were running towards a house when shots came from all the cellar windows. A few metres to the left of me a comrade was hit in the throat – blood was spurting out – it was horrible. Another comrade got a chest wound – in his breast pocket was a photo of his girlfriend and the bullet went right through the picture ... we took cover and ran to the right ... kicked the cellar windows in and threw in hand grenades. There was a horrible explosion – it's terrible when a hand grenade explodes in such a small space – I'd experienced that myself. The Englishmen appeared; a few of them had been wounded, some had been killed. Four of them came out and I took them back with us... I realized that the captives were afraid of being executed – they relaxed a bit when we exchanged cigarettes. They were young boys and still suffering the mental strain of urban fighting.

Renner's comrade and fellow Normandy veteran, Albert Sturm, was involved in the same fighting, and at one point had a British truck filled with wounded men lined up in the sight of his panzerfaust:

> I grabbed the panzerfaust, flipped up the sight and sized them up – and then suddenly there was a block in me. Fighting a tank – cold steel – the enemy firing wildly as it ran us down ... all of this I had experienced many times ... they had wounded men in the truck, I couldn't just blow them all into the air... I put the panzerfaust down and an older Obergefreiter patted me on the shoulder. 'Yeah Albert, war is shit.' And that was that, we didn't say anything more about it.

A couple of days later Sturm was badly wounded in a mortar blast:

> I neither felt the explosion nor the fact that the blast flung me into the air... The one thing I could move without pain was my right arm. There was blood everywhere else, it had hit me worst in my leg. My right combat boot was shredded from my leg, the bone showing through – my left knee joint was swollen, full of shrapnel, both thighs were full of iron, everything was just blood and mangled flesh. A large piece of

shrapnel was stuck in my left upper arm and pain wrenched my chest –
I had two broken ribs ... my face and mouth were full of blood ...
no-one could help my No. 2 gunner – there was nothing in the place
where his head had been.

Somehow, Sturm's comrades managed to pull him into cover and get him
to a medical post for treatment.[15]

As the British advance slowed, so German reactions speeded up. The
Reichbahn's[16] *blitz* system kicked into gear again, and almost eighty-
thousand troops would arrive in the Netherlands in less than a week;
the impact on *Market Garden* was devastating. Even the Luftwaffe –
long considered an absentee parent by the *landsers* – took a hand.
Some one hundred and twenty Luftwaffe aircraft raided Eindhoven in
the dimming light of dusk that first day and caused chaos; over nine
thousand houses were destroyed or damaged, and 227 people were
killed. The destruction was added too by a chance hit on a column
of four Allied ammunition trucks, which blew up with devastating
consequences for their crews and anyone near them. *Hauptmann*
Johannes Kaufmann and his flight of Bf 109G's also took a hand: 'We
took off for our first patrol of the Nijmegen-Arnhem corridor. Our
brief was to search for any enemy transport aircraft attempting to
drop supplies...we strafed the landing zones – destroying a number of
abandoned gliders – and shot up the neighbouring areas of woodland
where enemy activity had been reported.'[17] A corresponding attack
on British positions at Arnhem by a solitary Focke-Wulf was less
successful – the single bomb it dropped failed to detonate, and then
the pilot proceeded to clip the tower of Arnhem's tallest building – the
fourteenth-century *Grote Kerk* – and cartwheel into a nearby lake to
'great joy all round', according to one British para.[18]

Arnhem now became a cauldron, with Frost's men desperately hanging
on at the bridge, and the rest of their comrades trying to hold their landing
zones and reach Frost. On Monday morning – the 18th – the Germans
attempted to force the issue by seizing the bridge from Frost's battalion.
The man responsible for this decision was *SS-Hauptsturmführer* Viktor
Gräbner. Gräbner was short, dark-haired, popular with his men and peers
alike - and impulsive. A latecomer to the armed SS – he had only transferred
over from the Army in 1943 – he soon found his feet and earned himself
a Knight's Cross for his exploits in Normandy, which he received the
very morning of his attack. He commanded the *9. SS-Panzeraufklärungs
Abteilung* (9th SS Armoured Reconnaissance Battalion), a unit viewed
as an élite even within the testosterone-fuelled confines of a Waffen-SS
panzer division. Unaware that he was facing an entire dug-in battalion,
Gräbner decided to charge the bridge and try and capture the north
end by a frontal assault, utilising the speed of his twenty-two vehicles

and their combined firepower. At 0900hrs the thirty-year-old SS officer climbed into his captured British Mark IV Humber Scout car and gave the order, '*Marsch!*' At full speed – but with no covering fire or support – the Germans sped across the bridge and promptly came under a barrage of anti-tank, machine-gun and small-arms fire, as one of Gräbner's men – *SS-Rottenführer* Mauga – detailed: 'Suddenly all hell broke loose ahead of us. All around my vehicle there were explosions and noise, and I was right in the middle of this chaos ... the commander had disappeared for good, we could not recover him.'[19] Gräbner had indeed been killed, almost certainly at the very beginning of a fight that went on for some time as the SS grenadiers tried to force a way through. Many, like Mauga, were in open-topped half-tracks and were very vulnerable to grenades thrown into them from the upper storeys of buildings occupied by Frost's men. Two of Gräbner's vehicles tried to withdraw out of the killing zone, only to crash through the side-barriers and fall off the edge of the bridge down onto the road below, killing everyone on board. Seventy panzer grenadiers lost their lives alongside their commander. Twelve of the original twenty-two attacking vehicles were now just wreckage that made the end of the bridge almost impassable – but one diehard refused to give up and continued to fire at the British paras from his burning vehicle, as nineteen-year-old James Sims recalled with horror:

> The paras shouted to the SS man to come out, promising to spare his life, because they were impressed by his fanatical courage. The only reply was a further burst of fire. As the flames got to him, we could hear his screams of agony, muffled by the steel turret, but none the less disturbing for that. They seemed to go on for an awfully long time before this brave soldier died for Führer and Fatherland.

With desperate courage, the rest of the British division tried again to reach the bridge from the village of Oosterbeek to the west of Arnhem itself. Paul Müller was a young SS NCO at the time, when he saw a group of paras come towards him: 'Two bursts from my machine-gun caused an explosion among them, its effect was devastating, only one of the Tommies remained standing, the rest were rolling and moaning in a heap on the ground.' The sole survivor kept on coming, and a now-wounded Müller threw a grenade at him even as his own comrades ran away and left him: 'This Englishman was indestructible.' Remarkably the para didn't stop: 'I just had enough strength to throw my pulled grenade at the Tommy before I blacked out.' Coming to, Müller thought to himself, 'You've got to get away fast now or Tommy is going to do you in completely.' Jumping out of his foxhole as he tried to wipe blood from his eyes, a British grenade landed in the now-empty hole, peppering his back with shrapnel.[20]

With the British pushing hard to get to Frost, the Germans needed to liquidate the paras toehold on the bridge. The fighting became vicious, as one SS officer remembered: 'We fired at everything, from room to room, from the ground floor up, from garden to garden, and from tree to tree.' Twenty-one-year-old Alfred Ringsdorf said the same: 'This was a harder battle than any I had fought in Russia – it was constant, close range, hand to hand fighting. The English were everywhere ... we fired at each other from only yards away. We fought to gain inches, cleaning out one room after another, it was absolute hell.'[21] Another Alfred –Ziegler – also talked about just how intimate the fighting was: 'We were never certain where our men were and where the British were. We were so close once that I heard them transmitting Morse code "dit-da-da-da-dit-dit" – we ran – it had to be the British because we didn't have any transmitters.'

By now, Montgomery's carefully worked-out timetable was shot to bits. XXX Corps wasn't big enough to bulldoze through the German defences, and it lacked the drive of a Patton at the helm to spur it on to the extraordinary efforts that were required if it was to reach Arnhem before the paras' position became untenable. As it was, an altogether unhealthy – and unwarranted – paranoia set in that the Germans were somehow preparing to burst out of the *Reichswald* forest in the east to take the advance in the flank. This was delusional – but it was a delusion the Allies would increasingly become prone to in the following months, with dreadful consequences for their armies. In reality, the Germans initially had just two battalions in the forest; one of untrained ex-Luftwaffe ground crew, and another of disabled 'ear and stomach' soldiers.

Scrambling to react to the Allied offensive, local commanders managed to scrape together three small *kampfgruppen* (battle-groups – KGs) of about a thousand men each, supported by a handful of anti-aircraft and artillery guns, five armoured cars and a few mortars and machine-guns. They were, as one of their officers said, 'a motley crowd', but their appearance sent alarm bells ringing at Allied headquarters. Perhaps they would not have done so if SHAEF had heard a conversation between one of their number – an elderly reservist who had fought in the First World War – and his new officer. 'Can't you see that it's up to us old boys to run the whole show again, and we will do it exactly as we did back then. First of all, we have got to get Tommy on the run (the enemy were actually American paras of the 82nd Airborne) and then we've cracked it!'

Incredibly, the assault succeeded in bursting through the American perimeter and overrunning some of the landing zones before being forced back by determined counter attacks.

With time ticking way, the fighting at Arnhem worsened:

One terribly wounded German, shot through both legs, pulled himself hand over hand towards his own lines. We watched his slow and painful progress with horrified fascination … he pulled himself across the road, and over the pavement, and then he dragged his shattered body inch by inch up a grass covered slope … he must have been in terrible pain, but he conquered the slope by sheer willpower. With a superhuman effort he heaved himself up to clear the final obstacle – a rifle barked next to me and I watched in disbelief as the wounded German fell back, shot through the head. To me it was little short of murder, but to my companion, a Welshman and one of our best shots, the German was a legitimate target.[22]

The Germans replied with heavy weapons to blast the paras out, as Horst Weber described:

Buildings collapsed like dolls' houses. I don't know how anyone could live through that inferno. I felt truly sorry for the British. [Watching a panzer demolish a house] …the roof fell in, the top two storeys began to crumble and then, like the skin peeling off a skeleton, the whole front fell into the street … the din was awful, but even so above it all we could hear the wounded screaming.

As an SS trooper told a newly arrived artillery officer, 'The only way to get the British out is to blast the building down, brick by brick. Believe me, these are real men. They won't give up that bridge until we carry them out feet first.'[23]

In the heat of battle both sides sometimes behaved badly, spurred on by seeing their friends and comrades fall, as the *Frundsberg's* Rudolf Trapp knew all too well when his company commander was killed: 'Vogel was shot in the heart … a medic was killed trying to reach him and this made the boys really angry! We were determined to do the Tommies in!' Nevertheless, both sides also showed incredible restraint given the ferocity of the battle, as one para, John Hall, witnessed at first-hand when he looked up from bandaging a wounded comrade to see an SS trooper pointing his gun at him: 'I honestly thought I was going to die there and then; we sometimes didn't take prisoners, so I didn't expect them to either … he spared me. I didn't ask why.' Mercy was often a two-way street as Wolfgang Dombrowski saw:

What we were to do with our wounded? A Red Cross flag was produced, and casualties approached; slowly, step by step. To our astonishment the firing ceased immediately. Stretcher-bearers picked up the wounded, moved off, and the shooting started again. We couldn't understand this as we were used to conditions on the Eastern Front – these Paras were meant to be hard men, we knew they were! Yet we were allowed to pick up our wounded. The other side was then given the opportunity to do the same.[24]

The *Das Reich* panzer officer, Fritz Langanke, had said much the same thing about the Normandy fighting. He recalled that in Russia both sides would simply have driven over the wounded in their tanks.

By now, the rest of 1st Airborne had given up trying to reach the bridge and were focusing on survival. That effort wasn't helped by the Germans overrunning the re-supply landing zones and otherwise interfering with the dropping of ammunition, food and medical stores, as Rudolf Lindemann of Lippert's SS NCO School unit explained: 'We watched the supply drops every afternoon, we expected them at about 1600hrs. Having discovered that the key to signal the aircraft was by using coloured panels, we would set them out just before. The aircraft always dropped onto the panels – we always had enough supplies, but the British didn't get anything.'[25] In fact, of the fifteen hundred tons of supplies dropped to the 1st Airborne during the operation, less than two hundred tons reached them, the rest fell into grateful German hands, leading to senior officers saying Arnhem was the cheapest battle they ever fought because they were supplied by the British; sixty-six Allied transport planes were shot down. Even the Luftwaffe made its presence felt, with Johannes Kaufmann's unit 'claiming three RAF Typhoon fighter-bombers in the Arnhem area for the loss of one of our own'. They wouldn't be the last as '…we were sent to attack enemy jabos in the Arnhem area, where we met again large numbers of English and Ami fighters, and although we claimed three Spitfires and a P-47 Thunderbolt, we lost four more of our own comrades; two killed and two reported missing.'

Down on the ground, the paras were soon hungry and short of ammunition, forcing them to use any weapon they could lay their hands on, as an SS soldier recounted: 'After two to three days it was no longer possible to identify friend or foe from the weapons – ours generally fired faster than the British, but both sides used each other's.' The trooper in question was himself using a British Sten-gun![26]

Attempts were made to reinforce the British by air; most notably by the often under-appreciated 1st Polish Independent Parachute Brigade, led by the lion-hearted and irascible Stanisław Sosabowski. On the afternoon of Tuesday 19 September glider-borne elements of the brigade tried to land within the shrinking British perimeter. The Polish war correspondent Marek Swieciki witnessed the horrific results as Luftwaffe Bf 109 fighters tore into the unprotected gliders:

> Several gliders caught fire and, rolling over from wing to wing, dived in mad flight to the ground… One of the gliders broke up in the air like a child's toy, and a jeep, an anti-tank gun and men flew out of it – we had never expected things to be so bad, so very bad.[27]

Needless to say, the operation failed.

To the south, the Americans had now crossed the Waal by virtue of a courageous daylight river assault, carried out under withering fire. Reaching the far bank, the American paras stormed the bridge, shooting German snipers hidden in the upper steelwork, and leaving them dangling by the ropes they'd used to secure themselves to their perches. Not all died in combat though, as one disgusted German officer wrote in his diary: 'The Americans behaved as they always do, throwing our wounded from the bridge into the Waal, and shooting the few prisoners.' Almost three hundred German dead were counted on the bridge.[28]

Meanwhile, the fighting at Arnhem was reaching a crescendo, as Rudolf Trapp describes: '

> We were told to get some wounded or dead SS men out of the enemy field of fire...putting down covering fire with two machine-guns ... we would race down the street, open the half-tracks' rear door, pull our comrades in, and fire away as we sped back to cover ... the British fired very accurately. In one case they shot a man in the heart straight through his Soldbuch [German paper record carried by every soldier detailing pay/rations/awards etc].

Not every venture ended in success for Trapp and his comrades. Ordered to take his half-track and try and establish contact with a neighbouring unit, the crew knew they would have to run the gauntlet of a dug-in British anti-tank gun that had already claimed several victims:

> Bernd Schultze-Bernd was our driver, a farmer's son from Sendenhorst ... he was one of three *alte Hasen* (literally 'old hares' the nickname given to front veterans) in the Kompanie. During the orders there were tears in his eyes, he told our Kompanie commander that this wasn't going to work, but an order is an order ... we raced past the crossroads and got hit on the left, near Bernd's seat. The vehicle came to a halt. Bernd was dead, a direct hit from the shell.[29]

Heinz Harmel of the SS-*Frundsberg,* now decided that only a systematic building-by-building approach would work in Arnhem, as he personally directed artillery and panzer fire: 'Aim right under the gables and shoot metre by metre, floor by floor, until each house collapses.' On Thursday 21 September, Frost's remaining men were overrun and resistance ceased at the bridge. Charles 'Freddie' Gough – who had taken over command from Frost when the latter was wounded – was interrogated after the fighting by an SS-*Sturmbannführer:* 'I wish to congratulate you and your men. You are gallant soldiers. I fought at Stalingrad and it's obvious that you British have a great deal of experience in street fighting.'

Gough replied 'No, this is our first effort, we'll be much better next time.'

Frost himself was of the same mind: 'The Germans, and particularly the SS, were complimentary about the way we had fought the battle, but my bitterness was unassuaged.'

The weekend arrived, several days after the deadline for XXX Corps to reach Arnhem. The British advance had liberated Eindhoven, Nijmegen and a host of smaller Dutch towns and villages, but clearly wasn't going to reach the main objective before disaster overtook Urquhart's command. Joseph Enthammer, captured by the paras early in the battle, watched his jailers closely: 'The British soldiers were very close and informal with their officers ... there was no saluting, they simply talked normally – we would never have been allowed to conduct ourselves like that – we realised that these men must be élite soldiers.' Funnily enough, Enthammer would have observed the same behaviour among the Waffen-SS troops, as the *Wiking's* Ivar Corneliussen confirmed:

> Of course we saluted and all that in barracks, but at the front it was different. We greatly respected our officers as we knew they had been through the same training as us, and they never gave an order for us to do something they wouldn't do – we talked as equals and shared our rations – there was no big divide like in the Army.[30]

Despite the incidents of dubious or even criminal behaviour, one of the seemingly odd things that is said by many – although not all – participants in the battle, was that a sort of mutual respect grew between the two sides. A British para even joked with a captured German about the lack of fuel that the Wehrmacht was suffering from.

'You Jerries have developed a new tank with a crew of a thousand.'

'Impossible!'

'Oh, it's true – one man to steer it, one to command it, one gunner to fire it – and the other 997 to push it!'

The situation inside the perimeter was now critical, and with ammunition running out British courage was turning into desperation, as one German soldier remembered: '...a young Britisher began to dodge about to draw our fire, while another tried to come at us from the side with a knife. One man leaped at us swinging his rifle like a club.'

Finally, the decision was taken. Browning ordered Urquhart to withdraw his surviving men on the night of Monday 25 September – more than a week after they were dropped. In filthy weather, and forced to leave their wounded behind, the survivors ghosted past German outposts and reached the bank of the Rhine. There, they were ferried over to the southern side and safety, although not all were who they seemed, as John Stanleigh discovered when he quizzed a man walking down to the river with him who was wearing a German helmet.

'Why are you taking that home?'

'Vass?'

He looked at him and the penny dropped: 'Are you German?'

'Ja, yes.'

'What are you doing here?'

'I've had enough of this war, thank you. I want to be a prisoner.'

As dawn broke, three hundred paras were still marooned on the northern bank, having run out of time to be evacuated. Some tried to swim it and drowned. Eventually realising their enemies had flown, the Germans pressed forward, scooping up around six hundred men still in the perimeter – mostly wounded, although some had been out of contact with their own command and so hadn't known about the withdrawal. A cross-eyed German NCO approached Lieutenant Tom Ainslie: 'Good evening, that was a lovely battle, a really lovely battle. Have a cigar, we are human too.'

Bitter at being taken prisoner, one paratrooper said to his SS captor: 'The Russians'll give you lot some stick after the war for the way you've treated them.' The German spoke some English and replied, 'We treat them the same way you British treat the Irish.'

Market Garden had failed. In human terms the cost was relatively high by Western standards, but low in comparison to the slaughter in the East. As it was, the British 1st Airborne Division was more or less destroyed. Of the ten thousand or so men landed north of the Rhine, some 2,300 escaped – including one hundred and sixty Poles – leaving behind around two thousand dead and over six thousand captured – mostly wounded. American casualties had been lighter, but still numbered several thousand. XXX Corps, meanwhile, had lost fifteen hundred men and some eighty tanks. The *Westheer* had lost around half the Allied total, but in the end it wasn't the numbers that really mattered. What mattered was that the Germans had won. For the first time in what seemed an age, back in the *Heimat* (the German homeland), they could toast a victory against the Allies.

Everyone could now see the Anglo-Americans weren't invincible, their airpower wasn't completely dominant, and they were as fallible as anyone else. This mattered, because it shored up the support at home that might have crumbled if the *Westheer* had suffered another defeat. Conversely, it was a major blunder by the Allied high command. At a time when the British and American armies were decrying their lack of frontline infantrymen, they opted for an operation that squandered thousands of the very best they had. Paras are many things – sometimes not all of them good – but what they are at their core are highly aggressive, superbly trained, extremely well-motivated light infantry – as the American 101st would resoundingly prove at Bastogne three months later. There was no need to throw them away in the Netherlands on a mission to nowhere. The 1st Allied Airborne Army was an unnecessary luxury after Normandy. Its component divisions should have been used as the point of the spear (a *schwerpunkt*) for a decisive Allied advance on the main effort, alongside heavy armour, to maximise their effectiveness. Instead they were made to kick their collective heels on air bases in England, growing increasingly frustrated as operation after operation was cancelled. Looking at *Market Garden* it seems almost as if a mission was *found* for a force – rather than what it should have been, a mission *needing* a force.

As the Allies licked their wounds and wondered what exactly had gone wrong after their golden summer, the *Westheer* got on with readying themselves for the next round. For the Germans, Arnhem was in many ways a Waffen-SS battle; large contingents of Army men had been involved, as well as *fallschirmjäger*, but it was the men of the armed SS who had led the initial reaction to the landings, and who had then played the leading role in frustrating the vital British task of capturing the bridge over the Rhine. If nothing else, it proved that Eisenhower's comment after the Normandy slaughter that 'the SS element fought itself to extinction at Falaise' was a little premature. In fact, Hitler's black guard would have one, final role to play in the West that coming winter.

In the meantime, Heinz Harmel's *Frundsberg*, the main hammer at Arnhem, was withdrawn back to Siegen in Germany to rest and be refitted. Reinforcements arrived, a full thirty per cent of them being former Luftwaffe and Kriegsmarine personnel, none too pleased to be drafted into the ranks of the armed SS, as one of their new officers, *SS-Obersturmführer* Steinbach, realised: 'At first the transfer to the Waffen-SS made them shudder, but our welcome ... soon made them feel part of us.'[31] Remarkably, by 1 November, the division had a strength of 14,861 men equipped with almost sixty panzers and self-propelled guns, and over a hundred armoured half-tracks, with another sixty half-tracks and almost ninety panzers scheduled to be delivered.

Where did all this equipment come from? The *Westheer* had basically left everything it had in the fields and ditches of France, and von Rundstedt himself had told Berlin that as *OB West* he only had about a hundred or so panzers at the beginning of September, and now – barely two months later – whole panzer divisions were being reconstituted. This was the other autumn miracle for the Wehrmacht to sit alongside the purely military one in the Netherlands and at Arnhem; and this one was made at home – in the Reich itself.

The first part of the turnaround came in Germany's factories and forges. Albert Speer's rationalisation and transformation of the Reich's industries was coming into full effect, and finally – after wasted years of playing at it – the country was on a proper war footing. Panzer production was a case in point; in 1939 Germany manufactured just sixty-two a month, in the autumn of 1944 that number hit 1,524.

In fact, weapons output reached its highest point of the war in the period September to November 1944, helping boost the number of panzers and assault-guns rolling off the production lines to 8,328 of the former and 5,751 of the latter for the year.[32]

It wasn't just the quantity either, but the quality of those armoured vehicles that would make a difference. The *Panther* – or to give it its proper title the *Panzerkampfwagen Panther* – was over its initial teething troubles, fully on-stream and was now the main battle tank of the *panzerwaffe*. The more advanced second generation of tank destroyers, the *Jagdpanzer IV*, the *Hetzer* (Troublemaker) and the *Jagdpanther*, were also coming off the line, replacing their predecessors and providing their crews with some of the best machines of the war.[33] It wasn't just the panzer-men who were happy at the new equipment they were getting, it was their comrades in the infantry too. The *landser* had begun the war carrying the Kar98k – basically an updated version of the rifle his father carried in the First World War – and had often found himself on the wrong end of an unequal battle as his enemies were increasingly equipped with a better weapon, such as the American's semi-automatic M1 Garand. Now, German industry had an answer; the *Sturmgewehr 44* (assault rifle 44), more commonly known as the *StG 44* or *MP 44* – the world's very first mass-produced assault rifle. Offering its user the ability to fire single shots or switch to fully automatic, it provided the humble *landser* with a sea-change in firepower. Some 425,977 were produced before the war's end, the only complaint being they couldn't make enough of them. So successful was it that the Soviets copied it as the basis for the ubiquitous AK-47 assault rifle of modern times.

However, the greatest change came not for the Army, but for its much-maligned sister service, the Luftwaffe. Working in tandem with Erhard Milch, Speer totally re-engineered German aircraft production. The numbers are staggering: in 1940 Germany built 1,870 single-engine fighters, by 1943 that had only grown to 9,626, but in 1944 the figure shot up to 25,860, with September's monthly output hitting 3,103![34] It wasn't just a tale of the same tired old models either, October would see the introduction into frontline squadrons of the new *Bf 109K-4* – an upgrade on the G-variant, with heavier armament and increased pilot protection – to help counter the Allied bomber fleets. However, a far greater leap forward in technology was provided by the arrival into service of not one but two ground-breaking aircraft: the *Me 262 Schwalbe* (Swallow) jet fighter and the *Me 163 Komet* (Comet) rocket fighter.

To understand just how advanced these aircraft were for the time it's important to grasp the limitations of what had come before them. With level flight speed being probably the most important measure of a fighter's overall performance, the key is that this speed is determined by the balance between *thrust* and *drag* – drag being the resistance of the air.

That drag increases at the square of the speed; so doubling the speed produces four times the drag, and with propeller efficiency falling away sharply at high speed, the two factors combined to effectively plateau the possible speed of a 'normal' aircraft to around 400mph (for example the British Spitfire's top speed was 370mph). This plateau had been reached by pretty much every major combatant nation by 1944. The only way forward was through a revolution – the use of a turbojet or a rocket. The former was simpler and lighter than a standard engine, with constant power output at all speeds, while the rocket was simpler and lighter than both. The two German engineers and aircraft manufacturers, Ernst Heinkel and Willi Messerschmitt, competed to build the new types with Heinkel's *He 280* prototype losing out in the government's eyes to Messerschmitt's *Me 262*. Development had been desperately slow though, a situation not helped by Hitler's insistence that the new aircraft be a fighter-bomber, and not a pure fighter – Hitler's argument being that a fighter is a *defensive* weapon, while a bomber is an *offensive* one. The *Komet* had its problems too, not least with its propellant; High Test Hydrogen Peroxide, HTP, was a very unstable and highly corrosive chemical mixture that was extremely difficult to handle. HTP's general unsuitability had been demonstrated in horrific circumstances back in December 1943 during a test flight, when the pilot – *Oberleutnant* Josef '*Joschi*' Pöhs, an Austrian with forty-three victories to his name – took off and released his landing gear as required, only for it to bounce, hit the plane and cut the engine. Somehow, Pöhs managed to keep control of the aircraft and land it safely, however by the time the emergency crews got to him the caustic HTP had leaked and filled the cockpit; Pöhs was dead and literally seeping through the seams of his flight overalls.[35] Nevertheless, the performance of the new types was nothing short of remarkable. The 262 jet could reach 530mph, while the *Komet* dwarfed even that by hitting over 620mph. Neither design was perfect, and both aircraft had their flaws – the *Komet* in particular – but what they offered the Luftwaffe was the *possibility* of a solution to its most pressing problem; the dreaded fleets of Allied *Viermots* (German slang for the Allied four-engine heavy bombers) and their escorts, which were devastating Germany's cities and industries, and killing her pilots at a rate of two for every bomber shot down. It was a situation Heinz Knoke was all too familiar with:

> The Americans are approaching central Germany. I am only able to take five aircraft into the air as losses recently have been very heavy. More than one thousand enemy aircraft are reported … they come over in groups of thirty to forty via a route we call 'bomber alley'… accompanied by Unteroffizier Krüger, who was posted to us just two days ago, I attack a Fortress in a formation of about thirty Viermots… In a frontal attack I put my first salvo directly into the flight cabin.

I then attack again, this time diving down upon my victim from above the tail... I pull in close beneath the monster fuselage and continue blasting away with all I have in my magazines ... the crew of the Fortress bale out, the fuselage is a blazing torch... At that moment a second aircraft comes hurtling down out of the sky ... it was my wingman, the young Unteroffizier.

Knoke and his fellow *jagdflieger* were under enormous pressure: 'The Staffel loses another six killed today in a dog-fight with Thunderbolts, Lightnings and Mustangs covering another Viermot attack. Our little band grows smaller and smaller. Every man can now work out on the fingers of one hand when his own turn is due to come.'

On the ground beneath them, more workers were needed from a labour pool that had already fallen from thirty-nine million in 1939 to twenty-nine million in 1944, mainly due to conscription into the Wehrmacht. To help counter this impact, Minister for Propaganda Joseph Goebbels proved as adept at introducing drastic economic measures as he was at manipulating public opinion. Appointed as Plenipotentiary for Total War by Hitler two days after the July Bomb Plot, Goebbels revelled in his new appointment: 'It takes a bomb under his arse to make Hitler see reason.' The key – as he saw it – was to do what Great Britain had done several years previously, and substantially increase female participation in the workforce; get German *hausfraus* out of the home and into the factory. Under the slogan 'The German Woman Helps Win', he firstly increased the upper age limit for women to be liable for service in war industries from forty-five to fifty-five years of age, and then began a campaign to encourage women in particular into industry. *Aktion B* teams, as Goebbels christened them, consisting of a speaker and two other Party members – *Volksgenossen* – toured their districts, visiting restaurants, coffee houses and social clubs, exhorting patrons to volunteer for war work, as radio and news reels bombarded the populace with the same message. The effects were substantial, with the number of women in the total workforce climbing to almost fifty per cent by the autumn of 1944. To add extra impetus, he also turned to non-German female labour; the army of women working in domestic service in German households, many of whom were forced labourers kidnapped from their home nations. Some four hundred thousand were 'reassigned' away from households and into the war economy. Non-German men fared no better than their female counterparts, with almost six million foreign labourers toiling away in German factories and farms, alongside two million POWs – forced into work that was against the provisions of the Geneva Convention.

Overall, by September 1944 a full quarter of the Nazis labour force were non-Germans, many of them coerced, with nothing to incentivise them bar the overseer's whip. They weren't comparable of course, but even conditions for native German workers were no bed of roses, with the standard working week being a full sixty hours, except in panzer and aircraft factories where it was seventy-two. Holidays were a thing of the past, and the queues at the shops kept on getting longer as food became scarcer and of lower quality; by the autumn of '44 the weekly food ration for a German adult was 2,525 grams of bread, 362 grams of meat and 218 grams of fats – in food-starved Britain the meat ration was almost twice that and there was no limit on bread. Real coffee was a rarity in German homes, with *ersatz* coffee made out of acorns or hickory being the only type on offer. Even the hallowed German *wurst* wasn't sacred, with the meat content of Germany's national dish gradually reduced and replaced by breadcrumbs and even sawdust. Albert Speer saw at first-hand the impact on the population: 'When people can't take anymore they just become numb ... when I saw them going through the streets in the morning to work they were like ghosts ... but work went on, morale was still there.'[36]

Speer instinctively understood the importance of the home front. Twenty-six years earlier it had been the collapse in people's belief in victory that had doomed the *Kaiser*, and this time round the Nazis were determined to avoid the same mistakes.

The Nazi approach to maintaining German morale was carrot and stick. The stick was the threat of direct action against any transgressors and defeatists by the power of a police state. Although ever-present in the Nazi era, it was nowhere near as pervasive as was commonly thought, with the all-seeing *Gestapo* only numbering thirty-two thousand employees in 1944, spread over more than half of Europe. They made their presence felt though, and everyone had a *Gestapo* story to tell:

> One of my patients, a very decent fellow called Probst, by chance ran into an old girlfriend at the station. The conversation soon turned to the war and Probst said he wasn't sure it could still be won. A few hours later he was arrested as he was having dinner with us. Three days later he was dead – executed for 'demoralising the war effort.'[37]

This sort of occurrence was unusual, with most tip-offs to the *Gestapo* never even followed up, let alone acted upon. In most instances the *fear* of the threat was greater than the threat itself. However, fear itself wasn't enough. Joseph Goebbels – with his intimate knowledge of the German mass psyche – knew that the population needed to have *hope* in order to carry on; that hope may be slim and even illusory, but it had to exist nonetheless. That need for a positive was perfectly captured in the Nazi idea of *Wunderwaffen* – 'Wonder Weapons' – of which the Germans were enamoured, as the twenty-three-year-old East Prussian, Lisa-Lotte Küssner, admitted: 'I believed in the wonder weapons; that our army would protect us; that the Russians could be stopped.

I had faith.'[38] This was a widely held view among the population as an internal report from the Frankfurt office of the SS's own security service – the *Sicherheitsdienst* or *SD* – made clear in its findings: 'One older labourer remarked that the revenge weapons would now bring victory.' It wasn't just civilians who believed that the new weapons would bring final victory, many in the Wehrmacht thought so too, including the naval officer Armin Weighardt: 'The new weapon is going to win the war! I believe in it!'[39] and *Feldwebel* Kunz of the *404. Infanterie-Regiment*: 'If the V-2 is operating the war will end in our favour.' The *Leibstandarte-SS's* Erwin Bartmann heard the same message from his family: 'My father exclaimed, "This is the Wunderwaffe, our scientists have done well with their rockets ... but it would really surprise the British if they put a special bomb in a rocket."'[40]

Goebbels carefully fostered these delusions through the use of state media, such as the weekly newspaper *Das Reich,* which trumpeted the advent of the first V-1 attack on London with the declaration that this was 'the day that eighty million Germans have been passionately waiting for.'[41] The ex-sailor and unemployed stormtrooper Fritz Mühlebach read the headlines with glee:

> With the use of our new wonder weapons the Führer would force a decision. There was a lot of talk about the wonder weapons. We learned that our scientists had developed entirely new types of planes ... and these were now ready to go into action... That was why we were almost crazy with joy when we heard the first secret weapon, the V-1, was at last being used against Britain ... any fears we might have had when the final decision didn't come immediately were soon dispelled when news came through that the V-2 had come into action... It was said that very soon the bombardment of America would start with an improved model. As usual there were the grumblers and fault finders ... but the morale of the people was lifted tremendously. They knew that these weapons couldn't fail to turn the course of the war.[42]

Landsers at the front agreed with Mühlebach, as a letter home from one made clear: 'Even if our allies abandon us we must not lose courage, once the Führer has his new weapons deployed then the final victory will follow.'

It's easy to look at this belief in retrospect and criticise it as clutching at straws, but even among those who should have – and did – know better, the myth was incredibly seductive. Albert Speer, the man with overall responsibility for producing these wonder weapons, said of the time:

> We possessed a remote-controlled flying bomb, a rocket plane that was even faster than a jet plane, a rocket missile that homed in on enemy planes ... a torpedo that reacted to sound and could thus pursue a

ship ... development of a ground to air missile had been completed ...
we were literally suffering from an excess of projects...[43]

Speer wasn't alone in the Nazi hierarchy in his wonderment at the
possibilities. Robert Ley, head of the German Labour Front and a
vicious anti-Semite and persistent drunkard, buttonholed the urbane
former architect on the matter: 'Death rays have been invented! A simple
apparatus that we can produce in large quantities ... there's no doubt
about it. This will be the decisive weapon!'[44]

Goebbels would have been pleased to hear of Ley's faith in the
propaganda, but he wasn't the audience the diminutive minister was
aiming at. The audience Goebbels wanted was typified by Inge Molter, an
unassuming *hausfrau* who wrote to her serving soldier husband Alfred,
'We've got to keep going until the new weapons are ready, it can't be
that the enemy will force us to our knees before that happens.' Time
and again Nazi propaganda hammered the message home and, whereas
in the victory years the headlines were all about the latest Wehrmacht
conquest, now the mood music switched to 'What We Are Fighting For?'
The glossy magazine *Signal* led the way. It asked its readers the question
'Has Germany a programme for which she is fighting? Answer: what the
German soldier is defending is not a programme. It is the very substance
of his existence, the richness and variety of his civil life in peacetime ...
the fulfilment of his claim that an individual shall be respected for his own
sake.' The dreadful hypocrisy of these words given the Nazis wholesale
denial of life – let alone respect – to anyone they deemed unworthy of
it, is staggering. To compound the infamy, *Signal* then went on to list
what it regarded as the main reasons for the *landsers'* continued struggle,
including 'Man's right to culture', 'Rights of Nationalities' and 'the final
solution of the question regarding workers rights' – the wording of the
last point in particular is beyond tragedy.

There was another aspect to sustaining German morale that played its
part that momentous autumn, and that revolved around the *alternative*
to continuing the war; the dangers of peace itself. A standing joke
among the *landsers* since before D-Day was 'make the most of the war,
because the peace is going to be hell!' Extraordinary as this sentiment
may seem to us now, at the time it carried a lot of sway. It was given
initial impetus by the decisions taken by the Big Three of Churchill,
Roosevelt and Stalin at their January 1943 conference in Casablanca
in north Africa. There, Roosevelt publicly declared that the aim of the
war was Germany's 'unconditional surrender', a term that evoked fear
and loathing among the German populace in equal measure. For many
it signified that the Allies wanted nothing less than the humiliation of
their country – a stripping of its national pride – something that played a
not insignificant role in sparking Germany's move to war in 1939 in the

first place. Needless to say, Goebbels seized on the American President's announcement: 'It means slavery, castration, the end of Germany as a nation.' Patton thought it a mistake too: 'Look at this fool unconditional surrender announcement. If the Hun ever needed anything to put a burr under his saddle, this is it. He'll now fight like the devil ... it will take much longer, cost us more lives and the Russians will take more territory – sometimes we're such goddamned fools it makes me weep!' Then came news of the so-called Morgenthau Plan. Henry Morgenthau Jr was Roosevelt's Secretary of the Treasury. A brilliant financier and administrator, he had played a major role in the New Deal programme that had helped the United States overcome the after-effects of the Wall Street Crash of 1929. Now, as the fighting raged, he penned a memorandum entitled *Suggested Post-Surrender Program for Germany*. As a serious policy proposal, it is extraordinary.

It called for nothing less than the dismemberment of Germany as a nation, with the creation of two separate German statelets in the south and north. Large tracts of the country would be annexed and handed to Poland and the Soviet Union, with France ceded the whole Saar region. De-industrialisation would be enforced, with people encouraged to migrate away from the Ruhr, and factories and mines either dismantled and shipped abroad or destroyed. The memo wasn't adopted by the US government as policy, but when the details were leaked, Berlin Radio trumpeted to the nation, 'The Jew Morgenthau sings the same tune as the Jews in the Kremlin.' For many at the front there seemed no other option but to fight on, as one of their number explained: 'We few old infantrymen no longer believed in the whole bag of tricks. For us it was clear; we could no longer win the war, therefore there was nothing left for us to do but sell our lives as dearly as possible.' The Waffen-SS NCO Max Wind agreed: 'The Allies' biggest mistake was "unconditional surrender". If there had been a chance of a deal we would have taken it... It was common knowledge what the enemy would do if they won ... knowing that, we only wanted to fight.'[45] Max Wind would get his wish.

With industrial production soaring, what the Wehrmacht needed was the men to wield the output of the factory gates; and here again Joseph Goebbels proved an unlikely champion. As foreign labour in the home released more German women for war work, so more German men could be conscripted from hitherto protected occupations. To produce even more men for service, in late August Goebbels ordered large-scale redundancies in local government and administration across the Reich, as well as radically cutting the entertainment and media industries; public orchestras were shut down, theatres, music halls, and cabarets were closed, as were newspapers and magazines, and even mail deliveries were restricted to one a day to release postmen for the front. The only publishing houses allowed to stay open were those printing

Hitler's *Mein Kampf* or medical textbooks to train doctors and nurses for the Wehrmacht. The conscription age – having already dropped from nineteen in 1940 to seventeen in 1943 – was further reduced, with a big drive to encourage volunteering among boys born in 1928. Local *Hitlerjugend* leaders were ordered to promote enlistment among their young charges, and their bi-monthly magazine, *Der Pimpf* (The Young Scamp) was full of slogans and stories extolling the virtues of joining the Wehrmacht, such as 'To conquer and die for the Führer's idea is the greatest honour,' and that the graves of the fallen were 'silent witnesses of the selfless willingness and soldierly spirit of our youth. Young hearts carry this belief and this spirit of the immortal battalions onwards.' Higher education was targeted, with Goebbels effectively shutting up shop on Germany's university campuses; sixteen thousand students were drafted into the Wehrmacht and another thirty-one thousand conscripted into war industries.[46] Teenagers weren't Goebbels's only target – the upper age limit for compulsory service was extended to fifty. Non-Germans within the borders of the Reich didn't escape the drag net either, with thousands of ethnic Poles in particular drafted in, as one Nazi official made plain: 'There were many cases where whole villages or towns were compulsorily entered in the register according to fixed quotas laid down... For example, a local branch leader or mayor was instructed to enter eighty per cent of his village as German although it was actually eighty per cent Polish.' In these border areas, refusal to be 'Germanised' became a crime, made punishable by deportation or imprisonment. The *Deutsche Volksliste* (*DVL*) or German People's List system, in use since the Nazi-Soviet partition of Poland back in 1939, was widened. *Class 1* was for ethnic Germans who had retained their mother tongue and were actively pro-German; they were granted German citizenship and could even join the Nazi Party. *Class 2* was for people of 'German racial descent' – *Deutschstämmige* – who had maintained their German characteristics, such as speaking German but who had 'remained passive' under Polish rule. *Class 3* included Germans in mixed marriages and their children and 'indigenous persons considered as partly Polonized' – *Eingedeutschte* – *or* 'voluntarily Germanized'. They received green ID papers and were essentially on probation, while *Class 4* was for those who had 'actively worked in a manner hostile to Germany' – they got nothing. Nevertheless, the presumption was that *everyone* – even a Class 4 – was a German deep down. The results spoke for themselves; in the heavily Polish Danzig-West Prussia region some 1,153,000 people were registered on the DVL; 150,000 in Class 1, 125,000 in Class 2, eight thousand in Class 4, and no fewer than 870,000 in Class 3 – officially, well over ninety per cent of the population were now classed as Germanized and liable for conscription.

The impact of all these measures was dramatic. An additional one million men entered the ranks of the Wehrmacht between September and December 1944, taking its overall strength to the highest it ever reached, but with one in six of them over thirty years of age, and most serving in companies lucky to field a single officer. Those same companies were overwhelmingly in a new category of formation, created in late 1944 to help the Wehrmacht turn the tide of the war; the *Volks-grenadier Divisionen* (Peoples Grenadier Divisions), or VGDs.

Before D-Day the German Army had undergone a transformation with the establishment of the new *M1944-type* infantry division. Trumpeted as the field army's response to the greater availability of firepower – and lessons learned at the front – in reality, it was a fairly transparent attempt to boost the number of divisions on paper by significantly reducing the number of men in each formation. So, the third battalion of each rifle regiment was disbanded, and the artillery regiment was downsized too. The result was a unit with roughly the same amount of punch but with only 12,772 men; thirty per cent fewer than before. It had been these M1944 divisions which had been crushed in Belarus and France in the summer, and their time was now up.

In their place would be something envisioned as truly revolutionary; a new, avowedly National Socialist army, as the head of the SS, Heinrich Himmler, wrote in an article for the Nazis' own *Völkischer Beobachter* newspaper: 'True marriage between Party and Wehrmacht has today become a living reality... The Army that must win this war MUST be the National Socialist People's Army.' This radical change was long overdue according to Fritz Mühlebach:

> We all felt very optimistic about these last changes, the regular Army officers had been too arrogant for too long, they were only interested in their own comforts, and they were inefficient and snobbish. They received a wonderful shaking, and we enjoyed noticing it and felt pleased when the order came out that they had to use the Hitler salute to remind them all the time who was the real master in Germany.[47]

So was born the *Volks-grenadier*; a name explicitly chosen to appeal both to German nationalism and its concept of the *Volk*, and to the country's military traditions of the *Grenadier* – there was even an echo of the Red Army's use of the *Guards* title to confer something akin to an élite status.

Ever since the end of the war, the accepted historical view of the *VGDs* has been overwhelmingly negative. They have been criticised as poorly trained, ill-equipped and badly led, little more than a last throw of the dice by a desperate regime – the reality is far more complex. Never envisaged as cannon-fodder, instead they were intended to embody a new Army shorn of class and hidebound tradition, and imbued with

National Socialist zeal. Initially, Himmler personally reserved the right to appoint *all* new officers into the *VGDs*, to ensure those selected were true Nazis. Needless to say, this stipulation was very quickly abandoned as impractical, given the first wave alone was nineteen divisions strong, with a further six formed in mid-September, and another twenty-four in October. Nonetheless, the bar for officers to serve in the new divisions was set very high indeed. To command a battalion or regiment required the holder to be a combat veteran, and to have previously been awarded either the German Cross in Gold or, preferably, the much-coveted Knight's Cross. Just to be sure, Himmler then deleted the post of divisional chaplain – there was no need for God in the Nazis' world – and added to the roster the *National-Sozialistischer Führungsoffizier* (*NSFO*) – the National Socialist Leadership Officer; a direct copy of the Red Army's commissar no less.

Smaller again than the M1944 type, a *VGD* had an establishment of 10,072 men, with its fusilier battalion reduced to a single company. Each would have three grenadier regiments of two battalions, plus a reconnaissance company on bicycles, an integral armoured element of self-propelled guns (either *Hetzers* or *StuG IIIs*) and no fewer than fifty-four artillery pieces.[48] The divisional cadres – the *Stammeinheiten* – were to be based on the remnants of frontline units shattered in the summer's fighting; so, 272. *VGD* was based on the experienced 272. *ID*, after the latter had been badly beaten up in Normandy. This meant that the new formations had a hard core of veteran officers and NCOs at their very heart – for example, forty-six men transferred from the 272. *ID's* old Fusilier Battalion to form the basis of the new 272. *VGD's* Fusilier Company – they were in fact the only survivors from the original 708 fusiliers.[49] The new recruits to fill the ranks were to be the cream of the crop that Goebbels had managed to squeeze out of the manpower pool – preferably the youngest and fittest from the 1926 and 1927 birth years. This did happen, but so urgent was the need for men that thousands of personnel were mass-transferred from the Luftwaffe and Kriegsmarine to make up the inevitable shortfalls – for the latter it was almost thirty per cent of its entire strength.

Lacking infantry training and combat experience, these men were hardly the stuff of the intended élite. Neither were some of their comrades who were ethnic Poles or Czechs from Class 3 of the DVL, or convalescing soldiers whose official period for recovery was drastically curtailed to get them back to the frontline. 272. *VGD's* forty-six-strong Fusilier Company, for example, was bulked out with sixty men from the normal training and replacement units, along with thirty-six unemployed U-boat crewmen from Wilhelmshaven. These latter 'volunteers' were less than enamoured at being forcibly transferred from what they viewed as a premier service and downgraded to mere infantrymen. However, their inclusion on the roster helped keep the average age of the company to twenty-four years of age – full of old men the *VGD*s were not.

To help redress any shortcomings amongst the ranks, it was decided that firepower was the answer – and lots of it. Single-shot *panzerfaust* anti-tank weapons were liberally handed out, and no fewer than twenty-six of the new *StG 44* assault rifles were issued per company, along with eleven MG42 machine-guns; the *Spandaus* so dreaded by Allied infantrymen. The result was a *VGD* company that fielded far fewer men than its predecessors earlier in the war but could put down an incredible 570kg weight of shot per minute on an enemy, compared to just 135kg back in 1941. Although this put huge strain on German industry's ability to supply the required amount of ammunition, as Speer recognised in an edict he sent out in late October: 'It appears that the Machine-Pistol Model 44 is being issued to Volks-grenadier divisions in great quantities without ensuring that the requisite ammunition is available. It is wrong to give out this machine-pistol to units to enter battle without first guaranteeing that sufficient ammunition is at hand.'

Just as concerning for the new formations as shortage of ammunition was their lack of training, motorised transport and communications equipment. With so many of the recruits hailing from the Army's sister services or from the factory floor, it was essential that they received proper training to enable them to perform at their best at the front, but necessity often prevented this from taking place, as von Rundstedt himself admitted: 'The state of training of the existing troop units and the newly-arrived VGDs is poor due to insufficient time ... the situation demanded that these units be immediately committed to combat.'

As for transport, *Volks-grenadier* battalions were as reliant as the old M1944 divisions on the horse rather than the internal combustion engine, being supplied with 430 of the former and just nineteen of the latter – ten of which were motorcycles. The situation was not much better in the now-combined support regiment, where 171 trucks were available to supply all the division's logistical needs; the American equivalent had 1,440. As for radios, the Germans were issued one per company, and more often than not had to rely on landlines or runners to communicate if a loss or mechanical fault occurred. This lack of modern radio sets was especially problematic when it came to calling in fire support from the artillery; not a problem the Allies laboured under, with their own infantry units handsomely supplied with sets and able to call down fire seemingly at a moments' notice, hence the *landsers'* belief in the 'never ending Ami artillery fire'.

Despite these drawbacks, it's clear that the *VGD*s were not as ramshackle as often portrayed, rather they were a last concerted effort by the Nazi war machine to produce a force capable of swinging the fighting back in Germany's favour.

The *VGDs* weren't the only structural innovation undertaken by the Army that autumn to prepare itself for future campaigning. It also greatly expanded its roster of *Panzer-Brigaden* and assault artillery, the so-called *Sturm-artillerie*. The former were nothing new on the German Order of Battle (OOB), having been in existence in one form or another since 1939. The concept behind them was to establish a unit which was armour-heavy and able to act – and react – far faster and with greater flexibility than the larger and more cumbersome *panzer division*. Modelled on *Oberst* dr. Franz Bäke's *Schweres Panzer Regiment Bäke* (Heavy Panzer Regiment Bäke), which had proven its worth in the Cherkassy Pocket fighting, the first wave of ten brigades was created by a Hitler order in July 1944. Numbered from 101 to 110, they contained forty to fifty panzers and assault guns, and a battalion of panzer grenadiers in armoured half-tracks. A further three – 111 to 113 – were formed in September, with this wave having double the number of panzers and accompanying grenadiers. The new brigades' stable mates were to be the *Heeres-Sturmartillerie-Brigaden* – the Army Assault-artillery brigades, first proposed back in 1935 by Erich von Manstein – then a lowly *Oberst*. Each was to have thirty assault-guns and an additional fifteen assault-howitzers, and were designed to provide mobile fire support to the infantry, although by the autumn of 1944 they were far more useful as defensive tank destroyer units, as attested by the Belgian Flemish Waffen-SS crewman, Herman Van Gyseghem:

> The Sturmgeschütze were lower and faster than normal panzers and were almost invisible. They had no turret. A normal panzer like a Tiger could turn its turret, and it had a crew of five, whereas we had to do our job with just the four of us. I was the radio operator – the *funker*, and I sat on the right side in the *Hetzer*, and I had to use the machine-gun on top of it, on the outside. I also had to load the main gun. During the fighting the cabin interior was overloaded with 7.5cm shells for the main gun. The most dangerous place was reserved for the driver. He sat down below and had nothing more than a narrow slit to see through. I was lucky, I was never wounded… Serving in panzers like we did, meant you didn't easily get wounded like the infantry guys would. In the infantry, you have man-to-man fighting. In our 'assault guns' things were quite different. You are driving around, and firing at other tanks and vehicles, not at men. It's all technology, mechanical, and you know; it's either them or us. In the panzers it was all or nothing – dead or alive.[50]

With fresh blood, and new equipment, the Wehrmacht had received a new lease of life. The Anglo-Americans had had their chance, but the failure at Arnhem had proven to be a double-blow for the Allies; having handed a much-needed victory to the Wehrmacht, and given the Third Reich precious time to reorganise and rebuild their forces. Germany's armed forces had come close to collapse – very close in fact – but weren't finished yet, as one of them made clear:

> We got two hundred ex-Luftwaffe men to help fill the ranks – some were former pilots, but most were ground crew – they had no infantry training these guys, they were useless. I was told I had four days to train them, that was it, just four days! They didn't have a chance and didn't last long – they were all killed soon enough … but there were still quite a few of us *frontschwein* left and we were ready to fight on.[51]

Nevertheless, the initiative still lay with the Anglo-Americans, the question was – how and where would they exploit it?

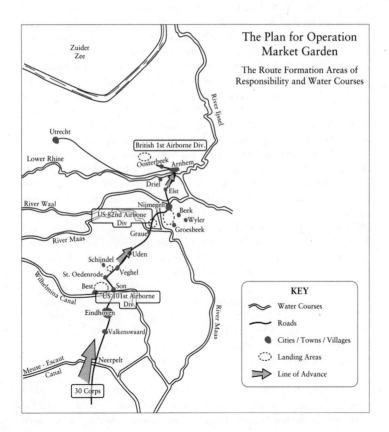

The Plan for Operation Market Garden

The Route Formation Areas of Responsibility and Water Courses

KEY

Water Courses
Roads
Cities / Towns / Villages
Landing Areas
Line of Advance

4

The Battle of the Border

Back in 1940, the Wehrmacht won a spectacular series of victories and conquered most of Western Europe by employing a new military strategy; *blitzkrieg*. The actual name wasn't used at the time, but the concept was clear – the massing of force at the enemy's weakest point to break their line, and then a headlong rush into his rear areas, paralysing his ability to resist until a cascade of collapse occurred. By the summer of 1944, the Anglo-Americans and Soviets had mastered the theory and developed it to a point way beyond that of the 1940 Wehrmacht. As a result, Germany had tottered, and the end of the war seemed tantalisingly close. Then, Soviet pre-occupation with the shape of post-war Europe, and Allied fumbling, had ended that dream. However, all was not yet lost for the Anglo-Americans. German industry had finally crunched into gear after years of half-hearted effort, and the training depots were full again, but the Germans weren't yet ready to seize the initiative. The ball was still in the Allied court as it were – and they proceeded to try and kick it into their own goal by undertaking a series of operations along Germany's western border that for the most part were as inexplicable as they were dreadful for those involved. These battles are little-known, and even less remembered, as the eminent British historian Max Hastings wrote:

> The American battles around the Siegfried Line in September and early October have attracted nothing like the historic attention lavished on Normandy, Arnhem and the Bulge. Yet in those days, and in that area, perished the last realistic prospect that the Allies might achieve a breakthrough to the heart of Germany in 1944.

One of these forgotten battles was fought at Aachen – the cathedral city, Charlemagne's city, the seat of the Holy Roman Empire and the place where no fewer than thirty-one Kings of the Germans had been crowned. Aachen was a city right on Nazi Germany's western border; a hop, skip and a jump from the border with Belgium and the Netherlands. Another battle would be fought some one hundred and forty miles south of Aachen as the crow flies, at Metz; another medieval architectural jewel, and capital of Lorraine, then a German province annexed after Paris's surrender in 1940. But it was the conflict in the green heart of the Hürtgen forest that would stand out as the epitome of Anglo-American senselessness that winter.

There were no British or Canadian troops advancing towards this stretch of frontier in autumn '44, only the Americans of Patton's and Alexander Patch's Third and Seventh Armies respectively, and the Frenchmen of Jean de Lattre de Tassigny's *Armée B* – soon to be renamed the *1re Armée*. Patch and de Tassigny's troops were all part of Jacob Devers's Sixth Army Group, as it motored up from southern France chasing the remnants of *Generaloberst* Johannes Blaskowitz's *Heeresgruppe G* towards the borders of the Reich. Harried by Allied airpower and newly enthusiastic *résistants* and starved of fuel, ammunition and supplies, Blaskowitz somehow managed to shepherd 140,000 men, two dozen panzers and 165 guns to a new defensive line roughly aligning with the border-as-was. Once there they turned and fought, as *Major* Georg Grossjohann of *198. Infanterie-Division* explained:

> Immediately across from the position of our heavy-gun section, several Ami tanks suddenly appeared in the dense bush. Our short-barrelled 150mm guns were basically only used for high-angle fire, but as the surprised gun crews had to protect themselves they aimed directly at the first two enemy panzers and fired…the distance amounted to not much more than fifty metres – the effect was horrible – the two Amis were hit and literally exploded into pieces, and the others behind them immediately shifted into reverse. Unfortunately, these 'moments of success' became more and more infrequent.[1]

Not far from Grossjohann's *198. ID* was another unit that had been heavily involved in the fighting in France, Edgar Feuchtinger's *21. Panzerdivision*. Having failed to push the Allies back into the sea on D-Day – partly due to the absence in a Parisian fleshpot of Feuchtinger himself – the men of *Rommel's Zirkus* as it was nicknamed, had distinguished themselves in the Normandy battles before escaping the Falaise disaster and heading east. With Feuchtinger absent – again – and another regimental commander, Josef Rauch[2] having been sent home due to illness, it was left to Hans von Luck to lead what was now in reality *Kampfgruppe (KG) von Luck*. 'On 9 September after an eleven-day march we reached the area west of Strasbourg, we were all dead tired after being in action without a break for over three months.

We needed rest, and, urgently, replacements of men and equipment. The strength of my grenadier companies was down to fifty men each. Our assembly area lay between the Vosges and Strasbourg, between the Maginot Line and the Westwall.' Von Luck's wish was at least partly granted, with several wagonloads of fresh reinforcements arriving to fill the ranks. With them came the aristocratic panzer officers' divisional commander, who proceeded to pin a Knight's Cross on von Luck's surprised chest: 'I can and will accept this award, but only on behalf of all my men. Without them I could never have succeeded in achieving what you are honouring me for.'

Feuchtinger agreed, then replied:

Give your men a little rest, some supplies; a Luftwaffe replacement battalion has arrived – among them fully-trained pilots without aircraft and boys of sixteen and seventeen, how are we supposed to stop the Allies now with their inexhaustible matériel when we're only sent such cannon-fodder as replacements?

Clearly the errant general felt his role was to dole out awards and bemoan the state of affairs generally rather than command his unit properly. Von Luck had no such luxury: 'I instructed Major Kurz to see to it that our experienced NCOs took the replacements in hand quickly and got them used to combat conditions.'

Touring the area to get the lie of the land, by chance von Luck then met his new army group commander, the diminutive live-wire Hasso von Manteuffel; a panzer commander as different from Feuchtinger as it was possible to be. Von Luck knew him from before the war, and Manteuffel chatted away easily to his new subordinate:

Montgomery has taken the offensive again ... but far more dangerous is Patton and the Amis of the Third Army ... without regard for his right, southern flank he has pressed on, reached Verdun and is advancing on Metz, Nancy and the Moselle ... the Sixth United States Army [Manteuffel is slightly confused here as the Sixth was an Army Group, whereas the Seventh was just an army] and the 1st French Army are approaching from southern France to link up with him – the remains of our armies from the Mediterranean are still holding a wedge as far as Dijon, but for how much longer?

It was a good question. Georg Grossjohann would probably have answered – 'not long'!

My soldiers brought in a seriously wounded comrade whose abdominal wall had been completely ripped open by a shell splinter. Since we had to retreat, we considered taking him along ... the moment we started to drive he screamed in pain. So, we took him out of the jeep and laid him on the ground ... a young French woman ... came out of the neighbouring house. She made us understand that he would die in a short time ... she promised to stay with him to the end ... when we left, she was sitting on the ground with the boy's head in her lap.[3]

As hard-charging as ever, George Patton's plan was to reach the River Moselle, leap it in one bound, bypass Metz and head straight for the Rhenish cities of Mainz and Mannheim, deep in the Third Reich. He achieved the first part of his plan on 2 September, when his spearhead reached the clear waters of the Moselle – Germany lay before him even before Allan Adair had entered Brussels, far to the north. Then Third Army ran out of gas, literally. Infuriated, Patton screamed for fuel – and got 25,390 gallons – one-eighteenth of what he'd asked for. Eisenhower's *broad-front* strategy now hit home hard. As Montgomery's XXX Corps celebrated the liberation of the Belgian capital, the best attacking Allied army in the field ground to a halt one hundred and fifty miles to the south. With no guarantee of sufficient fuel to continue the attack, Patton looked around at what to do – and his eye settled on Metz. Originally built on a number of islands in the Moselle River and surrounded by hills, it was well-protected by a ring of forts constructed to defend it from French revanchism in the late nineteenth century. The fortifications were now outdated, but still formidable, and it had long been rated as an outstanding defensive position. However, the city was barely defended. Hitler's reaction was swift; Metz was declared a *Festung,* and Otto von Knobelsdorff and his *1. Armee* were given responsibility for its defence, an army that had only just escaped from its pre-D-Day bases on the southwestern coast of France. Shepherded across the country and back to the German border by its then-commander Kurt von der Chevallerie, it's paper strength of around sixty thousand hid the fact that most of those men were service and support troops and non-combatant paramilitary personnel. The reality – according to Friedrich von Mellenthin – was that Knobelsdorff could only muster around ten combat battalions, less than two dozen panzers and assault-guns, and perhaps two to three batteries of artillery. Once more the trains rolled as *blitz* transports ferried men into the area from as far afield as Denmark and northern Italy.

Some of the arriving troops were good quality, such as the *3.* and *15. Panzergrenadier-Divisionen,* while others were of more dubious value. In this latter category was Kurt Pflieger's *416. Infanterie-Division,* its 8,500 men having an average age of thirty-eight, with many having either stomach complaints requiring special diets, or too used to the soft life of occupied Denmark – leading to the unit being nicknamed the *Schlagsahne,* or 'Whipped Cream' Division.

By the time Third Army moved north and south of the city to surround it, they found all the bridges blown and the best part of four divisions now manning the fortifications. This included the remnants of *17. SS-Panzergrenadier-Division 'Götz von Berlichingen'* under *SS-Standartenführer* Otto Binge, which Knobelsdorff pushed west of the city to block the Verdun-Metz road and delay Patton's advance. Not that it was in any real shape to try and hold the Americans, as one of its members recalled:

> The composition of the regiment at that time was very mixed... I Bataillon was commanded by a police hauptmann, the company commanders were all Army leutnants from Metz officer school, most of the NCOs were Waffen-SS, but a few were from the Luftwaffe. As for the enlisted men, the Luftwaffe men-turned-panzer grenadiers continued wearing their Luftwaffe uniforms ... some men came from the police ... our position was protected by wooden box-mines, captured matériel from Russia... Our communications trenches and some of our strongpoints were underwater.

The issue of who commanded the city garrison itself soon became an unseemly row between the SS on one side and the Army on the other. Himmler, as *Reichsführer-SS*, appointed *SS-Standartenführer* Ernst Kemper, late of the *SS-Wiking* and now head of the nearby SS Signals School. However, the Army opted for *Generalleutnant* Walther Krause, the newly appointed commander of *462. VGD*, the resident garrison unit. The Army won out, and Krause set to work preparing the city's defences.

With Patton's attention now focused on Metz, Berlin thought it sniffed a chance to counter, and a plan was hatched to attack in the south into the American flank. Hans von Luck witnessed the preparations.

> 'Three newly-created Panzer-Brigaden arrived, a new concept from OKW (Oberkommando der Wehrmacht – Armed Forces High Command) – they are certainly well-equipped with the latest weapons like Panthers, and they have experienced commanders, but they don't know each other and have never trained together, after our heavy losses why don't they give us the new matériel?'[4]

The new units were the *111., 112.* and *113.Panzer-Brigaden* – formed only a few days before. On 12 September the *112. Panzer-Brigade* went into action against Philippe Leclerc and his superb *2e Division Blindée (2ᵉ DB*, French 2nd Armoured Division), and in a four-day battle described by the American historian Hugh M. Cole as '...a brilliant example of perfect air-ground co-ordination, not only was it an outstanding feat of arms but it also dealt a crippling blow to Hitler's plans for an armoured thrust into Third Army's flank.' Von Luck was right to rue the diversion of scarce resources to new units, rather than tried and trusted ones. The 112th lost sixty panzers – two-thirds of its strength – and hundreds of grenadiers. By the end of the month it could field a single Panther, six Mark IVs and a handful of infantrymen – it was virtually annihilated.

Worse was to come for the new arrivals when the other two panzer brigades went into action; this time trying their luck against the Americans near the town of Arracourt a few miles east of Nancy. Initially the attack went well, the surprised American 4th Armoured Division being hard-hit and pulling back in some confusion with the loss of over twenty tanks, as fog and low cloud prevented Allied aircraft from intervening. However, their experienced commander – John Shirley Wood, a former American football quarterback and Chemistry teacher whose nickname was 'Tiger Jack' – was no push-over, and soon turned things round. The attacking brigades were pounded from the air and eviscerated by Wood's fast-moving Shermans and Stuarts. Burnt-out panzers and half-tracks littered the fields and roadways. The *111. Panzer-Brigade* was reduced to just eight panzers and eighty panzer-grenadiers, and the *113.* lost its commander – *Oberst* Erich von Seckendorff – killed in action. The German offensive was smashed. Von Manteuffel's *5. Panzerarmee* could barely field twenty-five serviceable panzers, although his Chief of Staff Friedrich von Mellenthin wrote that 'Although our attacks were very costly it appeared at the time that they had achieved their purpose and had effectively checked the American Third Army.' No Nazi, Mellenthin was known for putting a brave face on German military performance – Hans von Luck was no Nazi either, but far less likely to sugar-coat. He was asked by one of his officers after the Arracourt disaster, 'Do you believe the rumours that Hitler is trying to make a separate peace with the Western Allies so he can have his back free for a fight with the Russians?' von Luck replied, 'No. Churchill and the Amis are out to destroy Hitler and his regime, there's no room for a separate peace.'

By now von Luck's division was a shadow of its previous self, and Mellenthin declared, 'It had virtually no panzers and was now only a second-rate infantry formation.' He wasn't wrong. In early November it reported a strength of nineteen panzers and fewer than three hundred panzer grenadiers. With *5. Panzerarmee* effectively gutted after Arracourt, the way was open for Third Army to roll over its remnants and reach the Rhine. All Patton needed was gasoline and ammunition. He got neither. Montgomery had persuaded Eisenhower to back *Market Garden*, and the bulk of available supplies went there. Frustrated by his Army's immobility, Patton turned back to Metz and launched the least inspired and most wasteful battle of his extraordinary career. Sweeping armoured thrusts, clever manoeuvring and brilliant improvisation gave way to infantry slog and massed artillery barrages. One of the men under those barrages was Max Wind, who's battered *17. SS-Panzergrenadier-Division*

'Götz von Berlichingen' had now been reduced to a few *kampfgruppen* as it fought in Metz's defence. 'We were still pretty good ... there were some young lads, but we also had some very experienced men. We respected Patton, because we knew he respected Germany, but the Ami was nothing like the Russian ... they lacked the motivation we had.' Not that all of Wind's fellow panzer-grenadiers necessarily felt the same, as one of his own regimental commanders knew only too well. Vehicles 'kept breaking down because the petrol was poor – there was water in it – that's the way we were supposed to fight a war! I had absolutely no artillery at all, you know, when our soldiers have to continually haul their own guns around they soon say "you can kiss my arse, I'd rather be taken prisoner."'[5]

The fighting at Metz dragged on with the Allies achieving not very much at all, except lengthening casualty lists. Committing relatively small forces and resources, the Germans tied up Third Army throughout September, all October and into a wet and cold November. Eventually XX Corps, under the command of the pugnacious Walter Walker, began to force the issue after undergoing a series of training programmes behind the lines to help them prepare for the assault. The Germans responded by sending a new garrison commander to the city to replace Walther Krause and inject more vim into its defence; the hawk-faced *Generalmajor* Heinrich Kittel – a veteran of the Russian front. It was too little too late for the defenders. Kittel himself was badly wounded and consigned to the underground field hospital where he surrendered the city to the Americans on 22 November[6] – although Fort Driant held out until 8 December and Fort Jeanne d'Arc even longer, its remaining five hundred men only capitulating on 13 December. Six thousand troops went into captivity alongside their commander, but that was scant return for almost three months of time wasted by the Allies, as Blaskowitz himself acknowledged:

A direct attack on Metz was unnecessary .... in contrast a swerve northward in the direction of Luxembourg and Bitburg would have met with greater success and caused our 1. Armee's right flank to collapse followed by the breakdown of our 7. Armee.

Blaskowitz's insight didn't save him; he was sacked by Hitler for the second time in the war. An inflexible and upstanding son of the Manse, Blaskowitz received no praise for being the man who handed George Patton his first battlefield check at Metz. Neither did he receive any accolades for helping to force Third Army – probably the best fighting formation the American Army possessed at the time – onto the defensive and thereby give his own command a desperately needed breathing space, as Mellenthin, the new chief of staff of *Heeresgruppe G*, related: 'The Third Army received categorical orders to stand on the defensive.

The rights and wrongs of this strategy do not concern me, but it certainly simplified the problems for *Heeresgruppe G*. We were given a few weeks grace to rebuild our shattered forces and get ready to meet the next onslaught.' Blaskowitz's success can only be considered the greater when it is remembered that Third Army was a quarter of a million men strong, while his own army group couldn't muster half that number.

As a headlong advance through Lorraine was turned into a brutal slog-fest at Metz, so yet another entire American army, this time Courtney Hodge's First, blew another opportunity in the north at Aachen. Metz was a city disputed between France and Germany, but Aachen had no such identity crisis, it was German, and hugely symbolic for the German people and Hitler himself. If it fell, it would be the first major German city to be occupied by the Reich's enemies; a propaganda gift for the Allies, and a major blow to German morale. Needless to say, Hitler had declared it a *Festung,* and ordered it held 'to the last man and the last bullet'. However, the dictator had not reckoned with the man in charge on the ground as American troops headed for the city, *General der Panzertruppe* Gerhard Graf von Schwerin-Krosigk. Schwerin was in many ways an enigma. A Prussian aristocrat who had been decorated for gallantry in the First World War, he had then personally contacted British Intelligence in early 1939 while working in the German Embassy in London, urging the British government to end appeasement and face down Hitler. This approach proving fruitless. He then received a prestigious appointment in the Army's élite *Grossdeutschland Regiment*, going on to have a distinguished wartime career, ending with command of *116. 'Windhund'* (Greyhound) *Panzerdivision.* Described by a fellow officer as 'intelligent, though this often proved a handicap'. He was a convinced anti-Nazi, but nevertheless played no active part in the 20 July Bomb Plot. Withdrawing his division east from France after the Falaise defeat, he reached the outskirts of Aachen in early September with barely six hundred panzer grenadiers and a dozen panzers still operational. Arriving at the city, he decided not to stand and fight and turn the city into a charnel house, but to quietly surrender it to the Americans.

> At Aachen I tried to find a way of ending the war as quickly as possible... I tried to use Hitler's order for me to stay with my division and defend Aachen to the last, to stay and be overrun by the Americans... But unfortunately the Americans didn't advance, they stopped short of Aachen and made no attempt to occupy the city. That wasn't understandable, and was very disappointing.[7]

Schwerin actually left a hand-written note for the advancing American commander at the main Post Office, declaring – in defiance of Hitler's direct orders – that Aachen was an open city: 'I ask you, in the case of an occupation by your troops, to take care of the unfortunate population in a humane way.' An SS unit found the note and reported it to Berlin. Amazingly, Schwerin wasn't executed for treason but only relieved of command and posted to another appointment in Italy. In his place appeared the fifty-five-year-old *Oberst* Gerhard Wilck. His arrival was inauspicious to say the least – he reported to Model and bluntly told him that in his opinion the city couldn't hold out and should be abandoned, to which the monocled field-marshal replied, 'The Führer has commanded that we will not give up one inch of ground – his command is holy for us!'

Wilck was then given a typed sheet declaring he would never surrender the city, and that if he did, then his wife and children's lives were forfeit – the straight-backed West Prussian officer was handed a pen and signed – such a document could only exist in a totalitarian dictatorship such as Nazi Germany. To further pile pressure on the new garrison commander, Rundstedt himself telephoned to remind him; that he 'will hold this venerable German city to the last man. If necessary, he will allow himself to be buried in its ruins.' But Model and von Rundstedt knew their man. Wilck was one of a new breed of middle-ranking German officers who had fought in the First World War as young men, before really learning their trade in the bitter battles in Russia over the preceding three years. More and more of these men were now being given commands that previously would have been the preserve of general officers. Partly this was because the new commands were smaller than they were in the war's early years, and partly it was because of their experience and ability; they were used to fighting battles against superior odds without the benefit of support, and they were accustomed to their units taking often massive casualties and then being rebuilt – this was the lot of the Wehrmacht in late 1944. Preparations to defend the city began in earnest, as Wilck exhorted his men to 'fight to the last man, the last bullet in fulfilment of our oath to the flag. Long live the Führer!' Next, the city's citizens were evacuated – whether they liked it or not – as one soldier explained:

> They put up notices or announced that unrationed bread would be available at such and such a place from two to four, and when the women had taken up their place in the queue, trucks drove up and they were loaded onto them...then they just took them out of the immediate danger zone, put them down on the road and left them to their fate.[8]

Just as at Metz, German reinforcements were rushed to the city, including a small *kampfgruppe* from the *Leibstandarte-SS*, led by the young *SS-Obersturmführer* Herbert Rink. Described by one of his senior NCOs as a 'tough, experienced officer, well-respected and liked by his NCOs and men', Rink's first meeting with his new boss at his headquarters in the Hotel Quellenhof went as badly as Wilck's earlier encounter with Model. 'I take my orders directly from *Reichsführer-SS* Heinrich Himmler, Herr Oberst. For that reason, I can only place myself conditionally under your command.'

Wilck shot back: 'You are directly under my command, *Obersturmführer*! I am battle commander here, and you are serving in this section of the front. How you combine that with any special orders you may have received is your problem!'

Despite the poor start, Wilck recognised that Rink's men were the best he had, and he made them his mobile reserve and 'fire-brigade' – available to be rushed to wherever the fighting was fiercest. Most of the rest of Wilck's garrison were a rag-tag bunch, including a number of former policemen and hastily drummed up *Volkssturm* militia, as a certain *Major* Heimann recalled:

> I had three battalions there who needed to move towards the city by night, but actually only the staff returned consisting of fifteen men, the rest had gone over to the enemy. They were all men aged forty to fifty-years-old who said, 'We're not going into the open,' how can you defend Aachen with people like that!

Not all of Heimann's men were of such doubtful quality though. 'Some of them were the most excellent troops, half of whom were naval personnel intended for the U-boat arm.'[9]

Hodges adopted the same approach to Aachen as Patton did at Metz; surround the city and try and avoid having to take it by direct assault. Initial moves soon stalled as *Market Garden* took precedence and supplies were choked off, and by the time Hodges was ready to attack it was early October. Initial air raids by over four hundred bombers and *jabos* smashed much of Wilck's mobile forces. '*Most of the few assault-guns we had were put out of action straight away.*' Parts of the city were reduced to rubble, as a German reporter later noted: 'In almost every street a building was burning like a huge torch.' An American ultimatum to surrender was rejected, and on the 10th another huge air raid dropped over sixty tons of bombs on the defenders, followed by the same two days later. Artillery joined in as well, before the assault proper began on 13 October. Three days later the city was surrounded.

The Americans then began the bloody process of clearing the defenders out house by house, and even room by room. As ever in urban warfare, casualties were high, and although the Americans received replacements, most were pretty poor quality having not received enough training prior to being committed to combat. The results were predictable, with as many as half of all replacements becoming casualties themselves in their first week. By 19 October, Wilck had just twelve hundred men and one assault-gun left, and the last rations were issued; a small piece of sausage with a hunk of bread half made of sawdust, washed down with a mug of *ersatz* coffee. Wilck sent a final message to his men: 'The defenders of Aachen will prepare for their last battle. We shall fight to the last man.' He then abandoned his Quellenhof headquarters; by now, its cellars were full of wounded and it was in the front line. A small detachment of defenders held on, but with ammunition running out they were reduced to throwing champagne and wine bottles at the attacking GIs. Most were killed when the frustrated Americans brought up an artillery cannon and used it to fire directly into the hotel.

Herbert Rink's *kampfgruppe* was now just fifty men strong, having lost ninety per cent of its members in a fortnight. Fighting in the ruins – almost eighty per cent of the city had been turned to rubble – Rink and his men became separated from the rest of the garrison, and in a final attempt to save the survivors, he led them in a break-out through the American lines.

Wilck had now lost most of the city except a small, shrinking section in the west. To try and keep up morale he recommended no fewer than 162 of his remaining eight hundred men for the Iron Cross. The Americans were within six hundred yards of his command post.

The next morning – Saturday 21 October – tank destroyers were brought up to fire point-blank at the remaining German positions. Wilck sent a final radio message to his superiors: 'All ammunition gone after severe house-to-house fighting. No water and no food. Enemy close to command post of the last defenders of the imperial city. Radio prepared for destruction... We are reporting out. Best wishes to our comrades and loved ones.'

With that, the radio went dead.

Wilck was more practical in reality than his radio message let on: 'When the Amis start using 155s as sniper rifles, it's time to give up.'

He sent two American prisoners, Sergeant Ewart Padgett and Private First Class James Haswell, out to tell their fellow GIs that he was willing to capitulate – despite his 'no surrender' declaration. Just after noon it was all over. Five thousand German soldiers had been captured in the fighting, with another five thousand killed or wounded, around the same number as were lost at Metz. The battle cost the Americans two thousand men killed, and another three thousand wounded. Yet again though, their biggest loss was time.

The Allies were now finally closing up to the Third Reich's last man-made defensive line, the *Siegfried Line* so beloved of 1940 British ditties, although actually called the *Westwall* by the Germans themselves. Originally built back in the 1930s to face France's far grander Maginot Line, the *Westwall* stretched for three hundred miles from Brüggen in the north down to Weil am Rhein on the Swiss border. Trumpeted by German propaganda as a major barrier to French aggression, in reality it was a rather amateurish affair, consisting of little more than a series of small bunkers, with enough room to stand and fire at any attackers, and hammocks strung up behind as makeshift sleeping quarters. With Hitler's arrival in the Chancellery accelerating Germany's re-armament, the order came down from Berlin to turn propaganda into action, and the *Limes Programme*[10] was instituted in 1938. Its main feature was the building of 3,471 new *Type 10* bunkers. The Type 10s were far more robust than their predecessors, with walls and roofs one and a half metres thick, and purpose-built accommodation for ten to twelve men. The Type 10s were supplemented by larger *Type 107* bunkers, designed to mount twin machine-guns which could only fire to the sides, in an effort to make them invisible to any attacker from the front. The 107s were big beasts indeed, with concrete walls over three metres thick and heavy metal blast doors at the back for access. Due to the time and resources needed to build them, they were concentrated in the Aachen-Saar area as this was the traditional invasion route into Germany; something the Allies had seemingly forgotten in 1944. Interspersed between the larger bunkers, smaller pillboxes were built, and roads and tracks were covered with tank traps, known as *Höcker* (humps). These were rows of reinforced concrete dragons'-teeth designed to be impassable to tanks and other armoured vehicles. At first, private construction companies were hired by the government to carry out the work, but conditions on site were very poor and after a while it was decided to bring in the Nazis' own construction arm; the *Organization Todt (OT)*. With thousands more workers, the building went on apace; anti-tank ditches were dug and filled with water, bunkers were camouflaged to look like farm buildings, and the *Westwall* itself was extended almost another hundred miles to Kleve on the Dutch border. Guns were fitted into emplacements, fields of fire were cleared and ammunition was stockpiled ready for use. To help guard against air attack, the Nazis also built the *Luftverteidigungszone West* (Western Air Defence Zone), which was a series of concrete anti-aircraft emplacements and flak turrets. Goebbels' propaganda machine went into overdrive, claiming that the fortifications were impervious to air attack and now included more than eighteen thousand bunkers, with miles of barbed-wire and underground tunnels linking them all together. The reality was not quite so rosy; the high-grade steel-plating required to protect the guns in their embrasures was in short supply, so was substituted with inferior material, or not fitted at all. Many of the bunkers went unfinished due to lack of time or manpower, and many that were completed were rudimentary, being built with wooden logs and topped with earth. When Alfred Jodl went to inspect it all in 1939 in his role as the Wehrmacht's Chief of the Operations Staff, he described it as 'little better than a building site' and von Rundstedt just laughed at it. Having said that, the sum of 8.5 billion Reichsmarks was spent on pouring eight million tons of concrete and laying a million tons of iron and steel and the same of wood – at the time it was Germany's largest ever construction programme.

Mercifully though for the Germans, the French never put it to the test, and following the fall of France in the summer of 1940, the whole project was shelved. The guns and ammunition were stripped out, as were the more expensive materials such as armour plating, steel doors and heating and ventilation systems. Loaded onto trucks and trains they were then shipped west to be used again, this time in the new *Atlantikwall*. The bunkers themselves were then locked up, the keys given to local officials, and most were then hired out to nearby farmers and small businesses as storage sites for crops and tools. In the ensuing four years, the poor and hurried construction of much of the line proved its undoing, as a lack of maintenance facilitated a marked deterioration in many bunkers, which began to crack and scab. Anti-tank ditch walls caved in, hundreds of dragons'-teeth were paved over or removed, and vegetation grew over much of the rest.

None of this mattered as long as the Allies were on the other side of the English Channel, but after D-Day and the Falaise calamity, Hitler ordered that the *Westwall* once again be given immediate priority as a defensive bulwark. Twenty thousand forced labourers were sent in, as were thousands of young men carrying out their obligatory pre-conscription *Reichsarbeitsdienst* (*RAD*, Reich Labour Service). They were joined by large contingents of *Hitlerjugend* boys and their female equivalent in the *Bund Deutscher Mädel* (League of German Girls), as well as local civilians pressed into service. By early September there were well over one hundred and fifty thousand people working on the *Westwall*.

Hans von Luck and his panzer division would be some of the first troops to man the fortifications: 'The next day we were sent south to occupy the approaches to the Westwall at Saarlautern (modern-day Saarlouis). As we crossed the Franco-German border it came home to all of us that from now on we would be fighting on our native soil.' The hard-bitten von Luck was less than impressed by what he and his men found:

A quick inspection of the Westwall fortifications confirmed our fears … armaments and communications systems had been dismantled and reinstalled in the Atlantikwall, and … a wild growth had sprung up with trees, bushes and flowers … it would take weeks to put the installations in a defensible state , to say nothing of arming them with heavy guns, anti-tank guns and minefields.[11]

One of von Luck's fellow officers also arriving at the frontier fortifications was Herbert Rink, who had managed to thread his few dozen men through the eye of the needle at Aachen and get them safely to the *Westwall*: 'At last we would be safe. We were shell-shocked and exhausted. Once behind the Westwall, we could join all the defeated, decimated German units, all those who had made it through ... horrifying, crushing battle.' However, on seeing the wall itself, Rink was far from pleased: 'Damn it! Where are the bunkers? Silence over the fields and nothing else!' After a few days rest and recuperation, he changed his tune, relieved just to have escaped Aachen and finally to have some measure of defence available.

> We were able to stabilise the situation at the Westwall – we had a continuous frontline, sufficient habitable bunkers, and adequate combat installations – and we, who had come depleted and exhausted from the inferno at Caen, through the break-out from the pocket at Falaise, through the nerve-wracking retreat across France and partisan-plagued Belgium – we had gathered our strength and rebuilt our confidence.[12]

To be fair, the *Westwall* was a decidedly mixed bag. Much of it was indeed a paper tiger, but some parts were formidable, as the American 39th Infantry Regiment discovered when attacking a bunker atop a hill south of Aachen in mid-September. Coming under machine-gun fire from the embrasures, the assaulting troops first fired bazookas at the firing slits to try and knock them out. When this had no discernible effect, charges were placed on the end of poles and stuffed into the firing ports; again, with no impact. Gasoline was then poured under the steel doors at the back and set alight, and an explosive charge thrown down the ventilation shaft on the roof – no result either. They then brought forward a job-lot of forty German *Teller* anti-tank mines, which were stacked at the base of one of the walls and blown up. The blast was ear-splitting, but the bunker remained intact. Next, flamethrowers were used to try and burn the defenders out. Fast running out of ideas, three hundred pounds of TNT were packed into a depression in the roof and fired – the blast was huge. As the dust settled the bunker was still standing, but the doors finally opened, and, with the first man waving a white flag, some thirty German soldiers came out with their hands up.[13]

With the line breached, Leonard T. Gerow's V Corps tried to follow up the 39th's success with a thrust towards the city of Trier. The Germans scrambled to react. A hastily assembled *Alarm* battalion was ordered to counter-attack, but melted under fire, with only one company showing any real fight. Its commander, *Hauptmann* Karl Kornowski, was a Russian front veteran: 'I found my commander huddled in a trench, he was too busy crapping his pants to show us where to counter-attack.' Nevertheless, Kornowski led his men forward and managed to retake eight *Westwall* bunkers before being captured himself. It was just enough though to check the Americans – much to the disbelief of Siegfried Westphal: 'If the enemy had thrown in more forces, he would not only have broken through the German defensive line – which was still in the process of being built up in the Eifel – but in the absence of any considerable reserves on the German side he would have affected the collapse of the while Western front within a short time.' Once again it would seem the Allies came close to affecting a general immolation of the *Westheer*'s position but failed to put the final nail in the coffin. Having said that, it's also true to say that Westphal's statement was made with the benefit of hindsight in 1951, but even so, it begs a mighty *what if*.

As it was, the *Westwall* held again. Along its length, weary *landsers* ended their retreat from France by finding refuge in its bunkers and were joined by freshly trained recruits or pressed men from other services. For the first time in weeks – as Herbert Rink had pointed out – they were relatively safe, but manning the *Westwall* meant fighting in Germany itself, and for many *landsers* that was a very unsettling experience, particularly when they had to deal with the local populace, as the twenty-year-old Otto Henning – an *Unteroffizier* in Fritz Bayerlein's *Panzer-Lehr-Division,* soon found out: 'We'd wondered what would happen when the fighting reached Germany. The civilians asked us what do do, "should we flee or stay?" We told them what we had seen in France, that if the enemy moved quickly through a region nothing would happen, but that if the front stabilised in a region everything would be destroyed.'[14] Otto Wölcky, a comrade of Herbert Rink's in the *Leibstandarte-SS,* found himself quartered in the house of a local woman about a mile or so back from the bunker line itself. She was far from pleased about the situation, as she made perfectly clear to the young Waffen-SS officer: '"We thought that the Amis would advance quickly and that it would all be over at last, and now you've come here and there'll be fighting and all we have will be smashed up again!" I should have taken some action against the woman, but I could well understand her feelings.'[15]

Not all returning troops were quite so sympathetic. A regimental commander in the 17th SS in Lorraine felt compelled to circulate a written order to his men: 'The reputation of the Waffen-SS cannot tolerate the confiscation of bicycles and horse-teams at pistol-point. It seems to me that some NCOs and other ranks have still not recognised that they are in their own country again.'[16]

For many of these men, the *Heimat* they returned to was not the one they'd left – far from it. Always an orderly society, normal life on the streets and in the homes of most Germans was breaking down under the strain of war. Cases of theft had almost doubled between 1939 and 1944, and with the men away it was more and more down to women and juveniles; 46,500 women and 17,500 youngsters were convicted of crimes in 1939 in Germany – by 1942 that had exploded to 117,000 women and 52,500 juveniles, and the numbers continued to climb as the war went on. The courts struggled to cope, and the country's jails filled up – the prison population doubled to 197,000 in mid-1944 (in 2018 the UK prison population was 83,000). With food and goods in short supply, theft was by far the most common crime, although with so many men serving abroad, the number of murders and sex offences reduced significantly. But while sexual crime plummeted, casual sex rocketed. Societal barriers disintegrated with every new bombing raid and ration reduction, and the absence of so many fathers, husbands, brothers and so on, contributed to an atmosphere of sexual licence that the Reich had never experienced before. The nightly black-outs would see public parks almost carpeted in copulating couples, and in rural areas, the foreign labourers shipped to the Reich to till the fields, soon began to take on the marital duties of absent husbands. Morale on the home front hadn't broken down, but it was fragile. Belief in a happy future was now a rarity; the number of marriages fell by a third in 1944 to just over half a million, and the birth rate dropped by the same figure, despite Nazi propaganda and the *Mutterkreuz* (Mother Cross) awards for women who gave birth to the Reich's future warriors. The Nazis were genuinely worried about the situation, and commissioned reports to try and understand what was going on across the country – the findings made for difficult reading for the Nazi hierarchy. For example, one report highlighted the unintended role that generous government welfare benefits were having:

> [With] the comparatively high benefits given to soldiers' wives and widows ... these women do not have to find a job, since ... family benefits guarantee them a higher standard of living than that which they had before the war. The time and money at their disposal seduce them into spending their afternoons and evenings in coffee houses and bars ... and they are in a position to treat men – mainly soldiers.[17]

These women could be picky though, with *Ostfrontkämpfer* (East front fighters) much preferred to their *Westheer* counterparts, as one woman described in a letter: 'The feeling of the civilian population towards the soldier on the Western front is not altogether good, and I too am convinced that if the soldier of the Eastern front had been in the West then the breakthrough would not have happened.'[18] One *landser* returning to his unit from home leave in Heidelberg was more succinct: 'The mood there is shit, but the hatred isn't directed at the enemy, but against the regime.' For the first time in the war, morale was visibly deteriorating, and civilians were more open about their anger at it all: 'The civilians called us Kriegsverlängerer (war prolongers), and that wasn't just in one place either, but in fifty towns and villages in the West.'[19]

What the reports made clear though, was that by far the biggest factor in the overall drop in morale was Anglo-American bombing of the German homeland. In the wake of D-Day, the rush to send to France almost every aircraft that could fly had stripped Germany's skies of their fighter protection; the so-called Defence of the Reich (*Reichsverteidigung*) structure. Now, with the need to target the transport network between France and Germany gone, the Allied bomber fleets could turn their full attention to the Reich's towns and cities. The head of Britain's effort was Air Chief Marshal Arthur 'Bomber' Harris. An intense and often brooding figure, Harris believed utterly in the primacy of the heavy bomber and its ability to win the war, as long as the politicians and other senior Allied commanders stopped interfering and left him to it.

Earlier on in the war, Britain had invested huge resources into building a strategic bomber fleet, partly as the only way it could hit back at the German homeland after the *Blitz* and its successor campaigns. From 1942 onwards, air attacks against Nazi Germany steadily increased, with the aim being to damage industry and severely disrupt the flow of armaments to the front. Unfortunately, early claims about the accuracy of bombing proved to be illusory, so Harris evolved the campaign, building a case for what would become known as 'area bombing'. His argument was simple: killing, maiming and de-housing the German civilian workforce would have the same overall effect as was intended by the precision bombing of industry. So, with the latter unable to be achieved, the campaign should focus on the former. As Harris himself explained, 'The aim of the Combined Bomber Offensive ... should be unambiguously stated ... the destruction of German cities, the killing of German workers, and the disruption of civilised life throughout Germany.' As for the indiscriminate nature of such attacks, he was very clear: '...in order to destroy anything, it is necessary to destroy everything.' He even cloaked his argument in Biblical terms: 'They sowed the wind, and now they are going to reap the whirlwind.' Harris was true to his word. Having had a list of the sixty most populous German cities and large towns drawn up, by the late autumn of '44 he could report with satisfaction that forty-five of them had been more or less reduced to rubble and ash. Exact figures are still disputed, but by the war's end Allied bombing would have destroyed over two million German homes, leaving seven million people homeless, while killing between four and six hundred thousand men, women and children. Agnes Erdös – a Hungarian Jewish slave labourer – was part of the clear-up in Bremen in November 1944 after one air raid:

> A nice little boy, about three years old, came carrying a toy shovel in his hand. He was completely uninjured. He started digging in the cold pile of ruins. 'What are you doing I asked?' He replied quietly, 'I have to dig up my mother.' It had been four days since the bombing.[20]

Not that the aircrew who had to carry out the campaign got away lightly – nothing could be further from the truth. The young men who did their duty in the bombers were carrying out one of the most dangerous jobs of the war. Ten thousand Allied aircraft were lost during the campaign, and with them some eighty thousand aircrew. The initial tour of duty for American crews was set at twenty-five missions – and only one in four lived to achieve that target, while forty per cent of RAF Lancaster crewmen didn't survive their first tours either. Nevertheless, the devastation they wrought on the ground was monumental:

I was given an assignment to escort another Danish Waffen-SS volunteer from Ellwangen to the Waffen-SS administration centre at the Lützowplatz, not far from the Admiral-von-Schröder Strasse in Berlin. This guy had had a mental breakdown at the front and wasn't allowed to travel alone. During our train ride together we spoke a lot, and it was my job to see we got something to eat and drink too when we stopped at stations. He was happy he was going to undergo treatment in Berlin and was hoping to be deemed unfit for further service so would be discharged and sent home. Shortly after we arrived at the Anhalter Bahnhof in Berlin, the air raid alarm sounded and we ran for cover in the nearest shelter, which was in the basement of a large apartment block, but in the chaos I got separated from my comrade. The bombs wrecked the entrance to the shelter, so we were buried alive. At the time I was only thinking about myself and how I could get through this Armageddon. It took us two days of digging to break through into a neighbouring basement and finally find a way out. When we came out above ground it was a total mess. There was rubble everywhere, so many houses had collapsed, the asphalt on the roads had melted in the heat of the fires and they were still digging dead bodies out. I was in shock, and fear of the bombs was still lodged in my mind as I could remember the whistling sounds as they fell. I was also hungry and very thirsty, but couldn't get my bearings in the middle of all the destruction. I thought, 'Where should I go?' So, I followed other survivors from the basement and saw a sign that said "Anhalter Bahnhof". I set off. Entire neighbourhoods were demolished, but I had survived. My only thought was to get out of this hellhole and find the nearest Red Cross station to get something to eat and drink.[21]

The Luftwaffe – reeling under the impact of fighting a superior enemy with too few aircraft and too few pilots – was firmly in a death-spiral, as the terrible lack of aviation fuel curtailed training to the point where new fliers were little more than cannon-fodder, as *Feldwebel* Rudolf Hener saw for himself:

We had dog-fights at altitudes far above 10,000m in our Bf 109 G-14s against a ten-fold numerical superiority of Mustangs, Thunderbolts etc., and generally got home reduced to half the number that took off. These operations were simply a slaughter, as is illustrated by the fact that of the sixty pilots making up I Gruppe after its refurbishment in August 1944, only five survived the war. Due to the heavy losses we suffered on every mission we were often totally flattened. Then, as replacements, we received very young and poorly trained pilots from the flight schools, and most of these only survived for a single day. Those that remained were always the same handful of old and experienced fighter pilots.[22]

No wonder that, as one *jagdflieger* put it, 'Each time I close the canopy before take-off, I feel I'm closing the lid of my own coffin.'[23]

The raids deeply affected the *landsers*. Every mail call was eagerly awaited, but also dreaded in equal measure for fear of the bad news it could bring, as the panzer officer, Richard von Rosen, knew:

If sad tidings were received from home there was always special leave no matter what the situation was at the front. It now frequently happened that soldiers had to be given leave if news came that their family had been bombed out. When those same soldiers returned to the Kompanie one had to take a special interest and keep a close eye on them. The more tragic the circumstances back in the Heimat, the more the Kompanie became a 'substitute family' for the men.[24]

Even as he was fighting at Aachen, Courtney Hodges gave the order to commence one of the most ill-conceived and unnecessary offensives of the whole northwest European campaign – the capture of the Hürtgen forest. Courtney Hodges was a native of the state of Georgia, and in American military parlance a 'mustang', that is an officer who began his career as an enlisted soldier. Prickly by nature, notoriously fastidious about his own appearance, he lacked tactical imagination and felt no urge to innovate in his approach to battle – a failing his men would pay for repeatedly. In an Army that was well-known to be unforgiving towards those officers deemed to have underperformed, it was seen – even at the time – to be something of a miracle that Hodges retained his command and Eisenhower's confidence. Short on supplies, and with an entire Corps investing Aachen and its few thousand defenders, Hodges now decided that there was a major threat to his flank from an area of Germany some twenty-odd miles southeast of Charlemagne's city – this was the *Hürtgenwald*, the Hürtgen forest. Convincing himself that the *Westheer* could mass troops amidst its phalanx of conifers, ready to attack him when he was at his weakest, Hodges decided to act first; clear the forest, seize the huge dam that lay beyond it and neutralise the threat. In reality, that *threat* was *Oberst* Karl Rösler's 'Horseshoe' 89. *Infanterie-Division* – the same division whose remnants had been scooped up by

Kurt Chill in the Netherlands a couple of weeks before. With one of his grenadier regiments reduced to just 350 men from its original three thousand, and his entire artillery complement down to six guns, of which only one was German, Rösler – who had taken command when *Generalleutnant* Conrad-Oskar Heinrichs had been killed near Liège – had been reinforced with thirteen hundred middle-aged replacements and sent to the Hürtgen. OKW thought it would be the perfect place for the shattered division to rest and refit, prior to taking the field once more.

As it turned out, OKW's view of the Hürtgen was far more accurate than Hodges'. The forest itself is like so many that garland the western border of Germany with its neighbours in France, Belgium, Luxembourg and the Netherlands, 'extensive, thick and nearly trackless forest terrain' as one German officer put it. A little over fifty square miles in size, it had been intensively managed for decades. Mostly pine, neatly lined row upon row, and so thickly strewn that no daylight filters in from above, there were also patches of oak and beech climbing the hillsides and crowning the ridges. These ridges are a feature of the forest, plunging sharply down to thick brush and undergrowth-choked ravines. Roads are few, but the whole forest is criss-crossed by logging tracks and firebreaks, used by the locals to access and harvest the wood. Those locals lived an isolated life, with villages and towns few and far between and small in size – one of the largest, Vossenack, could barely muster a couple of thousand people. Part of the *Westwall,* there had been little fighting there due to the nature of the terrain, and not a great deal of effort had gone into its defences – surely, no-one would attack it, what would be the point? What would be the point, indeed.

The point as Hodges and his fellow commanders Bradley and Eisenhower saw it, was that on the eastern edge of the forest was the *Rurstausee;* the Rur Reservoir, the second biggest artificial lake in Germany. Headed by a seventy-seven metre high dam (the *Rurtalsperre Schwammenauel)* built in 1939, Eisenhower's concern was that the Germans would release the waters and flood the land to the north, greatly delaying the planned crossing of the Rhine. Given that the shortest distance between the American lines and the dam was straight through the Hürtgen, and that by clearing it the danger of a German counter-attack through it was also removed, the decision was made to take it. Logic-wise, this argument is pretty thin gruel. If the goal was to capture the dam intact, why not swing north or south of the forest (or both) and take it that way – that would also stop any German offensive materialising from it as well. In truth, Hodges failed to understand the awful conditions his men would face in the Hürtgen, or come up with a plan that was anything more than a blunt, frontal slog. As one of the new *volks-grenadier* officers – *Leutnant* Rolf-Helmut Schröder – said, 'With the Allies it was always the same ... they attacked in daylight, starting with artillery, then the tanks ... the Allies would never move without reconnaissance and preparation ... the last time we attacked in Russia we formed up on the start line straight off the train.'

The battle began in mid-September with Louis A. Craig's 9th Infantry Division attacking on a broad front. Craig was a West Pointer and his division – nicknamed the 'Old Reliables' – was an experienced outfit, having landed in North Africa during *Operation Torch*, and then going on to fight in Normandy. Despite initial success in the north of the forest, where there was only light resistance, the division got sucked into brutal close-quarters fighting with Rösler's grenadiers further south around the small village of Lammersdorf. Woefully unprepared as Rösler's men were, Craig's 9th was in no better state, as all the Americans usual advantages of dominant air power, excellent communications and mechanization, were negated by the conditions; low cloud and fog kept the air force on the ground, and even when they could go up the pilots struggled to identify their targets in the almost-jungle like canopy. Unable to make their usual impact on the frontline, they took to hitting anything moving towards the Hürtgen:

> Jabos took every opportunity to attack trains during the day ... they didn't even shy away from shooting at farmers working in the fields. There was no longer any differentiation between combat troops and civilians. The German people were very uneasy due to the constant air attacks and the feeling that in spite of everything it no longer seemed that this war could be won.[25]

Radios didn't work among the trees and hills, and the flow of information between units and commanders dried up. Tanks were brought up, but only in small numbers owing to the Americans belief they weren't fitted to the terrain. This seemed to be confirmed when a few of them were sent down unsuitable tracks and either became stuck in the mud or were picked off by grenadiers armed with *panzerfausts*. In a battle like this it was going to come down to the humble American infantryman stumbling forward, and his equally humble *landser* opponent holding firm in his earthen bunker.

Those American infantrymen soon found themselves in an alien environment they quickly came to hate and fear. Away from the tracks and firebreaks, the forest itself was pitch dark. The earth was soft underfoot and covered in a thick carpet of pine-needles and leaves which deadened all sound. It was always damp – there was no sun to dry up the land – and the air was thick with the smell of mould. Line of sight was usually twenty metres or less, and in the perpetual gloom a man had the unpleasant feeling he was totally alone. In the darkness amongst the trees were the bunkers the American infantry had to capture; purposefully built deep under the canopy where light didn't penetrate. Constructed and camouflaged to blend in with the forest, they were sunk into the ground so only a few feet showed above ground, making them almost invisible. As for the *landsers* waiting in them, it was unnerving to stand in silence, transfixed by the sight of their enemy coming closer and closer, oblivious to their presence. Then the firing would begin.

The leading Americans would be cut down by machine-gun fire, and then – as usual – they would call in their artillery, only to see the rounds explode in the treetops above them before they could penetrate through the foliage. The veteran American infantrymen threw themselves to the ground for cover as masses of metal and wooden splinters were hurled across the forest floor, causing dreadful injuries and wreaking havoc. But in throwing themselves to ground the Americans soon discovered that they presented a far larger target for shell and tree shrapnel than if they'd remained standing – it was counter-intuitive, but that was the Hürtgen. The *landsers* – sitting in their bunkers with overhead protection above them – were much safer than their exposed counterparts, and, with fewer guns available, used mortars far more, where their elevation proved as useful as it had in the Norman *bocage*. The results were predictable; casualties amongst Craig's division swiftly reached a thousand, with conditions on the frontline that beggared belief. One American medic described how the only way to find the wounded was to feel your way forward in the dark with your hands, and on finding a casualty it was 'like putting your hand in a bucket of wet liver'.[26] The Germans were not much better off, as attested to by a letter from one grenadier to his parents: 'We squat in an airless cellar, the wounded lie on blood-stained mattresses ... one has lost most of his intestines from a grenade.'[27]

When the Americans paused for breath at the end of the month, the German 7. *Armee* commander, Erich Brandenberger, realised they were serious about taking the Hürtgen, and that this ill-judged decision was a god-send to his overstretched command – if the Amis wanted to throw away all their usual advantages and fight on ground more or less made for the defender, then let them; as Napoleon himself said 'Never interrupt your enemy when he is making a mistake.' Brandenberger decided to feed just enough men into the battle to keep it going – that would be victory enough. That strategy saw *Generalleutnant* Hans Schmidt – an officer described by the historian Charles MacDonald as 'physically robust ... level-headed and never rattled under fire' – lead his 275. *Infanterie-Division* into the forest. Having been almost annihilated at Falaise back in August, the 275. *ID* now absorbed the remnants of Paul Mahlmann's 353. *Infanterie-Division*, to give Schmidt a strength of six and a half thousand men, a dozen howitzers and six assault-guns. When Craig renewed his attack – this time towards the ridge-top village of Schmidt some three and a half miles southeast of the town of Hürtgen itself – the *landsers* were ready, as one of their officers described: 'We became accustomed to leaving only an outpost screen in front of them to bombard … so that their initial attack hit thin air.'

On that very first day, 6 October, one of the leading American battalions suffered one hundred casualties without engaging a single *landser* with small-arms fire. A sick joke was soon doing the rounds in the 9th Division that they were taking the Hürtgen one tree at a time. Ten days later Craig's exhausted men were taken out of the line. The Old Reliables had taken a month to advance just three thousand yards, losing 4,500 men killed and wounded in the process.

Next up was Norman Cota's 28th Infantry Division. 'Dutch' Cota himself was already a legend in the American Army, having landed on Omaha on D-Day as a mid-ranking officer and inspired his men to get off the beach and overwhelm the defenders. Rewarded with a divisional command, he had led the experienced National Guardsmen of the 28th since their previous commander – James Wharton – had been killed in action back in the summer. Now, he was detailed to continue the stalled advance and finish the job. Starting on 2 November, his regiments moved off, with torrential rain turning the ground into a quagmire and hampering both the advance and resupply. The attack was a disaster for the Americans.

OKW had reinforced the area – even committing the remnants of von Schwerin's old *116. Panzerdivision* – and the Americans ran straight into a prepared and aggressive defence. After some initial success, including the capture of the villages of Schmidt and Kommerscheidt, the Germans countered, and the 28th almost fell apart. In less than a week Cota's men suffered 6,184 casualties; one of his regiment's – the 112th – lost over two-thirds of its men, with many surrendering after being surrounded. The shock within First Army was profound. Cota retained command of the division, but his reputation was badly tarnished and would never fully recover.

By now, Aachen had fallen, and the siege of Metz was entering its final days. It was now obvious to Allied senior command that there would be no German counter through the Hürtgen. To continue the forest offensive was simply to invite more casualties and waste precious time. The *raison d'être* for the whole affair had evaporated.

So, even at this late stage, could the Allies still end the war that winter? It wasn't unthinkable. The Red Army had amply demonstrated that winter offensives were not only possible but could change the course of the war; think of the Soviet counter-offensive in front of Moscow in December 1941, and even the Stalingrad attack in late November 1942 that doomed *6. Armee* to destruction. Winter in Germany could be tough, but it wasn't anything like Russia's 'General Winter', and the Anglo-Americans were masters of supply. Even the politics would be easier now that Montgomery had shot his bolt in the Netherlands – the infamously acidic field-marshal couldn't now begrudge the Americans leading the charge into Germany through the Aachen-Saar gap – even if it was led by his arch-rival Patton. A swift end to the war was the carrot dangling in front of the Anglo-Americans; now was the time to focus, to concentrate. Bradley's Twelfth Army Group would be allocated pretty much every gallon of gasoline and every bullet and artillery shell that the Allied logistical system could supply. Patton's Third Army would be the point of the spear, with First and Ninth following up. Jacob Devers' Sixth Army Group would take over responsibility for the line to the south, and the Anglo-Canadians would hold in the north. It was about 350 miles from Aachen to Berlin as the crow flies – Heinz Guderian's race to the sea in 1940 from Sedan to Abbeville was 140 miles, and he'd covered that in a matter of days, while having nothing like the military muscle now available to the Allies. A decision needed to be made – a leader had to grab the campaign by the scruff of the neck and throttle the Third Reich to death.

Step forward Omar Bradley. His plan – *Operation Queen* – called for eighteen divisions; mostly American from the First and Ninth Armies, but also some British troops from Horrocks's XXX Corps, to advance to the Ruhr River and then on to the Rhine and into the very heart of Germany. Bradley – desperate to escape Patton's shadow and finally prove himself an exceptional field commander – called *Queen* 'the last offensive necessary to bring Germany to her knees'.

Delayed by poor weather, it was finally launched on 16 November, and preceded by the largest tactical air bombardment of the war, with a staggering 4,500 aircraft involved – including over seventeen hundred heavy bombers. A number of German towns were flattened, including Düren, where one SS grenadier described seeing 'German women literally smeared against the walls of houses by the bombs'. In a terrible stroke of misfortune, *Generalleutnant* Max Borck's *47. Volks-Grenadier Division*, its ranks full of seventeen- and eighteen-year-old youngsters, was in the process of transiting through Düren at the time of the attack and was gutted. A *feldwebel* who survived and was later captured by the Americans said of it: 'I never saw anything like it. These kids … were still numb forty-five minutes after the bombardment. It was our luck that your ground troops didn't attack us until the next day. I couldn't have done anything with those boys of mine that day.' However, apart from the unlucky *47. VGD*, German troop losses were relatively few, with the bombing causing a great deal of destruction but failing to subdue the defenders. The American assault divisions were met with stubborn resistance, and in just two days it became obvious the great breakthrough envisioned by Bradley simply wasn't going to occur.

Back in the Hürtgen – a focal point for *Queen* – all that was left was the objective of capturing the *Schwammenauel* dam. While useful, it was hardly a goal that would bring the war to a rapid and successful conclusion. Hodges refused to change tack though, and the 28th Infantry Division was rotated out, and the offensive was ordered continued; this time with the 4th Infantry in the vanguard. Hans Schmidt's rag-tag *kampfgruppe* had been more or less destroyed by now, its troops having done more than could have been possibly asked of them. Several other formations had been drafted in, primarily the new *volks-grenadier* creations, including *Oberst* Georg Kossmala's 272. *Volks-Grenadier Division*, and even elements of Friedrich von der Heydte's *FJR. 6*. Both units would have good cause to remember their time as *die Hölle im Hürtgenwald* – Hell in the Hürtgen – an epitaph Hans Wegener would readily agree with:

> Then came the inferno; panzer against panzer, hand to hand combat, panzers burning... Feldwebel Brockmann shot a Sherman with a panzerfaust, but the warhead fell off in mid-air, rendering it useless. He was immediately killed by the panzer ... men falling everywhere... My people shot up a Sherman which started to burn. One of the crew members tumbled out and staggered beside his burning tank, I screamed 'don't shoot!'... they brought him to me and he appeared unwounded, though he was blinded ... we had to retreat.

Only fourteen of Wegener's forty-strong platoon were left standing after that attack. Their American opponents were in just as bad a shape, as one wrote in his diary: 'Virtually all of the men were in a state of shock. Their nerves were shot, their physical energy had long since disappeared. They crouched dazedly in their foxholes ... waiting for the Germans to come back. They could never hold another counter-attack like the last one.'[28]

Another *volks-grenadier*, the Romanian ethnic German Eduard Zacharuk, recalled the ferocity of the battles:

> We had no cover at all... In the fighting that followed ... my comrades and I fought like programmed machines without thinking much at all. I felt we accepted the assignment as certain death, and a fatalistic attitude set in. There were no heroes that day, at least no-one set out to become a hero... During this fighting I realised just how much of a firepower advantage our enemy possessed ... everyone from the heavy machine-gun section who could run, including me, fled from our positions into a ravine to escape the killing artillery fire. After a short while this horrible fire stopped and me and two others ... returned to our positions. From where I stood, I observed the approach of a group of Ami prisoners ... thirty or so I think, being escorted by several comrades from the Kompanie.[29]

Overwhelming American firepower was finally beginning to have an effect, as one German medic recalled: 'The earth trembles, the concussions take our breath away. Two wounded are brought to my hole, one with a torn-up arm, the other with both hands shot off. I am considering whether to cut off the rest of the arm – I'll leave it on. How brave these two are. I hope to God all this is not in vain.'

The Americans then attacked: 'Machine-guns begin to chatter, and here come the Amis. In broad waves you can see him come across the field. Tanks all around him are firing wildly... Can't stick my head out of the hole. Finally, three German assault-guns appear...we can see several tanks burning ... the attack slows. It's stopped.' But not for long. A few hours later, the Americans attacked again: 'Unbelievable that with this handful of men we can hold out ... our people are dropping like tired flies ... suddenly hordes of Amis are breaking out of the forest... We shoot until the barrels sizzle... There are only five of us left ... we can't hold them any longer.'[30]

Despite this seeming success, 4th Infantry Division fared little better than its predecessors; as an official US Army report admitted: 'After heavy fighting, primarily by the 4th Infantry Division, VII Corps' attack ground to a halt.'

Hodges's answer was yet another rotation, this time it was Donald Stroh's 8th Infantry Division that was fed into the heat of the battle – although Stroh himself was temporarily relieved of command following the death of his pilot son in action and his subsequent near-breakdown. The 8th was a veteran unit (like its unsuccessful predecessors) and had earlier liberated the ruins of the Breton port city of Brest, its deputy commander – Charles Canham – accepting the surrender of the garrison and its para leader, Hermann-Bernhard Ramcke. Arriving in the Hürtgen, the men of the 8th soon realised they were entering a different world. They were lucky to advance six hundred yards in a day, as their attacks were met with determined resistance from men like the para NCO, *Obergefreiter* Alfons Krüsch:

Late in the afternoon – it must have been on around 15 December – three Amis were trying to destroy one of our machine-guns with their own machine-gun fire. A comrade pointed out that something was moving up ahead; I let the Amis get into position by a small brushwood pile and then my submachine gun came up and I fired a complete magazine from a distance of twenty-five metres. I changed the magazine, pulled the trigger again and gave the medics something to do. In the next few days the Amis attacked again and again but couldn't break through.

Their opponents were just as tough as Krüsch and his comrades; Staff Sergeant John W. Minick of the 8th's 121st Infantry Regiment found himself and his men facing a minefield covered by a German machine-gun post. Leading four men through the mines, he attacked and destroyed the machine-gun nest. Continuing to advance he then shot up a group of Germans, killing twenty and taking another twenty prisoner. Carrying on once more, he found himself in yet another minefield where he accidentally stepped on a mine and was killed – he was posthumously awarded the Medal of Honor.

By now, German leadership in the forest had undergone a change, with Georg Kossmala replaced by *Generalmajor* Eugen König; the same Eugen König who had taken command of *91. Luftlande-Infanterie-Division* after Wilhelm Falley had been killed by American paratroops on the morning of D-Day. His subsequent performance was highly praised by his superiors: 'The newly-organised division, which had not yet been fully-trained and equipped, performed well owing to the energetic leadership of König.' The new broom brought fresh energy to his tired and depleted command, as the *landsers* settled down to a Christmas and New Year in the dark of the Hürtgen: 'On Christmas Eve we had something to eat for the first time in a while; a loaf of kommissbrot (German Army black bread), a sausage and a bottle of Bols liquor for every ten men.'[31] One of König's *volks-grenadiers*, Kurt Klein, was feeling festive: 'Tomorrow is New Years, we've got ourselves a goose!' Writing in his diary the next day, his celebrations were tinged with sadness: 'A new year has begun… I wish I could have gone to church. How nice it would be if there were no war.'[32] Shattered, the 8th Infantry Division was pulled out. As they trooped out of the forest their condition was described by a watching officer: 'The men are physically exhausted … the physical ability to continue is gone … shivering with cold their hands are so numb that they have to help one another with their equipment. I firmly believe that every man should be evacuated through medical channels.' With no hope of the same relief, *Oberst* Bremer saw how it was for his own men: 'In some cases, soldiers were found dead in their foxholes from sheer exhaustion.'

Hodges' generalship of the Hürtgen fighting continued to lack any inspiration or subtlety. He simply sent in one division after another into the forest, waited until they were decimated and then rotated them out; the 1st and 78th were the latest to enter the meat-grinder. With more men and equipment than the Germans, such a battering-ram approach was bound to win in the end, but the human cost of such an approach negated the offensive's very objective. *Oberleutnant* Karl Bolzmann of *272. VGD* tried to describe it in a letter home:

The icy cold creeps through the boots and into the feet of the solider standing watch behind the machine-gun … a feeling of defeat comes over him … he knows that he still has to keep standing for another half an hour. Then his comrade will arrive to relieve him and he will be able to crawl back into his foxhole and get some sleep... Tomorrow afternoon it is the grenadier's turn to pick up hot food for his squad at the Company command post, located in a basement where there is a warm stove... The position must be held at all costs ... one night not long ago Oberst Burian had come by, since it was impossible to move during the day, and had asked each man if he could rely on him to do his duty. 'Jawohl Herr Oberst!' each of them had said. Then he passed out cigarettes ... in Russia things were much worse, that was the only consolation, there you had to pay more attention, so that you didn't immediately get frostbite. Yes, the Oberst could rely on him, just as he had in Russia, and in Normandy at Caen... There are no songs to sing and no words to describe the quiet, hard and taciturn life of the infantryman in combat.[33]

The young officer's description of his men's devotion to duty is touching, but wasn't shared by every *volks-grenadier*, as Hans Gunkel understood: 'The enemy has increased his level of activity, including the use of artillery... The complete German defeat in the west is now only a matter of time.'[34] Gunkel's fellow *gefreiter*, Helmut Lürkens, agreed with him and said so in a letter home to his wife, Lena. Perhaps forgetting that all mail was censored, Lürkens was given three-days close arrest for his inked outburst.

By 16 December, the Americans had been hammering away at the *Westwall* for three months. Hodges's First Army had taken the brunt of the campaign, but Bill Simpson's newly arrived Ninth Army, and Patton's Third, also took their punishment. American fighting casualties in the border battles had now almost reached seventy thousand, with twenty-four thousand in the Hürtgen alone. Just as shocking was the fact that as many men again were lost to sickness, disease and accidents, with thousands of cases of exposure and trench-foot. In the Hürtgen, one in every four GIs became a casualty, with the 4th Infantry Division so badly mauled it was officially declared incapable of further offensive action, and subsequently sent to a quiet sector of the front to rest and refit; the Ardennes. As for the *Westheer*, its losses were at least as high as the Americans in terms of killed and wounded, but far higher overall when the 95,000 men who were captured are factored in. Eugen König's 272. VGD for example, lost almost three-quarters of its original roster, but, incredibly, was still receiving replacements, men like Günther Ecker, a seventeen-year-old Rhinelander who'd volunteered for the Wehrmacht's famed *fallschirmjäger* after his compulsory *RAD* service. Sent to FJR. 6 in Normandy, he'd fought throughout the campaign before finding himself transferred to 272. VGD in late November, complete with para smock, rimless helmet, jump boots and StG 44. With him went his friend Wilfried Wilts, an ex-Kriegsmarine sailor, whose minesweeper had been sunk off the Normandy coast back in June, forcing Wilts to fight with the paras ever since. In Ecker's view, 'the Hürtgenwald was hell.'

Charles MacDonald – an American infantry captain who fought in the Hürtgen and would go on to become a distinguished historian – said of it, 'a misconceived and fruitless battle, that could have, and should have, been avoided.'

For the Allies, it is hard to see the *Westwall* battles as anything other than a mistake at best, and a massive blunder at worst. Three months and a hundred and forty thousand men had been spent taking two cities and a tract of forest – all of which could have been bypassed. Summer's charge had become autumn's trudge, and Berlin had gained time and space to prepare for the invasion of Germany proper. At the end of November, Montgomery, whose personal and professional faults had been laid bare that autumn, wrote to his superior and supporter, Alan Brooke, regarding the possibility of ending the war that year: 'There is a feeling of optimism at SHAEF ... there are no grounds for such optimism.'

On this occasion, the British field marshal's opinion was entirely correct. Yet he was as much to blame for that reality as anyone within Allied high command. His original sin of failing to secure the Scheldt estuary at the beginning of September had haunted Allied military decision-making ever since. Much-needed supplies were still being trucked all the way from the D-Day landing beaches to the front, even as the US Army's daily needs alone grew to some 20,750 tons. Criminal gangs and corrupt officials were doing a roaring trade on the black market in everything from gasoline, to tyres, to tents, socks and everything in between, and the culture of waste within the American forces in particular was prodigious – the countryside was littered with their detritus. Staff officers at various headquarters were scrabbling to re-draft logistical requirements as it was realised that previous planning assumptions were wildly optimistic; for example, boots and blankets were found to be wearing out in half the time planned for, and the need for new uniforms in general was far higher than even America's ability to produce them. Capacity on the beaches was so limited that ships laden with cargo could be sat at anchor for weeks waiting for their turn to be unloaded, and once that had been done those same supplies could then sit in dumps ashore for weeks more, waiting to be transported forward. Anything perishable treated like this was likely to spoil, and hundreds of tons of food especially had to be destroyed.

As casualties mounted in the *Westwall* fighting, no fewer than six entire American divisions kicked their heels in the rear, unable to move or fight due to lack of supplies. Winter would only make things worse, with additional kit such as cold-weather clothing needed for a huge number of men. Eisenhower's team at SHAEF sent a memo to the Pentagon back in Washington stating that the troops would need *3.5 billion pounds* of food to sustain them through the winter; including four thousand head of beef cattle and more than a million eggs per day! In total, it was estimated that a fleet of 340 Liberty ships would be needed solely to ferry the food across the Atlantic, plus several times that number for gasoline, ammunition, tanks, guns, aircraft and every other item an army in the field consumed.[35]

The answer to the Allies' logistical dilemma was Antwerp and its intact facilities – and, at last, Montgomery realised it. To carry the weight of what was bound to be a difficult operation, he turned to the same men who landed on Juno Beach on D-Day and had fought so well throughout the subsequent Normandy campaign – the volunteers of the First Canadian Army. An excellent outfit, the First was, in many ways, an oddball army right from its inception. With its 'only volunteers' rule, the biggest problem the Canadian Army had was getting enough Canadians to serve in it. Desperate for the political kudos of having their own field army, the Canadian government and high command lobbied furiously for the creation of the First, and indeed, it could boast a strength of over 250,000 men in the run up to D-Day. However, the decision was then made to send seventy-five thousand of those same men to the Italian front, leading to something of a scramble to find others to fill the gap. In came Stanisław Maczek's 1st Polish Armoured Division, Jean-Baptiste Piron's Free Belgians, and the Dutchmen of the Princess Irene Brigade. Even with this polyglot patchwork of allies the roster was still dangerously low, so the Americans contributed the 104th 'Timberwolf' Infantry Division, and the British an entire Corps, John Crocker's First. To command Canada's only field army, Ottawa chose the slight and unassuming Harry Crerar. An able staff officer, Crerar was not known for his charisma or battlefield experience – it was no secret that Montgomery would have much preferred the energetic and decisive Guy Simonds – and it's fair to say that Crerar's leadership of the First Army can best be described as unlikely to inspire comparisons with Alexander the Great. As it was, with the majority of major British formations involved in the aftermath of *Market Garden*, or deployed further south and east, Montgomery ordered Crerar to clear the Scheldt estuary by any means necessary.

Crerar's first task was to clear the Breskens Pocket, *Scheldt Festung Süd*. Lying in wait for them was the inveterate smoker, Kurt Eberding, and his ten-thousand-strong *64. Infanterie-Division*. Beginning their assault – codenamed *Operation Switchback* – on 2 October, the Canadian 3rd Infantry Division managed to establish bridgeheads over the steep-banked Leopold Canal under heavy fire. With progress slow, an ambitious amphibious landing was made a few days later to the east at the small village of Hoofdplaat, to try and draw defenders away from the Canal fighting, but dreadful weather hampered Allied air support, and enabled Wilhelm Daser, over on *Festung Walcheren*, to send two companies of his own men over the estuary to reinforce Eberding. With the help of specialist *Wasp* flamethrower tanks, the Canadian infantry finally managed to cross the Canal in numbers, only to find themselves in a landscape that Eberding himself described as 'a maze of ditches, canalized rivers and commercial canals, often above the level of the surrounding countryside ... which made military manoeuvre almost impossible except on the narrow roads built on top of the dykes. Each of these roadways were carefully registered for both artillery and mortar fire.'

Despite their lack of military pedigree and training, the men of *64. ID* put up a vigorous defence, contesting every yard of ground. They were helped by having been left a plethora of guns by the rest of *15. Armee* as it escaped across the Scheldt weeks before, including dozens of 20mm anti-aircraft guns and superb 88mm tank-killers. Nevertheless, by 18 October, the Canadians had taken over three thousand prisoners, and German resistance was beginning to crack. Breskens itself fell on 21 October, with only the Napoleonic era Fort Frederik Hendrik still holding out on the estuary's edge. An initial attack by the North Nova Scotias was repulsed the following day, and scant hours before another was made a German deserter told the Canadians there were only twenty-three defenders left alive in the fort. Sent back with an ultimatum, those twenty-three surrendered, despite Eberding informing the remnants of his command that 'German soldiers who retreated without orders were to be regarded as deserters and summarily executed... In cases where the names of deserters are ascertained, their names will be made known to the civilian population at home and their next of kin will be looked upon as enemies of the German people.' Just days after issuing this vengeful proclamation, Eberding was captured unharmed in a pillbox at Het Zoute on 1 November, without firing a shot. His remaining men laid down their weapons the next day, having lost over thirteen hundred killed in the battle. The Canadians suffered over two thousand casualties – mostly wounded – but with more than five hundred dead. The region around Breskens was devastated, with a third of all buildings flattened, major flooding, and some six hundred locals killed in the crossfire. In the Operations Log for the 3rd Infantry Division, the entry for 9.50am on 3 November 1944 read 'Op Switchback now complete.' Someone had added next to it, 'Thank God!' In one of the most blatant examples of Montgomery's inability to either admit his own mistakes, or empathise with others, he had appeared at the division's headquarters a few days previously and savaged its officers and men for what he regarded as their sluggish performance in clearing the pocket. He forgot to mention his own negligence in not prioritising the operation back in September when it should have been launched.

With the estuary's southern bank in Allied hands, it was the turn of *Festung Walcheren*. The German garrison on the island and the adjoining south Beveland peninsula was another scratch outfit; *Generalleutnant* Wilhelm Daser's *70. Infanterie-Division* and some naval gun batteries and their sailor crews. Daser's unit was unflatteringly nicknamed the *Weissbrot* (White bread*)* or *Magen* (Stomach) division by its peers, due to the fact that it was mustered from men hitherto exempted from military service, as mentioned previously, due to severe stomach disorders and disabilities. As such, the division was allocated a special diet for its 7,500 men. *OB West* didn't consider it likely that the *70. ID* would hold out that long, so had also positioned several thousand *fallschirmjäger* – most notably a *kampfgruppe* from Friedrich von der Heydte's *FJR. 6* – to the east, where the estuary narrowed as it neared Antwerp itself.

Even as Kurt Eberding meekly surrendered at Het Zoute, the Canadians landed on Walcheren Island in a seaborne assault, losing nine landing craft sunk and another eleven damaged. Wilhelm Daser's men fought far better than expected – despite their physical disabilities – and succeeded in holding the Allies back for a week, before Daser met with a lieutenant from the Royal Scots to discuss terms. However, a general of the German Army was never going to capitulate to an officer of such inferior rank, so the lieutenant awarded himself the 'local and temporary' promotion to lieutenant-colonel. With honour satisfied, Daser surrendered on 9 November and resistance more or less ceased, with *70. ID* effectively destroyed.[36]

Having described Eberding's *64. ID* as the 'the best infantry division we have met' in its official Intelligence Summary, it is slightly unnerving to consider what the First Army thought of Eugen Griesser, Alexander Schmidt, and their fellow *jäger* as they now battled with them further up the estuary. The British who fought them were pretty clear about their capabilities, saying the conditions they fought under 'would have undermined the morale of any but the staunchest soldiers, but the German paratroopers were capable of sustaining their desperate role.' However, they also recognised their lack of numbers: 'The seasoned paratroopers were now merely the nucleus of the force, and it was from the rest that the prisoners mostly came … officers were rare birds indeed.' Anton Richter was one of those 'seasoned paratroopers', having fought through the Normandy campaign. As part of an assault patrol, he and his comrades went tank hunting one night: '…crossed the canal in an inflatable boat … the front was quiet … nerves were on high alert. Two hulking dark shadows, next to them a double sentry, and the Shermans we had been looking for. Everything happened in a matter of seconds. Two panzerfausts roared, flames sparked and in a single detonation the tanks burst apart.'

Richter's comrade, Eugen Griesser, remembered it well: 'In Hoogerheide and Woensdrecht we fought the Canadians. You could recognise them by their uniforms which were greener and not as brown as those of the Tommies. The fight for the villages was bitter; often enough we weren't even fighting house-to-house, but room-by-room.' Griesser wasn't exaggerating. Von der Heydte received the following situation report on the fighting from his 6. *Kompanie*: 'In house number nineteen the Canadians have taken the kitchen – bedroom still in our possession.'[37]

The twice-wounded paratrooper *Oberstleutnant* was full of admiration for his Canadian foes: 'The Canadians fought – as a German I have to say this – superbly. Their officers – up to and including their brigadier-general – stood next to and with their soldiers in the front line.' An element of mutual respect grew between the two sides that sometimes brightened the savagery of the fighting, as nineteen-year-old Alexander Schmidt recalled from one incident in a forward post near the Dutch town of Bergen op Zoom: 'A Canadian tank that had broken through, drove over one of our mines and flew into the air, some of the crew were thrown clear and lay wounded.' Another tank then appeared. 'My comrade, who was with me, shot his panzerfaust at the Canadian tank and hit it straight on. Now we had two tank crews and no idea what to do with them.' Schmidt and his comrade decided to hand them back to their fellows. 'We salvaged a Red Cross flag from a tank and went into the village where the Canadians lay in position ... an ambulance came and picked up the wounded, when we said goodbye they gave us a pack of cigarettes in thanks.' Those cigarettes almost cost Schmidt his life when he was captured by the Canadians the following night. Thinking he had looted them from a dead Canadian his new captors demanded to know how he got hold of them – once his story was verified his guards relaxed and gave him coffee instead of shooting him out of hand. Schmidt's fellow *jäger,* Alfons Krüsch, who would later be sent to join the fighting in the Hürtgen, remembered the same battles: 'For the entire day the Canadian artillery covered the whole area with fire, including the positions of their own infantry. Around evening time, we figured out that their own soldiers must have had their lungs ripped apart by the artillery fire, as they lay unmoving in their foxholes.' Retreating north past Steenburgen to Dinteloord, the fighting didn't slacken as *Feldwebel* Wolfgang Langer recalled:

> Jabos were attacking non-stop ... the area lay under constant fire from heavy long-barrelled artillery... I lost some of my boys there, including little Schmidt, a Berliner with fire-red hair and an irrepressible sense of humour – a piece of shrapnel hit him in the chest and killed him instantly.'[38]

With both banks in Allied hands, a total of one hundred minesweepers (the vast majority from the Royal Navy) could get to work clearing the estuary of sea mines, in an operation that lasted three weeks – some 267 mines were blown up or deactivated – and finally, on 28 November, some eighty-five days after it was liberated intact, the first Allied cargo ship docked in Antwerp harbour and began to be unloaded.

First Canadian Army suffered between thirteen and eighteen thousand casualties clearing the Scheldt – the figures differ depending on the definition of what operations were included in the battle – but, terrible though this toll was, it was relatively low in comparison to American *Westwall* losses, in what were – arguably – a series of unnecessary battles, when set against the vital objective of opening Antwerp.

The three months where Antwerp's docks lay idle, weren't wasted by Hitler. Enraged at the city's liberation, he ordered that V-1s and V-2s be diverted from their primary mission of obliterating London and sent crashing into the Belgian port instead – it was the only time that Hitler sanctioned their use in such a way. The Germans rained down more than thirty of their revenge weapons on the city and its inhabitants per day.[39] The destruction wrought was dreadful; over sixty-seven thousand buildings were demolished or badly damaged, including two-thirds of the city's housing stock. Two cargo ships and fifty-eight smaller vessels were sunk at anchor, and more than ten thousand people were killed or wounded. Damage to the port meant that even by the new year, Antwerp was only handling about 10,500 tons of supplies a day – a fraction of its capacity. The *Westheer* may have lost over forty thousand men killed, wounded, or missing defending the Scheldt, but Berlin considered it a price worth paying to deny Antwerp to the Allies for three precious months.

With winter well and truly ensconced on the Western front, both sides could reflect as to their position, and what the next few months could hold. British Intelligence decided to interrogate some of the tens of thousands of prisoners taken in the recent Scheldt battles, and ascertain from them their views:

> Few thought that Germany had any hope of final victory; most had had their fill of fighting and recognised the futility of continuing the struggle. Nevertheless, they all fought hard. The deduction would seem to be that no matter how poor the morale of the German soldier may be, he will fight hard as long as he has leaders to give him orders and see that they are obeyed.[40]

There were other reasons the men of the *Westheer* gave for their continued resistance. The signaller, Albert Pretzel, no doubt spoke for many when he wrote home to his wife from the front: 'When will the new weapons actually be ready so they can be used en masse? Only they can bring us victory. I believe in them strongly. They must and will be a cataclysmic addition to technology and the conduct of the war. They will be something utterly new, something which our enemy will have no countermeasure for.'

Others agreed with the artillery officer *Major* Martin Jenner when he opined, 'The low strength of the Kompanies ... left little room for doubt, that with a renewal of the enemy attack large sections of the front line would be forced back ... if only the Allies could get to Berlin before the Russians do!' While others were increasingly nihilistic in their outlook, as one German prisoner explained when asked by his new captors whether he worried about the destruction of border regions like the Rhineland: 'Why not destroy it? It probably won't be ours after the war anyway.'[41]

As for the Allies, the euphoria of the summer had proven to be a chimera. Montgomery's pessimism as to the possibility of ending the war in 1944 had proven to be well placed, even though his own mistakes had played a large part in making that calamity come true. Omar Bradley – a general not usually given to prophecies of doom and gloom – told a visitor from the US War Department, 'It is entirely possible for the Germans to fight bitter delaying actions until 1 January 1946.'

Mercifully, Bradley's forecast turned out to be way off. But the Allies lack of focus and clear decision making over the autumn and early winter had given Berlin precious time to prepare one more giant surprise.

5

Wacht am Rhein –
Germany's Battle of the Bulge

In the wake of the disaster in France, Nazi Germany had roused itself to one last great effort to try and turn the war back in its favour. Albert Speer and Joseph Goebbels in particular had taken radical steps to provide the Wehrmacht with a powerful sledgehammer. Widening the age of conscription and sweeping changes in the industrial and agricultural workforce had freed up a million men for the front and the new *volks-grenadier* divisions. At the same time, the rationalisation and transformation of the war economy would provide those same men with a mass of new and deadlier weapons. Some 1,430 Messerschmitt Me 262 jet fighters rolled off the production lines, along with 370 even faster Me 163 rocket-fighters. They would fly alongside 1,500 new Bf 109K-4s – designed specifically to combat the hated and feared *Viermots*. Two hundred and twenty-eight *Jagdpanthers* – arguably the finest tank destroyer of the war – would line up with almost five hundred 70-ton *Tiger II* behemoths, both armed with the superlative long-barrelled 8.8 cm Pak 43/3 L/71 gun, capable of knocking out any other tank of the time at a range of two thousand metres. They would join several thousand Panthers as well as two thousand *Hetzer* tank destroyers and the even more numerous *Sturmgeschütz IIIs (StuG IIIs)*. The Wehrmacht's panzer fleet could now count on 3,220 new and refitted vehicles delivered in November and December. Forty-six thousand trucks had been built to transport troops and supplies, and in September alone thirty-five thousand tons of explosives were manufactured. Winter was coming, and whilst gasoline was in short supply and strictly rationed, the mines of the Ruhr and Upper Silesia were disgorging mountains of coal to keep the forges and home fires burning as the weather turned. All of this was happening even as the Allied bomber fleets stepped up their attacks on the Reich to unprecedented levels. Scarcely believable as this was in many ways, the picture was not as rosy as it seemed.

Yes, Germany's mines were disgorging mountains of coal, but instead of being efficiently transported to factories and homes, the black bounty piled up at the pit-heads as the goods trains it should have been on were blasted off the tracks by Allied bombing. The shortages grew so bad that steel production in the Ruhr halved from October to November, and electricity generation dropped by a third. Explosives were only being manufactured at half the rate at which they were being used, and while forty-six thousand trucks did indeed join the Wehrmacht's transport fleet, it lost 118,000 during the same period; mechanisation in the Nazis armed forces was going backwards.[1] Weapons production was its highest ever that autumn, but to put the numbers in context, the Soviet Union alone made over forty thousand aircraft, almost twenty-nine thousand tanks and a staggering 129,500 artillery pieces in 1944 – never mind the twenty thousand tanks and one hundred thousand aircraft the United States built that same year. The new Bf 109K-4 was indeed a powerful machine, but with aluminium stocks low its entire tail section was made out of wood, and as for the Me 163, the *Komet* was revolutionary but had a disturbing tendency to catch fire on take-off or landing.

It wasn't just in the air where Germany's weapons had problems; the Tiger was a formidable panzer, often adored by its crews, men like Werner Block:

> You had to be really strong and tough to survive in a Tiger unit. I loved my Tiger so much I gave him a kiss every day. We nicknamed him 'Leo', and Leo saved me so many times – saved all of us – the frontal armour was so strong you see. Shells would hit us and bounce off, it was like a miracle. We were hit twenty-seven times by enemy shells and survived all of them.

However, the Tigers own mechanical complexity and huge weight often counted against it, as one of its commanders explained: 'When a Tiger became temporarily immobile, it could only be towed by another Tiger. Such targets were very conspicuous to the enemy ... and they would soon draw fire.' Werner Block reluctantly agreed:

> The Tiger had problems mechanically. It just wasn't reliable. If you had to go fairly long distances you had to load it onto a railcar – trying to drive it was not a good idea; the tracks and drive system in particular would break, or the suspension would go. I can't tell you how many track pins we had to replace; it was dreadful.

As for the new formations, the *volks-grenadier* divisions were flexible and equipped with impressive firepower, but corners were cut everywhere –

literally when it came to their uniforms. With cotton, leather and wool in short supply, anything deemed non-essential was removed, so out went pleats, facings and cuffs. Semi-synthetics were used to patch the gaps – basic military service dress which had a wool content of 85% at the beginning of the war, now only had fifteen per cent or less, with the bulk made up of cellulose-based fibres like rayon. This hugely reduced the clothing's heat retaining qualities, and when wet it lost its shape completely. Germany's soldiers would shiver on the front that winter. Even that universal symbol of Nazi oppression, the leather jackboot, had more or less disappeared, to be replaced with the far cheaper hobnailed ankle boots with canvas leggings.

In truth, the *Westheer* was fragile, and it wasn't just because of cheap boots and cheap tunics. It's official Order of Battle listed sixty-three divisions, forty-eight infantry and fifteen panzer or panzer grenadier – four more than on the eve of D-Day – but most of these formations were shadows of their former selves, with many being at twenty-five per cent strength or less. Hans Behrens of 9. *Panzerdivision* remembered, 'We regrouped on the western side of the Rhine ... we stocked up – or at least tried to ... we didn't have enough of anything.'

They faced the Allies' forty-five far larger divisions, brimming over with tanks, guns and all manner of equipment. The only two real weak spots in Eisenhower's forces were his lack of infantry – especially in the Anglo-Canadian units – and the still-shaky situation in the new 250,000-strong French 1re*Armée*. With little in the way of domestic manufacture, the task of equipping and supplying the quarrelsome French fell mainly to the Americans, and merely increased their logistical problems. At the same time, de Gaulle was trying to integrate well over a hundred thousand former *résistants* into the ranks and withdraw some of its African units to help prevent disorder at home from gun-toting irregulars, and to 'whiten' France's only field army. In overall terms though, the Allied Supreme Commander significantly outnumbered *OB West* in manpower and artillery, and by an astonishing twenty to one in tanks and aircraft.

Regardless, Hitler knew he'd been handed a huge opportunity by his armaments and total war supremos; not only did the Wehrmacht now have the strategic reserve it had lacked since Kursk, the Allies knew nothing about it. The question was how and where to use it.

There were three options: Italy, the West, or the East. Italy could immediately be discounted. The difficulties of the terrain and the lack of any major strategic objectives meant there would be little point in committing additional forces. That left a straight choice; East or West. The East was where the bulk of the Nazi war effort had gone since the launch of *Unternehmen Barbarossa* (*Operation Barbarossa*) back on 22 June 1941. While the British were facing two panzer divisions in North Africa in 1942, the Red Army had been facing twenty. The campaign had then followed something of a pattern; a major German offensive in the summer, followed by a Soviet counter-offensive in the winter. That situation had continued up until Kursk in 1943, when the Soviets were strong enough to move over to the attack in the summer once they had defeated the *Ostheer*'s latest assault. The next year had then radically moved the goalposts once more, when the D-Day landings blocked any possibility of a German summer offensive in the East. Moscow had taken advantage by launching its own attack – *Operation Bagration*. In two months *Heeresgruppe Mitte* (Army Group Centre) – the fulcrum of the Nazi war effort in Russia – had been more or less wiped out. By year's end over three and a half million German soldiers had been killed, wounded or captured on the Russian front since the invasion began. Belarus was now liberated, and eastern Poland had swapped one occupier for another. Realising far earlier than London or Washington that the Third Reich's defeat was now only a matter of time, Joseph Stalin turned to the post-war European settlement he was determined to achieve. Above all, the Soviet Union needed security from any possible future invasion, and to achieve that the communist dictator would extend Russia's empire into the Balkans, and as far west into Europe as his armed forces and Anglo-American complacency would allow. The Soviets would therefore not look to launch their next offensive across the Vistula River just yet. First, they would go on an all-out power and land grab in the East.

In the aftermath of the *Ostheer*'s disaster in Belarus, it is sometimes forgotten that the Wehrmacht still had two entire army groups, *Heeresgruppen E* and *F*, in barracks across Romania, occupied Greece, Albania, and Yugoslavia-as-was. Neither was in any way equivalent to the frontline army groups fighting in Russia, but nevertheless they still contained a quarter of a million German troops and several hundred panzers, guns and aircraft – although most of these were, like the troops, second-rate. The diminutive Alexander Löhr's *Heeresgruppe E*, for example, fielded in its ranks a single Luftwaffe field division and no fewer than twenty-two penal battalions for soldiers convicted of crimes, while his compatriot Maximilian von Weichs's *Heeresgruppe E* contained a hotchpotch of non-German anti-communist units, including monarchist Serb *chetniks*, fascist *Ustashi* Croats, White Russian Cossacks and Waffen-SS formations drawn from the Moslem peoples of Albania and Bosnia. However, amongst this medley of odds and ends there were a number of very viable formations that could have been usefully employed elsewhere, not least the four infantry and mountain divisions under Löhr's command, and especially the excellent *22. Infanterie-Division*, more or less marooned on the island of Crete since being sent there in the summer of 1942 – as the German field marshal Manstein said,

'Though one of our best formations it was to lie more or less idle for the rest of the war.' Sending these units north to Russia would not have averted the *Bagration* calamity for the Germans, but it might have cushioned the blow and enabled a more orderly withdrawal. Just as before D-Day, German dispersion of effort was momentous, with tens of thousands of troops sitting in subsidiary fronts hundreds of miles away from where the war was being won and lost.

The Germans were spread pretty thinly as the Red Army reached the eastern border of Romania, and partisan activity grew relentlessly across the Balkans. Hitler himself had once memorably compared the Soviet Union to a dilapidated house, and that all he had to do was kick the door in and the whole rotten edifice would come crashing down; one could forgive Stalin if he used the same analogy of the German eastern front that summer. As *Bagration* kicked the door in, so everything else began to crumble. The young King Michael of Romania had seen his armies annihilated during the Stalingrad disaster, and now had vengeful Soviets on home soil. In desperation, he had his *Conducător* (Romanian version of *Führer*) Ion Antonescu arrested, sued for peace and switched sides; along with several hundred thousand Romanian soldiers went the vital Ploieşti oil-fields. The biggest gasoline tap to the Wehrmacht was now shut off. Having fought side by side with the Romanians since the launch of *Barbarossa*, many *landsers* felt betrayed by Bucharest's actions, and took it out on their former comrades when the Soviets pushed their new allies forward into the fray:

> We could just make out the enemy approaching through the smoke ... no tanks this time just infantry, suddenly the cry went up: 'Romanians! The treacherous bastard Romanians!' The blood pressure nearly lifted my helmet from my head!... Every man on our side used a machine-gun. The Romanians were withering under the murderous fire ... without any orders, we jumped up and clubbed, stabbed and shot the Romanians in an orgy of frenzied hatred and fury ... no more than a dozen of them reached the safety of their own lines.[2]

On almost the same day as Ploieşti fell, unrest in Slovakia escalated into a full-blown uprising against the Nazis that would require the best part of fifty thousand troops to put down. After Slovakia, Bulgaria was next to go. Always diffident about the war, Bulgaria had already declared itself neutral at the end of August, and then on 9 September Sofia officially put its forces at the disposal of the Red Army. To the north, the Warsaw Uprising had exploded into life on 1 August, only to be starved of outside support by Stalin's intransigence and crushed on the ground by one of the most barbaric and brutal operations the Nazis undertook in the war.[3]

Further north still, Helsinki had taken Finland out of the war via an armistice signed on 19 September, after its forces almost bled to death halting the Soviets' Karelian Offensive. The Wehrmacht still had an entire army in the country on armistice day, *20. Gebirgsarmee,* one of whose newest recruits was the Norwegian volunteer Stål Munkeberg.

When I finished my training I was sent north to Finland, to the SS-Skij*ä*gers, but I was only there for fourteen days before the Finns made peace. I hadn't heard a shot fired in combat, and then we were told we had to go home. It was a 1100km walk back – 1100km, can you imagine that! It was very, very hard indeed. We had hardly any food, no change of clothes or anything, it was awful. My feet were always in pain, I was always hungry – dreadful, absolutely dreadful. I finally got back to Bergen on 24 April 1945 – and I was just happy to be alive I can tell you![4]

Simultaneously, Moscow ordered its armies to drive the *Ostheer* from northern Russia all together and 'liberate' the Baltic states. The Norwegian Waffen-SS volunteer Bjørn Lindstad faced that offensive:

The Russians broke through near Riga – we were the furthest troops east at that point and on 18 September 1944 we retreated. Estonia is very flat and we could see soldiers and vehicles everywhere, lots of horses too, and lots and lots of civilians. As we drove down the road the horses and civilian cars would get out of the way, and then when we got close to Riga we attacked the Russians. We held the Russians until all the refugees had gotten away. We then packed everything away, the cannons were taken off as well, and all the time the infantry were coming past us saying they were the last ones and there were only Russians behind them. Then a wagon came back to get us and took us to a farm. I was with my two volksdeutsche (ethnic German) friends... I heard them say 'Bubi' and that was my nickname so I knew they were talking about me. They were saying that Bubi has to join them for something but I didn't know what. Theft was strictly forbidden you know, but it turned out to be stealing a chicken from a coop. We went and one of the volksdeutsche 'hypnotised' one of these chickens and off we went with it. We ate well that night for a change.

Lindstad and his comrades were driven back into the Kurzeme peninsula in western Latvia – the so-called Courland Pocket.[5]

We were cut-off in Courland, and General Steiner wanted us all to evacuate the place, to escape, but Hitler said no, we had to stay.

All those lives were lost for nothing. I knew then that we had lost the war, in fact I never thought we were going to win, not ever, not since before I volunteered. It's never been good to be on the losing team in a war! Most of my comrades didn't agree, they believed in Hitler's 'secret weapons' and were always talking about them. Some also thought that when the Russians advanced into Germany itself then the Allies would join the Germans in fighting the communists – they thought the Western Allies and the communists was an unnatural alliance that would fall apart pretty soon – but I never really believed that... One night I was digging in and I was talking to my comrade – another Norwegian – about what would happen when we lost the war, even though we didn't really think we would survive that long, but we both wanted to see what would happen at the end. That's why we carried on fighting, to try and survive.

Constantly under attack from the surrounding Soviet forces, Lindstad and his fellow Waffen-SS men were taking enormous casualties:

We were fired at and I jumped down into my hole and fell asleep, and woke up when someone was shouting at me that we were retreating and we had to go – it was my Norwegian friend from the next-door hole. I grabbed my stuff and began to run, and after a few yards I saw that he had been shot in the head and was dead. I took his ID disc – it was difficult to break off – so at least his family would know what happened to him... I remember always being tired – we never got enough sleep – and, of course, there was never enough food either, but it was the lack of sleep that was the worst thing... My commander, Abels, he was killed on 28 October 1944, and I had to take over, and then I was wounded on 1 November 1944. I was near my hole and a volksdeutsche was in the hole next to me, and I was walking to the telephone when I heard Stalin's Organs[6] being fired at us. It was a very imprecise weapon and usually when they tried to hit us in the front line they hit their own men too, so they normally used it to fire at our rear areas. But I'd forgotten we were slightly further back than normal and so we were in the firing zone for the rockets. One landed near me and the explosion knocked me back into my hole. I was covered in blood – I'd been hit by shrapnel at the top of my right leg – but I didn't pass out. I got up and was shaking from shock. My comrades put me on a sledge and dragged me out to a field dressing station, and then I was taken further back through an area under fire from Russian artillery ... that was a very painful journey. I was so thirsty and kept on calling to another soldier to give me water. I was on my back, lying in my own blood – it was a *Heimatschuss* (a 'Homeland wound', the type of wound that meant you were sent home and could be out of the war) – but I didn't think it was possible to be evacuated as we were surrounded, but we were sorted into categories depending on how badly we were wounded. I arrived at the hospital for surgery and there was a big line waiting to be operated on – there were Russians waiting to be treated too, but they weren't prioritised. The surgeons were working on two tables each and their aprons were covered in blood. There wasn't any anaesthetic, someone put a cigarette into the surgeon's mouth and then he turned to me to start the operation. An orderly was holding me down and the surgeon took out the shrapnel in my leg – the wound it left was 6cm by 2cm – and he also took out bits of shrapnel in my right shoulder and lower down in my right leg. He left some smaller bits in me and over time they moved around and just disintegrated, it looked like I had 'rust'![7]

Lindstad wasn't the only Norwegian SS man in Courland feeling the strain. Gustav Palm had already been wounded once before returning to action:

A Russian tank crashed through the underbrush and into the same clearing where we were … everything just stopped … the tanks turret began to swing towards us. There was no protection and no time to flee into the woods. Our Untersturm grabbed a panzerfaust from one of us, took it off safety, swung it up onto his shoulder, spun round and fired – all in a single motion … the tank rumbled to a stop, inside was a small bright light – like a welder's torch – and then came an explosion. The Untersturm ordered me and another soldier to check the tank while the others stood ready. We climbed to the hatch and opened it – all the crew were dead.

Palm and his comrades paid a high price for successes like this though:

By now the Kompanie was reduced from 140 grenadiers to just twenty soldiers and two NCOs – one of whom was now the company commander… I had a Hungarian comrade who was wounded, so another soldier came to replace him – he only lasted two days and then shot himself in the foot. The doctor reported him, and he was arrested and sentenced to five years hard labour. So, a new soldier came – this time a Romanian… Another soldier was hit by a mortar shell that exploded right next to him. He screamed again and again for someone to help him. The medic who arrived a minute or so later looked at the wounded man from a distance but didn't try to help him. One leg had been completely blown off, and he had shrapnel injuries all over his body. He was bleeding profusely, and the ground around him was stained red. Gradually the screams subsided, and the soldier died... Thus the war continued, with no end in sight.

In a little over a month the *Ostheer* had lost most of the Baltic states, been ignominiously bundled out of its last toehold in Russia proper, and Berlin had lost Romania, Slovakia, Bulgaria and Finland from the Axis. Now it was the Magyar's turn, and that threat galvanised Hitler to extraordinary action, as recalled by Heinz Guderian, the OKW Chief of Staff, from a conversation he had with the dictator: 'If something happened down there it's over. That's the most dangerous point. We can improvise everywhere else, but not there.' Why this alarm? What did Hungary have that was so vital? 'I can't improvise without fuel ... the panzers won't be able to move and the aircraft won't be able to fly... I can't hang a generator on a panzer.' That then was the answer; Hungarian oil. It might not be a great deal, but after losing Romania, and with the German synthetic fuel industry being pulverised by Allied bombers, it was all Hitler had. He would remain obsessed with it almost to the very end.[8]

In Budapest, uncertainty reigned. The Regent – Admiral Miklós Horthy – was war-weary. His eldest son István – a fighter pilot – had been killed on the Russian front back in '42 in a flying accident, and not long after Horthy had watched as the greater portion of the Hungarian Army had been destroyed at Stalingrad along with the Romanians and Italians. Wary of Budapest's lack of enthusiasm for the war, Berlin had ordered the country occupied by German troops in March 1944, so when the Admiral went on national radio in mid-October to announce Hungary was following Romania and Bulgaria out of the Axis, Berlin could act swiftly, and the old man was deposed. Fresh German troops were ferried into the country to secure it for the Axis and to try and hold back the advancing Soviets. One of those soldiers was the panzer officer Richard von Rosen. He and his men had now been re-equipped with brand-new Tiger IIs – *Königstigers* – before being hurriedly packed off to Budapest, where their presence was used to intimidate the waverers into sticking with the Reich. That job done, Rosen and his battalion went east to push back the Red Army and their new Romanian allies. In concert with *24. Panzerdivision,* Rosen took part in an attack near the River Tisza (in German the *Theiss).*

Shortly after we crossed the main German frontline the first Romanians came towards us. We reached the main village quickly, the Romanians attempting to flee in vain. We waved them aside since we had no time to bother ourselves taking prisoners. There was a barrier of anti-tank guns, which we crushed, and with that, we had gone through their entire defences ... enemy rear-echelon units were surprised, whole columns of traffic swept off the roads, nothing could stop our advance.

Still pushing forward the next day, they had now advanced over fifty kilometres, but then came up against Russian troops and began to take hit after hit: 'It was a grim feeling to be sitting in a panzer, see a muzzle flash ahead and then wait for the hit ... we could receive a hit so powerful that it stunned us all.' Werner Block knew the feeling too: 'When a shell hit us the noise inside the Tiger was incredible, it was a huge sound, like a bell being struck and the whole Tiger would shake, and we would scream in fear, but we survived. I remember some guys pissing themselves in fear – they'd be there, their legs covered in piss, it was horrible.'

Fighting their way onwards, the Germans lost more and more of their precious *Königstigers* to breakdown and damage; Rosen's own panzer lost the use of its gun from a direct hit: 'The Kompanie had now put thirty-six enemy anti-tank guns out of action. We had to fight for every kilometre; the Russians fought us more bitterly than I had ever experienced before.'[9] The weather was terrible, pouring rain turning the landscape to a sea of mud that the German leviathans sank into, requiring them to be towed out again and again, as well as making life in the panzers themselves very uncomfortable. 'One might think a panzer was watertight – on the contrary – water always found its way in. If it rained all day it was very unpleasant inside. Constant drips falling on your head or neck could drive you mad... I saw that the ground was swampy, and my panzer had begun to sink in. Two of my other panzers had already stuck fast.'[10]

The earlier Russian advance had captured the town of Gyongyos, which higher command decided had to be taken back. By now Rosen and his men were attached to *1. Panzerdivision*. A night attack was planned. To support the assault and provide cover to Rosen's remaining five *Königstigers,* a handful of armoured half-tracks with a hundred infantrymen were allocated: '"Oh my God" I thought when I saw the infantry. They were convalescent walking-wounded cases, poorly armed and lacking any motivation.'

The attack went ahead, despite Rosen's obvious concerns, and soon he and his panzers were fighting through the town as the Russian garrison put up a stubborn defence. Anti-tank guns were firing from some of the houses, and it was obvious that his accompanying infantry weren't clearing them out as required. Unable to get hold of them on the radio, Rosen climbed out of his panzer and went looking for them: 'Finally I found their commander, an Oberleutnant, he was helpless and had no control over his men. Then a brave Unteroffizier arrived with a small group of men and offered to clear out the houses either side of the panzers. Upon entering the first courtyard, he was hit and fell dead ... the other infantrymen disappeared, and I stood there utterly alone.'[11]

Rosen and his men weren't the only Axis soldiers fighting the Red Army in Hungary. Despite political uncertainty in the capital, many members of Hungary's army – the *Honvéd* – were determined to defend their country against troops they saw as invaders. One such man was Edömér Tassonyi, commander of the 1st Hungarian Parachute Battalion. Trying to hold off a number of strong attacks on his line, Tassonyi had little choice but to call down fire on his own positions:

> I turned to the German artillery observer: 'Shoot to kill at reference point A!'
> 'But that's your position.'
> 'Never mind, do it, at once!'
> I looked at my watch – seventeen seconds later our position and the area in front of it was under fire from fifty-two barrels... This barrage scored a direct hit on the Russian infantry within assault distance ... the paras told me they'd known the barrage was their own ... some had peeped out and seen Russian bodies flying through the air, and other Russians manically trying to dig in. Miraculously we lost only seven dead and a few wounded.

The German cavalryman Werner Sass was another involved in the fighting:

> We were employed as infantry ... the Russians launched their anticipated offensive against us, and we were initially forced to give up our positions in the village... In the fierce house-to-house fighting we lost contact with the unit on our right... I was wounded in the knee. The platoon leader and two comrades took me to the aid station ... my right knee was shattered, and I was taken by ambulance to Budapest. There they told me that my leg couldn't be saved and would have to be amputated.

South of Rosen, Sass and Tassonyi, there was little to stop the Red Army advance into Yugoslavia, and on 20 October Belgrade was liberated by a joint force of Tito's Partisans, Bulgarian troops and the Soviets. Both *Heeresgruppen E* and *F* were now in desperate straits. Their only option was to retreat northwest as fast as they could before they were cut off in Greece, Albania and southern Yugoslavia. The key town was Kraljevo; the railway line from there could transport them north to safety. The race was on as to who could get there first and hold it. The winners were the Germans, who managed to get the grenadiers of *7. SS-Freiwilligen Gebirgs-Division 'Prinz Eugen'* there in the nick of time. Formed from Yugoslav ethnic Germans, the *Prinz Eugen* had proven itself a fearsome opponent to its partisan adversaries – too fearsome sometimes, as a number of alleged atrocities confirm – but it was neither equipped nor trained as a frontline division. Regardless, its members realised the importance of the task they'd been given: 'We arrived to find the German command in desperate need of fighting forces to hold the fragile bridgehead at Kraljevo to allow the retreat of the vast majority of Army and occupation personnel, along with a host of fleeing chetniks, Croatian soldiers and other refugees who'd worked with us.'

Friedrich Umbrich was a trooper in the *Prinz Eugen*:

> The procession from the south was a sorry sight ... the evacuated forces travelled through the mountains on roads little better than goat trails ... even compared to the normal standards of roads in the Balkans, this one was poor. Dust, stones, bogs ... resulted in broken axles, clogged filters and overturned vehicles... air raids, fierce enemy assaults and an acute fuel shortage meant it was no easy journey – panzers were forced to tow each other to save on fuel.

Issued *panzerfausts* for the first time, Umbrich and his fellow grenadiers dug in. His position was in a graveyard, where, as he was excavating his foxhole, he unearthed a keg of local plum brandy, obviously buried there by the owner for safe keeping. He proceeded to get roaring drunk and had a dreadful hangover the following day.

> Then the rain started ... our foxhole filled with water to our knees ... we used our helmets to bail out the water... as senior machine-gunner I had to keep the gun itself dry under my tarp except when I was using it, and I had to keep it clean and maintained... One dark night I heard a noise as if someone was slithering over the ground outside my foxhole. Unable to see, I fired in the direction of the sound. When daylight came I cautiously raised my head ... a dead Russian soldier lay about a metre away from my foxhole.[12]

Umbrich and his comrades ended up defending the area for almost five weeks in terrible conditions. 'We lived like moles underground. I can count the number of times I came above ground.' He had good reason to be wary:

> I remember Toni Schillinger, a cheerful, friendly man only a year or two older than I was... I warned him to whisper and to stay low since the

Russians were only twenty to thirty metres away and had snipers … he said, 'I want to see' and peered above ground. I heard a loud bang and saw a lightning-like flash. He sank down. 'Are you alright? I asked, all I got in reply was a hiss and a gurgle. When I turned to grab him, I saw a hole in his forehead and two uplifted eyes wide open. I knew he was dead.[13]

Kraljevo held. The withdrawal was largely successful, although it didn't end there, as the Partisans and Red Army continued north, driving the battered German forces ahead of them in the direction of the southern Austrian border.

The loss of the Balkans hit morale at home hard, but the biggest shock for the German population at large came on their very doorstep. Nemmersdorf in East Prussia (present-day Mayakovskoye in Russia) was a quiet village of fewer than a thousand people on the banks of the Angerapp River. Close to the border, it was nevertheless taken by surprise on 21 October, when soldiers from the Red Army's 2nd Battalion, 25th Guards Tank Brigade entered the village without a shot being fired. The following day the Soviets abandoned Nemmersdorf as the Germans counter attacked. Karl Potrek, a *Volkssturm* militiaman present at the time, testified at a tribunal in 1953 as to what he and his compatriots discovered:

In the farmyard stood a cart, to which more naked women were nailed through their hands in a cruciform position… Near a large inn, the 'Roter Krug' [Red Cross] stood a barn and to each of its two doors a naked woman was nailed through the hands, in a crucified posture… In the dwellings we found a total of seventy-two women, including children, and one old man seventy-four years old – all dead… Some babies had their heads bashed in.

Medical examinations confirmed that all the women and girls – aged from eight to eighty-four – had been raped. Some fifty French and Belgian POWs trapped in the village were also murdered. One of the *landsers* who recaptured the town wrote: 'The sights are so terrible that some of our recruits ran out in panic and vomited.'

Goebbels and his Propaganda Ministry went into overdrive and 'Nemmersdorf' quickly became a byword for what the Nazis declared would happen to all Germany if the Soviets weren't beaten. Always a major reason for the continuation of German resistance, the perceived threat from the Soviet Union now grew to fever pitch. Hildegard Trutz was a baker's daughter, married to an SS man, and mother to four children: 'Surely anything was better than falling into the hands of those sub-human Slavs, who raped every woman and child as a matter of course. The wireless had warned us that any especially pretty blondes were always picked by the Jewish commissars for their army brothels, and whenever I felt like turning back I reminded myself of this.'[14] Trutz joined the throng of refugees heading west – her four-month-old daughter Heidrun died of the cold on the journey. Rolf Munninger, an *Afrika Korps* veteran on the staff of *Heeresgruppe B* in the West, remembered a fellow officer: 'He was a very good pianist, and I can still see him playing Beethoven's Moonlight Sonata and crying like a child ... he was an East Prussian and he had lost contact with his whole family.'[15]

Fear was heightened by the Nazis' publication of a leaflet said to have been distributed to all Soviet troops approaching the Reich:

> Kill, you troops of the Red Army, kill!
> Because there is no-one among the Germans who is not guilty, not the living and not the unborn. Kill! Follow the advice of our Comrade Stalin and trample down the Fascist beast in his cave, forever. Break the racial pride of the German women! Take them for yourselves as your rightful booty![16]

Little wonder then perhaps, that the attitude of so many *landsers* on the Eastern front was typified by Helmut Grund, a Waffen-SS cavalryman: 'Better dead than Slav!'[17]

With the Eastern front under such pressure, surely this was where the Wehrmacht's last strategic reserve would go? Even Hitler had had to abandon his *Wolfsschanze* (Wolf's Lair) headquarters at Rastenburg as the Soviets came closer. Berlin had always been clear that it was in the East where the war would be won or lost – the choice was obvious.

After leaving the *Wolfsschanze*, Hitler and his entourage moved west to another purpose-built headquarters complex, this time in the Taunus Hills near the town of Bad Nauheim; this was the *Adlerhorst* – Eagle's Eyrie. It was there that the dictator sent out invitations to his senior military commanders for the decisive conference. Five-times wounded *SS-Sturmbannführer* Heinrich Springer was on the guest list: 'I was first orderly officer to Generalfeldmarschall Walter Model, and he asked me to accompany him to a high-level briefing in December 1944 at the Führer's Adlerhorst HQ.' Springer and his boss were driven to a secret location where a bus was waiting to take them on the last leg to the headquarters. They were joined by a number of senior officers who had earlier congregated at Rundstedt's headquarters before taking their seats on the bus. They were all then driven round the mountain roads for miles to confuse them as to their final destination. After a while, Springer looked up out of the window and couldn't help but notice that the road they were on was hidden from the air by a camouflage canopy suspended from the trees on either side – they were getting close. Suddenly, they were there.

The bus pulled up into what looked like a well-kept farmyard. Around the yard were seven half-timbered buildings; the sort you could see anywhere in the Taunus. The only thing that marked it out was the double row of SS guards who suddenly appeared and formed a cordon from the bus to a building that Springer later found out was called *Haus 2* – also known as the Adlerhorst Officers Club. Stepping off the bus, the passengers strode towards the doorway, most dwarfed by the *Leibstandarte* men forming the cordon – although not Springer, who was a giant at almost two metres tall and a *Leibstandarte* man himself. Relieved of their side-arms and briefcases – as was now routine following the 20 July Bomb Plot – they were escorted through some ante-rooms; deer antler trophies on the walls, flower baskets on the mantles, oak floor-lamps and pine panelling, all adding to the charade of this being the home of a well-to-do *burger* - and then on into a large briefing room wrapped around an enormous, rectangular wooden table. Once in the room they sat down: 'An SS guard assumed a position behind each chair, glowering with a ferocity that made one of the generals – Fritz Bayerlein – fear even to reach for his handkerchief.' Moments later, Hitler entered the room and sat down. One of the assembled generals remembers the moment: '…a broken man, with an unhealthy colour, a caved-in appearance … his hands trembling, his left arm subject to a violent twitching which he did his best to conceal … sitting as if the burden of responsibility seemed to oppress him … he often stared vacantly, his back was bent, and his shoulders sunken… When he walked he dragged one leg behind him.'

He then began to speak, as Springer described:

> Hitler stood and spoke for just under an hour, it wasn't a briefing in the normal sense, with recommendations and conclusions, but rather it was an address on Frederick the Great at the battle of Leuthen[18]… I can still clearly recall his closing words. 'Meine Herren, if we don't succeed with this breakthrough we will face a bloody end to this war.'[19]

This was the most important conference Hitler had held with his senior commanders since the 17 June meeting at the *Wolfsschlucht II* (Wolf's Ravine II) near the tiny hamlet of Neuville-sur-Margival, in France's Aisne *département*. At that session, von Rundstedt and Erwin Rommel had desperately tried to persuade their *Führer* to save the deteriorating situation in France by abandoning Normandy and the south, and withdrawing the *Westheer* back behind the Seine – even going so far as to imply that some sort of political negotiations with the Allies were needed. The ramrod Prussian and the 'African' upstart failed. Hitler had decreed such a course of action was impossible, and instead had doomed his army in France to a battle of attrition it was already losing. Now, six months later, he had laid out his intentions for the Reich's final push – having already begun to plan it four months earlier with an order to his Chief of Operations Staff, Alfred Jodl: 'Prepare to take the offensive in November when the enemy's air forces cannot operate... Main thrust; around twenty-five divisions must be transferred *to the West* (author's emphasis) in the next one or two months.'[20] While resting to recover from his Bomb Plot injuries, Hitler was sitting up in bed listening to one of Jodl's daily map briefings when he confirmed his vision by declaring, 'I have made a momentous decision. I am taking the offensive ... out of the Ardennes. Across the Meuse and on to Antwerp.' Hitler then directed his sharp-faced subordinate to dig out the operational plans for Manstein's 1940 offensive from their resting place in the Leignitz archive.

He had discussed his intentions with Joseph Goebbels, as the Propaganda Minister confirmed in his diary entry for 24th August: 'By the autumn we will form seventy new divisions, which for the most part will be sent to the West. For here we want to go over to the offensive again – in fact not only there, but also in the East, as soon as the opportunity presents itself.'

OB West's Chief of Staff, Siegfried Westphal, had also been taken into the dictator's confidence to begin planning the operation:

> On 24 October I was ordered to report to Hitler at his HQ at Rastenburg in East Prussia, where he told me that we would receive strong reinforcements by the end of November or the beginning of December; he named twenty infantry divisions, ten panzer divisions and a lot of special troops, and he promised that we would be supported by three thousand aircraft – but we were totally surprised that these forces weren't intended for the defence of the Western front, but for an offensive!'[21]

The *Führer* had made the decision – the Wehrmacht would attack in the West.

The operation was called *Wacht Am Rhein* – Watch on the Rhine, the title of a popular German folk song. Purposefully, the name suggested a defensive posture – Hitler wanted to keep the Allies off the scent – because *Wacht Am Rhein* was anything but defensive; in fact it was a stunning gamble. The intent was to launch two panzer armies – with an additional infantry army in support – through the forests and hills of the Ardennes region to the River Meuse (the *Maas* in Dutch), cross it, and then drive to Antwerp. They would then seize the port city and cut the Allies off from their largest, and newest, supply base, and in the process split the Anglo-Canadians in the north from the Americans and French to the south. Hitler envisaged nothing less than a giant Dunkirk, with the wholesale surrender or evacuation of Montgomery's army group, and Great Britain and Canada more or less knocked out of the European war. He could then switch his forces to the East and take the offensive once more against the Red Army. In terms of ambition it was one of the most daring plans of the war – perhaps only Manstein's Sedan operation back in 1940 was its equal in that regard, and that too had had the Ardennes as its starting gate. But this wasn't 1940, this was the end of 1944. In 1940 the Germans had flung forty-four divisions through the Ardennes – now they could field only two-thirds that number. The Wehrmacht that had won the dazzling victory of 1940 was palpably *not* the Wehrmacht standing in the snow that December – and just as importantly, the armies they now faced weren't Maurice Gamelin's under-performing French.

For Hitler, the reaction to his plan from his own senior officers was cool to say the least. Model said: 'It hasn't got a damned leg to stand on!' and Hasso von Manteuffel – the very picture of Prussian discipline – also expressed his doubts to his Führer, to which the dictator admitted to '…a certain disparity between the distant objective of Antwerp, and the forces which were to capture it. However … this was the time to put everything on one throw of the dice.' Manteuffel persisted, questioning in particular the claim that the Luftwaffe could commit three thousand aircraft to support the offensive: 'Mein Führer on our sector of the front we never see or hear a German aircraft these days.'

Hitler replied, 'Goering has reported that he has three thousand fighters available for the operation. You know Goering's reports; discount one thousand and that still leaves a thousand to work with you and a thousand for Sepp Dietrich.'

Hitler may have been sanguine about his plan, but Sepp Dietrich was not. The commander of 6. *Panzerarmee* was at the *Adlerhorst* conference, and was blunt with his leader:

Hitler: 'Is your Army ready?'

Dietrich: 'Not for an offensive.'

Hitler: 'You're never satisfied.'

The old Nazi Party street-brawler was not so polite about the attack in private:

All the Führer wants me to do is cross a river, capture Brussels, then Antwerp, and all this during the worst period of winter when the Ardennes are waist deep in snow, when it doesn't get light until eight and is dark again at four, where there isn't room to deploy four panzers abreast let alone six divisions, and with those same divisions being recently rebuilt and composed mainly of raw untrained recruits, and to do it all at Christmas!

Not exactly a ringing endorsement for the offensive. Von Rundstedt had once memorably described Dietrich as 'decent but stupid', but now found himself agreeing with his subordinate: 'It was a nonsensical operation … if we reached the Meuse we should have gone down on our knees and thanked God – let alone try to reach Antwerp!'

Just as at Neuville-sur-Margival back in June, von Rundstedt detailed to Hitler the weakness of his command for the assigned task – he reported being short of four thousand officers and over one hundred thousand men, with deficiencies in everything from ammunition to bridging equipment, to panzers, and most especially gasoline – and so proposed an alternative solution to his leader; this time in concert with his Chief of Staff, Siegfried Westphal: 'We proposed a little solution at Aachen … we compared it to a game of bridge, the plan to take Antwerp was a "grand slam" while the Aachen plan was a "little slam" – but unfortunately Hitler didn't play bridge.'[22] The Aachen 'little slam' would have seen the Germans attempt to trap and destroy Hodges's First Army, but Hitler was having none of it, describing it as a 'half solution'. As Hasso von Manteuffel explained, 'The plan for the Ardennes offensive was … sent to us as a cut and dried "Führer Directive"… it was Hitler's idea … he had decided to stake everything on one card because Germany needed the breathing space, a defensive struggle could only postpone the decision and not change the general situation for Germany.'[23] Rundstedt – in his general order to the troops on the eve of the offensive, could barely conceal his lack of belief in the operation: 'Soldiers of the Western front, your great hour has struck. We are gambling everything! You carry with you a holy obligation to give everything to achieve things beyond human possibilities for our Fatherland and our Führer!'

Why not the East then? Jodl was clear: 'The Russians had so many troops that even if we had succeeded in destroying thirty of their divisions it would have made no difference. On the other hand, if we destroyed thirty divisions in the West, it would amount to more than a third of the whole invasion army.'

Actually, it would have been half. But was this supposition true? Would an offensive in the East have been pointless? The Third Reich was being crushed in a vice from the west, east and south, there was no way it could change the fortunes of war and grab victory at this late stage, but could something else have been achieved? In all probability, no. However, it was obvious to every man, woman and child in Germany that defeat and occupation by the western Allies was far, far preferable to the Soviet alternative; after what the Nazis and the Wehrmacht had done to them, they could expect no mercy whatsoever – Nemmersdorf had shown that. Would an offensive in the East have done the job? Would it have given the Anglo-Americans the time to advance and defeat Germany before the Red Army could intervene?

Consider this: at that time the Soviet armed forces were some thirteen million strong, with only a small fraction of that number facing the Japanese in the Far East. Just in the operational area north of the Carpathians the Red Army had some 2.3 million men facing four hundred thousand Germans, with six thousand tanks versus 1,100, thirty-two thousand guns against four thousand and a superiority in the air of eighteen to one. Grim reading as these figures undoubtedly were for any offensive planner in the *Ostheer*, the underlying picture was, perhaps, not so forbidding. The Red Army was a two-tier organisation, as Andreas Fleischer knew all too well:

> They had excellent units, called Guards,[24] they had different uniforms from their normal infantry, we could tell when we were up against the Guards because they had proper belts – leather belts – while the rest – we called them 'second-line units' – they just had rope holding up their trousers. They weren't well-trained or well-armed like the Guards, not all of them even had weapons. They were told before they went into an attack, 'take the weapons from the dead'.[25]

It was these 'second-line' units that made up the mass of the Red Army, and increasingly their ranks were being filled with hundreds of thousands of males of all ages – from fifteen to fifty – scooped up from newly liberated regions, and issued with a tunic, a cap and a rifle (if they were lucky!), and pressed into service. Their longer serving comrades often referred to them as 'booty Ukrainians'. One report to Stalin detailed that of 110,000 civilians in a single liberated region, investigations were underway to establish how the people had behaved under Nazi occupation, and that seven thousand had already been drafted for frontline service. As can be imagined, casualties among these poor souls were truly horrendous; in the year July 1943 to July 1944 the Red Army suffered 1.9 million men killed and three times that number wounded – Bagration alone cost them over three-quarters of a million casualties. With losses of that magnitude, even the Soviet colossus was beginning to creak – hence why a full ten per cent of the ranks were now filled with women.

Back in the spring of 1943, after the extermination of Paulus's 6. *Armee* at Stalingrad, a victorious Red Army had swept westwards into the major industrial city of Kharkov (modern-day Kharkiv in Ukraine), threatening the entire southern wing of the *Ostheer*.

Disaster loomed for the Germans, and into the breach stepped the commander of *Heeresgruppe Süd*, Erich von Manstein. With barely 120,000 men, he comprehensively routed the two hundred thousand troops of no fewer than fifteen Soviet armies (including four Tank Armies) – the Soviets suffered ninety thousand casualties to the Germans eleven thousand, and the whole front was stabilised by Manstein's 'miracle on the Donets' as it quickly became known.

Imagine then what Manstein could have done with a strike force of twenty divisions – seven of them armoured – with double the number of soldiers and panzers he had on the Donets, especially enjoying the element of surprise. After all, Manstein had almost succeeded at Kursk despite facing probably the greatest defensive array ever created; a system of defences only established because the Soviets knew the attack was coming. Imagine as well that Manstein's offensive was carried out to the north of the mass of Soviet armies fighting in the Balkans and southeast Europe – a series of envelopments that could have torn the heart out of the Red Army in Poland.

Instead, Hitler had sacked Manstein on 30 March 1944 with the words, 'I have decided to part company with you ... the time for operating is over – what I need now is men who stand firm.' Model was given Manstein's command, and the victor of Kharkov was fobbed off with the award of the Swords to his Knight's Cross – he never again held a field command during the war. As the Waffen-SS officer, Rudi von Ribbentrop, said of the decision to head west and not east: '...the fact that this operation was executed in the West and not against the Red Army, underlined to me how unreal Hitler's perceptions were.'

Although many senior officers were not enthusiastic about the offensive, their view was by no means universal, as one officer in a spearhead division recalled:

> ...we had the feeling that this huge build-up might enable us to reach our final objective of Antwerp .... the weather was foggy and so American and British air superiority didn't matter and in addition we had the support of a whole artillery corps, we had never known such support before ... therefore we believed we would be successful.[26]

After so many defeats and retreats, it was amazing that such optimism was felt among veterans who had already seen so much. However, for the offensive to be successful, two factors in particular needed to be considered and overcome. The first was the terrain. As Sepp Dietrich sarcastically outlined, large tracts of the Ardennes were seemingly designed to discourage armoured warfare. The north – where Dietrich's army would form the main punch – was criss-crossed by numerous rivers and streams that, though not wide, were deep and fast-flowing, and so only crossable on a few bridges, which channelled attackers and concentrated them at choke points. Roads were few, and not built to cope with masses of tracked vehicles, especially 1944-era panzers touching seventy tons. Pretty soon they would be chewed up very badly, and the Germans wouldn't be able to switch to cross-country movement, as most of the roads themselves were flanked by thick, dark forest impassable for vehicles. While true that using such an area for an offensive gave the attacker the element of surprise, a few determined defenders could cause havoc by holding a handful of bridges or road junctions. The south Ardennes is quite different, with a lot of arable farmland, pasture and high plateau – a far more amenable area for manoeuvre.

It was the second factor though that was keeping German commanders up at night; shortage of fuel. The paucity of gasoline had long been a brake on Wehrmacht operations, and by the autumn of 1944 that scarcity had become a veritable drought. Armoured divisions are very thirsty beasts – particularly when fighting or traversing difficult terrain; and if they're doing both their needs are prodigious. Model's own staff calculated that the offensive would require four and a half million gallons to reach the Meuse, plus an additional five million to get to Antwerp. OKW came up with a far lower figure. It worked out that twelve tank-fillings per vehicle would be enough to cover the expected duration of the battle – with this number based on one filling per hundred kilometres of driving on dry and level road. So OKW only stockpiled some 3.8 million gallons. Worse still, because of Allied air activity, a large proportion of that fuel – over two million gallons – was stuck east of the Rhine in rail sidings, rather than in depots near the front. The result was that when the offensive began, the petrol tankers bringing fuel forward were having to drive all the way to the front from the dumps near Cologne. When confronted with Model's calculations, Keitel blustered as usual, telling the front commanders that they had enough fuel and should just get on with it, despite Jodl admitting that Keitel held some fuel back deliberately and that only three fillings per vehicle had actually been issued, 'on principle, otherwise commanders would have been too extravagant with it.' Manteuffel, whose 5. *Panzerarmee* would form the southern attacking prong, was told his fuel allowance at a conference in Berlin on 23 November by the OKW Chief of the Army Staff, *General der Infanterie* Walther Buhle. The five-foot two-inch tall Prussian exploded, demanding to know if Buhle had seen the ground over which his panzers were expected to fight. Buhle replied that the spearheads had already received their allocated fuel, and as the first phase of the advance was only 150 kilometres and given a Panther's range on a single tank was two hundred kilometres,[27] there might be no need to refuel in any case. Manteuffel, with 6. *Panzerarmee's* Sepp Dietrich standing next to him, was aghast. He told Buhle to cover that first 150 kilometres he would need enough fuel for five hundred kilometres. Buhle shrugged his shoulders – they would have to work with what they'd got – that was the end of it.

And in a way he was right – that was the end of it. Panzers don't move without fuel, and the Wehrmacht didn't have the fuel it needed to reach its objectives; hence, the attack would fail – regardless of what the troops themselves did, and even regardless of what the enemy did. To put it another way; the Allies *could* just get out of the German's way and let them advance, and they would run out of gasoline before they reached Antwerp. Patton would grasp this reality soon after the offensive was launched: 'Hell, let's have the guts to let the sons of bitches go all the way to Paris. Then we can really chew 'em up!' Hitler's offensive was bold, it was daring – and it was doomed to failure before a shot had been fired. Clearly exasperated, when challenged by some of his officers on the lack of gasoline and basic supplies, Model snarled back: 'If you need anything, take it from the Americans!'

The die was cast. Delays had pushed back the start date of the offensive, so *Wacht Am Rhein* became *Herbstnebel* (Autumn Mist), and under strict secrecy the assault formations began to take up position. Three armies would take part; the northern shoulder would be Sepp Dietrich's 6. *Panzerarmee*. It would be the *Schwerpunkt*, the main effort, and within its ranks would be much of the cream of the Waffen-SS; Wilhelm Mohnke's 1. *SS-Panzerdivision 'Leibstandarte Adolf Hitler'* (LSSAH), Heinz Lammerding's 2. *SS-Panzerdivision 'Das Reich'*, Hugo Kraas's 12. *SS-Panzerdivision 'Hitlerjugend'* (HJ), and Sylvester Stadler's 9. *SS-Panzerdivision 'Hohenstaufen'*. Dietrich also had a *fallschirmjäger* division, 3. *Panzergrenadierdivision*, and five of the new *volks-grenadier* divisions. The southern shoulder would be Manteuffel's 5. *Panzerarmee*, with a further five *volks-grenadier* divisions and four panzer divisions, including Fritz Bayerlein's *Panzer-Lehr* and Meinrad von Lauchert's 2. *Panzerdivision* – the latter had a complete battalion of Panthers and was reckoned to be the finest panzer division left in the Army.

Forbidden to carry out reconnaissance for fear of discovery by any sharp-eyed American observers, *der Kleiner* – as Manteuffel was known to his friends – went anyway:

> I went to the front line disguised as an infantry Oberst, and was there for thirty-three hours ... one hour after darkness I saw the Americans went to the villages, their rooms or their girls ... then one hour before the sun came up they went back to their trenches ... there was no-one covering their positions at night, and it was for this reason I proposed to Hitler that we start the attack early.

In support of Manteuffel and Dietrich's two armoured fists was the competent and capable Erich Brandenberger and his resurrected 7. *Armee,* with a mass of infantry in eight divisions. In total, the *Westheer* would initially throw at the Ardennes some twelve hundred panzers and a quarter of a million men, supported by two thousand guns. Some of those troops were less than enthusiastic about the operation, one such was staffer Gerda Ehrhardt: 'The mood wasn't euphoric – quite the opposite, we were desperate.' Ehrhardt's boss was one of Brandenberger's commanders, *General der Kavallerie* Edwin Graf Rothkirch und Trach, and having known Ehrhardt since their days in Russia, he felt able to be open with her:

'Hitler is crazy! It is the "Desperation Offensive".'

Ehrhardt asked: 'Why then do you play along when you know everything has become pointless?'

'I don't want to be put up against a wall.'

Rothkirch knew what he was talking about. When in Russia he had been responsible for security to the rear of *Heeresgruppe Mitte* and had seen for himself what the SS and Nazi authorities were doing. He admitted as much to Hermann-Bernhard Ramcke, when the two were later secretly recorded as prisoners at Trent Park. Rothkirch said, 'I wanted to take some photographs – it's my only hobby – and I knew an SS leader quite well, and as I was talking to him about this and that he said: "Would you like to photograph a shooting?" and I said "No, the very idea is repugnant to me." The SS man replied, "Well, I mean, it makes no difference to us, they (the Jews) are always shot in the morning, but if you like we still have a few left over, and we could shoot them in the afternoon if you want."'

It wasn't just senior commanders who had serious misgivings about the offensive either, junior officers like Rudi von Ribbentrop were unconvinced as well: 'In view of the ratio of forces and the supply situation, the offensive was an irresponsible gamble – as regimental adjutant of the panzer regiment of the right wing division, I experienced at first hand the hopeless inferiority in men and matériel – not least the lack of air support.' The *jagdflieger* Heinz Knoke – slated to help provide air cover for the offensive – agreed with Ribbentrop's assessment:

No replacement pilots or aircraft have arrived yet ... the vast majority of experienced fighter pilots have either been killed or wounded ... we are slowly bleeding to death in defence of the Reich ... almost every synthetic fuel factory has been destroyed, and the fuel shortage has become a matter of grave concern... I have come to the conclusion that victory can no longer be achieved.

Nevertheless, the formations rostered to take part in the offensive prepared themselves. For those units which had fought in France there was a great deal of work to be done as new equipment arrived and reinforcements had to be integrated. One such formation was the famed *Panzer-Lehr*, whose remnants were stationed near Paderborn. Originally composed of instructors and demonstration troops from the *panzerwaffe's* training schools, it had taken enormous casualties in Normandy and needed to be completely rebuilt, as its rather doleful commander, Fritz Bayerlein, explained:

> I received sixty new panzers, and demanded more flak guns in view of my experience air attack, and in training I stressed anti-air discipline ... by this time our fuel shortage was such that much of our actual manoeuvre was theoretical. I got no fuel for training – legally. To get my division ready I wangled fuel through personal connections.[28]

Panzer-Lehr wasn't the only division in need of drastic infusions to get it battle-ready, its stable mate for much of the Normandy fighting – the *Hitlerjugend* – was if anything in even worse shape after France. Formed from a cadre of experienced veterans from the *LSSAH*, its ranks filled with seventeen- and eighteen-year-old Hitler Youth volunteers, it had almost bled out battling the Anglo-Canadians at Caen. Its celebrity boss, and youngest divisional commander in the Wehrmacht, Kurt 'Panzermeyer', had escaped the Falaise Pocket to lead his shattered unit back through Belgium in early September, when he came under fire from American advance units and local *résistants* in the village of Durnal. Having played cat and mouse with his pursuers and hidden in a chicken-coop for several hours, he found himself cornered and out of options: 'It was over...I threw my pistol's magazine into one corner, and the pistol itself into another. What a horrible feeling it was being taken prisoner.'[29] Into Meyer's boots stepped his namesake, the divisional operations officer, *SS-Sturmbannführer* Hubert Meyer:

> The division was a shell of itself ... of an original strength of twenty thousand men, about ten thousand men, including twenty-one unit commanders, were lost. The artillery was practically without guns, there was virtually only light infantry weapons left, and the vehicle complement had shrunk to a quarter. The situation offered little hope, but nevertheless training and refitting started at once ... we received men from the Kriegsmarine, Luftwaffe ground personnel and even flight crews. They had hardly any infantry training and their integration into the formations wasn't easy.[30]

Other officers didn't put such a brave face on it and lamented the quality of the reinforcements: '...mostly Ukrainians who don't even speak German. There is a shortage of everything here, but it is the men who count ... if only we just had one division trained and equipped ... like we both knew in 1939.'[31] Having said that, the division in question, the 9. *SS-Panzerdivision 'Hohenstaufen'*, went from being a burnt-out wreck in September to having almost twenty thousand men in the ranks and a full armour complement by the time the offensive began.

Two men who perhaps considered themselves less than lucky with the men they were given to fulfil their roles in the assault were Friedrich von der Heydte and Otto Skorzeny. Heydte, now promoted to *Oberst*, was summoned from his post at the parachute school at Alten to meet his boss, Kurt Student, whereupon Student ordered him to create a *kampfgruppe* for a special mission. That mission was codenamed *Unternehmen Stösser* (Operation Hawk) and its job was to jump onto the High Fens in the Ardennes just before the main assault and capture the crucial Baraque Michel road junction for the attacking troops of the *Hitlerjugend*. Heydte immediately asked for his old command of *FJR. 6* to do the job, only for Student to refuse and insist instead he form a composite unit from one hundred men from each of the *fallschirmjäger* regiments in *II Fallschirmkorps*. 'I was horrified; a troop built from a mix of forces and units is seldom good ... but my fear that I would receive a "pile of pigs" turned out to be unfounded. The spirit of the assembled kampfgruppe was good and the core personnel were excellent.'[32] The veteran para officer may well have been putting a brave face on it though, as he returned no fewer than one hundred and fifty of the 'volunteers' to their parent units as unsuitable. Heydte was also told by Dietrich: 'Don't worry, be assured that I will reach you by 1700hrs on the first day ... behind their lines are only Jewish hoodlums and bank managers.'[33]

As for Skorzeny, he was already a celebrity within the Wehrmacht, having come to prominence for taking part in the rescue of the deposed Benito Mussolini from his mountain prison back in 1943. The giant Austrian then went on to carry out some very high-profile operations, including the kidnap of Horthy's playboy son, Miklós Junior, in an attempt to try and keep his father beholden to Berlin. Now, he was given the mission for which he would become most notorious; to form a unit of English speakers who would operate behind the Allied lines in American uniforms, spreading disinformation and causing confusion and chaos. Secrecy was the key, although this wasn't helped by the circulation down to divisional level of an order from Berlin that read: '...the formation of a special unit ... to be employed on reconnaissance and for special tasks on the Western front... A knowledge of English is essential and American dialect terms and military technical terms is required ... captured American clothing, equipment, weapons and vehicles are to be handed in to equip these volunteers.' The paper then named Skorzeny personally as the officer responsible for the new unit, and gave the address of his headquarters. Naturally, Allied Intelligence had a copy before some of the divisions it was sent to – Skorzeny's cat was well and truly out of the bag. Under the cover name of '*Panzer Brigade 150*', Skorzeny went about recruiting and equipping his force, only to find the gap between his needs and what was available was a chasm. For example, he requested 150 captured American Jeeps and light cars, and got fifty-seven, many of them broken down or smashed up. Of the fifteen US tanks asked for, he got five – all German. When two captured Shermans did eventually turn up, only one had a working engine, the other had a broken gun and no radio equipment. In desperation, thirteen Panthers were requisitioned and converted to look like American tanks using wooden frames and by painting them olive-green with American markings. Skorzeny famously said of them that they could deceive only 'very green troops, at night and when seen from a great distance'. The panzer crews drafted in to man these 'Shermans' were less than impressed as well, especially as they had to make room for a supposedly English-speaking cuckoo in their metal nest:

> The loader was a 'speaker'... His job included operating a medium-wave radio with an umbrella aerial on the turret. The deployment of 'speakers' in panzer crews was controversial as they hadn't had any specialist panzer training. We were afraid that they would make mistakes in combat ... our 'speaker' didn't know the first thing about the duties in a panzer. Leutnant Gertenschläger was keen to get rid of him at the first opportunity.

Obergefreiter Gries wasn't the only concerned panzer trooper – one of his officers, *Hauptmann* Scherf, shared his angst: 'I regret to say that it seemed to me that parts of the offensive could hardly be described as well-planned or organised ... the concept we were given was far too optimistic and so once the attack was underway there were a lot of disappointments and problems.' As for Skorzeny's English-speaking, gum-chewing commandoes, only ten volunteers – all former Brandenburg special forces soldiers – were fluent and capable of passing as Americans. There were thirty to forty others whose English was good enough to get by if not pressed, one hundred and fifty who could understand English but couldn't speak it much, and a final two hundred who could understand simple English phrases if spoken slowly – this was not the force that was intended.

Despite the obvious original security lapse regarding the commando force, *Unteroffizier* Georges saw the draconian nature of other measures put in place:

> We had an official meeting and were told that we are an élite troop. All the Wehrmacht are represented; airmen, sailors, fallschirmjägers, and also civilians... Every offence can be punished by the death penalty... One of our comrades, who had to leave camp to get some spare parts, took letters with him which hadn't been censored and posted them outside the camp. This came to light in an inspection and he was shot as a result.

For once, German operational security did indeed fool the Allies, who neither believed the *Westheer* was capable of mounting an offensive, nor was contemplating one. To buttress this perception, troop movement was forbidden during the day, and men were only moved forward at night to avoid the prying eyes of Allied aircraft. Headquarters were constantly shifted around, and commanders weren't told their objectives until the eve of the attack. Hitler even tried to have all ethnic Alsatians removed from the first wave assault divisions in case they deserted and gave the game away, although this measure wasn't carried through.

Many of the men involved in the offensive, especially the officers, knew just how important this attack was. Jochen Peiper, a former adjutant to Heinrich Himmler and much-decorated *Leibstandarte* veteran, was put in charge of Dietrich's spearhead and given the job of driving hell for leather for the Meuse crossings to secure them for the follow-on troops. On the eve of battle, Hermann Priess, the owl-like commander of *I. SS-Panzerkorps*, went to see him at his forward headquarters. After being briefed on the situation by his subordinate, Priess fixed Peiper with a stare that bore into him and gripped the younger man's arm: 'Don't worry about your flanks. If you only get to the Meuse with one damned panzer Jochen, you'll have done your job!' Peiper grimaced, he thought the roads his battlegroup would have to travel on 'only broad enough for a bicycle'.

Gefreiter Guido Gnilsen of *2. Panzerdivision* remembered the hours before the offensive began: 'We were all sitting quietly by the light of candles, looking around the walls of our shelter you could see the white and serious faces of my comrades.'[34] Finally, at 5.30am on the morning of 16 December, it began, as Gnilsen recounted:

> After five o'clock we were woken by tremendously loud explosions. I thought the world was coming to an end! It was our mortars shooting

rockets out of their many barrels ... the earth was trembling as if there was an earthquake... As far as you could see there were the flashes of artillery fire. It was like being in Hell – something you never forget – and it must have been a lot worse for the enemy.

A German gunnery officer described the scene with evident delight: 'It was all so peaceful, as it can only be in the hills where fir woods quietly whisper ... then as far as the eye could see the sky lit up! Thunder filled the air and the earth shook under the impact of the blows. At first, I was dumb, but then I couldn't contain myself any longer, I shouted and danced and laughed!'

Fallschirmjäger Rudi Frühbeisser was in the same position:

0530 hours; short commands are given along the entire assault front. The Kompanie lines up in an open formation looking westward. We are shivering with excitement. Watches have long been synchronized ... 20 seconds ... 10 seconds ... 5, 4, 3, 2,1 ... Fire! The muzzles of several thousand guns, howitzers and launchers roar together almost as if they were a single detonation. The flashes light up the sky to the east behind us so that it is almost as bright as day ... 0600 hours; all at once this hell of a noise stops. Then the command is given, 'Charge!' We start running forward!

Hans Baumann was a young *Jagdpanzer IV* crewman in the *Hitlerjugend*: 'I hadn't planned on joining the SS, in fact I wanted to be a policeman, but when I was in the recruiting office in Aachen before the city was destroyed of course, I was approached by an SS man who told me that "real men" joined the SS and not the silly police force. He was very persuasive, so that was it, I joined the SS.' Now, months later, he was full of optimism as he climbed into his driver's seat: 'The weather, particularly the low cloud and mist, is on our side. Those Amis haven't got a chance.' Writing to his sister, a young grenadier in the same division could barely contain his fervour:

Dear Ruth, my daily letter will be very short today – short and sweet. I write during one of the great hours before an attack, full of excitement and expectation of what the next few days will bring. Some believe in living, but life isn't everything! It's enough to know that we attack, and will throw the enemy from our homeland. It's a holy task. Above me is the terrific noise of artillery, the voice of war.

On the back of the letter he had hastily scribbled 'Ruth! WE MARCH!!!!' He had just been given the order to advance.[35]

The effect back home when the news broke was just as electrifying, as Fritz Mühlbach recalled:

> Suddenly ... the news that we'd been waiting for came at last – the German armies in the West had gone over to the attack... The Führer had finally given the word. He had bided his time patiently, collected immense forces, thousands of planes and panzers ... keeping them back until he was certain the moment of the attack had come. Now he was leading us to final victory ... all would turn out well in the end as long as we trusted in the Führer.[36]

Manfred Thorn – a panzer driver in the *LSSAH* – was a little more circumspect after his experiences in Normandy: 'When people read about the experience of serving in a panzer regiment they rarely imagine what it's like actually driving one ... they can't imagine how the war looks through a twenty-five square centimetre window ... that's how it was on 16 December in the early hours of the morning when we left the cover of the Schmidtheimer forest and struck off west.' Hans Herbst of the *116. Panzerdivision* was just as sanguine as Thorn:

> When we first set off I vividly remember seeing von Manteuffel standing on a Panther shouting at us 'Faster, faster!', it was bitterly cold and there was no heating in our half-track, so we did as best as we could to keep warm ... we picked up supplies left behind by the Amis so we had plenty to eat and lots of cartons of Lucky Strike cigarettes.

Flying through the night sky just hours before the assault began was Heydte and his scratch *kampfgruppe*. The majority of his men had never jumped before, and they were now going to fling themselves out at night, onto wooded hillsides, with strong cross winds. For the experienced minority this was going to be their first operational jump since Crete back in 1941. The pilots were no better than their passengers; all young men who had never dropped *fallschirmjägers* before, and whose night navigation training had been rudimentary at best. As was expected, Heydte was leading from the front. 'I was in the first plane, because I was convinced that as the leader of such an attack I had to jump first – it was less important that I show a good example, but rather getting on the ground first meant I could see the terrain and any situation with the enemy and then could organize the troops that followed.' *Feldwebel* Rudolf Hener was one of the fighter pilots flying escort: 'We flew an escort mission for Ju 52s that dropped paratroopers behind the enemy lines in bad weather. The paratroopers were all very young boys and most of them were captured almost immediately after jumping and landing.'[37]

Hener was not quite accurate, but he was right that the mission was an unmitigated disaster. Heydte had a premonition something was wrong while still in the belly of the aircraft: '...a flash from the artillery, burning houses. I looked at the light on my watch ... according to the calculations of the pilot, based on the weather reports, we should have already been over the drop zone, had we flown too far?' Jumping with his right arm strapped to his body, as it hadn't healed properly from an earlier wound, the para officer landed awkwardly, but got up and began to gather his men together: 'I unbuckled myself, stood up and stretched with a wonderful feeling in my heart ... the feeling of power, the joy of being grounded again, the expectation of adventure and the lust for action. At first, I was alone. I oriented myself by the smouldering fire-bombed fields and made for the fork in the road that was the designated rally point.'

Unfortunately for him, the dreadful weather and anti-aircraft fire had made pilot navigation a bit of a lottery, and in consequence men were dropped all over the place – two hundred came down as far away as Bonn, over fifty miles away to the northeast! After over an hour on the ground, Heydte had been joined by just six men. An hour later there were twenty-six, and by the following evening just 125 men had made it to the rally point. The rest were scattered for miles. A quick equipment check confirmed they only had six drop containers of weapons, ammunition and other supplies, one mortar and one radio set – which had been smashed on impact.

Unable to contact anyone, and nowhere near strong enough to carry out their mission, they were helpless. Heydte – in terrible pain after being shot in his already-injured right arm when jumping – was eventually joined by another 150 men who had been gathered up by *Oberleutnant* Kayser, although this just worsened the supply situation. The mission having clearly failed, Heydte made the only decision he could, and resolved to lead his men back to the safety of German lines. By now there were American patrols out everywhere hunting the *fallschirmjägers* down, and the main force was simply too large to be able to slip east unnoticed.

After a sharp skirmish with an American patrol on 21 December, the order was given to break up into three-man groups to make their own way home. Heydte was now alone with his adjutant and a single messenger. Creeping through the woods, another group of young *jägers* appeared and asked to join them. 'They thought I was the surest way for them to reach the German lines. They didn't understand it when I rejected them harshly and forbade them to follow me. They didn't see the tears in my eyes that welled up against my will as I watched them walk away.' Exhausted and hungry, Heydte and his comrades reached the town of Monschau on the night of 23 December. It had been one of the first objectives for the offensive and so the para officer had reasoned must be in German hands – it wasn't. The three men split up, and Heydte knocked on the door of the Bouschery family house. Seeing he was close to collapse, the secondary school teacher and his wife took Heydte in, fed him and put him to bed. The fever from his wound was now very high, and in desperation Heydte scribbled a note to the Americans that the Bouschery's son took to their local headquarters at the Hotel Horcheim. 'I am surrendering myself because I am wounded and at the end of my physical strength. Please be so kind as to send me a doctor and an ambulance as I am unable to walk.' The house was surrounded by a company of troops, Heydte was captured and treated by American medics.

As for Skorzeny's men, whilst his *Panzer Brigade 150* tried to pass itself off as an American armoured unit, forty-four men in American uniform from the *Einheit Stielau* (Stielau Unit) were sent behind Allied lines to sow confusion and try and capture one or more of the bridges over the Meuse. Their presence soon became known to American troops who reacted by interrogating every GI they came across whom they didn't know. Detailed questioning led to a large number of mistakes, with real GIs arrested at gunpoint for not knowing who came bottom of the baseball league in 1938, or some other minutiae of life Stateside. One American officer was forcibly detained as he was found to be wearing German boots. Even Montgomery wasn't exempt; the field marshal was stopped in his Jeep and questioned. He told his driver to carry on, only to have his tyres shot out and to find himself frog-marched to a nearby barn under arrest until his identity could be confirmed. One of Skorzeny's teams was captured near Aywaille on the Amblève River on 17 December, when they failed to give the correct password. By now, the rumour had got out that the real objective for the commandoes was Eisenhower's assassination, and amidst the paranoia the trio had little chance. Tried and found guilty as spies, two days later, *Unteroffizier* Manfred Pernass, *Oberfähnrich* Günther Billing and *Gefreiter* Wilhelm Schmidt were tied to posts and shot by firing squad. Thirteen more were executed over the following three weeks. On 14 June 1945, *Einheit Stielau's* leader, Günther Schulz, was shot by the American occupation authorities in the city of Braunschweig. Courtney Hodges gave the go-ahead for all the executions.

German special operations may have been misfiring, but it seemed to many that the offensive itself got off to a great a start, as one soldier explained when he wrote home: 'We shall probably *not* have another Christmas here at the front, since it is absolutely certain that the Ami is going to get something he did not under any circumstances reckon with... Even I, as a poor private, can easily tell that it won't take much longer until the Ami throws away his weapons ... everybody is retreating, he runs away and can't be stopped anymore.' A *Leutnant* Rockhammer was even more emphatic: 'Today we overtook a fleeing column and finished it off ... it was a glorious bloodbath, vengeance for our destroyed homeland. Our soldiers still have the old zip, advancing and smashing everything. The snow must turn red with American blood ... victory was never so close as it is now!' Both letters were retrieved from the corpses of their authors.[38]

Seasoned campaigners too found cause for optimism – Russian front veterans like Heinrich from the *Hohenstaufen*: 'The woods in Belgium and Germany seemed to be even darker than the woods in Russia... The first days ... were fast and furious, we were advancing at such a speed we thought we would be in Antwerp in a few days.'[39]

Leutnant Behrman, an artillery officer with *18. Volks-Grenadier Division*, recorded in his diary: '18 December: The infantry is before St Vith. The men hear the wildest rumours of success.' Even Manteuffel – never the offensive's loudest cheerleader – wrote of the initial assault: 'My storm battalions infiltrated rapidly into the American front – like raindrops.'

Not all were so euphoric though. *Major* Frank was an ex-flight instructor, now serving as a battalion leader in *FJR. 16*. Frank knew the twelve officers under his command had no combat experience, and the majority of his NCOs were 'willing but inept':

> On the very first day we stormed ... a fortified village, we got to within twenty-five metres of the 'bunker' but were stopped and my best company leaders were killed. I was stuck fast there for two and a half hours, five of my runners were all shot ... what a show for young boys, making their way over a plain without the support of heavy weapons![40]

Despite Frank's lack of success, it did seem that the *Westheer* had found the Allies' weak spot. There were only some eighty thousand American troops covering the Ardennes, mostly either green, inexperienced troops, or units sent there for a rest after bitter fighting elsewhere on the border. Amongst the latter were Dutch Cota's 28th Infantry Division, badly mauled in the Hürtgen in November, and among the former were Alan W. Jones's 106th Infantry – having only arrived in France some ten days before the offensive. So sure was SHAEF that the Ardennes was a quiet zone, they had disregarded their own rules and assigned Jones's men a front almost twenty-one miles longer than the five their own service manuals recommended.

The results were predictable. Attacked by massed German forces, the 106th was overwhelmed. Their situation made worse by Jones's lack of judgement. Lacking information on his enemy, and forced to cover a ridiculously long frontage, Jones proceeded to move his fighting regiments and their supporting units to almost exactly the wrong place at the wrong time. He wasn't helped by the behaviour of several other American officers who broke down under the strain. One, Colonel Mark Devine commanding the armour of the 14th Cavalry Group, burst into Jones's headquarters and blurted out, 'General we've got to run, I was practically chased in here by a Tiger tank!' Devine was sent to the rear to get a grip of himself, only to be later found dazed and confused and personally directing traffic in the village of La Roche-en-Ardenne. The 106th wasn't helped either by a certain amount of sluggishness in Allied senior command. Omar Bradley – whose troops were taking the brunt of the attack – was in Paris seeing Eisenhower when the assault kicked off. Taken aback, he struggled to come to terms with it in a timely fashion, as one of his own staff officers recounted. 'General Bradley, who almost never used profanity of any kind, said, "Where in the world did that son-of-a-bitch get all of that stuff?"' His decision to then move his headquarters further back from the front was a sensible choice in some ways, but ill-timed to say the least – communication and command almost froze, and an impression was created of senior command almost running away.

Back at the front, two of the 106th's three regiments; the 422nd and 423rd, were surrounded and surrendered en masse on 19 December. Six thousand American soldiers marched into captivity, as recorded in his diary by the *18. VGD's, Leutnant* Behrmann:

> 19 December: Endless columns of prisoners pass; at first about a hundred, then another group of about one thousand. Our car gets stuck on the road. I get out and walk. Generalfeldmarschall Model himself directs the traffic. (He's a little, undistinguished-looking man with a monocle.)… The roads are littered with destroyed American vehicles, cars and tanks. Another column of prisoners passes.

The men of the 106th didn't realise at the time of course, but they were one of the largest mass surrenders in American military history; almost fifty per cent higher than at Kasserine in Tunisia back in 1943.

The 106th's sole surviving regiment, the 424th, was in trouble too. One of its members, PFC Jim Forsythe of Company 'A', was defending Winterspelt in the southern sector of the division's front when his unit was attacked by Friedrich Kittel's *62. Volks-Grenadier-Division (64. VGD)* – Kittel's older brother, Heinrich, had been Metz's garrison commander. Forsythe's company was surrendered by its captain – rather too quickly in his view – and the young private found himself a prisoner: 'The one who searched me was polite. The first thing he did was to take two cigarettes from a pack of four in my coat pocket. He put one in his mouth and one in my mouth, lit them, and put the remaining two in my pocket. He spoke good English, told me to put my arms down, and that if I behaved I would not be harmed.'

Despite the near extinction of the 106th Division, not everything was going the Germans' way, as Guido Gnilsen of *2. Panzer* saw for himself: 'Our battalion suffered many losses when the Amis counter-attacked ... we lost many good men; Feldwebel Bacher killed, our communications feldwebel, the Adjutant – Leutnant Fietner and his clerk ... we were beginning to ask ourselves when our number would be up.'

Would Hitler be proved right, would the American front collapse, was Dietrich correct when he said the opposition were just Jewish hoodlums and bank managers? *Leutnant* Behrmann seemed to think so:

20 December: The American soldiers have shown little spirit for fighting. Most of them often said, 'What do we want here? At home we can have everything much better'. That was the spirit of the common soldier. If their officers thought that way??? A rumour has been started that Eisenhower was taken prisoner. It will probably prove to be only a rumour.

Unknowingly, the young artillery officer had hit upon a major issue which had been bubbling up since D-Day itself and would play a critical role in the Ardennes; were the Germans simply better soldiers than the Anglo-Americans? Senior British officers, who had had their views shaped by their collective experiences in the First World War, often thought so. The Ulsterman, Alan Brooke – as Chief of the Imperial General Staff – was Britain's most senior soldier and had always made clear his view on their abilities: 'There is no doubt that the Germans are the most wonderful soldiers.' Hubert Essame – the well-known post-war historian and broadcaster – was a brigadier in 43rd Wessex Division during the northwest Europe campaign: 'He who has not fought the German does not know what war is.' Such views were widely held, and in concert with a determination not to repeat the mass slaughter of the trenches – Brooke refused to even utter the word 'attrition' – this led to a desire on the part of the British to win through *matériel*, 'pitiless industry' as it was termed, or as Brooke himself coined it, 'the results of Passchendaele without its cost in blood'. By the autumn of 1944, with British manpower reserves just about gone, this attitude carried even more weight – the country simply couldn't afford to lose lots more fighting men. No wonder then that the British even described their own way of fighting as

...thorough and methodical, but slow and cumbersome. In consequence our troops fight well in defence and our set-piece attacks are usually successful, but it is not unfair to say that through lack of enterprise in exploitation, we seldom reap the full benefit of them. We are too flank-conscious, we over-insure administratively, we are by nature too apprehensive of failure and our training makes us more so.

As for the Americans, questions over the capabilities of their fighting men had hung over them since the United States' entry into the war. In many ways this was entirely predictable. Prior to the outbreak of war, the Army of the United States comprised just 175,000 men with relatively little combat experience. Its expansion into a multi-million-man behemoth was bound to lead to huge strain, especially regarding providing enough officers and NCOs to lead it in battle. Something the Germans readily took advantage of: 'The Amis seemed very green to us ... they operated by the book. If you responded by doing something not in the book, they panicked.'[41] It was a description that no lesser a person than George Patton echoed: 'I can never get over the stupidity of our green troops.' The Americans didn't help themselves with their own enlistment process, which deemed it a waste of good quality men to put them in infantry units. Instead, the best recruits were funnelled towards service support units; intelligence, logistics, transport and so on. In many ways this was logical given the American objective to win any war by out-supplying and out-thinking the enemy, rather than outfighting him per se. However, this approach is less defensible when it's considered that almost ninety per cent of recruits steered into the Army's own Finance Department – and a full third into the Military Police – were graded as I and II in educational testing. Only a quarter of infantry recruits received these top grades, with half being the lowest IV or V grades. To put it bluntly, the US Army thought infantrymen were expendable. The campaign in northwest Europe showed them that was a fundamental mistake. Normandy had shown the way, with a host of 'green' divisions bloodied and learning their trade, but it was in the Ardennes – undeniably an American battle – where the American fighting man showed what he was really capable of.

The key to the battle – as with so many others – was speed. Attacking on such a narrow front, in an area with a very limited road network, meant that to win, each side had a very clear approach. For the Germans, the objective was for their spearheads to break through the defences as quickly as possible and charge ahead, literally dragging their follow-up units behind them to then fan out and disrupt Allied rear areas. For the Americans, it was all about slowing those spearheads down; to stymie them and force a log-jam where the Germans were unable to deploy and bring their attacking power to bear. At first, it seemed that the Germans were achieving their goal – at least that was what it looked like to the commander of *KG Peiper*'s reconnaissance group, *SS-Hauptsturmführer* Werner Sternebeck, whose panzers and armoured cars rolled into the village of Honsfeld, taking the American garrison by surprise, capturing fifty vehicles intact and taking a number of prisoners, who were then forced to pour their own gasoline into the tanks of Sternebeck's thirsty column: 'The enemy was in total confusion ... there was no organised resistance apparent.'[42] Even so, there were signs not all was going to plan for the Germans, as Max Hansen said of his own lead unit of the *LSSAH* when ordered to divert due to American roadblocks: 'I became very angry ... because I had been able to advance rapidly along my assigned route up until then, and I wasn't facing strong enemy resistance.'

That resistance was starting to make itself felt. For perhaps the first time since D-Day, American troops were finding themselves outnumbered, on the defensive, and without the close air support they were used to. Some, like Jones's 106th Division, shattered into pieces, but others stood their ground and fought. Often it was small groups, a few infantrymen with an anti-tank gun or two holding a crossroads or a bridge – but the impact was far-reaching, as one of *KG Peiper*'s officers, *SS-Untersturmführer* Arndt Fischer, recalled during his 17 December assault on the village of Ligneuville on the River Amblève:

> The bridge was strategically important to us... As we had no other armoured vehicles immediately available, my Panther and Obersturmbannführer Peiper in his SPW [armoured half-track] followed the spearhead as fast as we could... At the bend before the bridge I was shot up from behind, and my Panther went up in flames. We got out of the panzer under machine-gun and rifle fire coming from nearby houses. We were burning like torches as only a couple of hours before we had refuelled, including our jerry cans .. .in doing so we had soaked our clothing in petrol. My driver never managed to get out and was burnt to death... Peiper gave me covering fire ... and bandaged me as well as he could and handed me over to a doctor.[43]

The *Hitlerjugend* was having much the same problem at the village of Rocherath, as described by Willi Engel, a Panther platoon commander:

> I sensed disaster as I was expected to act against the elementary rules of combat, that a built-up area should be bypassed if at all possible without the security of accompanying infantry... I could survey the main street, the knocked-out panzers were a distressing picture ... at that moment a single panzer approached the command post, suddenly, only about one hundred metres away, it turned into a flaming torch.

Engels fellow platoon commander, Willi Fischer, was involved in the same fighting:

> When I reached the vicinity of the church, a gruesome picture was waiting for me. Beutelhauser's panzer was knocked out … his loader was killed by rifle fire as he bailed out… Brödel's panzer stood next to me, burning lightly. He sat lifeless in the turret. In front of me, farther down the street, more panzers had been put out of action and were burning.[44]

Even at this early stage of the offensive, severe delays due – more often than not – to stubborn American defenders or lack of gasoline, were wrecking the timetable and throwing the plan into confusion. *SS-Obersturmbannführer* Richard Schulze saw it at first-hand: 'Since the men were largely without combat experience, only the deployment of the officers at the front could help. In the first hours all the company commanders were lost, either killed or wounded – senior NCOs took over the Kompanies.'[45] Otto Ernst Remer, commander of the *Führerbegleitbrigade* (Führer Escort Brigade): 'The brigade had constant fuel difficulties and most of the tactical decisions made were dependent on the fuel situation.' Hubert Meyer with the *Hitlerjugend* saw the same problems: 'The attack soon stalled in the difficult wooded terrain east of Krinkelt. Part of the division had to pull back to its original positions.'[46] Two of Meyer's officers, Helmut Zeiner and Max Sölner, were more forthright. Zeiner: 'I only had some forty panzer-grenadiers, and each of my jagdpanzers only had ten high-explosive shells left – our fuel supplies were very low – we had also taken some eighty prisoners – tactically our situation was hopeless.' Sölner's experience was more chilling: 'We took a direct hit in the front of the turret … the explosion virtually ripped our driver Karl-Heinz to pieces. Our radio operator Gottfried Opitz lost his left arm … the legs of Hannes Simon ended up full of shrapnel. I was sitting in the cupola, my legs pulled up, so I got away with just a fright.' Hans Baumann was driving one of those *jagdpanzer*:

> My Kompanie encountered very strong resistance at Krinkelt and Rocherath, and we suffered a great many casualties. I could hear the shells whizzing past and some exploded close by and shook my vehicle. We were well-trained but didn't expect such a strong fight from the Amis. Suddenly, I felt a tremendous crash as a shell hit the side of my jagdpanzer… I struggled to free myself and open the hatch. Most of my crew managed to jump out like me and run for cover. But our radioman was stone dead. A big bit of shrapnel was sticking out of his abdomen and his intestines were spilling out of the wound, steaming in the air.

Despite Baumann's belief in his own training, in truth, the *HJ* was only a shadow of its former Normandy self, and although its hasty rebuild had almost brought it back up to strength in terms of men and machines, it would never again scale the heights of combat proficiency it reached in France. Shuffled from one sector to another in the Ardennes, it failed to make much of an impression, as Meyer had to concede: 'A new attack was launched on 21/22 December, after initial success it too bogged down after it became light due to artillery fire ... there were heavy losses.'

Not that it was the only German division to underperform. Meyer said of his neighbour, Gerhard Engel's *12. 'Wild Buffalo' VGD*: 'The failure of the first attack by 12. VGD on the heavily-fortified positions at Losheimgraben led to a decisive delay to KG Peiper.' Having said that, US Intelligence later rated *12. VGD* as the best infantry division in *6. Panzerarmee*. Of Peiper himself, he felt strongly that initial failures to break through cost the German offensive dear: 'I had the disgusted impression that the whole front had gone to bed instead of waging war.' Neither were the delays confined to the SS, as the former *Panzer-Lehr* officer, now *Generalmajor*, Heinz Kokott of *26. VGD*, noted all too sadly, 'The long resistance of Hosingen resulted in the delay of the whole advance of 26. VGD, and thereby Panzer-Lehr, by a day and a half.'

As euphoria turned to frustration, some *landsers* reacted with barbarism: 'Our battalion advanced to Stavelot and on to La Gleize ... our Sturmführer just shot prisoners outright ... there were twelve of them the first time. He just shot them because they were in the way.'[47] In the Stavelot fighting, an SS company commander came across one of his subordinates:

> I passed Untersturmführer Siebert, my 3rd platoon commander, who reported he had repulsed the enemy after heavy fighting and that he had had to shoot some Ami prisoners. He didn't state the exact number. I asked him why he had had to shoot prisoners and he explained that his platoon consisted of only nine men and he couldn't spare anyone to guard them.

Civilians were also murdered in over half the villages the attackers went through. Perhaps the assault troops felt they were traitors as they had remained behind after being ordered to evacuate back into Germany a few weeks previously – the area was partly ethnic German and had been annexed into the Reich in 1940, with its young men conscripted into the Wehrmacht. Or, perhaps, the perpetrators were the growing breed of 'crazy Helmuts' as men were called who had lost loved ones to Allied bombing: '...soldiers on leave from the front came and asked after their families and relatives, and you had to tell them that they're dead – your wife is dead, your children are dead, your parents and grandparents are dead.'[48] Jochen Peiper himself acknowledged the problem: '...after the battle of Normandy, my unit was composed mainly of young, fanatical soldiers. A good many of them had lost their parents, sisters and brothers during the bombing... Their hatred for the enemy was such, I swear it, that I couldn't always keep it under control.'

Regardless of the horrors of strategic bombing, it was no excuse for what was nothing more than foul murder – especially of civilians who in no way could have been said to bear any guilt whatsoever. However, the Germans weren't the only ones responsible for atrocities, as an American officer fighting in Stavelot admitted:

A new man who had only been with the Company a couple of weeks heard a noise in a cellar, he called 'HERAUS!' ('COME OUT!') but panicked when there was no reply. He pulled the pin and rolled a grenade down the steps – the cellar was jammed with civilians – after the wounded were carried out our aid men went to work – the rest of the men walked away, unable to watch.

Dreadful though the consequences were, it's clear that this incident was a tragic mistake rather than a deliberate act, but – just as in Normandy – there were also cases of German soldiers being gunned down in cold blood.

The big news though, was the lack of a clear and decisive breakthrough, as *Generalleutnant* Otto Elfeldt lamented to his fellow prisoners at Trent Park as he chewed relentlessly on his cigarette-holder: 'It's Wednesday today (21 December) and if they have advanced only forty kilometres in five days I can only say it isn't an offensive, a slow-moving offensive is no good at all because it allows the enemy to bring up reserves far too quickly.' Elfeldt was a veteran of the Russian front and knew what he was talking about. Sepp Dietrich knew it too. 'According to the original plan I was meant to reach the Meuse on the second or third day.' *Hauptmann* Erwin Kressman – a company commander in 1. *Schwere-Panzerjäger-Abteilung 519* (Heavy Tank Hunter Battalion 519) – was attached to Dietrich's Army, and could see the attack stalling: 'We knew we were not making the progress we should...there was an atmosphere of desperation about it all.' Manteuffel, felt the same. 'I never expected to reach the River Meuse in two or three days, rather I felt that if everything we went well we could perhaps reach it in four to six days.' Even this proved a vain hope.

After the initial shock wore off, the Allies reacted decisively; Eisenhower gave Montgomery control of American forces north of the German thrust – unarguably the correct decision but one that riled Omar Bradley no end – and ordered Patton to break off his attacks in Lorraine and drive north into the German's southern flank. Reinforcements and firepower were poured into the line too, and as the sky overhead cleared, the Allied air forces once again made their presence felt. Heinz Kokott remembered the day the sky turned blue on 23 December: 'The first enemy jabos appeared towards 0900hrs, swooped down on communication roads and villages, and set vehicles and farmyards on fire.' At Hompré the *jabos* attacked the paras of *5. Fallschirmjäger-Division*. 'Houses caught fire, vehicles were burning, wounded men were lying in the street, horses that had been hit were kicking about.'[49] Johannes Kaufmann led his Bf 109s up into the Ardennes sky:

> The Ami jabos would have great difficulty in distinguishing friend from foe amongst the densely wooded hills and valleys, and this, plus the weather conditions – I hoped – would reduce both their numbers and effectiveness... I was to be sadly disappointed ... we had just flown over Malmédy ... when our small formation of about twenty Bf 109s was met by a much larger force of P-47 Thunderbolts. The encounter immediately erupted into a series of fierce dogfights ... the Gruppe lost a third of its aircraft; six Bf 109s shot down, plus a seventh badly damaged and forced to make a belly-landing. Three of our pilots had been killed... In return we had brought down three of the enemy.

As in Normandy, the *Panzer-Lehr* seemed to be singled out for special treatment by the Allied fighter-bombers that had made life in France so terrible for them, as their commander Fritz Bayerlein recalled: 'Both my panzer recovery vehicles were destroyed from the air ... my panzer repair shops were heavily bombed, gasoline was scarce and had to be brought up by truck, and I lost thirty panzers in the advance – bogged down, in need of repair or out of gas – in addition to those lost to enemy fire.' In truth, Bayerlein was a doleful figure even before the offensive, his nerves shot through after the North African campaign and the attrition of Normandy. One of his subordinates, *Major* Helmut Ritgen, had served with him in France, and was subsequently injured in an air attack that autumn, only to leave his hospital bed early to re-join the unit and lead his men in the Ardennes: 'We tried to find fuel, but we found only empty jerry cans. We could go no further. The armoured cars had to give us their fuel, so at least the divisions panzers could move. As long as there was rain, fog and snow we were alright, but as soon as it cleared up the jabos came and that was very unpleasant.'[50] An officer candidate with the *Leibstandarte* said much the same as Ritgen:

> We were part of that operation until we ran out of ammunition and gas ... we were very successful for the first week because the Amis couldn't use their air force, but the minute the skies cleared we just knew that was the end for us ... we had no fuel and no logistics could get through to us ... we blew up our panzer and fought as grenadiers.[51]

At St Vith, a German *leutnant* wrote in his diary, 'The Ami jabos keep on attacking everything that moves on the roads ... they hang in the air like a swarm of wasps.'[52] In just four days the Allied air forces flew fifteen thousand sorties against the German spearheads.

At St Vith, it wasn't just air attack that was pounding the Germans, but the growing weight of American artillery fire. On 20 December the defenders could call on the support of five field artillery battalions that fired over seven thousand rounds on that single day. An NCO in the *Hohenstaufen* said of it: 'The number of shells that were fired at us was beyond imagination ... try to imagine a rain of fire above your head, hitting everything that is above and beside you, trees falling down, fires everywhere and bullets flying all over the place.'[53] Rudolf von Ribbentrop – a veteran of both Russia and Normandy – was taken aback by the barrages he and his division were subjected to:

> The Americans threw everything at us, particularly artillery ... it put everything that we had previously undergone into the shade. One of our battalions was stuck right under some of the heaviest fire ... and while I was standing on the back of the commander's panzer to give him fresh instructions, he said to me, 'It's too windy out there, you'd best come into the panzer.' I hadn't quite closed the hatch when a shell exploded on the rear of the panzer... I would have been mincemeat if I had been a second slower. As it was, all I got was a splinter in the face. The commander was killed a short time later carrying out the orders I had given him.

Of the German's own air force, *Generalmajor* Siegfried von Waldenburg, commander *116. Panzerdivision,* said: 'Of the German Luftwaffe nothing was to be seen or heard.' It was just like Normandy, the troops on the ground felt betrayed and forgotten by their sister armed service, but again, just as in Normandy, that wasn't the whole truth – far from it.

The Luftwaffe in the autumn of 1944 was a pale shadow of its former self. Starved of aircraft, fuel and pilots, and with too many of its scarce resources frittered away on peripheral theatres, the fighter force in particular – the *jagdwaffe* – was close to breaking point. In the East, after years of air superiority against inferior machines and inferior pilots, the Soviet Airforce – the *VVS* – now had the upper hand as large numbers of their opponents were withdrawn and sent West. D-Day significantly accelerated that process as Berlin's contingency plan to respond to a landing – *Drohende Gefahr West* (Threatening Danger West) – went into operation and squadrons in droves were shipped to France in a vain attempt to try and combat Anglo-American air power. It wasn't enough.

By then, the advantages enjoyed by the Allies – especially the Americans – were so great that they crushed the Luftwaffe's response. Coupled with the Anglo-American decision in spring that year to actively hunt out German fighters across the Reich itself, the *jagdflieger* were shot out of the sky; during 1944 the USAAF alone destroyed 3,706 German aircraft over the Reich.

With France liberated, *Viermot* raids across the Reich were stepped up. Germany's cities were being pulverized. *General der Jagdflieger* Adolf Galland and his fellow commanders tried everything to try and turn the tide – or at least arrest it. One idea was the *Gefechtsverband* concept (Battle or Combat group); this would be a mixed force of Messerschmitts and Focke-Wulfs to go after the American heavies and their escorts during daylight hours. Half the fighters would be Bf 109Gs or Ks, tasked to climb high and hold off the escorts, while the other half would be Fw 190A-8's *Sturmbocks* (Battering rams) to go after the *Viermots*, their noses packed with additional armour to protect them during either a conventional stern approach or a riskier frontal attack. On 7 July the new force was tested, with about one hundred fighters of *Jagdgeschwader 300* (*JG 300*) sent up to intercept an eleven hundred-strong force of B-17 Flying Fortresses, B-24 Liberators and their escorts, whose targets were aircraft factories near Leipzig and the synthetic fuel plants at Leuna-Merseburg, Boehlen and Lützkendorf. The cigar-chomping Walther Dahl was in command of the Bf 109s, and he spotted that a squadron of Liberators (it turned out to be the 492nd Bombardment Group) seemed to be flying without any escort cover. Immediately, he got on the radio and told Wilhelm Moritz and his *Sturmbocks* the good news. Moritz seized his chance, leading his pilots to point-blank range before opening fire. It was a massacre. In less than two minutes all twelve Liberators had been destroyed. The rampaging *jagdflieger* went on to down a further sixteen enemy aircraft, losing nine of their own. It was a success, but by itself not a big enough one to make a difference.

As it was, with attrition rates cripplingly high, Berlin was forced to send up pilots with next to no training – with all-too predictable results. Nineteen-year-old *Unteroffizier* Fritz Wiener was a fighter pilot over the Reich in late 1944: 'The young pilots, who had only a limited chance to survive in air combat, were massed as cannon-fodder... the majority had only minimal flying hours and no combat experience at all. It wasn't uncommon for replacement pilots to arrive in the frontline having never flown the Fw 190 ... firing the MK 108 cannon and MG 151 machine-guns prior to going into combat was also a rare feat.'[54] Helmut Rix – two years Wiener's senior – was one of those cannon-fodder, having done some initial training on multi-engine night-fighters, before being given the choice of converting to day-fighters or transferring to the *fallschirmjäger*!

> We were limited to five take-off and landings each day due to fuel shortages and Allied fighter activity... My introduction to frontline flying wasn't good, my fellow pilots and I had hardly had time to meet before the 'scramble' order came through – eight out of ten of my comrades didn't return! Things were getting very bad, with shortages of everything. We newly trained pilots were supposed to get some flying experience before being sent into action, but that didn't happen. We were just thrown straight into combat.[55]

The failings of the Luftwaffe could more or less all be laid at the door of its own senior leadership, but that didn't stop the most senior of them all – *Reichsmarschall* Hermann Goering himself – from assembling his top fighter pilots at the Reich Air Defence School at Gatow to harangue them on their performance: 'I've spoiled you, I've given you too many decorations, they've made you fat and lazy. All that about the aircraft you've shot down was just one big lie ... a pack of lies I tell you! You didn't make a fraction of the kills you reported.' The view of the flabbergasted audience was summed up by one of their number, Johannes *Macky* Steinhoff: 'For sheer cynicism and arrogance he outdid himself.' Gatow was so offensive it helped spur on a number of the most senior *jagdflieger,* including Steinhoff, to try and have Goering replaced a few months later in what became known as 'the fighter pilots' revolt'.

Away from Goering's rants, Galland was evolving his thinking following the Dahl/Moritz success in July. The answer, as he saw it, was size; if a *Gefechtsverband* of one hundred fighters could destroy twenty-eight *Viermots,* then what could five hundred or a thousand fighters do? In essence, it was something of a replication of Leigh-Mallory's 'Big Wing' idea from the battle of Britain; that concept being much the same – mass as many fighters as you can and concentrate them in one huge blow to check the enemy. Galland called his idea *der grosse Schlag* – the Big Hit. To husband his resources as much as he could, Galland ordered his fighters dispersed all over Germany, there to sit under cover and await the order to attack. The factories were squeezed for aircraft and the flight schools for pilots – much to the chagrin of Ernst Schroeder as he struggled to master the complexities of the Bf 109G:

> To train a pilot on it took longer than on the Fw 190, and time is what we didn't have in 1944... I couldn't see behind me in the Bf 109, and the all-round visibility was poor... The rear-view mirror was near useless due to excessive vibration in flight ... it lacked electrical equipment ... and the cockpit canopy was difficult to jettison ... the aircraft tended to swing on take-off or landing, and although experienced pilots soon grew accustomed to this ... novices often found themselves brutally pulled to the left, which caused countless accidents.[56]

To his relief, he was switched to Fw 190s.

By mid-November, everything was ready. Galland had massed no fewer than nine entire *Jagdgeschwader* – fighter wings – in the Reich, leaving only four each on the Western and Eastern fronts.[57] Almost two thousand German fighters were awaiting the order for *der grosse Schlag*. The young Luftwaffe general calculated that his force would shoot down between four and five hundred *Viermots* in one go – roughly half the attacking force – while losing perhaps four hundred aircraft of their own, and maybe a hundred to one hundred and fifty pilots killed. The losses would be acceptable for the Germans, and catastrophic for the Americans, causing them to suspend their attacks. The Luftwaffe would then have bought itself time; time to train new pilots and build new aircraft.

Then came the order that shattered Galland's hopes; *der grosse Schlag* was suspended indefinitely. Instead, his carefully husbanded fighters were to be readied to cover the Ardennes offensive and fulfil Hitler's pledge to Dietrich, Manteuffel and Siegfried Westphal to support the attack with three thousand fighters – he was only one thousand short. In disbelief, Galland broke the news to his pilots – his verdict was clear: 'The Luftwaffe received its death blow in the Ardennes.'

On the ground in the Ardennes, all eyes turned to the point of the German spear: *KG Peiper*. If Jochen Peiper could reach the Meuse at Huy and force a crossing, then the Germans had a chance. The operation wasn't going to plan – but then what operation does – and in any case, there were still enough follow-on forces to spread out on the other side of the river and cause the Allies major problems, as long as Peiper got the Huy bridge.

The route to that bridge was a nightmare. In effect, it ran along the valley of the River Amblève, forcing the SS men to criss-cross the river several times, and leaving them extremely vulnerable to delay by handfuls of obstinate defenders. Those defenders were made even more determined by an incident that would hang over Peiper and his entire unit long after the war was over, an incident that has gone down in the annals of infamy – the Malmédy Massacre. Around noon on 17 December, Peiper's lead vehicles approached the crossroads at Baugnez, a few miles from Malmédy. An American convoy was already there, as Manfred Thorn recalled:

> Horst Pilarcek was our crew commander, he was two ranks higher than me, but hadn't come from a panzer unit and wasn't even an officer. He saw an Ami convoy moving over the Baugnez crossing... 'Manfred, what should we do? I don't have any experience at this.' I gave the order to 'Fire!' to our gunner and we destroyed the first two vehicles ... the front of the column had already passed, but the trucks coming up behind crashed into the wrecked vehicles.

With no escape, the Americans – mainly men from an artillery observation battalion – had little choice but to put up their hands and surrender. Panzer grenadiers scooped them up and marched them into a field next to the road. Peiper swept by, his focus on pushing his panzers to their objective. Behind him, over a hundred defenceless American prisoners stood in the snow, when suddenly a machine-gun chattered into life. Immediately it was followed by others as the troopers standing as guards became executioners. Needless to say, the prisoners panicked and many tried to flee to the nearby woods. Most were shot as they ran or where they stood. Once the shooting was over, some of the SS grenadiers walked among the bodies, finishing off the wounded and anyone they found trying to feign death. In all some eighty-four Americans were murdered. Thorn later vehemently denied the slaughter had occurred, claiming it was a set-up by American intelligence – this is patently untrue. As for Peiper, he didn't take part in the massacre, he wasn't there when it happened, and – according to the evidence from the post-war trial – he didn't order it either, but it was his men who carried it out, he was responsible. All that was to come. At the time, several dozen men escaped and told their stories to other American units – as early as that same evening rumours of the slaughter were circulating among American troops. The reaction to the news can be imagined. Officers, NCOs and men told each other it was better to die fighting than be butchered like cattle; Peiper's men had shot almost a hundred prisoners – and had also shot themselves in the foot. Not least if they were unlucky enough to fall into captivity, as was made plain by an order sent out by the headquarters of the US 328th Infantry Regiment: 'No SS troops or paratroopers will be taken prisoner but will be shot on sight.'

From then on it seemed that *KG Peiper* was dogged by bad luck, as well as a vengeful enemy. Their next objective was the village of Stavelot and its bridge over the Amblève. The bridge itself was a multi-arched, stone-built affair, capable of taking the weight of even Peiper's heaviest panzers. The Americans were as keen to deny it to the Germans as the SS were to capture it.

Heinz Tomhardt's panzer grenadiers were tasked with storming the all-important bridge, as the senior NCO, *SS-Hauptscharführer* Rudolf Rayer remembered:

> 11. Kompanie was given the order to take the bridge ... only 1st and 2nd Platoons were available; due to mechanical problems the rest of the Kompanie was further back. The bridge was taken but couldn't be held ... we were in a very difficult position, enemy panzers continued to move around and we expected a counter-attack. We were fired on from all sides but couldn't do much about it. We had quite considerable losses including Tomhardt, Horn [one of the platoon commanders] and several others... I took over the Kompanie.

The opportunity to *bounce* the bridge was gone, so Peiper ordered up mortars and artillery to soften up the defenders before trying again, and this time the panzers would lead the way. Peiper knew it was going to be a difficult assault: 'The terrain presented us with great difficulties, and ... there was a short curve at the entrance to Stavelot where several Shermans and anti-tank guns were zeroed in.' The young officer gave Eugen Zimmermann the unenviable task of leading the charge:

> Obersturmbannführer Peiper himself detailed my panzer to lead the attack through Stavelot ... at first light. The whole crew was given a very precise briefing: 'Immediately after the bend there's an anti-tank gun – you'd better go in fifth gear. There's one of our officers lying in the middle of the bridge. Don't know if he's dead or wounded. Watch out for that officer... Drivers Go!' We met no resistance, the anti-tank gun was standing there and we rammed it out of the way. On to the bridge! No officer. No sooner were we over the bridge than we were hit ... our gun was pointing crazily at the sky after the hit. Driver 'Accelerate!' We drove over the trail of the anti-tank gun, it broke and ended up on the driver's hatch ... we were through.[58]

Karl Wortmann remembered the fighting: 'The Amis had committed all the heavy weapons available in Stavelot to protect the bridge. Several of our panzers lost a few feathers here! Worse was the fact that one of our panzers was shot and blocked the bridge access.'

Regardless of this difficulty, Zimmermann's dash had secured the all-important bridge and the *kampfgruppe* pushed on towards their next goal: Trois-Ponts and its bridge. Behind them, the Americans began to filter back into Stavelot – *KG Peiper* was in danger of being cut-off. Eugen Zimmermann was in the vanguard again:

> We came upon the railroad, and the order 'sharp left' came over the radio. At that moment we were hit, but thank God, it was only a graze – apparently we were moving too fast! I saw the anti-tank gun that had hit us and aimed our main gun at it directly through the barrel at a stone wall right behind it. One high-explosive round and that was it. We drove cautiously through the underpass, as I thought there would be another anti-tank gun, but it was all quiet. However, the bridge had been blown.

This was very bad news for the Germans. As the advance stalled, the lead panzers began to run out of gasoline. Worse still, there was little hope of any resupply as the Americans began to infiltrate back in to Stavelot behind Zimmermann and the spearhead. Friedrich Pfeifer, one of the *Leibstandarte* officers following up, found himself caught up in the next bout of fighting at Stavelot the following day: 'We maintained our position on the other river bank for about eighteen hours, but only had one machine-gun left and very little ammunition...when dawn came we began our retreat across the Amblève, downstream from the bridge under heavy fire – I remember it cost twenty-three men their lives.'[59]

Meanwhile, Peiper had moved his troops onto another road and had reached Stoumont, further up the valley. As at Stavelot, Rudolf Rayer was in the thick of the action:

> Our leading panzer was knocked out by an anti-tank gun at the station. I was ordered to take the station on foot. We did this after light resistance and took two prisoners...we were then ordered to take out enemy panzers and anti-tank guns on the right of the road, but we failed in close combat and only withdrew with great difficulty and losses.[60]

Peiper was stuck; unable to move forward, running out of fuel and ammunition and cut-off at his rear. By dawn on 20 December the offensive's main effort had ground to a halt some thirty-odd miles short of the Meuse.

Back at Stavelot, Wilhelm Mohnke was desperately trying to force the Americans out and re-establish communications with Peiper. Friedrich Pfeifer – recently transferred from the *Totenkopf* – led his panzer grenadiers into the fray:

> I gave orders to dismount because the artillery fire became too heavy, and I preferred to go through the town on foot ... when I returned from

my reconnaissance, Obersturmbannführer Sandig [Rudolf Sandig, his regimental commander] appeared suddenly on a motor-cycle and said things were going too slowly. I told him I needed fire support from the heavy weapons of 4. Kompanie, however it had been delayed, so I had to risk the attack with my 1st and 3rd Platoons, whilst my 2nd and 4th provided fire support. When half of us reached the north side of the bridge we were shot to pieces... The heaviest fire we received was from a building marked with the Red Cross.[61]

American reinforcements were soon arriving in strength, and by the afternoon of the 21st, Mohnke's men were clinging on in desperation:

In the afternoon we came under heavy attack supported by panzers ... the enemy succeeded in carrying the attack to about fifty to eighty metres of our positions. He was, however, repulsed ... there were only a few men left in our platoon and we hadn't either eaten or slept for several days ... we were totally exhausted. One man suffered a nervous breakdown. In the evening we had to dig out two or three men from a machine-gun crew who had been wounded and buried by shellfire.[62]

Elements of *KG Peiper* were spread out from Stavelot to Stoumont, with Peiper himself gathering most of his remaining men and vehicles into the hill-top Walloon village of La Gleize. The Americans began to close in, drawing a noose around the SS men. Increasingly hungry, with hardly any gasoline, an air drop was planned for the morning of 22 December. With a few notable exceptions the Germans weren't known for their success at air-lifts; this was not one of those exceptions. The few Junkers Ju 52 transports that managed to reach the village pushed out a few containers, but it was nowhere near enough to make a difference. The following day Peiper himself radioed high command: 'Position considerably worsened. Meagre supplies of infantry ammunition left ... this is the last chance of breaking out.'

At 2am the next morning – Christmas Eve – Peiper led the remnants of his *kampfgruppe* out of La Gleize, boots and weapons wrapped in rags to muffle any sound. Before leaving they had tried to destroy or at least disable their remaining vehicles, but many were simply abandoned – without fuel or ammunition they were just so much scrap. Those too badly wounded to join the escape were left behind to be treated by the Americans. At dawn it was clear the Germans were gone, and the victors cautiously made their way into the village.

It was a great haul we captured in that town ... twenty-eight tanks and seventy half-tracks... Lots of it had been knocked out by our artillery ... and the rest the Germans had destroyed themselves. The Germans began to come out onto the streets. These Hitler boys were sad looking sights; heads bandaged and hands, legs, chests and backs badly wounded... I would judge that all of them were between eighteen and twenty-four.[63]

Cold, hungry and bedraggled, fewer than eight hundred of Peiper's original force made it back to the safety of German lines; having lost over four thousand men killed, wounded or missing, more than a hundred panzers including a number of Tiger IIs, as well as almost one hundred and fifty half-tracks and sixty guns. *KG Peiper* – the spearhead for the entire offensive – had been annihilated. In defence of its performance, the inability of follow-on units to maintain contact with it and provide re-supply was a killer blow. Having said that, it had barely covered two-thirds of the distance to its objective and had achieved little despite its obvious punching power. It is difficult to conclude anything other than it was a huge disappointment.

Elsewhere in Dietrich's sector the picture was a mixed bag. Lammerding's *Das Reich* made solid, if unspectacular, progress. Lack of gasoline was proving its biggest issue, and, astonishingly, it wasn't until 22 December – six whole days after the offensive began – that a convoy of fuel trucks arrived and it received its first full replenishment. A company commander in the 3. *SS-Panzergrenadier-Regiment 'Deutschland'* wrote in his diary about those following few days:

> In the early evening a patrol was sent out to locate crossing places for the panzers ... the weather changed and became a bright, moonlit night ... moving over open ground without the protection of white clothing the men could be seen as dark spots and were soon under fire. The patrol withdrew bringing back three wounded, one seriously.

Christmas arrived. 'There was a piano in a large room and one of our comrades began to play a carol – there was some half-hearted singing but we had no Christmas spirit in us.' One of his fellow officers felt much the same: 'All the Spiess (senior NCO with quartermaster responsibilities) can offer us on Christmas Eve is a meatless stew,' but what especially aggrieved him was the flagrant disparity between the firepower available to each side: 'he (the American) withdraws slowly under the cover of a barrage fired by hundreds of guns... Our guns, in an orgy of spendthrift recklessness, reply with eight rounds – and then cease fire – we have to save ammunition.' The capability of American artillery was something he and his men were forced to adjust to:

> Strehl, our company clerk, lit a fire in the grate of an abandoned house to warm his frozen fingers. The enemy notices the thin column of

smoke and opens fire. When the barrage ends, we have fresh air coming through new holes in the roof and walls. Strehl now warms his fingers by rubbing them between his knees.

The two SS officers then found themselves in the village of Grandmenil when it came under artillery fire:

> We moved into another house outside which were a couple of panzers. Inside we found some forty badly wounded comrades. The blast from a massive explosion just outside lifted the concrete ceiling of the cellar where the wounded were being treated ... we rushed outside ... the partially camouflaged panzers had been attacked by jabos. One bomb had fallen between the two panzers ... the panzers themselves showed no signs of damage. Then about 1215 the shelling stopped and the Ami infantry attacked.

Attempting to escape, the same SS officer found himself under fire from the hull machine-gunner of a Sherman as he hid behind a smithy wall:

> The pillar I was behind was about forty centimetres wide, and machine-gun bursts tore out whole bricks. Then the tanks main gun opened up, the first armour-piercing shot passing straight through the smithy wall... The next shot was a high-explosive round – there was smoke, dust and shrapnel... I was unhurt and raced across the yard ... we rushed around the corner intending to attack the Ami tank, but a corporal had already destroyed it with a panzerfaust.

Despite this small success, the battle wasn't over, as he discovered when he reached his battalion headquarters: 'The commanding officer told me the battalion was surrounded ... and we were practically out of ammunition and supplies... In view of the shortages of ammunition, fuel and rations, our own attack had to be called off and instead we had to fight our way out of the encirclement.' His comrade was in much the same position:

> By this time the Kompanie had been reduced to just twenty men, and I put them into all-round defence ... we were now under fire from all sides and I decided to hold the remaining five houses and chapel until the last ... we were then involved in house-to-house fighting of an intensity which I had never come across before in all my frontline service. My grenadiers fought for every wall and every pile of rubble.

Outnumbered, the struggle couldn't go on for ever: 'The Shermans were firing high-explosive and armour-piercing shells at us, and then

I received a report that there was no more ammunition for the machine-guns or the personal weapons... A final signal was sent to battalion – 'Ammunition used up. Documents destroyed. Situation hopeless. No escape possible.' I then ordered the set to be blown up using our last grenade. The enemy was now in the front room of the last ruined house.' At that moment a barrage from a nearby *Nebelwerfer* battery landed right in the middle of the village, giving the SS men just enough cover to allow them to escape 'under cover of the smoke and exploiting the shattering effect of the shells'. As it turned out both officers managed to lead their men through the American lines and re-joined the rest of the division.

Other *SS-Das Reich* units were having better luck; Ernst Barkmann, still lauded by Nazi propaganda after his exploits in Normandy at 'Barkmann Corner', found himself leading a column of Panthers near the village of Manhay, some fifteen or so miles south of La Gleize. Even as Peiper was leading his break-out to the north, Barkmann found himself coming through an American artillery barrage to find himself alone and with unknown numbers of Shermans on the lanes around him. He quickly destroyed three – having to reverse to fire at one as he came round a corner and found himself too close to it to fire a shot! He then drove past two columns of American vehicles without being recognised as German, until a Jeep tried to flag him down. Crashing into it, he then accidentally rammed a Sherman before his engine cut out. Quickly re-starting it, his driver reversed and broke away from his interlocutor and raced away. He was reunited with his battalion as it bluffed its way into the centre of Manhay, helped by the presence of a captured Sherman out front. There, standing around, engines idling, were elements of the American 7th Armoured Division. Almost mirroring Michael Wittmann's feat at Villers-Bocage nearly six months earlier, the young SS NCO proceeded to shoot up everything he could see. To add to the mayhem his company commander, *SS-Hauptsturmführer* Ortwin Pohl, and fellow NCO Franz Frauscher, joined in, their 7.5cm cannons and machine-guns spraying vehicles and men alike. Within minutes, twenty Shermans, two tank destroyers and a dozen or so soft-skinned vehicles were burning wrecks. The SS didn't lose a single panzer. Frauscher was awarded the Knight's Cross for his part in the action.

By comparison, Hugo Kraas's *Hitlerjugend* was still struggling. Shifted south after its lack-lustre showing at Elsenborn, it was sent into the attack in the densely wooded hills near Dochamps, five miles south of Manhay. Its Chief of Staff Hubert Meyer, described the situation: 'Because of the aerial situation the attack would have to be carried out through broken, forested terrain at night ... panzers, SPWs and wheeled vehicles couldn't be taken ... only mortars and panzerfausts would be available to fight off tanks, effective artillery support would be close to impossible due to uncertain communications in the hilly terrain.' After this inauspicious start, *SS-Unterscharführer* Günther Burdack described the unfolding nightmare

> The SPWs were left behind in a ravine south of Samrée ... the road was totally clogged by abandoned and destroyed enemy vehicles, mostly artillery, and was under constant heavy shelling ... the villages couldn't be observed as they were higher than our own location ... the frozen ground didn't allow us to dig in, the battalion didn't have any heavy weapons, only rifles and machine-guns – harassing artillery fire covered the whole area.[64]

The attack failed. Though as Meyer made clear, he didn't feel the division itself was at fault: 'We were forced to operate out of character by conducting frontal attacks in bogged-down situations ... we had the further bad luck of being committed every time against a fresh and numerically superior enemy.'

With the armed SS floundering, was all lost for the Wehrmacht? Well, not quite. The Waffen-SS have always grabbed the headlines for the Ardennes offensive – and, as at Malmédy, sometimes for all the wrong reasons – when in fact well over half the forces involved were regular Army, and not Hitler's black guard. To Dietrich's south was 5. *Panzerarmee* and its Lilliputian commander, Hasso von Manteuffel. In its ranks were four panzer divisions, all of great renown and hugely experienced. Like most of the *panzerwaffe* by the end of '44, all had been decimated at least once and rebuilt – most more than once – but now were re-equipped with some of the newest weaponry to roll off the production lines, and with a cadre of veterans, they were still a force to be reckoned with. None more so that Meinrad von Lauchert's 2. *Panzerdivision*. Lauchert himself was still under forty years of age when he was handed command of one of the Wehrmacht's founding panzer divisions; tall, almost gaunt, an inveterate smoker, he had won the Knight's Cross while serving with 4. *Panzerdivision* in Russia in 1941. The division he took over on the eve of the offensive had distinguished itself throughout the war, capturing Abbeville in the French campaign of 1940, and Athens the following year. Taking part in *Barbarossa*, some of its members reported seeing the towers of the Kremlin before they were thrown back by the Soviet counter-offensive that December. It remained in Russia for the next two years, suffering terrible losses, until sent to France in early 1944 to rest and refit.

Caught up in the Normandy fighting, it took part in the ill-fated Mortain counter-attack before being crushed at Falaise, only to be withdrawn back to Germany to be rebuilt once more. By then, the ranks were filled with men from all over the Reich, and not just from its original recruitment areas in Austria. It even absorbed the remnants of 352. *Infanterie-Division* – the same unit that had come so close to rebuffing the American landing at Omaha beach on D-Day and had subsequently fought at Arnhem. Equipped with a hundred and thirty-three panzers and assault-guns – including fifty-eight brand new Panthers – it was set to play a leading role in the Ardennes as Manteuffel's spearhead formation. One of its officers described how 'the fighting spirit was better than in the early days of the war' – an optimism that confounded even von Rundstedt's view that 'their strength in panzers was low – it was largely paper strength.'

Manteuffel's plan was to harness Fritz Bayerlein's resurrected *Panzer-Lehr* alongside Lauchert's 2. *Panzer*, in a powerful corps grouping; *XLVII Panzer Korps*, under the overall command of Heinrich Freiherr von Lüttwitz. Lüttwitz was the monocle-wearing scion of one of Prussia's oldest *Junker* families, and although a Knight's Cross holder, had not distinguished himself during the war so far. A rather self-satisfied character, he was not an obvious choice to command Manteuffel's most important formations, with Bayerlein especially critical of him as 'not sufficiently coherent and energetic'. Unfortunately for the *Westheer* the jaded Bayerlein would be proved correct in his estimation.

At first, Manteuffel's attack went well. Eschewing the lengthy artillery bombardment recommended by Berlin, 5. *Panzerarmee* slammed into their opponents, broke through their lines and drove towards the village of Longvilly. Bayerlein reported on a tank battle he saw in the gathering dusk: 'Panzer-Lehr, with their barrels turned northward, passed by this impressive spectacle in the twilight which, cut by the tracer bullets, took on a fantastic aspect.' With the village secured, the *Lehr* headed for neighbouring Bastogne. Bastogne was the junction for pretty much every road in the area, and as such was a vital objective for both sides. Lightly defended, it was an easy target, however in the first sign that Lüttwitz wasn't up to the job, the panzer general failed to adequately order his packed troops into a sensible priority on the roads, leading to total chaos as panzers became horribly mixed up with horse-drawn artillery, infantry and even engineers and supply wagons. The lack of gasoline – and Keitel's miserliness when issuing what OKW did have – now hit hard as dozens of trucks and other soft-skinned vehicles ran out of fuel and had to be abandoned, blocking every road for miles. This dreadful congestion slowed the advance, and the opportunity to take Bastogne was missed. By the time the Germans had sorted themselves out, the Americans had won the race to reach the town, and the hastily assembled paratroopers of the US 101st Screaming Eagles were digging in around the place where they would create a legend for themselves in the coming days. Typically, Lüttwitz refused to shoulder responsibility for what turned out to be a monumental error, instead blaming Bayerlein for not pressing the attack with enough vigour. This was a hard argument to agree with, given that even at this stage – just two days after the beginning of the offensive – the *Lehr* was already having to siphon the gasoline from captured American vehicles to fill their own thirsty tanks. As one German officer wrote, 'Because of the traffic jams ... fuel, and ammunition for the panzers, is not coming up, to say nothing of rations.' With Bayerlein more or less stuck at Bastogne, the emphasis shifted to Lauchert's division some five miles north of Bastogne at the village of Noville. Defended by Major William Desobry and the four hundred men of his 20th Armoured Infantry Battalion, they had been reinforced by a battalion of paratroopers sent from Bastogne when 2. *Panzer* hit them on the morning of 19 December. The divisions leading Panthers had already made short work of a column of 9th Armoured Division's Shermans, their excellent gunnery virtually annihilating their opponents, and now it was the turn of Desobry and his men.

At first, using bazookas and an anti-tank gun, the Americans managed to brew-up two Panthers and sent the rest scuttling back up the slopes surrounding the village. Realising it couldn't be taken quickly, Lauchert ordered his artillery into action, as one of the defenders, William J. Stone remembered: 'Noville was taking a beating. The Germans were pounding the village (and us) with everything they had. The piercing whistle of incoming projectiles followed by the sounds of their explosions assaulted our ears. Their blasts buffeted our bodies. The sharp, bitter smell of the exploded powder invaded our nostrils.' Desobry's headquarters was hit and the major himself badly wounded, forcing his evacuation to Bastogne.

The following day, the decision was taken to abandon Noville and the surviving defenders climbed into their vehicles and headed out, only to drive straight into a 2. *Panzer* attack. The Germans reacted first, their cannons and machine-guns raking the Americans and causing chaos. Within minutes eleven Shermans were on fire and over two hundred Americans were killed. A GI described the scene: 'Dead were lying all around on the road and in the ditches ... our trucks and half-tracks were either burning or had been torn to shreds.' *Gefreiter* Guido Gnilsen then entered Noville. 'We drove into the middle of the town – what a sight met our eyes; the red glow of burning houses, the church was on fire and brewed-up tanks were silhouetted against the sky... I saw knocked-out Shermans and other blown-up wagons, and cases of provisions – like tins of carrots – as far as the eye could see.' It hadn't been a walkover though, as Gnilsen readily acknowledged: 'I saw all our dead lying in rows ... in a few hours we had lost twenty panzers and half the panzer grenadier regiment... Our battalion was now at company strength and we had lost all our senior officers.' Nevertheless, in triumph, Lüttwitz ordered Bayerlein and Lauchert to continue their advance and bypass Bastogne – despite their strenuous objections. With little urgency, Lüttwitz then turned to the bespectacled figure of Heinz Kokott and ordered him to besiege and capture Bastogne with his 26. *VGD*: '2. *Panzerdivision* have taken Noville, the enemy is in flight-like retreat to the south, 2. *Panzer* is in steady pursuit ... after taking Foy 2. *Panzer* will turn west and drive into open country.' As an example of hubris this takes some beating. The Americans were most definitely not in 'flight-like retreat', and in fact were being heavily reinforced by the experienced 2nd Armored Division and the first elements of the British 3rd Royal Tank Regiment (3 RTR), arriving from the north. As for his own troops, Lüttwitz seemed to be in a state of denial as to their situation. That wasn't an accusation that could be levelled at Manteuffel:

> By the time the reserves had been given to me they couldn't be moved. They were at a standstill for lack of petrol – stranded over a stretch of a hundred miles – just when they were needed ... the spearhead of 2. Panzer were pinned down to lack of fuel ... and enemy air activity was steadily increasing.

Somehow, Lauchert managed to drive his division on until it reached the tiny hamlet of Buissonville, some thirty miles to the northeast. There, his supplies were nearing exhaustion. Increasingly hungry, his men were forced to knock on the doors of local houses and beg for food, while gasoline was drained from any vehicle deemed non-essential in an attempt to at least try and keep the panzers moving, as Guido Gnilsen recalled with evident frustration: 'Here was the spearhead, the panzers were all ready to go, all lined up, but we couldn't go any further because we were waiting for gasoline.' *Lehr* was south of 2. *Panzer*, and Harald von Elverfeldt's 9. *Panzerdivision* was meant to be following on from behind, but neither were able to support Lauchert, leaving his formation pretty much cut-off and increasingly isolated. For Lauchert the frustration was palpable; his men were just eighteen miles short of the bridge over the Meuse at Dinant – just eighteen miles – he couldn't stop now.

At *Heeresgruppe* headquarters Model felt it too, and in desperation he sent the following command: 'If necessary, elements of the reconnaissance battalion were to capture the Dinant bridge on foot in a coup de main.' Lauchert had little choice, he needed to somehow push on, and so he took the momentous decision to split his division into three; one *kampfgruppe* would be commanded by *Major* von Böhm and would be based on his own armoured reconnaissance battalion. They would form a northern prong and head for Dinant by any route they could find. Setting off that night, they made steady progress until they ran into a 3 RTR Sherman Firefly which blasted the lead Mark IV panzer and an ammunition truck following it. The British withdrew in the ensuring confusion, leaving Böhm thinking he had run into a strong enemy force. Dog-tired, and unwilling to risk his *kampfgruppe* in the inky blackness, the major halted the advance, and his men laagered up around the hamlet of Foy-Notre-Dame, shivering in their vehicles as the thermometer plunged to almost twenty degrees below zero. Back at Buissonville, a second *kampfgruppe* was formed around *Panzergrenadier-Regiment 304*, reinforced with a battalion of *Panzer-Regiment 3,* all Lauchert's artillery and most of his anti-aircraft guns. Under the leadership of *Major* Ernst Cochenhausen, this *KG* contained the majority of the divisions punching power, and was sent on a southwards route to Dinant, where it was scheduled to meet up with *KG Böhm.* Lauchert himself would stay in Buissonville with the remainder of the division, waiting for supplies to reach them, and would then follow on.

With most of the division's remaining gasoline, *KG Cochenhausen* pushed on, and as Christmas Eve dawned the leading Panther reached the village of Celles, just five miles from Dinant. There, it ran over a solitary mine and blew up. When questioned, local villagers lied to the panzer commanders that the Americans had sown thousands of mines in the area, spooking men who were at the end of their tether, and had neither eaten nor slept for the best part of forty-eight hours. The news that *KG Cochenhausen* was within touching distance of the Meuse electrified the *Adlerhorst,* and Hitler himself sent a message of congratulations to the officers and men of 2. *Panzer.* He didn't, however, understand the true position of those men; just like *KG Peiper* they were almost out of fuel and food, and ammunition was scarce. Finally understanding what was going on, Lüttwitz recommended to Manteuffel that 2. *Panzerdivision* be withdrawn for re-supply, while 9. *Panzer* move into its place, but there was no way that request was going to be agreed to at the very moment Hitler believed Lauchert's men were about to bring him victory. There was also the fact that 9. *Panzer* itself was terribly low on fuel, and in no position to come to its sister division's rescue, as *Oberstleutnant* Rüdiger Weiz – Lauchert's operations officer – recounted: 'Towards the evening … the commander of 9. Panzer arrived at the divisional command post. He revealed that his division had been held up for twenty-four hours owing to lack of gasoline.' This would be 9. *Panzerdivision's* high watermark. Hans Behrens:

We were at our most westerly point between Bastogne and St Hubert … we were coming down a hill and on the left side was a Sherman with its turret open. I don't know why but I got out of my vehicle and looked down inside it. What I saw was a young man absolutely charred black, and one clean hole in the side of the turret. At that point I realised that this man could be me, and that he had a mother and a father. It became hard to carry on.

The supply situation would be considerably eased if the seven roads through Bastogne could be used; accordingly Heinz Kokott was told in no uncertain terms – take Bastogne! This was easier said than done. The American defenders resolutely stood their ground and, supported by a mass of artillery, decimated every attack made on them. When Kokott heard Anthony McAuliffe's famous 'Nuts!' response to Lüttwitz's call to surrender, his own words were, 'In the course of the day news arrived from Korps to the effect that the commander in charge of Bastogne forces had declined to surrender with remarkable brevity.' He then went back to trying to break through the American lines, but by now his casualties were so severe that he was plugging gaps in his assault companies with men combed out from his artillery batteries and the divisional supply battalion.

Finally reinforced with *Oberst* Wolfgang Maucke's under-strength *15. Panzergrenadier-Division*, Kokott tried again on Christmas Day; his men and Maucke's storming forward into the teeth of American fire – the Germans suffered eight hundred casualties, and *15. Panzergrenadier* was practically annihilated as a fighting force. As for *26. VGD*, its companies now averaged twenty men apiece, and one of *Volks-grenadier-Regiment 78*'s battalions was down to just forty survivors. As one of Kokott's officers lamented: 'We were nine hundred metres from the edge of Bastogne, and just couldn't get into the town.'

KG Böhm and *KG Cochenhausen* were now effectively two pockets, more or less stranded in the Belgian countryside just outside Dinant, as Guido Gnilsen (in the latter) described: 'Leutnant Baier was wounded and Oberfeldwebel Schmelzer took over the Kompanie. It was a wonder we got through to where we did… I saw a sign that read "Dinant 9 kms" – it was just nine kilometres to the Meuse, our objective! … we were stranded with the same complaint as always – no gasoline, and the enemy was preparing to surround us.' Their only hope of survival was to be reached by a relief force that could either re-supply them or open an escape route. Rüdiger Weiz saw their dilemma at first-hand. 'Since both pockets reported that their supply of ammunition and fuel wouldn't allow them to continue the battle much longer and since the fuel available at the front wasn't sufficient for the withdrawal of the forces, the nearly unsolvable question arose of how to bring help to the elements fighting in the frontline.' Hans Behrens knew *9. Panzerdivision* would be no help: 'Things started to turn very bad for us … we suffered great losses, food was becoming difficult to get hold of, and so was gasoline... I was eventually captured. I remember I was sending a message from the back of my panzer when the door opened and there was an Ami with a sub-machine gun.'

At this point, the Allies threw Ernest Harmon's 2nd Armored Division straight at 2. *Panzer,* with devastating results for Lauchert's advance. Harmon was an aggressive, determined commander, who expected his men to fight hard and fight fast. Calling on every artillery piece within range – including British guns now in the area – 2nd Armored began to crush the two German pockets. Manteuffel could do nothing but sit in his headquarters and listen to his attack die in the snow:

> The forces of the Division ... soon had to repulse increasing pressure from the enemy from the north and northeast. This brought the advance to a standstill ... the connection to the rear was also lost. In villages and hamlets security detachments and supply train elements ... fought desperate defensive battles against superior enemy forces. These small groups were the first to be destroyed ... the lack of fuel and ammunition soon made itself felt.

With no fuel and ammunition running out, and under attack from experienced American armoured troops, all was lost for Lauchert's division. *KG Böhm* was especially hard hit, and on Boxing Day, Böhm and the remaining 148 men of his command surrendered. In desperation, Lauchert assembled a *kampfgruppe* from among the rest of the Division and despatched it west under the command of *Hauptmann* Friedrich Holtmeyer in a last-ditch bid to reach *KG Cochenhausen* in Celles. Weiz was with them: 'In spite of strong enemy artillery, and even stronger armoured superiority, we came up to within nine hundred yards of the pocket by the afternoon of 26 December.' They would go no further. Harmon's men counter-attacked and called in air attacks which stopped the relief force; Holtmeyer was killed. Gnilsen was in the pocket: 'The fighting went on for three days, and then came the jabos to finish us off and push us backwards ... the grenadiers had been in their foxholes, in the snow and ice, holding their positions as well as they could, pushing back every attack... The Ardennes offensive was lost.' Finally, Manteuffel authorised 2. *Panzer* to withdraw. Celles was liberated for the second time that same day. *KG Cochenhausen* was shattered; 2,500 of them were killed or wounded and another 1,200 captured. The Americans counted eighty-two panzers, the same number of guns and several hundred soft-skinned vehicles, most abandoned through lack of fuel. Ernst von Cochenhausen himself managed to break out and head east with six hundred of his men. 2. *Panzerdivision* was finished.

Unteroffizier Otto Henning from the *Panzer-Lehr*'s reconnaissance battalion remembers their escape:

> Our unit leader, Oberfeldwebel Keichel, came and told us that some officers were going on reconnaissance and we had to accompany them – we had to move out towards the Meuse... Keichel found the bridge we were to secure for the divisions advance ... it was extremely cold ... then we noticed shadows coming towards us... I crouched down and heard Keichel order 'fire!' in a loud voice, but the approaching group started to shout 'don't shoot! don't shoot!' I was sent to check these men – they were from 2. Panzerdivision. They were older than us and completely exhausted. Some of them just fell to the ground, shaking all over ... we continued our march the next day but received new orders by radio ordering us to return. Our unit was supposed to reinforce 2. Panzer but the enemy's artillery fire was so intense we didn't dare move out of the forest... We knew that the Ardennes offensive had failed.

Henning was right. The defeat of 2. *Panzer* spelled the end of 5. *Panzerarmee*'s advance, and with *KG Peiper* wiped out too, the offensive was done. Lauchert's men had gotten the furthest west – some sixty miles – and had been tantalisingly close to the Meuse at Dinant, but even if they had reached it and taken the bridge, they were too weak to exploit its capture and push on to Antwerp. By then, strong American and British forces were converging on the area and unless the Germans could affect an orderly withdrawal they risked being smashed in their own cul-de-sac.

At first, this looked to be the case, but much to Rüdiger Weiz's relief, 'Luckily the enemy was slow in following up and didn't attack the route of retreat in any way worth mentioning.' Hitler refused to accept the inevitable and insisted the offensive be continued much to the chagrin of almost all his senior officers – Rundstedt, Manteuffel, Guderian and Dietrich among others – his obstinacy was only supported by the likes of Keitel and Jodl, who couldn't bring themselves to see their massive gamble had failed.

The orders came down from Berlin; take Bastogne. This time it was the Waffen-SS who tried once again to overcome its defenders; men like the 9. *SS-Hohenstaufen*'s *SS-Hauptsturmführer* Appel:

> We lie before Bastogne ... through inadequate training of the men and very serious shortages of supplies, in particular clothing and boots, I have very heavy casualties. They are mostly due to artillery and, whenever the weather clears, from jabos. Yesterday I received two

hundred replacements, but unfortunately almost all are old men from the Ukraine, some of whom neither speak nor understand German. Everything is lacking... I have already experienced what it means to have to attack without any heavy weapons ... as they couldn't be brought forward due to a lack of prime movers or because they had to be left, stuck fast in the frozen ground, as target practice for jabos. The Kompanies have only a fraction of their fighting strength ... on average about forty to fifty men.[65]

The *Hitlerjugend*'s Ewald Rien was as enamoured with the fighting as Appel:

The commander of 7. Kompanie was among the many men already killed or wounded, however they couldn't be rescued because of the heavy fire ... orders arrived from battalion to dig in. Of the 4th Platoon led by Hauptscharführer Müller, which had remained at the corner of the woods, no-one was found again ... by 2000hrs the 2nd Battalion was only about sixty NCOs and men strong.[66]

Across the Ardennes, the *Westheer*'s last strategic reserve was bleeding to death. The *SS-Das Reich*'s Erich Heller, having proudly brought fifty of his men out of the Falaise disaster, found himself fighting for his life when ordered to attack a village without any chance for reconnaissance, and no heavy weapon support:

I gave the order for our attack to begin. We made good progress and the enemy lost possession of the first few houses, however the group on our right made the mistake of rushing forward and were spotted by the enemy. They soon came under fire from a tank in the centre of town, as well as machine-gun fire, and quickly suffered heavy losses ... the attack would have to be called off ... three men with a panzerfaust and a machine-gun would stay behind with me to cover the others... Just as we were about to make our way back the house we were in was hit by two high-explosive shells ... part of the roof crashed down on me and I lost consciousness.

Heller woke to find himself dazed and alone. Within minutes he was taken prisoner by the Americans.[67] As the Germans were pushed back, morale began to crack for some, as Otto Henning witnessed:

On one occasion I had a run-in with a battalion commander who just lost his composure and shouted at me: 'I don't need reconnaissance, I need soldiers, I need weapons, I need ammunition!' He had lost almost all his men, only one hundred and fifty remained from his battalion.

These heavy losses, particularly among the infantry, affected the morale of the troops.[68]

Manteuffel was distraught: 'Instead of withdrawing in time, we were driven back bit by bit under pressure of Allied attacks, suffering needlessly. Our losses were much heavier at this later stage than they had been earlier. It spelt bankruptcy because we could not afford such losses.'

Frustration at the failure was keenly felt among the *landsers*. Sigmund Landau and his men had been assigned to join Dietrich's 6. *Panzerarmee*:

> In the Lorraine area of France, here, at a huge depot, under cover of darkness, we took possession of three modified Wespes ['Wasp', this was the Sd.Kfz. 124 self-propelled artillery gun] with high-velocity 7.5cm guns, which penetrated all known armour of the day]. We arrived at headquarters and were told we were too late, the show had started, so we chased off in search of Ami tanks... After an endless number of redirections by the Feldgendarmerie we found ourselves among 5. Panzerarmee, ran out of petrol and were ordered to blow up our new, hardly used Wespes. We were in a murderous mood, and I was glad we hadn't taken any prisoners as our despair and frustration could have driven us to some really ugly deeds. We were once again withdrawing, and, yet again, relying on nothing but small arms.[69]

The *Lehr*'s Helmut Ritgen was just as disappointed as he watched the retreat. 'An almost unbroken snake of vehicles of all types, panzers and guns wound its way through the hilly, icy, roads to the east.' Heinrich, an NCO in the *Hohenstaufen* was, perhaps, a bit more philosophical:

> Our advance got stopped abruptly and we had to pull back... I remember that the enemy fire – and the fighting in general – was a lot heavier than on the Eastern front, and also that we were much more aggressive ... probably because we were fighting close to the borders of Germany itself. At no cost could the Allies reach Berlin, we had to stop them, no matter what... But you get used to it ... and every time you escape death you get that adrenaline rush through your body – incredible! One day there was a wave of enemy soldiers attacking our positions, and, luckily for us we had several MG42s and one Tiger, positioned on a small hill ... it looked like a suicide mission on their part, we were just waiting for them to get closer so we could open fire.[70]

The fighting in the Ardennes dragged on into the new year, with men bleeding out in the snow and mud of a battle that had already been won and lost.

For the Americans – who far and away did the bulk of the fighting, despite Montgomery's rather crass comments to the press afterwards – it was the costliest battle fought in the European campaign. Figures vary, depending on the date taken as the end of the battle, but in broad terms the Americans lost over eighty thousand men; with over ten thousand killed, almost fifty thousand wounded and a further twenty-three thousand missing – almost all captured. As well as the men, the US Army lost well over seven hundred tanks, a similar number of guns and some 647 aircraft. British losses totalled less than fifteen hundred, with two hundred of those dead.

As for the *Westheer*, Omar Bradley claimed to have inflicted a quarter of a million casualties on it – a ludicrous exaggeration – while the official German estimates of the time at forty-five thousand were an equal falsehood. The accepted figures put German losses at about the same as American at eighty thousand men killed, wounded or missing, with some six hundred panzers and assault-guns lost as well as 644 fighters and 478 pilots; with half of those falling in the three days before Christmas – so much for the view that the Luftwaffe didn't fight.

The numbers hid a stark truth. Despite the Anglo-Americans problems with the manning of their infantry units in particular, they could – and did – make good their losses in a few weeks. By the beginning of January they had pushed over half a million men into the Ardennes, with over two thousand guns and almost three thousand tanks and tank destroyers. While for the Germans, their position was neatly summed up by Rolf Munninger in Model's headquarters: 'It was the coup de grace for our army in the west. This catastrophe took our best divisions.'[71]

In the Ardennes the Wehrmacht had tried something it had never done before; a major winter offensive. It had selected undoubtedly the weakest point in the Allied line, and for the first time in several years had managed to maintain operational secrecy as to its intentions. The weather – as predicted – had prevented Allied air power from playing a decisive role early on, and Berlin had concentrated some of its finest formations for the attack. It had then failed – and failed badly.

The biggest reason for that failure was simply that the Wehrmacht didn't have the resources to achieve the plan. There weren't enough panzers, there weren't enough men and, crucially, there wasn't enough fuel. As the Imperial Japanese Army had discovered earlier on that year in Burma, an offensive that relied on capturing the enemy's supplies to make up for your own shortfalls was unlikely to succeed.

The other main reason for the Wehrmacht's failure was a more nebulous one, but nevertheless just as important, and that was the fighting quality of the American troops. Since the war's beginning, the Wehrmacht had taken for granted that the officers and men who filled its ranks were the best soldiers in the world; partly this was due to the Nazi myth of racial superiority, and partly to training and the venerated military tradition in Germany. The Allies themselves were often complicit in this delusion. Captain William DePuy – an American infantry officer - analysed German small-unit tactics:

> They used cover and concealment, and they used imagination ... a handful of Germans could hold up a regiment by siting their weapons properly ... an American unit would stay there and fight all day against twenty-five men and two assault-guns – that happened all too often... In attack they were masters of suppression using machine-pistols. They'd spray our front, drive our soldiers to ground, and then they'd come into us.

DePuy wasn't alone in his admiration for the *landser*. George Turner-Cain, commanding officer of the British 1st Herefords wrote: 'The Germans ... fighting in penny packets and not in formations, were showing splendid spirit and defiance, fighting until told to withdraw,' in contrast to his own men where 'hard fighting and heavy casualties had a depressing effect on morale all round. Men became jumpy and unwilling to go forward in the face of fire or possible fire, unless led by their leaders.'[72]

Generalmajor Johannes Bruhn had been the commander of 553. *VGD* when he had been captured in the Saverne Gap in the Vosges mountains by the US Seventh Army back in November, and while being held at Trent Park back in England was secretly recorded expressing a view of the Americans typical of the Wehrmacht as a whole: 'The flower of our manhood is being mowed down by the aircraft and massed tanks of an army which has no real soldiers, and which doesn't really want to fight.' Hitler believed – as did many of his senior generals – that once confronted by a massed German offensive, the ordinary American soldier would either surrender or run – in the Ardennes, that belief was shown to be the fallacy it was. Willy Nissel, a flak gunner in a *volksgrenadier* unit understood this all too well: 'After a short artillery barrage ... we rattled up the road ... we fired the first explosive shells from our cannon. The German infantry pushed into the town, firing their assault-rifles as they went. The enemy defended himself vigorously. Our talk about the enemy being "too afraid to fight" was unmasked ... as a bloody fairy tale.' The GI in the Ardennes proved to be the sand in the Wehrmacht's engine, clogging it up and doing just enough to bring it to a grinding halt. Perhaps the most succinct view was expressed by a Waffen-SS NCO, a veteran of more than four years fighting on every front: 'They didn't need to take chances. Slow? They were just careful.'

Myths are tricky things though. George Patton – never a man to undersell himself or the men he led – wrote after the Ardennes: 'We can still lose this war ... the Germans are colder and hungrier than we are, but they fight better.'

It was going to be a long winter.

Last Gasps in the West

The Ardennes offensive was a massive mistake for Germany. Just as at Kursk back in the summer of '43, the Wehrmacht had seen its carefully husbanded reserves of men, machines and supplies thrown like water on rocks. The twin miracles wrought at Arnhem and in the Reich's factories and recruit depots were squandered. The *jagdflieger* Johannes Kaufmann said of the Ardennes: 'The offensive withered, and with it our hopes of turning the tide of war on the Western front.' Back in the East, the warnings were getting shriller as Moscow finished the job in the Balkans and eastern Europe, and turned its eyes back to Germany itself. The Eastern front was now the priority. Starved of reinforcements – only one fifth of armoured vehicles produced in the pre-Christmas period and less than half of the fifty-five *Volks-grenadier Divisionen* created were sent east – the *Ostheer* now resembled the Wehrmacht's poor relation. *Herbstnebel* hadn't achieved its goals – any of them – except it had bought some time at least, with the Anglo-Americans unlikely to go on the offensive in the depths of winter. Not so the Soviets, whose mastery of the winter attack was well-known. Berlin's choice was clear: shut down the Ardennes attack and switch all available forces east, ready to blunt the inevitable Soviet assault. This was definitely the view of *landsers* like Rolf-Helmut Schröder: 'We thought it impossible that the Amis would allow the Russians to sweep Europe. We thought that, when the Amis had defeated us, they would turn on the Russians, and we believed that we had to do everything possible to stop Russia from overrunning our country.'[1] Hans Bernhard of the *SS-Leibstandarte* agreed with his *volks-grenadier* comrade: 'Our motivation was simple, we had to keep fighting in the east, we had to keep the Russians out of our country.'[2] Fear of a vengeful Red Army weighed heavy on German minds: 'All those who had been in Russia knew what to expect if Bolshevism came to Germany ... if it had only been England and France we would have stopped earlier.'[3]

Nazi propaganda played its part too, with Joseph Goebbels painting an apocalyptic vision of the future in publications like the newspaper *Das Reich*:

> If the German people lay down their arms, the Soviets, according to the agreement between Roosevelt, Churchill and Stalin would occupy all of East and Southeast Europe along with the greater part of the Reich. An iron curtain would fall ... behind which nations would be slaughtered.

Perhaps Manteuffel offered a more military-minded view of the post-Ardennes situation: 'The result of the offensive mainly benefitted the Russians.'

So, it was the East again for the remains of the Wehrmacht. Except that didn't happen. After more than three years during which time the Eastern front was the Wehrmacht's very own black hole, sucking in everything around it and blotting out all other theatres, it seemingly disappeared off the agenda in a puff of smoke. Instead, it was now the West that dominated every conference and briefing. So much so, that even as the fighting in the Ardennes dragged on after Christmas, Hitler called another meeting of senior officers at the *Adlerhorst* on 28 December, where he declared his intention of launching a further, simultaneous, offensive some one hundred and twenty miles to the southeast in Alsace-Lorraine.

> This attack has a very clear objective, namely the destruction of the enemy forces. There is not a matter of prestige involved here. It is a matter of destroying and exterminating the enemy forces wherever we find them... With this done, Strasbourg will fall to our troops and the destruction of the enemy in Alsace-Lorraine will be complete.

Among the bemedalled coterie of officers present was none other than Edgar Feuchtinger, the less-than-dynamic commander of 21. *Panzerdivision*. Lucky to have kept his division after his infamous disappearing act to the fleshpots of Paris the night before D-Day, Feuchtinger sat open-mouthed listening to his *Führer*:

> He began as usual with a long speech and emphasised that we were waging an ideological war, the loss of which would destroy the German people ... he then came to speak of the Ardennes offensive, in which 'not all objectives had been achieved', but which had an 'incidental' consequence of weakening the American front opposite us ... he estimated the strength of the Americans to be only four or five divisions, which he proposed to destroy with eight offensive German divisions... Hitler then ended his address by saying 'It must be our absolute goal to settle the matter here in the west offensively.'

Stony silence greeted the dictator's announcement. Johannes Blaskowitz – once more commander of *Heeresgruppe G* after his premature sacking back in September – was as surprised as his subordinate, *General der Infanterie* Hans von Obstfelder. Obstfelder was now in charge of *1. Armee,* having previously had a solid if somewhat undistinguished war as a corps commander in Russia. Now he found himself appointed to lead an attack aimed at destroying not one but two Allied armies; Alexander Patch's Seventh US, and Jean de Lattre de Tassigny's French *1ʳᵉ Armée.*

As ever, Hitler promised his commanders a cornucopia of military riches to achieve the objectives he had set them for the offensive he christened *Unternehmen Nordwind – Operation North Wind.* As far as the troops committed were concerned, this was a chimera. OKW's main reinforcement to Obstfelder's existing force was *Oberkommando Oberrhein* (High Command Upper Rhine), led by the mass-murderer and head of the SS, Heinrich Himmler. A military virgin, the only time Himmler had heard a shot fired in anger (or slaughter) was when he watched an execution of one hundred Jews in Minsk, back in 1941, as Karl Wolff recalled:

> An open grave had been dug and they had to jump into this and lie face downwards. And sometimes when one or two rows had already been shot, they had to lie on top of the people who had already been shot and then they were shot from the edge of the grave. And Himmler had never seen dead people before and, in his curiosity, he stood right up at the edge of this open grave – a sort of triangular hole – and was looking in. While he was looking in, Himmler had the deserved bad luck that from one or other of the people who had been shot in the head he got a splash of brains on his coat, and I think it also splashed into his face, and he went very green and pale – he wasn't actually sick, but he was heaving and turned round and swayed, and then I had to jump forward and hold him steady and then I led him away from the grave.

Over lunch at the *Adlerhorst* after Hitler's briefing, the bespectacled bureaucrat expressed his confidence in the venture, without having the slightest understanding of what it entailed.

As it transpired, elements of seventeen *Westheer* divisions would be involved in *Nordwind,* including *6. SS-Gebirgs-Division 'Nord'* – a mountain division shipped south from Finnish Karelia – although most were units still recovering from their flight across France, like Hans von Luck's *21. Panzerdivision* or Hans Lingner's *SS-Götz von Berlichingen.*

The latter was typical of what Obstfelder had to hand; reduced to less than four thousand men by early December, a shipment of new assault-guns and an influx of barely trained *volksdeutsche* had brought it almost back to strength, but in no way could the division be considered anything other than mediocre at best.

Having said that, *Nordwind*'s major goal – the destruction of the American Seventh Army – was not as outlandish as it might have been. To counter the Ardennes offensive, Eisenhower had disengaged Patton's Third Army from the Metz area and sent it north to hit the Germans in the flank. He had also stripped other units from the Seventh and sent them north too, stretching the Army out to hold a line almost seventy miles long. If anything, the Americans had fewer troops in the region now than they had in the Ardennes on 16 December. Edgar Feuchtinger was still very doubtful though: 'We've received replacements and now have seventy-four Panthers and Mark IVs ... but two things are being overlooked; we have no air superiority and nothing to set against the massive US artillery.' However, on the former problem, Hermann Goering had a trick up his sleeve; one he believed would give the assault a winning advantage from the very start – *Unternehmen Bodenplatte – Operation Baseplate*.

Bodenplatte's concept was a simple one: replicate the Wehrmacht's offensive victories of 1940–41 by destroying the enemy's air forces on the ground right at the start of the attack. In Poland and Yugoslavia in particular, this tactic had been a huge success and it had helped bring the Wehrmacht to within an ace of victory in Soviet Russia in 1941. Now it would be the turn of the Anglo-Americans – or so the dazzlingly incompetent *Reichsmarschall* believed. Having steadily lost influence at Hitler's court since the Luftwaffe's failure to supply the Stalingrad garrison by air, Goering had gotten to the point where he no longer attended *Führer* conferences unless specifically asked, preferring instead to spend his time at his palatial residence *Carinhall*, northeast of Berlin, or at his hunting lodge at Rominten in East Prussia. Now, in an attempt to once more curry favour with his old boss, he proposed a mass dawn attack on Allied airfields across France, Belgium and the Netherlands, to cripple the enemy before they could get airborne. Hitler was dubious of his one-time favourite's plan: 'The hope of decimating the enemy with a mass deployment is not realistic.'

Having originally planned to launch the attack to coincide with the Ardennes offensive, the bad weather that had grounded the Allied air forces also forced the repeated cancellation of *Bodenplatte*. Now, Goering planned the attack to coincide with the launch of *Nordwind* – early morning on New Year's Day 1945 – thinking that Allied eyes would be bleary after the previous night's celebrations. Desperate to replicate the operational secrecy that had served *Herbstnebel* so well, he decreed that the frontline units over which his squadrons would fly should not be told of the attack. Crucially, this included the massed anti-aircraft batteries that were now such a feature of the German line.

By now, morale in the Luftwaffe had hit rock bottom. More aircraft than ever were being manufactured, but when not shot out of the sky while being flown by desperately under-trained young pilots, they were grounded through lack of fuel or spare parts. Large numbers of Allied fighters were sweeping the skies over the Reich, shooting up everything they could see in the air around them or on the ground. The bomber fleets were now so big and so well-protected that to challenge them was becoming a death sentence, as the experienced *Hauptmann* Heinz Knoke realised:

> The Yanks don't leave us alone. Today they attacked Münster in strength. Just when I am ready to pounce with my flight on a formation of Fortresses over the burning city, we are ourselves bounced by dozens of P-47s diving on us from above... At my first burst of fire a Thunderbolt ahead of me blows up, and my wingman downs a second, that brings the entire pack down on us – it was all we could do to shake them off.

Helmut Rix's flight wasn't as lucky. Having converted to Fw 190s with *JG 301*, he took off with his *Staffelkapitän* and two others to intercept a bomber formation. Before they could reach the *Viermots,* their fighter escort intervened. Hopelessly outnumbered, Rix and his fellow *jagdflieger* had little chance. All four were shot down – Rix was the only pilot who lived. Some didn't even make it into the air. Norbert Hannig had spent his war in Russia, and in December 1944 was asked by his old commander – and 275-kill *Experte* – Günther Rall, to convert a unit of Messerschmitt 410 '*Hornisse*' (Hornet) crews to Fw 190s. On arrival at their base, Hannig found out that on their previous mission the Hornets had been ordered to attack advance Soviet units, only to be bounced on their way there by American P-51 Mustangs coming from the West. Of the eighteen original crews only three escaped, and they were traumatised. Hannig called his boss to explain: 'They were jumped by Mustangs and all but wiped out... Converting the survivors onto single-engine fighters is out of the question at the present time ... they're simply not up to it.' Rall agreed, and Hannig went back to his war.

Even in the East, long the happiest of Luftwaffe hunting grounds, where the cult of the *Experte* – the air ace – had reached its zenith, with dozens of pilots wracking-up kill scores into three figures, the enemy was now gaining the upper hand. On Hannig's return to his squadron he shared his billet with an old friend Helmut Wettstein.

'"Norbert, when do you think the war will be lost?"

It was a simple enough question, but in those days to even utter such words was nothing less than sedition. Even to mention the possibility of defeat was regarded as subversion of military discipline and morale.'

To fulfil Goering's rash promise, these same pilots now began to fill hurriedly prepared billets in the West, gulping down mugs of *ersatz* coffee and eating plates of whatever their ground-crews had managed to scrounge up from local farmers. The mood amongst them was gloomy, as *Oberst* Hanns Trübenbach recalled: 'At the turn of the year 1944/1945 the crazy order was given, for all available German fighter units to attack the enemy air force on their European airfields and to destroy them in a single blow.'[4] The fliers themselves weren't the only ones with their doubts, as *Oberstleutnant* Johann Kogler discovered when he spoke to his old comrade Adolf Galland about the impending attack. 'He poured out his troubles to me, it was pretty grim.'

Regardless of what the pilots thought, the plan was set, and with the early morning sky still dark, a thousand of them climbed into their cockpits across thirty-eight separate airfields and started their engines. Taking off, a total of thirty-four *Jagdgruppen* (nineteen of them flying Bf 109Gs or Ks) turned their noses west and headed to their pre-assigned targets – ironically, many of them being previous Luftwaffe air bases. As they approached their own lines, surprised anti-aircraft gunners raced to their weapons and began pumping shells into the air – the Luftwaffe hadn't been seen in such numbers for months, and with no prior warning the gunners assumed the armada were Allied planes. Pilots cursed their own side as several aircraft were hit and tumbled down earthwards in flames; Herbert Ihlefeld's *Jagdgeschwader 1,* for example, lost four aircraft. Flying on, the *Jagdgruppen* reached their objectives at around 0920hrs. Unfortunately for them, due to navigation errors, what should have been twelve British bases in Belgium and the southern Netherlands and four American ones in France, were actually four American, nine British and Commonwealth, and three joint. Some Allied squadrons were caught unawares; at Eindhoven twenty-six RAF Typhoons were lined up on the airfield and destroyed as sitting ducks – but at many target bases not only were the ground defences alert but there were also alarm flights either in the air or ready to take-off. Arriving disorganised after negotiating their own flak corridor, the *jagdflieger* pressed home their attacks while taking horrific casualties. Having dropped their bombs and strafed anything they could see, the survivors headed for home, only to be subjected to yet more friendly flak. Unbelievably, Goering had also left orders stating that any returning aircraft that had failed to destroy any enemy aircraft had to refuel and head back west once more – the losses amongst those unlucky few were almost one hundred per cent, as the Allied lines by now resembled a hornets' nest the Germans had poked with a sharp stick.

By midday it was all over. The Allies had lost three hundred aircraft destroyed and an additional one hundred and ninety damaged,[5] including fifty *Viermots* – even Montgomery's personal plane was a burning wreck.

This was no small loss, but given production numbers it would only be a couple of weeks at most before these aircraft could be replaced. With most of the losses happening on the ground too, it meant that very few pilots became casualties – once they came out of their shelters and slit-trenches the survivors would have plenty of aircraft to climb back into. Not so the *Jagdwaffe*. For them *Bodenplatte* was an unmitigated disaster. Almost one in three of the aircraft that took off were shot down, however it was the pilot casualties that cut the deepest. Some 214 were killed or missing, with dozens more wounded. Even worse was the fact that so many experienced senior flyers were lost; three *Kommodoren* (Wing Commanders), five *Gruppenkommandeure* (Group Commanders) and no less than fourteen *Staffelkapitäne* (Squadron Leaders). One of the latter was Johann Kogler, flying with his unit *Jagdgeschwader 6,* his Fw 190 was mistakenly shot down by German anti-aircraft fire en route to Vokel airfield in the Netherlands. Managing to parachute out, he floated to earth and was taken prisoner by Allied troops on the ground. Hanns Trübenbach was left bitter by the debacle: 'The greater part of the remaining German fighters and their outstanding leaders were sacrificed. As it was thought that a surprise attack could be carried out at low level, many of our fighter pilots were killed by our own flak!' Johannes Kaufmann – spared having to take part in the attack due to his attendance on a formation leaders course – said of it in despair: 'Galland's carefully husbanded force was squandered on a costly low-level attack for no lasting gain and would never again pose any serious threat to the enemy... Bodenplatte sounded the death-knell for our fighter arm.' Hitler's Luftwaffe adjutant, *Oberst* Nicolaus von Below, agreed with Kaufmann: 'Our formations suffered heavy losses which could never be made good – this was the last major effort by the Luftwaffe.' Adolf Galland was more concise: 'We sacrificed our last substance.'

The impact of *Bodenplatte* was minimal, as the SS trooper Wilhelm Tieke recounted at the time: 'The supply situation had grown to catastrophic proportions. The enemy air force brought the railroad and highway traffic to a complete halt.' After the offensive, the West was stripped of fighters, with only one *geschwader JG 53,* left to cover the entire front. Everything else was deployed on home defence or sent to the East.

As for the ground offensive *Bodenplatte* was meant to support, H hour was one hour before midnight on New Year's Eve. After the crash of the opening artillery barrages, eight German divisions in the Low Vosges on the River Moder struck southwest, while Siegfried Rasp's *19. Armee* pushed up from Colmar on the west bank of the Rhine. Not that much could be expected from Rasp; when a visiting officer apologised to his adjutant – an *Oberstleutnant* von Amsberg – about appearing slightly the worse for wear for drink, the white-haired ex-cavalryman replied that 'it wouldn't be noticeable here as the general is drunk every night.' However, if the two jaws of the pincers met, an entire American corps and sizeable French forces would go into the bag, and Strasbourg would once more be a Nazi city.

At first, the attack made progress, the surprise total as American troops fell back in confusion. The initial advance even instigated something of a mini-crisis at Allied headquarters, where it aggravated latent resentments between the French and Americans. De Gaulle, *la grande asperge*, 'the great asparagus' as he was nicknamed in reference to his 6 feet 5 inches of height – was always keenly aware of French honour, particularly now that the Anglo-Americans had almost liberated his country. When told that Eisenhower was contemplating a temporary withdrawal in front of *Nordwind* that would abandon Strasbourg to the Germans, the self-proclaimed saviour of France reacted immediately, despatching his Chief of Staff, Alphonse Juin, to remonstrate with Eisenhower's deputy. The meeting did not go well for either party. Juin – almost as insufferably imperious as his boss – insisted that Strasbourg be defended at all costs, citing the damage to French prestige if it was lost. He even went so far as threatening French withdrawal from Allied command if his demands were not met; so much for French gratitude. Bedell Smith was so annoyed that when he reported to Eisenhower, he remarked that had Juin been American he would have punched him in the face! In a rare flash of anger, Eisenhower contacted De Gaulle with the uncompromising message that if he followed through on his threat, '...the French Army would get no ammunition, supplies or food unless it obeyed my orders.'

As it turned out, neither threat had to be actioned. With snow waist-deep, and the icy roads almost impassable, *Nordwind* was already in trouble, as a member of Lingner's *SS-Götz von Berlichingen* related:

Our company attacked Hill 382... At dawn the assault bogged down. We had no heavy weapon support and lay on the slope for hours without any cover. We took very heavy casualties from flanking sniper fire too. After about four hours, three panzers appeared and gave us some relief. The Amis withdrew and we hesitantly followed... Our panzers ran into a minefield right in front of a farm. But the attack continued to a ravine at the railway embankment. There we again suffered heavy casualties to artillery and mortar fire.

Heeresgruppe G's own War Diary acknowledged, 'The attack has lost its momentum.'

The *Westheer* looked to rejuvenate the offensive, as Hans von Luck described: 'Nordwind made no progress... A new plan was conceived. Our division and the 25. Panzergrenadier-Division ... were to break through the Maginot Line and trap the enemy in the Haguenau depression... One last dramatic battle lay before us.' The same day von Luck was told of the new plan, he was also told that Feuchtinger was being investigated for his conduct on the eve of D-Day, and for an additional absence on Christmas Eve, when he was found to be back in Germany celebrating whilst his division were engaged in bitter fighting for the *Westwall*. This proved to be the final straw for von Luck and his peers in the division:

> I was speechless...we knew of Feuchtinger's fondness for la dolce vita... We commanders had always maintained our loyalty to him whenever our friends in other panzer divisions had sneered at his style of leadership and way of life – now even I felt this to be the last straw.

Tasked with cutting through the old Maginot Line defences and severing Allied communications with Strasbourg, von Luck's operation had an inauspicious start: 'I asked for maps with exact locations of bunkers and other fortifications – there were none ... we were told that the Maginot Line was barely manned and constituted no obstacle.' This turned out to be little more than wishful thinking on the part of the German planners. 'Even before we reached the first bunkers we came up against fierce resistance and the concentrated fire of American artillery ... suddenly we could make out the first bunker, which received us with heavy fire.' Taking casualties, and in danger of becoming bogged down, 21. *Panzer* tried again two days later on 8 January. 'Hauptmann Herr with twelve Panthers, accompanied by grenadiers and pioniere (assault engineers), managed to force one Ami bunker to surrender, shot up three Shermans and took many prisoners, and only lost one Panther to mines. Then such heavy artillery fire came down that Herr lost twenty grenadiers and pioniere and had to withdraw.'

Unperturbed by this setback, the Germans tried again with a night attack: 'It was bitterly cold and snowing ... we had to cut through barbed-wire and clear mines, and for this we only had a few pioniere and young soldiers of sixteen and seventeen-years-old.' Somehow these few were successful: 'Toward four in the morning a path had been cleared – it was only another hundred yards to the bunker. On all fours the assault party worked their way forward ... the men crept round the bunker, the armoured door was closed, an NCO beat on it with the butt of his gun ... the Ami crew had been taken completely by surprise and were quickly overcome.'

With a tiny wedge driven into the Maginot Line, *kampfgruppen* from both the 25. *Panzergrenadier* and 21. *Panzer* strove to widen it, as *Major* Willy Spreu reported:

> At first light I moved up with my pioniere, while my heavy weapons fired non-stop at the gun-ports in the bunker... The pioniere threw hand-grenades into the ports, while others cut the barbed-wire and cleared mines. When we ran around to the rear entrance the door opened and a white flag appeared with five officers and 117 men. Four of the officers had suffered severe eye injuries from the firing at the ports. They were treated at once by the regimental doctor.

Badly wounded himself the following day, Spreu was evacuated and subsequently awarded the Knight's Cross for his bravery.

Elsewhere in the offensive, the twenty-year-old *jäger* Johann Voss and his comrades from the 6. *SS-'Nord'*, were arriving on the Western front for the first time:

> Ami artillery had already claimed casualties in our ranks ... in the afternoon heavy fire fell on our assembly area. It seemed as if our new enemy's resources in guns and ammunition were limitless ... they kept on hammering our supply routes, on our march to the front we saw the results; dead horses, destroyed carts and a dead mule-skinner spread-eagled in the middle of the road ... we walked a forest trail and passed a bunker ... a heap of dead bodies next to it, piled up like firewood.

Voss's sister Waffen-SS unit, the *Götz von Berlichingen,* found itself attacking the village of Rimlingen – which it captured – only to find itself struggling to capitalise on that success. The Americans vigorously counter-attacked, capturing the divisional commander Hans Lingner in the process, and inflicting dreadful losses among the SS ranks. As the battle around Rimlingen raged on, Johann Voss and his comrades were beginning to see that the fighting in the West was very different from what they were used to against the Red Army:

> I had seen our new opponents only through my binoculars. On our first day in the line we repelled a probe they had started, inflicting casualties on them. The action hadn't ended when they sent their medics and an ambulance right onto the battlefield to rescue their wounded – I couldn't believe my eyes, what kind of war was this? Nothing like that would have happened on the Eastern front, but here, some of the rules of war seemed to still be in place.

True though this undoubtedly was, it rarely diminished the ferocity of the fighting; von Luck:

> In Rittershoffen we were only twenty yards apart from the Amis. Sometimes we would be in the first floor of a house and they'd be on the ground floor – and vice versa... Both sides used artillery non-stop and flamethrowers... We took prisoners from the 827th U.S. Armoured Battalion,[6] which consisted almost entirely of blacks. They told us that they had instructions to shoot-up or set on fire, any house in which Germans – they said 'Nazis' – were to be found.

Conditions during the fighting were terrible, that winter being one of the coldest in Europe for many years, with frequent snowstorms. Even Johann Voss and his comrades – whose last posting was the far north of Finland – found it difficult: 'We were freezing, our hands shoved deeply in the pockets of our anoraks, caps and shoulders hunched under the hoods of our canvas sheets for protection from the sleet that swept through the forest.'

Nordwind was getting nowhere, but Hitler refused to cancel it – just as in the Ardennes. Instead, on 15 January, he left the *Adlerhorst* and headed to Berlin – he would never leave the capital again. Back at the front, the fighting continued unabated. 'The battle raged on ... their howitzers did not stop firing round after round on our positions ... we dared not imagine the casualties among our comrades, we had never experienced such massive shelling with the Russians.' Voss's 6. '*Nord*' wasn't the only armed SS formation in dire straits in Alsace, as a *1. Armee* report on *17.* '*Götz von Berlichingen*' made clear:

> Poor quality replacements and poor co-ordination between Divisional units... Numerous ethnic Germans from Russia have added to its problems. The Division suffers from being battle-weary after almost non-stop fighting... Strength is about three thousand men in two weak panzer-grenadier regiments ... insufficient ammunition, petrol supplies lower than operationally necessary. Division lacking enough vehicles to be called a panzer-grenadier division.

If anything, the gloom of the report was understating the situation – three days later the combat strength of one of the grenadier battalions was listed as eleven NCOs and thirty-two men, every single officer having been killed.

Von Luck's battle in Rittershoffen ground on remorselessly. 'My regimental doctor came to me angrily and said, "I have up to fifty wounded lying in a cellar in urgent need of medical treatment. I have no morphine left and hardly any dressings. In another cellar I have more than forty dead who can't be buried ... I'm also doing what I can for the civilians."' There was little von Luck could do as his unit was stretched to the limit: 'My orderly officer had to take the ammunition boxes forward to the grenadiers as all my other staff were in action... The dead lay about the streets, among them many civilians ... the cadavers of dead animals stank and infected the air.'

Johann Voss's regiment had surrounded an American battalion of the 157th Infantry Regiment: 'The worst area was on the summit of the hill, where the now-encircled Ami battalion was being pressed back into an ever-smaller perimeter.' Eventually their opponents surrendered:

> The Ami battalion gave up on the fifth day after our regiments attack had begun. That morning they made a last attempt to break out, only to suffer more casualties... They surrendered at the request of our regimental commander ... their losses were terrible – of the original five companies only about 450 men went into captivity, most of them were wounded.

Led through another section of the line into captivity, Voss and his comrades regretted not having the opportunity to congratulate the surviving Americans on their bravery: 'Our comrades behind the hill were forming something of an "honour guard" watching the captured GIs passing through ... all of them were handed a box of Scho-Ka-Kola,[7] a fine gesture by our commander.'

By now, even the Nazi dictator knew nothing more could be gained by *Nordwind,* and, on 25 January it was finally called off.

In terms of casualties, losses weren't far off being even, with the *Westheer* suffering over twenty thousand and the combined American and French lists not being too far below that. *Nordwind* didn't then – and still doesn't now – receive much attention from historians, eclipsed as it has been by the fighting in the Ardennes. However, for the men involved it was a bitter battle fought in dreadful conditions, with frostbite and trench-foot claiming almost as many men as bullets and shrapnel. Hans von Luck – a veteran of every major campaign the Wehrmacht had fought since 1939 – described it as 'one of the hardest and most costly battles that had ever raged on the Western front'.

For Johann Voss, having spent his service on the Eastern front, it was an eye-opener as to the Reich's perilous position. 'Troop movement had become practically impossible by day ... we saw that "Fortress Germany" as it was called in the propaganda, was a bastion without a roof, open and exposed to Allied bombers.' He was pleased to see that his friend Heinrich was still alive though: 'His number two gunner had fallen, shot in the neck when they brought an Ami attack to a stop thirty metres from their holes – the bullet ripped up the carotid artery... I had our medic take a look at my feet, he said I had two frostbitten toes – I was lucky!'

One of Voss's comrades – Bing – was an Alsatian, and it now hit home they were fighting on what had been, at least before, German soil.

Voss: 'You must feel funny coming home under these circumstances. Where is your hometown anyway?'

Bing: 'About twenty-five kilometres from here ... it's a small village.'

Bing then spoke about the fact that some of the troops they were fighting were French. 'If they took me alive, I would be shot right away for treason.' He was killed in action two months later.

The *Westheer* hadn't lost in the Alsace, it was more of a draw, and it wasn't ready to give up the ghost quite yet, as one *landser* made clear: 'Call it loyalty if you have to call it something, have we fought in Lapland, at the Volga, and in Africa just to throw away our weapons the moment the enemy enters the Reich?'

7

Avalanche in the East

On one thing we were all agreed, we didn't want our country to be under the heel of the Russians – after all, we'd seen the 'Soviet Paradise'!

So said one officer from the *SS-Das Reich*, and he might well have been speaking for almost every member of the Wehrmacht, including Andreas Fleischer, an NCO in the *SS-Totenkopf*: 'We had to stop the Russians – that was it – nothing else was as important as that.' His comrade, Herman Van Gyseghem, a fervent Catholic and Flemish Belgian volunteer, thought much the same: 'We'd always been told the choice was Rome or Moscow, and that's why so many of us enlisted, because we chose Rome, and Europe. Now the communists were coming, and if we didn't stop them, they could go all the way to Flanders.' A fellow Flemish nationalist, Dries Coolens, was of the same opinion: 'We respected Ivan as a fighter, he was tough, and didn't stop – just like us – but we shuddered to think what he'd do if we let him get into Europe.' The Dutch volunteer Jan Munk was no Catholic but saw the threat from the East as being very real: 'No soldier who'd fought in Russia could do anything other than want to stop them from getting into Europe – we'd seen what they were like.'

What *were* they like then? Josef 'Sepp' Allerberger, a sniper with *3. Gebirgsjäger-Division,* had fought on the Russian front since the summer of 1943. By late autumn the following year, he and his unit had been driven back into Hungary. He recalled, 'There were many incidents of extreme brutality perpetrated against civilians by Russian soldiers, while the corpses of horribly tortured soldiers became a routine sight.' In one truly dreadful story, he recounted how he found himself viewing the aftermath of the capture of the small town of Nyiregyhaza. Unable to move or open fire, as it would have given his position away, he witnessed the scene as a number of Soviet soldiers found a middle-aged man and a young woman, whom Allerberger believed was his wife, hiding in the ruins. Dragging them out, the man was hit over the head and tied to a streetlamp. The woman – screaming in fear – was thrown over the bonnet of a jeep, where one of the soldiers proceeded to cut her clothes off with a knife. 'Accompanied by the yells of his comrades he penetrated her... In order of rank every single Russian proceeded to rape the helpless woman one after the other as she lay motionless across the jeep... It took almost an hour for the twenty-three of them to finish.'[1] This is the vileness of man laid bare. Not that the *Ostheer* could lay claim to any sort of moral ascendancy – quite the opposite – as one of their number made clear when recorded talking to a fellow POW about how he and his comrades had treated women in Russia: 'I travelled everywhere in a lorry, and all over we saw women doing compulsory labour service... They were employed on road-making – extraordinarily lovely girls; we drove past, simply pulled them into the armoured car, raped them and threw them out again – and did they curse!'[2] This was the grim reality of the Russo-German war; a conflict that seemed to rival Europe's religious wars of the seventeenth century for brutality and sheer horror. Now, the *landser* could see that horror coming to his homeland.

Although for some, their homelands were already lost – men like the Latvian Mintauts Blosfelds, who had joined the Waffen-SS in 1943. Wounded in January 1944, he had returned to action to be issued 'new weapons': 'The light machine-guns were magazine-fed British Bren guns, made in Czechoslovakia, we also had Czech machine-pistols and grenade attachments for our rifles – hardly new.' Soon, the Red Army advanced into the small Baltic state, and Blosfelds realised he was unlikely to be able to go home – although that wasn't the issue that was uppermost in his mind at the time:

> We all have lice and decide to get rid of them. We mix quicksilver with lard and rub our bodies with the paste. The lice begin to leave our clothes straightaway, but in the evening we all feel ill, it's possible we have quicksilver poisoning ... the commanding officer spoke to us and warned us of the consequences of stealing and selling Army equipment.[3]

While some *landsers* like Blosfelds were threatened with military discipline, others, like Gustav Palm, were kept fighting via other – less traditional – means: 'To fortify our nerves, our NCO offered us a special drink ... and saw to it we drank it all. The narcotic drink was supposed to lower our anxiety, but it also made me fuzzy-headed and gave me tunnel-vision ... with our weapons off safety, our little drugged group was ready to go.' Palm soon found the drugs had their limits: 'My steel helmet flew off... I felt a sharp slap on my cheek, blood ran down onto my submachine-gun, which soon became completely red... Then bang! I felt it in my left thigh.' Palm would survive to fight on another day.

The *Leibstandarte* veteran, Erwin Bartmann, summed up his thoughts that new year:

The British and American armies had broken our attack in the Ardennes, and every day brought them closer to the Rhine. Disturbing accounts of rape and brutal mutilation recounted by refugees fleeing East Prussia were spreading like wildfire, and Allied bombers flew over Berlin day in day out. The Third Reich was on its knees.

The refugees Bartmann was talking about were a mix of 'native' Germans from Germany's eastern provinces – the so-called *Reichsdeutsche* – and 'ethnic' Germans – *volksdeutsche* – from half a dozen expat German communities spread out over eastern and south-eastern Europe. Often used by Hitler to justify his pre-war territorial demands and hoped-for expansion to the east, those *volksdeutsche* had been used as fertile recruiting grounds for the armed SS in particular during the war so far. Once the tide of battle turned against the Nazis, conscription was brought in, and then enforced call-ups. The large ethnic German communities in Hungary were some of the first to be drained of men. The Danube Swabians, for example, were the descendants of German settlers invited by the Hungarian monarchy to work and live in the valley of the River Danube as far back as the twelfth century. Calling themselves the *Schwowe,* there were as many as two million of them before the war. Several thousand voluntarily enlisted after the invasion of the Soviet Union, but in August 1944 conscription was introduced for all males between the ages of seventeen and fifty. Eighty thousand men were called up, and two entire new Waffen-SS divisions were formed: the *18. SS-Freiwilligen Panzergrenadier-Division 'Horst Wessel'*, and the *22. SS-Freiwilligen Kavallerie-Division 'Maria Theresia'*. The next Germanic region to be targeted was the *Banat*, also known as the *Bačka (Batschka)*, between the Danube and Tisza (*Theiss*) rivers. Thousands of men appeared at the call-up centres, and the *31. SS-Freiwilligen-Grenadier-Division* was formed under the command of Gustav Lombard – an American-educated Brandenburger and friend of the *Leibstandarte*'s Jochen Peiper. With the Red Army advancing and the Western front near collapse, the new recruits could be forgiven for finding chaos as they turned up: 'I volunteered for service in the Honvéd ... for a field artillery unit in Szeged. However, a few days later we ethnic Germans were singled out and sent home, where we were drafted into the Waffen-SS ... we were issued uniforms, tattooed, sworn in and assigned.' Josef Gratwohl was another willing recruit:

> I was inducted in Baja on 14 September... I was assigned to an infantry company as adjutant to the company commander, Obersturmführer Alfred Berger ... he was Sudeten German [from the Czech Sudetenland border region] and a very fine fellow. He had seen action in Finland with the 6. SS-Nord ... our NCOs were actually only NCO candidates, and were all ethnic Germans from Croatia. They spoke Croatian among themselves and were really rough fellows.

One of those NCOs – *SS-Rottenführer* Bennert – recalled the problems that arose from having new recruits who were perhaps not the élite of the élite:

> There was a great shortage of uniform tunics and belts in the required sizes for men of larger girth. So, from two belts one was made. Because of the tunic shortage the men wore overcoats which was very unpleasant in the heat. The train that was bringing the new uniforms was attacked by enemy aircraft and the car carrying the caps received a direct hit, so the men had to wear their steel helmets even off duty. Boots were in short supply too and some of the recruits had to shuffle around in slippers, the preferred footwear of local civilians.[4]

With little time to train, and equipment so scarce, the new unit struggled to get itself into any sort of shape. Then, with the Red Army resolutely advancing, the Germans were forced to abandon the *Batschka,* and all of a sudden the men had lost their homeland as their families either became refugees or stayed put and prepared to weather the Soviet storm. Little wonder then that when the division went into action in November, things went awry from the start, as one grenadier recounted:

> The situation was bloody awful ... things looked bad with the ammunition, we only had two hundred rounds for the machine-gun, so the order was given to let the Soviets come within fifty metres of us and only then open fire... Soviet aircraft had dropped incendiary bombs ... we were only just able to slip away out of the town through the gypsy quarter and so escape being encircled. But many men from my Kompanie remained there, many men from my home village.

By the end of the month the division was shattered.

Centuries-old ethnic German communities were under threat, as a Red Army that had seen for itself the horrors the Nazis had visited on their own lands came ever closer. Alfred Divisch saw what that meant when he returned to his home after it was sacked by advancing Russian soldiers. Almost everything of value had been stolen, all the remaining furniture had been smashed and the soldiers had urinated and defecated everywhere. He found a note from a Soviet officer hidden in a music book by the wrecked piano: 'Don't conclude, from the destruction here, that the Soviet people have an evil nature and no culture – everything that is happening here is for revenge.'[5]

Divisch joined the throng of refugees fleeing west, as the land emptied of its people. And those throngs were huge; the ethnic German population of central and eastern Europe numbered over ten million, with three and a half million in Czechoslovakia, over one million in Poland, eight hundred thousand in Romania, seven hundred thousand in Yugoslavia, and almost a quarter of a million in the Baltic states. The decision of the Big Three of Stalin, Roosevelt and Churchill, that Germany east of the River Oder would cease to exist after the war – as the lands would be given to Poland to compensate for territory it would lose to the Soviet Union – instigated the largest shift of European peoples in a millennium. Sixteen million east Germans were condemned to becoming refugees. Often refused permission to head west by local Nazi officials, they were then abandoned by those self-same officials who only sought to save their own skins and whatever loot they could carry with them as the Red Army got closer. Finally taking to the roads, the danger they were exposed to was horrific, as the Luftwaffe fighter pilot, Norbert Hannig, saw for himself as he helped escort a flight of Stuka dive-bombers attempting to attack a column of Soviet tanks near Gumbinnen on the East Prussian/ Lithuanian border:

> The Soviets took evasive action, churning tracks sent up flurries of snow as they charged straight into the refugee column packed tightly on the road. Panic broke out. Horses bolted, wagons overturned, people ran into the open fields. The Stukas circled helplessly as the enemy tanks used the refugees as a living shield. The snow was stained red where they ploughed over man and beast ... the attack was called off, it would only add to the carnage.

Other eyewitnesses described what happened to some poor souls fleeing Upper Silesia: 'On the road were lying a column of refugees several kilometres long, shot-up and bloodily squashed and flattened in the ditches by tanks.'[6] Gustav Palm found the scenes heart-breaking:

> To see small children cut to shreds with bomb splinters protruding from their bodies, women in bloody clothes, and horses dying in pools of their own blood, was horrifying. People stood in the ruins of their

burnt-out homes, their clothing in rags ... everywhere there was panic, shattered carts, dead animals, screaming children and the anguished cries of parents... My feelings had long since been dulled at the sight of maimed and dead soldiers, but to see a bloodied child crying over his dead mother was even now a heart-wrenching experience.

Werner Block thought the same:

The roads were full of refugees, totally full, pushing or pulling little carts, the lucky ones with horses and a wagon, all of them piled high with their possessions. We had to move them out of the way so we could get by – a Tiger takes up a lot of room you see – and they would plead for us to take them with us, I remember one woman holding a young child up towards us begging to take him or her to safety, but we couldn't of course. We were still fighting and couldn't look after a child. It was dreadful to see – afterwards we didn't talk about it, we just wanted to pretend it hadn't happened.

By the end of the war some eight million Germans had already fled the east – with approximately six hundred thousand dying in the attempt, and another million 'missing presumed dead'. The survivors would be joined by a further eight million in the years after the war as newly established governments forcibly evicted citizens they now saw as collaborators and traitors.

The Germany they were fleeing to was increasingly threadbare, as the very fabric of the country and society was burnt through by the war. By September 1944, some six hundred thousand tons of bombs had already been dropped on the Third Reich by the Anglo-Americans, killing over one hundred thousand people, injuring several times that number, and rendering three million homeless. Industrial production in Britain and the United States was now churning out far more bombers than the decimated ranks of *Luftflotte Reich* could shoot down, swelling Harris's strategic fleet to some fifteen hundred, and the American force, plus escorts, to a mind-boggling seven thousand. From now on, the bombing would significantly increase, with sixty per cent of the total tonnage dropped in the war falling in its last seven months – an astonishing eight hundred thousand tons – killing an additional quarter of a million people and making another four million homeless. Karin Busch was a schoolgirl at the time: 'At about half past nine I was sitting, sewing a bag for a friend, when I heard a roaring noise... Then hell broke loose, it was terrible, truly terrible.' Forced to abandon her shelter due to an unexploded bomb, Busch ran for safety:

Outside I was hit by an inferno of wind and fire, it was like looking into a huge burning oven. I saw my twin brother sitting down and holding his eyes, he couldn't see ... he had lost his sight from the heat, one eye later recovered, but the other didn't... There were bodies everywhere, and the gasmasks that people were wearing were melting into their faces ... we went back to the cellar where we had first taken shelter. Inside I saw a pile of ash in the shape of a person... I didn't know who it was but then I saw a pair of earrings in the ash. I knew those earrings – it was my mother.

For the survivors, life was grim. With the transportation system – especially the railways – severely disrupted, coal lay stacked up at the pit-heads while civilians froze in their unheated homes. Clothes were now nigh on impossible to buy, so shirts, trousers, shoes and coats became worn-out and patched. Night after night the air raid sirens would go off, and the tired and dishevelled masses would head underground for another night. Food was even more scarce than clothes or a good night's rest, with the bread ration slashed by more than half to 900 grams, meat by two-thirds to 137 grams, and fats to a miserly 75 grams. The black market was rife. People in the cities especially were noticeably getting thinner and thinner.

The impact of the bombing was visible to all – except perhaps Hitler himself who tried his best not to see it – and it undoubtedly badly damaged the Nazi war effort. It also forced the Wehrmacht into a number of actions it otherwise wouldn't have contemplated; the huge diversion of resources to manufacture and man thousands of anti-aircraft batteries and the prioritisation for the *jagdwaffe* of defending the Reich, to name but two – however, just how much the bombing campaign achieved has been the subject of huge controversy ever since. This in no way diminishes the bravery of the tens of thousands of young men who took part in it and often lost their lives – far from it. But it is important to reflect on its effects and the suffering caused to the civilian population in particular. Take for example the German U-boat industry. By 1944, the battle of the Atlantic had been comprehensively lost by the Kriegsmarine; the German surface fleet was either sunk or bottled up in Norway, and improved Allied tactics and equipment had defeated the submarine threat and sent the cream of Karl Dönitz's wolf packs to the bottom of the sea.

The key to reviving German fortunes – as Dönitz saw it – was technology. It had long been understood that U-boats were most at risk when on the surface – something they had to do to vent the exhaust gases from their turbines. Showing up on Allied radar, surface ships or aircraft would home in and destroy them before they could find safety in the depths. The Germans had now come up with a solution; the *Schnorchel*. This device was pretty much what you would expect, a snorkel that could be raised while the submarine was underwater, breach the surface and vent the boat, all while remaining safe under the waves, and with a radar signature too small to locate. *Schnorchels* were integral to a new series of bigger, faster boats, designed to be able to hunt down Allied shipping while staying hidden, and then wreaking havoc with a new generation of *Lut* torpedoes, capable of homing in on propeller noise. This would enable the U-boats to simply get within range of a convoy and fire off a fan-like spread of torpedoes that would automatically search out their prey and blow it to pieces. The new boats were christened *Type XXI* and *Type XXIII*, and orders were placed in mid-1944 for 360 of the former and 208 of the latter. The difference in performance between what the Kriegsmarine had -- the 'workhorse' of the U-boat arm was the *Type VII* with 709 built in total – and the new designs was dramatic. For example, the *Type VII* could teach a speed of about seven knots submerged – nowhere near fast enough to enable it to chase down a convoy while underwater – while the *Type XXI* could do seventeen knots, and the *XXIII* an unbelievable 25-plus. If produced in large numbers, these U-boats could still cause enormous damage to the Allied war effort in late '44 and early '45. The Allies had an advantage though; Germany only had a few yards where U-boats could be built, and a typical boat took twelve months to complete – admittedly this was down from twenty months at the war's beginning. The Anglo-American air forces could, therefore, throw an enormous bomb-shaped spanner into the works. However, when the Allied campaign was at its height in 1944, some 234 U-boats were built – this was only four fewer than in 1942 when the bombing was in its infancy. In fact, the highest ever monthly production total was achieved in December 1944, when no fewer than thirty-one submarines rolled off the lines.[7] One young shipyard worker remembers that time:

We lived near the border, near Christiansfeld [Denmark] and we from the German minority were asked to join a youth organisation, like the Hitler Youth, almost the same. We were told they met every Saturday, but my brother and I thought they just made loud speeches all the time. Then when I was fifteen in 1941 I got a job in Germany, in Flensburg, as an apprentice blacksmith. I was working in the dockyard there, where they built U-boats for the Kriegsmarine. Narrow things they were those U-boats, no room inside, I didn't like the idea of being in one of those things, not one bit... Yes, we were bombed, but not much, it was more of a nuisance really. The air raid siren would go off and we'd go into the shelters and then come out when it was all over. Sometimes we'd see a few craters, or a building that had been hit, but not that much. Then in 1943 I volunteered for the Waffen-SS – I definitely didn't want to go to sea in a U-boat that's for sure.

The impact on the U-boat industry might not have been what was wished by the Allied planners, but elsewhere in Germany's cities the effects were profound, as the massive numbers of internal refugees testified. The masses fleeing the East tended to head towards relatives first and foremost to try and find somewhere to live, but even there Nazi bureaucracy caught up with them and herded their teenaged sons into uniform as the conscription age was dropped once more, and those boys born in 1928 were called up. By a directive promulgated on 5 March, it would be reduced to the class of 1929.

Those youngsters would find themselves drafted into yet another army reorganisation, with the creation of the *M1945 Divisionen*. Simply a smaller unit than its predecessors, the new formations had five hundred fewer Germans on establishment – 10,728 compared to 11,211 – with almost the same number of *Hiwis* (*Hilfswillige* – 'willing helpers', mainly ex-Soviet POWs who'd volunteered to serve the Wehrmacht), at over six hundred. In reality, most divisions struggled to reach even this new, lower, figure.

By now, the noose was tightening around the Reich. Greece had been abandoned, as had most of Yugoslavia up to the Croatian capital, Zagreb. Eastern Hungary was also gone, and by Christmas Eve, Budapest itself was besieged. While this endangered Austria's eastern border, the real threat was over three hundred miles to the north, on the River Vistula in Poland.

The land lying west of the Vistula is the rolling north German plain of rich farms and prosperous towns, with no natural barriers of any real significance before the River Oder, just forty-five miles from Berlin itself. For three months the front had been quiet. The Soviets had focused on the south, and had now liberated – or occupied, depending on your point of view – most of eastern Europe and the Balkans. With Hitler's eyes firmly fixed on the Western front and the Ardennes, the Soviets had gone about building a force capable of staving in the German line and advancing all the way to the Oder in one single push. Now, at the beginning of January 1945, Moscow had massed no fewer than 160 divisions ready to attack. Almost two and a quarter million men, with seven thousand tanks, and fourteen thousand guns, supported by five thousand aircraft, would smash into the 450,000 men of *Generaloberst* Josef Harpe's *Heeresgruppe A*. Harpe's outnumbered divisions could call on just over four thousand guns and fewer than twelve hundred panzers, with only five of the *Ostheer's* seventeen panzer divisions positioned on the Vistula front. Warning after warning was given to Hitler about the impending attack, but just like Stalin back in June 1941, he refused to believe it, preferring his own fantasies instead. Heinz Guderian – Chief of Staff at *OKH* (*Oberkommando des Heeres*, Army High Command) and the man tasked with advising Hitler on the Eastern front – was clear:

> We calculated that the attack would begin on 12 January. The Russians' superiority was 11:1 in infantry, 7:1 in panzers, 20:1 in guns. An evaluation of the enemy's total strength give him a superiority of approximately 15:1 on the ground and 20:1 in the air, and this estimate didn't err on the side of exaggeration … the individual qualities of the German soldier, when well-led, more than compensated for such numerical superiority, but now, after five years of intensive fighting, with ever-diminishing supplies, weapons and above all decreasing hope of victory, the burden put upon him was indescribably heavy.[8]

This cut little ice with Hitler, who even went so far as declaring 'Who's responsible for producing all this rubbish? It's the greatest bluff since Genghis Khan!' Guderian wrote that this was 'Ostrich politics … combined with ostrich strategy'. To answer the dictator's question, the author was Reinhard Gehlen, intelligence head of *Fremde Heere Ost (FHO)* – Enemy Armies East, and while Gehlen was largely proven right by the subsequent Soviet offensive, there is more to this than some historians have explored since the war. Hitler's outburst has been oft-quoted as a clear demonstration of his irrational behaviour and pig-headed refusal to believe anything but his own delusions – and there is truth in that – however, against that view must be weighed the performance of Gehlen and the *FHO* in the war so far, which was poor to say the least – in fact, German intelligence in the East was a gigantic failure from the very beginning. Their initial estimates of Red Army strength proved woefully under-cooked; the Chief of the Army General Staff in 1941, Franz Halder, wrote in his diary, 'At the outset we reckoned on about two hundred enemy divisions … we have already counted 360 … if we smash a dozen of them, the Russians simply put up another dozen.' The *FHO* then failed to discover the movement of Stalin's Far Eastern forces from Siberia to carry out the December counter-offensive in front of Moscow – an event that signalled the defeat of *Barbarossa*. It then proceeded to miss the impending counter-offensive at Stalingrad in November 1942, before badly underestimating Soviet defences at Kursk the following summer, and then stating the Soviet summer assault in 1944 would be targeted in Ukraine and not Belarus. It is something of a struggle to find evidence of German intelligence success at any of the critical junctures of the Russo-German war. Given this background it is perhaps easier to understand Hitler's resistance to the advice given. The irony that at this point it was actually accurate would weigh heavily on the *landsers* of the *Ostheer*.

Oh the glory! Major-General Allan Adair – commander of the British Guards Armoured Division – salutes the cheering crowds from the turret of his Cromwell tank as he and his men liberate Brussels on 4 September 1944. (Author's collection)

With Antwerp's liberation, thousands of Germans march into captivity. (Author's collection)

Romania's Columbia Aquila refinery burning after being bombed by the USAAF. Ploesti's oilfields were vital to Nazi Germany's war effort and their loss at the end of August was a disaster for Berlin. (Author's collection)

Above left: Convalescing Flemish Waffen-SS volunteers wounded in the fighting on the Russian front, contemplate their future at a parade in Brussels. Many of these men would fight to the bitter end. (Author's collection)

Above right: The German military miracle of September 1944 was led by experienced officers like Friedrich *Freiherr* von der Heydte. The highly decorated *fallschirmjäger* would go on to command a scratch battlegroup during the Ardennes offensive. (Author's collection)

Above left: Belgium 1944; the *Spiess* – or chief supply NCO – of Herbert Rink's panzergrenadier company from the *SS-Leibstandarte*. Men like this worked minor wonders in re-equipping their units after the debacle in France. (Author's collection)

Above right: An artillery observer from the *17. SS-Panzergrenadier-Division, Götz von Berlichingen* waiting to call down fire on the advancing Americans near Metz in October 1944. The *Götz von Berlichingen* was the only Waffen-SS division to spend its entire wartime career on the Western front. (Courtesy of Jimmy McLeod)

Above left: A German *volksgrenadier* keeps watch on the *Westwall* near the city of Metz in October 1944. He is armed with a *Panzerschreck* – the German copy of America's famed bazooka. His decorations include the Iron Cross, the Infantry Assault Badge, the Wound Badge and the Close Combat Clasp. (Courtesy of Bundesarchiv Bild 183-J28180)

Above right: *SS-Standartenführer* Ernst Kemper – late of the *SS-Wiking* and nominated as the commander of Metz by Heinrich Himmler; he was superseded by Walther Krause of *462. Volks-Grenadier Division*, who set about preparing the city's defences. (Author's collection)

Above left: German *volksgrenadiers* advancing near the city of Aachen. Fighting for the city was fierce. (Courtesy of Bundesarchiv Bild 183-J28344)

Above right: Aachen in 1945. One of Germany's most beautiful cities, it was reduced to rubble by Allied bombing and bitter house-to-house fighting. (Author's collection).

A German infantry cannon provides supporting fire in the Hürtgenwald in 1945. (Courtesy of Bundesarchiv Bild 183-J28303)

Above left: Rudolf von Ribbentrop, son of Nazi Germany's Foreign Minister, Joachim von Ribbentrop, fought in the Ardennes in the *12. SS-Panzer-division*, 'Hitlerjugend'. (Courtesy of Rudolf von Ribbentrop)

Above middle: The commanding officer of *2. Panzerdivision* Meinrad von Lauchert. His division would advance the furthest of any German unit during the Ardennes offensive. (Author's collection)

Above right: *Major* Ernst von Cochenhausen of *2. Panzerdivision*. His *kampfgruppe* was formed around *Panzergrenadier-Regiment 304*, reinforced with a battalion of *Panzer-Regiment 3*, all the divisional artillery and most of its anti-aircraft guns. It would be stopped a few miles short of the River Meuse during the Ardennes offensive. (Author's collection)

German *volksgrenadiers* advance through woodland during the first days of the Ardennes offensive. The grenadier in the front centre is armed with the first-ever true assault rifle; the *Sturmgewehr 44*. (Courtesy of Bundesarchiv Bild 183-1985-0104-501)

Trent Park Camp in north London November 1944. Senior Axis officers captured by the Allies in Europe were sent there and secretly recorded discussing the German war effort. Back row, standing, from left: *General der Infanterie* Dietrich von Choltitz, *Oberst* Gerhard Wilck, *General der Fallschirmtruppe* Hermann-Bernhard Ramcke, *Generalmajor* Kurt Eberding, *Oberst* Eberhard Wildermuth. Front row, sitting, from left: *Generalleutnant* Rüdiger von Heyking (Luftwaffe), *Generalleutnant* Wilhelm von Schlieben, *Generalleutnant* Wilhelm Daser. (Courtesy of Bundesarchiv Bild 146-2005-0136)

SS-Obersturmführer Alfred Hargesheimer (on left), Panther company commander in *2. SS-Panzerdivision 'Das Reich'* in a captured American Willys Jeep near Bad Ems in late autumn 1944. Hargesheimer would later use this Jeep in the Ardennes offensive. (Courtesy of Jimmy McLeod)

Above left: *Königstiger 213* of *KG Peiper*. Abandoned by Peiper as his unit was forced to retreat on foot, it still stands in the village of La Gleize outside the museum dedicated to the Ardennes battle. (Author's collection)

Above right: The Baltic German aristocrat and panzer ace, *Leutnant* Richard Wilfred Harry Erich *Freiherr* von Rosen. A company commander in *schwere Panzerabteilung 503*, Von Rosen would spend most of the final months of the war fighting in Hungary against the Red Army. (Author's collection)

Above left: *Königstiger 323*, of Von Rosen's company, in Budapest, in late October 1944. Their presence was used to intimidate Budapest into sticking with the Third Reich as the Red Army approached. (Author's collection)

Above right: *Marshall* Károly Beregfy (third from left in glasses) visits positions of Joachim Rumohr's ethnic German *8. SS-Kavallerie-Division 'Florian Geyer'* near Budapest. Beregfy served as Minister of Defence in the 1944–45 Hungarian Arrow Cross Party Government, having been dismissed from field command for military incompetence in April 1944. Arrested by the Americans in late April 1945, he was handed over to Hungary's communists, tried, convicted and hanged on 12 March 1946. (Author's collection)

Below: In the aftermath of the Allied bombing of Dresden in February 1945, recovery teams gather up the bodies of victims in the Altmarkt Square to stack them in pyres ready for burning. (Author's collection)

The Courland pocket, November 1944. The crew of a German assault-gun pose for a photo. Seated on the StuG is the Austrian Knight's Cross winner *Hauptmann* Sepp Brandner. (Courtesy of Jimmy McLeod.)

As the Red Army relentlessly drove the *Ostheer* back towards the borders of the Reich, everything was thrown into the fighting, including these young Estonian Waffen-SS volunteers – most would not survive. (Author's collection)

Above left: The Flemish Waffen-SS man Theo D'Oosterlinck, who spent the war fighting the Red Army on the Russian front. (Author's collection)

Above right: The Flemish Waffen-SS trooper, Herman van Gyseghem: 'We'd always been told the choice was Rome or Moscow, and that's why so many of us enlisted, because we chose Rome, and Europe. Now the communists were coming, and if we didn't stop them, they could go all the way to Flanders.' (Author's collection)

Above left: Wounded SS men pose while convalescing. Standing with the crutch is the Flemish Waffen-SS volunteer, Oswald van Ooteghem. Van Ooteghem would later become a senator in the Belgian parliament. (Author's collection)

Above right: Jan Munk, from Leiden in the Netherlands, enlisted in the *SS-Panzergrenadierregiment 10 'Westland'*, which was established for recruits from the Netherlands and Flanders. (Author's collection)

Above left: Andreas Fleischer was an ethnic German from Denmark who served with the *3. SS-Panzer-division 'Totenkopf'* during the fighting in Hungary in early 1945. (Author's collection)

Above middle: Having fought in northern Russia and Courland against the Red Army, the Norwegian SS man Bjørn Lindstad deserted one day before the war ended. (Author's collection)

Above right: The young Danish SS volunteer, Ivar Corneliussen, lost his left eye fighting the Red Army on the River Dnieper, before taking part in the attempt to relieve the besieged Budapest garrison in 1945. (Author's collection)

A senior NCO of the German Army's élite *Panzergrenadier-Division 'Grossdeutschland'* instructs elderly *Volkssturm* recruits on the MG42 – the feared *Spandau* – somewhere in East Prussia, October 1944. (Author's collection)

An elderly *Volkssturm* militiaman fires a panzerfaust during his hurried training in the spring of 1945. Lacking equipment, more than 100,000 *Volkssturm* members were killed in action in the last few months of the war. (Courtesy of Bundesarchiv Bild 183-J31390)

Above left: Portrait of Ernst Tiburzy after winning the Knight's Cross as a *Volkssturm* commander. In February 1945 he was seriously wounded while defending his native city of Königsberg. The 34-year-old stayed at his post and personally knocked out five T-34 tanks with *panzerfausts* before leading his men in a counter-attack that pushed the Soviets back. He also shot one of his own platoon commanders for running away. (Author's collection)

Above right: *Hauptmann* Willi Bratge was commander of the makeshift defence of the town of Remagen and its famed Ludendorff bridge as the Americans approached in early March 1945. After the war he became a teacher in the town. (Author's collection)

Above left: *Major* Johannes Scheller, with his daughter. Dispatched by headquarters to Remagen to help ensure the bridge was destroyed, he arrived too late to ensure the job was done – the Allies were over the Rhine and into the heart of the Third Reich. (Author's collection)

Above middle: *Oberstleutnant* Karl Thieme led his *kampfgruppe* from *11. Panzerdivision* in furious counter-attacks to try to retake the Ludendorff bridge at Remagen after its capture by the Americans. For his leadership he was awarded the Swords to his Knight's Cross, but there was nothing he could do to stop the American surge. (Courtesy of Jimmy McLeod)

Above right: A portrait of the young Luftwaffe *jagdflieger* Heinz Knoke. Having scored 52 kills, Knoke would finish the war in hospital after having been blown up by the Czech resistance. (Author's collection)

The city of Wesel – objective for Montgomery's assault crossing of the Rhine in March 1945. Flattened by Allied bombing, some 97 per cent of the city was destroyed, with its pre-war population of 25,000 dropping to just 1,900 by May 1945. (Courtesy of the United States National Archives and Records Administration, NARA)

Above left: *SS-Obergruppenführer* Hans-Adolf Prützmann (right) would end the war commanding the Nazi *Werwolf* resistance organisation. In this picture – taken in September 1942 in Ukraine – he is meeting his boss, *Reichsführer-SS* Heinrich Himmler during a visit to the *SS-Wiking*. (Courtesy of the United States Holocaust Memorial Museum)

Above right: A *Jagdpanther* tank destroyer from *Panzergruppe Hudel* lies abandoned after being knocked out by an American M36 tank destroyer on 13 March 1945 near Kaimeg-Ginsterhain, Germany. (Author's collection)

Hamburg was bombed over seventy times during the war and virtually destroyed. British officials called it the 'Hiroshima of Germany'. (Courtesy of John Bathgate via Jimmy McLeod)

Berlin's last-ditch defenders included Frenchmen, Norwegians, Swedes and Danes; some of these Danish SS men (pictured in northern Russia) would be among them as they fought to protect the city. (Author's collection)

Above left: The mutilated bodies of the Italian fascist dictator Benito Mussolini and his mistress Clara Pettaci after their execution by Italian communist partisans on 28 April 1945. (Author's collection)

Above right: *SS-Oberscharführer* Rochus Misch was transferred to Hitler's bodyguard after being seriously wounded in the invasion of Poland in 1939. After helping to burn Adolf and Eva Hitler's bodies following their suicide, he ended up running a small painting and decorating shop in Berlin after the war. This photo was taken in 1944 at Hitler's Rastenburg headquarters in East Prussia. (Courtesy of Jimmy McLeod)

One of the last photos taken of the Nazi dictator on his fifty-sixth birthday on 20 April 1945. As the Red Army closed in, he left the bunker to congratulate teenaged Hitler Youth members in the Chancellery garden, many of whom had received bravery awards for fighting the Soviets. Hitler is shaking hands with sixteen-year-old Wilhelm Hübner. (Courtesy of Jimmy McLeod)

Wageningen, the Netherlands. *Generaloberst* Johannes Blaskowitz (right centre) surrenders the remaining German armed forces in the country on 5 May 1945 to Lieutenant-General Charles Foulkes (left centre), GOC 1st Canadian Corps. Acquitted of war crimes, Blaskowitz would inexplicably commit suicide in Allied captivity. (Courtesy of Library and Archives Canada/PA-138588)

Werner Block served as a Tiger tank driver on the Russian front. He christened his Tiger '*Leo*' and credited it with saving his life on multiple occasions due to its extremely thick armour. (Author's collection)

Surviving the war, Ivar Corneliussen served in the merchant navy before retiring to rural Denmark. He passed away in 2018. (Author's collection)

Above: The former *SS-Totenkopf* NCO Andreas Fleischer lives quietly in retirement in southern Denmark. (Author's collection)

Right: The ex-SS trooper Bjørn Lindstad stands next to a homemade Viking carving in his log cabin hidden away deep in the Norwegian forests. (Author's collection)

Many surviving Wehrmacht veterans clubbed together after the war to support and reminisce with old comrades. These are the last remaining members of the Flemish *Sneyssens* group; standing at rear, left to right; Oswald Van Ooteghem, Herman van Gyseghem (now deceased); sitting, front, left to right: Theo D'Oosterlinck, Lucie Lefever (Flemish volunteer nurse in the German Red Cross). (Author's collection)

The Dutch SS volunteer Jan Munk refused to needlessly sacrifice his teenaged charges from the Hitler Youth in 1945. He ended up marrying an English girl, Mauveen. They lived in south-west England until he passed away in 2010. (Author's collection)

As it was, that twenty to one advantage in guns came into its own on the morning of 12 January, when the Soviets unleashed their offensive with a crushing bombardment that lasted for over an hour, before the assault was begun by penal battalions composed of men convicted of crimes against military justice. Treated as cannon-fodder, these poor souls were massed as human waves and literally driven onto the German guns by pistol-waving commissars, who only too readily shot any who faltered or fell back. A Hungarian officer who had witnessed the same sort of attack in his homeland described the scene:

> The so-called Russian penal battalions attacked our positions ... the attack collapsed after a little while with huge losses. Hundreds of dying and wounded were lying in front of our positions. We could hear shouts of 'Bozhe Moi!' ['My God'], together with loud – but weakening – calls for help. Our stretcher-bearers tried to bring them in, but each time they were rewarded with machine-gun fire. These men simply had to die. We were unable to help them.

Tricked into thinking this was the main attack, troops from the main German defensive line – which, at Hitler's insistence was far too close to the outpost line – moved forward, only to be engulfed by another two hours of artillery deluge. Casualties among German artillery and infantry units were colossal; sixty per cent of the former and a quarter of the latter were killed or wounded. A battalion commander in *Generalleutnant* Paul Scheuerpflug's experienced *68. ID* was left reeling by the bombardment: 'I began the operation with an under-strength battalion ... after the smoke of the Soviet preparation cleared I had only a platoon of combat-effective soldiers left.' One officer – asked what was happening at the front – exclaimed: 'Front! Front! That's over. I'm the only one left from my Kompanie, the others are all gone. The whole regiment – all gone. I got into the woods and ran... Ivan will be here in a few hours.'

With *Nordwind* and the Ardennes fighting both continuing, the Wehrmacht's cupboard was almost bare as it frantically tried to find some reinforcements to send to the fracturing front. In the end two panzer and four infantry divisions were scraped together and pitched into the maelstrom; to little avail. Hitler played to type, and with a flick of a pen created a gaggle of *Festungen* that he ordered to act as breakwaters against the Soviet onrush. They included Breslau (now Wrocław), Danzig (now Gdansk), Gotenhafen (now Gdynia), Stettin (now Szczecin), Swinemünde (now Świnoujście), Kolberg (now Kołobrzeg), Küstrin (now Kostrzyn nad Odrą), Posen (now Poznań), and Frankfurt-an-der-Oder – still a German city, now sitting on the border with Poland.

This tactic had worked superbly in the winter of 1941–42 in front of Moscow, as *Heeresgruppe Mitte* came perilously close to disintegration; but this was three years later, and the Red Army was a very different beast – as was the *Ostheer*. Now, all this order did was fix German units in place and rob them of the mobility that might – possibly – have allowed them to avoid destruction. Bruno Friesen, a Canadian of German descent, was a gunner in a *Jagdpanzer IV* that January: 'Prussia was bitterly cold – 'Eastern cold' – in the winter, and the Jagdpanzer had no heating ... our billets were cold too, never a mattress, perhaps a bit of straw, a jacket in lieu of a blanket, for months I had cold sores above my upper lip.'

Thrown into the fighting on 15 January, Friesen and his unit found themselves counter-attacking near Bischofswerder. 'When our Jagdpanzer rounded a bend in a sideroad I was surprised to see a Soviet soldier running obliquely across the snow-covered road ... on his shoulder a single shell – were we close to an anti-tank barrier?... We hurriedly withdrew.' Part of a well-trained crew – Friesen was serving in Rommel's old command, 7. *Panzer,* the 'Ghost Division' – the Germans made a diversion and came up on the Russians flank and 'shot two 7.62cm anti-tank guns and their crews all to hell'. Advancing to the next village, Friesen and his comrades faced another challenge:

> Instead of anti-tank guns, there were Soviet soldiers standing around, at least two dozen of them ... we ordered them to stand with their hands clasped behind their heads in front of the largest shack in the hamlet ... those fellows knew better than to try to outdraw our MG42s... The Soviets were lucky – they were being treated humanely at a time when both sides disliked taking prisoners.[9]

The next day, Friesen and his unit took on a column of Soviets: 'Our fire did away with two T-34/85s, and our MG42s firing lots of tracer bullets caused the Soviets to scramble out of the two targeted trucks.' They next found themselves facing an SU-85 tank destroyer:

> I called Feldwebel Starke, our crew commander... he got aboard fast... I calculated the range, 600 metres... We would use armour-piercing ... it would be best for me to get our first round to hit the front of it dead centre... I pulled the trigger, firing the electric fuse of the shell in the breech... Immediately I saw a flash on the SU-85s frontal glacis, indicating a hit. I quickly let it have another ... the thing didn't seem to be burning, maybe some of the crew were still alive. There, at last, the smoke of burning diesel fuel, confirmation of its destruction.

Such successes were not enough for *Heeresgruppe A* that January, and within a few days, a hole 350 miles wide had been torn in the German line. Soviet tank armies rolled forward to exploit the situation and began to motor towards the River Oder. Army-strength formations also hooked north to the Baltic – cutting off dozens of German units, and towns and cities on the coast, including Danzig, Kolberg and Königsberg (now Russian Kaliningrad). One of those cut off in Kolberg was the French volunteer, *Unterscharführer* André Bayle of the *SS-Charlemagne*:

> What strikes me is the extraordinary beating of the artillery, of the rocket launchers and the aircraft, but also the masses of infantry, their acrobatic agility to heave themselves onto roofs, their automatic weapons which they fire in excess without a thought to the ammunition they use, and the snipers who take aim with great precision without being seen… We hopelessly resist, first from house to house, then from ruin to ruin, and finally from cellar to cellar, day and night, without respite.[10]

In their second *Jagdpanzer IV* – the first having had its gun mounting wrecked in an accident – Friesen and his crew mounted an ambush near the village of Lessen. Four T34/85s and two Stalin IIs came into view.

Crew commander (CC) *Feldwebel* Starke: 'When the time comes, give the lead vehicle a solid punch – fire at will.'

Gunner Bruno Friesen (BF): 'I already have the first T-34 in my reticule. Lead correct… Fire!'

CC: 'Direct hit low in the turret! Next, knock out the first Stalin … drive one into his superstructure, directly below his turret.'

BF: 'Hold six o'clock. Fire!'

CC: 'Direct hit on the superstructure! There's smoke rising out of his paunch!'

The other two tanks were swiftly dealt with, and the victorious panzer-men headed west. Unfortunately for them they blundered into a minefield, along with the other two vehicles of their troop. Luckily, only the tracks were smashed. However, the crews had no choice, they would have to abandon their *jagdpanzers* and head off on foot after first wrecking their precious tank destroyers. 'Each gunner waited until his buddies were close to the thickets away from the field, then they pulled the igniter of their one-kilo demolition charges and ran for it.'[11]

The Soviet offensive didn't only head west to the Oder and north to the Baltic, it also sliced to the southwest and the prize of Silesia. If the Ruhr was the Koh-I-Noor diamond in Germany's industrial crown, then Silesia was its Cullinan. Owned by the Habsburgs since the 1500s, it had been part of Prussia for two hundred years. Touched early by the industrial revolution, its abundant mineral resources had made it a cornerstone of German economic might ever since its first furnaces had been lit. By 1944 it was producing ninety-five million tons of coal and 2.4 million tons of steel per year, as well as two-thirds of Germany's zinc; vital for the manufacture of brass shell and bullet casings. The United Foundry at Kattowitz (modern-day Katowice) built most of the Wehrmacht's famed and feared '88s', and even the Iron Crosses hanging on the *landsers'* tunics were made in Gleiwitz (today Gliwice). So important was Silesia to the Reich that Speer told Hitler in no uncertain terms that without it, Germany couldn't continue the war.

The dictator's response was perhaps less than Speer would have wished. He broadcast to the nation one last time, but these were not his electrifying words of old, and neither was his audience the same, having heard talk of promised victory too often to believe it, as teenager Mehta Marschmanna recalled: 'His voice sounded shrill with despair.' The bottom of the manpower barrel was also scraped once more, as Russian front veteran Günter Korschorrek recounted with disgust when ordered back from convalescence to train recruits in the Silesian town of Grottkau (modern-day Grodków): 'The rabble to be trained in our Kompanie consist of a mix of older east Europeans of ethnic German descent, most of whom are heads of families, and naval personnel who, because of the shortage of ships for them, are to be retrained to become panzer grenadiers.'[12]

In a desperate bid to make up for the *Ostheer's* weaknesses, Guderian pressed the emergency button, and on 14 January ordered the call-up and mobilisation of the *Volkssturm* along the entire Eastern front. The *Volkssturm* –People's Storm – was the Third Reich's version of Britain's Home Guard. Formally created by Hitler in a decree announced on 25 September the previous year, it was envisioned to be a national home defence force imbued with Nazi fervour, able to strike fear into the hearts of any enemy who dared approach the sacred territory of the Reich – or so the propaganda declared. Every male German between the ages of sixteen and sixty who didn't have a criminal record, or wasn't already a member of the Wehrmacht, was liable for service. Berlin calculated that there were six million men and boys who fit the bill, who were then sub-divided into four distinct *Aufgebote*, or Levies. The first *Aufgebote* would be over a million-strong, its members aged twenty to sixty, and men who weren't engaged in essential war work and were assessed as physically fit – this was a very loose description indeed by early 1945. They would be dragooned into 1,850 separate battalions and would be liable for service outside their home district. The second *Aufgebote* would be almost three million men – again aged twenty to sixty – but this time composed of those men who were normally exempted from service due to the essential nature of their war work. These men would only serve in their home area. The third *Aufgebote* were the nation's youngsters; the six hundred thousand boys aged between fifteen and sixteen trained in the so-called *Wehrertüchtigungslager* (Military Training Camps). One of these boys was the Fleming Julien Hertenweg, whose family had fled Belgium before the Allies liberated it:

I was enlisted by the local Nazi Party leader – a certain Herr Wünnenberger – into the German Hitler Youth in Ludwigsdorf. I had never been a member of the Flemish Hitler Youth in Flanders. On my papers he suddenly made me fifteen instead of twelve! Of course, I wasn't worried about that, I was happy enough to be a 'soldier' like everyone else at the time – and we didn't have much choice either. I was given a black Hitler Youth uniform and cap – everything was a few sizes too large of course, and my parents weren't told anything when they just sent me away to the front. Our first tasks were to help transport mail and ammunition to the front line. One day I was ordered, together with a Wehrmacht soldier, to drive a 'panje-wagon', a horse-drawn cart, forward to the front with ammunition. I sat next to the Wehrmacht soldier on the running board. On the way we were suddenly shot at and there was blood splashing over me – I thought I was hit – but it was the soldier next to me, it was his blood and he had been fatally wounded. His German shepherd dog 'Waldi', who was always with him and sitting behind us, had also been hit and killed. I didn't hesitate for a second and jumped on the drawbar of the wagon between the horses and drove the wagon full speed ahead – I hoped they would hit the horses and not me – but somehow, I got through with the horses unharmed. Arriving at the front line in a forest, I immediately told the soldiers waiting for me. They sent out a spähtrupp to try and find the Russian sniper. When I drove back I came across those men, they told me they had managed to find the Russian and kill him. Later we were sent to Posen, I think for about four weeks. This was for some training, which mainly consisted of learning how to handle weapons and explosives – mostly hand-grenades, mines, adhesive mines and panzerfausts. From there we were sent to the front at Breslau where we were up against Russian tanks. The older soldiers were smarter and left this dangerous work to us, we children were still brash.[13]

The fourth *Aufgebote* were the 1.4 million adult men graded as unfit for active service; given that thousands of men with terrible eyesight, serious hearing impairments and intestinal illnesses, as well as those missing a limb, were already at the front, one shudders to think what ailments the Nazis regarded as making someone *unfit for active service*. All in all, the *Volkssturm* was established as containing a remarkable 10,180 battalions. Needless to say, the Reich did not have the ability to arm, equip, train and deploy such a force in the depths of the winter of 1945. This situation wasn't helped by the appointment of Martin Bormann as their chief organiser. A creature of the Nazi Party, Bormann had never seen active service himself, and the only talent he had demonstrated was his skill as a back-room manipulator and political in-fighter – hardly the qualities needed to inspire and lead Nazi Germany's last-ditch hope. Otto Henning of the *Panzer-Lehr,* back home in the city of Lübeck on leave after the Ardennes fighting, saw the result at first-hand:

I saw a military band marching one Sunday – a group of soldiers with civilians behind, some of the civilians had steel helmets and some had guns... I asked someone next to me 'Who are they?' he replied, 'That's the *Volkssturm*, the People's Defence of the Fatherland.' I went home and asked my father about the *Volkssturm* and he told what it was all about and that he was in it too – in the second line. My father had lost a foot during the First World War ... but he maintained that the 'second line' was the most important in the *Volkssturm* because men like him couldn't run away.[14]

Henning the elder's view would be funny if it wasn't so tragic.

Hermann Voss – a fifty-year-old businessman – was caught up in the mobilisation: 'I was called up for the Volkssturm... I couldn't avoid it... I was given command of a Kompanie (Voss had been an officer back in the First World War) and spent three very unfortunate weeks supervising the building of fortifications around Zossen.'[15]

In Silesia the *Volkssturm* paraded as instructed. It was biting cold, but most men turned up without adequate warm clothing – they didn't want to ruin their only good winter coat – and so would shiver through their service, as there was certainly nothing for them from the Wehrmacht's stores except an armband identifying them as *Volkssturm*. In Ratibor (modern Racibórz), the ex-First World War *feldwebel,* Georg Bednarek, was called to the colours once more:

> Everything went so quickly. Whether or not you were properly trained in the use of a weapon was something they didn't ask... Whoever had held a military rank beforehand had to come forward... I got two stars pressed into my hand [indicating a platoon leader]... We went by railway into the Tschenstochau area ... a Hauptmann there was in despair, he had neither spare weapons nor ammunition ... he gave us this advice, 'Best you go home!'

It was good advice. Instead, Bednarek and his men found themselves deployed to Lublowitz: 'Foxholes and trenches were dug at the last minute, we received rifles, panzerfausts, grenades, machine-guns and mortars, but not all the Volkssturm men got weapons, there were only a few panzerfausts, and the rifles were for the most part worn-out and foreign – Italian – with just a handful of rounds each.'[16]

Some seventy miles north of Bednarek in Rosenberg – still in Silesia – was Dr Rudolf Pratsch. A former *Major* in the Wehrmacht, Pratsch had been invalided out of service back in 1943 due to ill-health, and now found himself not only re-classified as 'fit for active duty' once more but appointed as the local *Volkssturm* commander.

> Five battalions of *Volkssturm* were formed. There were no medical examinations... Many members of the *Volkssturm* secretly returned to their villages or joined the treks west... I myself wore a Major's uniform ... while all the other men were in civilian dress, only marked out by an armband ... most of the men were quite untrained, others hadn't been soldiers since 1918.

Pratsch described his men as standing 'in thin suits, without overcoats, in adequate shoes and some of them even without warm underwear'. The temperature was fifteen degrees below zero, but at least the weather had some advantages for the *Volkssturm,* as Pratsch saw during a Soviet barrage: 'Even for hits only three to five metres away the splinters were completely swallowed by the snow.'[17] This was a godsend, as artillery was the biggest killer at the front, as testified to by *Leutnant* Siegfried Bucher who was standing in the doorway of a command post with his commander, *Hauptmann* Willi Schülke, when he heard

> ...a thin buzzing, like that of a midge, not much more, but whatever it was Schülke suddenly toppled over ... a thin splinter had penetrated

the artery in the arm. The escaping blood had streamed directly into the arm and into the chest and caused shock from blood loss... Externally there wasn't much to be seen ... hit by the splinter he had bled to death internally.

The Germans were still capable of hitting the Soviets hard in Silesia, as Siegfried Baier of the *8. Panzerdivision* remembered when he and his fellow *Jagdpanzer IV* crews came up against a force of twenty Soviet tanks near the town of Bladen: 'Fire at will! Individual enemy tanks were hit simultaneously from three sides and flew apart. During the firefight, which only lasted a few seconds, everything that had come over the hill was destroyed... The entire field was full of wreckage; turrets blown off, gun barrels, engines, sumps, all torn apart.' The Soviets tried again, with the same result, and then once more: 'Towards 3pm, a third attack... It was one great field of destruction.'[18] Another officer in Baier's division; *Major* Jobst von Lossow, came up against a massive Josef Stalin II tank near Lauban (modern-day Lubań), in his Mark IV panzer: 'The Stalin tank, its tracks damaged by a direct hit, rolled out of control into a meadow and stopped ... the turret had also become disengaged because it didn't turn. Finally, the fifteenth shot on the same place on the sump burst though and set the Stalin on fire.' Lossow's luck didn't hold though. Later that same day, whilst conferring with his superior, *Oberst* Kurt von Einem, he noted, 'The air was full of steel because of massive enemy shellfire.' Minutes later a shell burst peppered the two officers, shattering Lossow's jawbone, and ripping into Einem's right arm and right calf – both were evacuated. Baier too, seemed to have used up his quota of good fortune when he was forced to tackle a group of Soviet tanks dismounted from his precious *Jagdpanzer*:

I aimed a panzerfaust at the nearest Soviet tank, pulled the trigger – misfire! The shot didn't fire! Quickly, another panzerfaust – and again a misfire! The third too misfired – the charge didn't fire, the grenade didn't fly away!... tucking two panzerfausts under my arm, I crawled with an NCO who gave me covering fire to within about forty to fifty metres of an enemy tank. Then up, aim, pull, but another misfire! The second panzerfaust – pull – misfire! Within thirty minutes that was five panzerfausts which didn't fire – was it sabotage?[19]

Sabotage or not, the Germans couldn't hold Silesia, and their line began to crack. An ethnic German grenadier in Georg Bochmann's *18. SS-Horst Wessel* recalled the fighting:

With the ground frozen solid, most infantry actions resulted in heavy casualties, as the Russians had outstanding snipers... After a daylight attack on the village of Klein-Ellgut had failed at the cost of eighty dead, the Kompanie received orders to retake the village in a night attack... The losses suffered by the Division were extremely heavy ... after four weeks of action our personnel strength was only a fraction of what it had been at the start. We had almost no heavy weapons or panzers, and we had frequent shortages of fuel and ammunition. Some of our losses were from a considerable number of desertions. The Russians made great use of these men, naming them in loudspeaker broadcasts and leaflets and declaring that they were already on their way home.

Some of the *Volkssturm* men also tried to leave their posts and head home to their families, as one of their number, Willibald Köhler, remembered: 'Often from our posts in the Volkssturm you could hear the sounds of the execution squads rifle shots hitting the brick wall. The deserters who were caught had to lay out the mats on which they would lie and be shot dead a few seconds later, then be dragged away and buried.' Some *Volkssturm* units fought well, and indeed four of its members won the Knight's Cross for bravery, including Ernst Tiburzy, the commander of *Volkssturm-Bataillon 25/82*, who single-handedly destroyed five Soviet T-34s while defending *Festung* Königsberg that February. However, overall the *Volkssturm* concept failed, and perhaps as many as 175,000 members were killed or captured, the majority of them in the east, for little military gain. Although it's difficult to criticise it when Heinz Guderian – himself a Prussian – summed up the reasoning behind it all and spoke for many of his countrymen from the eastern German provinces: 'It was our immediate homeland that was at stake, that homeland which had been won at such cost ... where lay the bones of our ancestors, land that we loved. We knew that ... our homes were lost.'

With the Red Army pushing hard into eastern Germany, Hitler finally agreed to withdraw troops from the failed Ardennes and Alsace offensives and send them east – to Hungary. Hungary? With East Prussia, Silesia and Pomerania all in danger of being overrun why send the few troops the Wehrmacht had to Hungary? Wilhelm Keitel gave an answer to this conundrum during his interrogation after the war before he was hanged for war crimes. 'The Führer attached decisive importance to securing Vienna and Austria ... it would be better to allow Berlin to fall, than to lose Hungary's oil and Austria.' Heinz Guderian agreed with Keitel as to Hitler's thinking:

The destruction of the greater part of our synthetic fuel industry meant that OKW now had to make do with such supplies as came from the wells at Zistersdorf in Austria, and from around Lake Balaton in

Hungary, which partly explains Hitler's otherwise incomprehensible decision to send the mass of forces freed in the west to Hungary.[20]

Budapest had been surrounded since Christmas Eve, its garrison besieged, and the German front line under severe pressure, as one of the officers involved, *Hauptmann* Helmut Friedrich, recalled: 'My battalion had to hold a sector a good twelve kilometres wide … the combat strength of my Kompanies had fallen to between twelve and fifteen men each.' However, some of the units sent to reinforce Friedrich and his comrades were not in much better shape, as confirmed by some of their members: 'We received replacements, more than fifty NCOs and men per Kompanie, formerly of the Luftwaffe … none of them had any infantry experience.' Another man said, 'More replacements reached us … this time they were exclusively Danube Swabians aged from seventeen to thirty-five … all of them had left their homes for the first time and were correspondingly depressed.'[21] Even the famed *SS-Hitlerjugend* fared no better in those sent to fill its battered ranks in Hungary, as Hubert Meyer saw for himself: 'Replacements joined their units at the railheads; some were the wounded from military hospitals, some Kriegsmarine and Luftwaffe personnel who were insufficiently trained for ground combat.'[22] Along with the *HJ* went its elder brother, the *SS-Leibstandarte*. *SS-Oberscharführer* Hans-Gerhard Starck:

After the Ardennes we were transferred east and headed to Hungary by train. All transport movements were constantly harassed by Allied jabos and we had to evacuate the train four times … one time I woke up to find the train halted and empty … the floor of the carriage all around where I had been lying was peppered with 2cm cannon holes… I had been so tired I had slept through the attack.[23]

The SS weren't the only exhausted troops sent to Hungary, Curt Vogt's *344. ID* was just as tired when he reported to his receiving officer, *Oberst* von Wietershausen: 'He was full of consternation on receiving a completely battle-weary division, instead of fresh troops ready for action.'

In Budapest itself, the Soviets had offered surrender terms to the garrison. *SS-Obergruppenführer* Karl Pfeffer-Wildenbruch was the man on the spot; a policeman with relatively little combat experience, he was unsuited to the role of leading the defence of a great European capital, and only too happy to wash his hands of responsibility and defer to Berlin. So, when a Soviet delegation presented themselves with terms, he sent them away with little more than a vague promise to ask for orders. The Soviet emissaries were escorted back to their own side by Josef Bader, an NCO in the mainly ethnic German *8. SS-Kavallerie-Division 'Florian Geyer'*:

> My commander ordered me to take the delegates back to no-mans-land where I had first met them. The closer we got ... the more intense the Soviet shelling became... I suggested to the Soviet captain – who spoke flawless German – that we should wait for the shelling to stop before we continued... But the captain said he had strict orders to return as soon as possible... I took off their blindfolds and told them I had no intention of committing suicide and wasn't going any further... I must stress that no-one on our side fired... The group started to cross ... when they had gone about fifty metres a shell struck from the side... When I looked up I could only see two soldiers, the third was lying motionless in the road.

Neither German/Hungarian resistance or Pfeffer-Wildenbruch's timorous leadership could deny the Soviets, and not long after their rebuff they closed in on Pest. The race was on to get across the Danube and reach relative safety in Buda. A German soldier recalled the chaos

> The infantry abandoned Pest by what was left of the two Danube bridges. They were running for their lives, oblivious of the heavy bombardment. The order to evacuate the bridges created a panic... A tangled mass of cars and trucks, peasant carts covered by tarpaulins, frightened horses, civilian refugees, wailing women, mothers with crying children and many – very many – wounded were hurrying towards Buda.

One of those *landsers* on the bridges recalled: 'We ran for our lives in the intensive artillery fire ... some people were naturally left on the bridges when they were blown up.' Helmut Schreiber was a Hungarian ethnic German cavalryman at the time: 'From Gellert Hill I was able to watch the blowing of the bridge over the Danube ... we were about out of ammunition for our guns... Our poor horses had already died of hunger or had been killed by shellfire or bombs. At least they benefited the hungry civilians who butchered them in no time.'

With Buda holding out, most of the German reinforcements reaching Hungary were used in an attempt to reach the city and lift the siege, as the *SS-Totenkopf's* Andreas Fleischer remembered:

> I was in 3. Kompanie, 3rd Battalion of Regiment Theodor Eicke. Totenkopf was a panzer division of course, and it was special I can tell you, we were an élite unit, and that was what we all wanted,

to serve with the best, to be the best. So, we were loaded up onto trains and sent down towards Budapest, in Hungary. We were sent with an Army division. When we arrived, I came across my brother – he'd escaped from Budapest – he told me that they had had to split up into small groups and escape that way – it had been their only chance. It was very good to see him, but we didn't get much chance to talk – that was the way things were at the front. Then we were moved from one place to another, we had to change our insignia – hide our SS insignia – you understand, all to confuse the Russians so they didn't know where we were or what we were doing. We carried quite a lot of rations too at that point – usually when we knew we'd be going into a fight we'd carry enough food for two to three days, but we had more then. Maybe they thought we'd have problems getting resupplied, I don't know. We were short of men, my Gruppe was meant to be twelve but we never had more than six or seven, we didn't get many replacements at that point in the war you see, in fact we got fewer and fewer replacements as time went on, and the ones we did get weren't as well trained as we were, most of them were barely trained at all. One lad we did get was so young, so inexperienced, he was going to get himself killed, I knew it. I had to teach this lad a lesson, to try and keep him alive. There was a Russian sniper around – their snipers were very good – and I used to warn my men 'don't stand up, don't put your head up,' but this young lad was going to forget my warning, so I put my helmet on a stick and told one of my men to put it up in the air, and at the same time I was looking at the Russian lines through the sights on my rifle. The sniper fired, and hit my helmet, but I didn't see him for a little while. Then he made a mistake, he moved, and I shot him. I'd got him. We had no more firing from him. The next day we attacked towards Budapest and cost the Russians 250 tanks! We had Tigers, Panthers and some old PzKfw IV's, and we attacked some of their Guards units – they were good – not as good as us, but good anyway.

The *SS-Leibstandarte* was also in Hungary at the time. 'Five Tiger IIs drove over the hill. What a sight! They appeared and immediately began taking fire from the Russian anti-tank guns. We saw the shells bounce off the front of the Tigers – that must've been a shock for the Russians – especially as the Tigers destroyed one gun after another.'

Alongside both divisions was the *SS-Wiking,* and in its ranks was Ivar Corneliussen:

We were ordered to pack up our gear and move to Hungary where the Russians were attacking Budapest. We were supposed to try and push them back, and we did some very heavy fighting around a brickworks factory... The biggest problem we had was the lack of gasoline and diesel oil. We only had enough fuel to fill up one panzer at a time, and that panzer then had to pull a whole string of other vehicles along behind it, how were we meant to fight like that?

Fleischer was injured in the fighting:

I was wounded then in Hungary. It was the second time I'd been wounded. What happened was that we attacked the first town we came to and there was a minefield there, the mines were in wooden boxes so they were difficult to find with mine detectors. Our panzers could then only use the roads, to stay away from the mines, but it meant that the Russians could hit the panzers from the flank, from the side, that's the best way to kill a panzer, from the side, the armour is thinner there. Anyway, a Tiger was hit, the commander managed to get out and we grabbed him and brought him back. There was so much machine-gun fire, it was like snow in the air. One round hit the panzer next to me like that, 'dummmm', that's the noise it made, it was so close. A shell landed just behind me then and shrapnel hit me here, in my right shoulder. The bone wasn't broken though, just scraped. I got a lift back to a small dressing station with a guy who had a little moustache – you know like Hitler – that was popular back then! The doctor I saw said it was lucky the shrapnel hadn't gone into my lung. I lay there in the dressing station – like I said, a small place with just two beds, me and another guy next to me. This guy next to me said 'hey, do you recognise me, do you know who I am?' and at first I didn't, he was all burnt up and bandaged, and then I realised who he was, he was the Tiger commander we'd grabbed. He was very worried though that they were going to take his legs off as they were in a mess. He kept on saying, 'please don't take my legs, please don't take my legs' – again and again he kept on saying it. The next day they told us they were going to send us back to a bigger hospital on a train. They loaded us up and he was there again, the Tiger commander, in the same wagon as me. We were waiting there on the railway track and I fell asleep. Then I woke up, and something was wrong. I opened the door and the Tiger guy said what's going on, and I said 'Shut up! Can you hear that, it's Russian fire!' He said, 'Are you crazy, how do you know?' and I said 'Trust me, I've heard it a lot of times before! That's Russian fire!' So, I then said that if another train doesn't come and take us away in twenty minutes then I'm off. Another train didn't come so I got out and left. I found out later what had happened; a Hungarian general had surrendered to the Russians and taken his whole division across with him, so there was a big hole in the line and the Russians had come through it, that's why they were so close to the train. Luckily, the train managed to get away anyway.

The German attempt to lift the siege failed, and Fleischer had soon recovered enough to be sent back to his division. 'That was when I was wounded for the third time, a bullet hit me on the left side of my face and my left ear – it hurt like hell I can tell you, and there was blood everywhere, I couldn't see much out of my eye.' Fleischer was one of the six per cent of *landsers* who were wounded three or more times at the front, with well over half of all German soldiers suffering at least one injury in the fighting. One of whom was the eighteen-year-old cavalryman, Helmut Schreiber, defending Budapest:

> During the house to house fighting I was wounded. First, I was hit in the head, luckily the bullet failed to pierce my steel helmet, but ten minutes later I was hit by another bullet which lodged in my right collar bone. A comrade took me to the aid station which was in the underground passageways beneath the castle ... the cellars were full of badly wounded men lying on the floor with no beds, all of them covered in paper as they'd run out of proper bandages.

Conditions in the ruins of the city were dire, as *SS-Hauptsturmführer* Jahncke wrote: 'Constant enemy attacks... Division too weak to launch an immediate counter-attack ... extremely heavy losses ... wounded receive just fifteen grams of legumes and half a slice of bread. These quantities are only available for the next two days.'

On the evening of 11 February, the surviving defenders of Buda tried to break out. A wounded Helmut Schreiber wasn't among them. 'The order came for all walking wounded to assemble in the castle's underground vaults ... word went around that those who could still fight were going to try and break out. Many of the walking wounded went along as well.' Organised into three waves, they set off into the darkness, desperate to escape a Soviet captivity they feared almost more than death. Helmut Friedrich was one of them:

> From all sides foot soldiers stream towards the north. Another mortar strike. Everybody seeks cover in doorways. More shouting, comrades have lost each other... It is painful for a commander to watch how this break-out attempt is developing into an act of madness, an almost animal act of despair obeying only the instinct of self-preservation, without being able to do anything about it... Left and right people jostle madly to start the break-out as soon as possible. They elbow their way ahead, pushing and kicking like animals.

With surprise on their side – despite the total confusion – quite a few of that first wave managed to get out of the city. Now alerted, the Soviets were determined that any successive attempts would be stopped in their tracks. It was into this bear-pit that the second wave crashed, as Ernst Schweitzer from *13. Panzerdivision* recounted:

> We move about three to four hundred metres west and reach an immense cluster of soldiers seeking cover behind a long barnlike building ... the square is dominated from both sides by Russian machine-guns and anti-tank guns ... it's strewn with wounded and dead. At our feet there are more than a dozen dead who bought it when they pushed out from the building ... now we are being forced into the firing line by those behind us. Without a moment's hesitation we run for our lives across the square. Bullets whistle past us... An SS officer staggered into the courtyard, announcing, 'I'm wounded, I'm going to end it all'... He shot himself.

He wasn't alone. The commanders of both SS divisions in the garrison, Joachim Rumohr and August Zehender, committed suicide – the latter after having his right leg blown off by a grenade. Around twenty-eight thousand men were involved in the break-out – most never made it out of the city – as Helmut Schreiber witnessed first-hand: 'Before long many returned in disappointment – the breakout had more or less failed.' *SS-Hauptsturmführer* Joachim Boosfeld was one of the lucky ones: 'On the rising meadow leading to the German positions we could clearly observe small grey dots – German soldiers ... the Soviet snipers shot down one escapee after another.' Buda fell on 13 February. Only some seven hundred men managed to reach German lines. Ernst Schweitzer was among them: 'My feet hurt so badly that I took off my boots ... on all fours I crawl towards the first houses. One of us goes ahead and reports back happily that the first house is a German billet – we've made it!' A grim fate awaited many of those left behind:

> A Russian officer asked which of us were Russians ... about fifteen to twenty men stepped forward. There were probably some Hiwis among them, but most were ethnic Germans from Russia who had served in the Waffen-SS. Before our eyes the Soviets set about them with their swords, and when they were lying on the ground, battered and stabbed all over, they were finished off with a sub-machine gun.

Schreiber saw much the same: 'On 12 February the Russians fetched us out of the cellars. What happened then was hell. Those who couldn't walk were shot ... we were taken via Romania and the Black Sea to Odessa.'

Meanwhile at the Yalta Conference in the Crimea, Stalin was able to declare to Churchill and Roosevelt that the Red Army had advanced some three hundred miles in three weeks, that East Prussia and Silesia were overrun, and Pomerania was on the brink. He also announced that he now had one hundred and eighty divisions facing just eighty German, and the Red Army was one hundred and twenty miles from Prague, eighty from Vienna and only forty-five from Berlin itself. What he didn't tell his fellow leaders was that the cost had been dreadful – the Soviets had suffered around three hundred thousand casualties,[24] three times what the Americans had suffered in the Ardennes battles. Even though, as Alfred Jodl acknowledged, 'With the Fifth and Sixth Panzer Armies committed in the Ardennes, the way was paved for the Russian offensive.' Once again, the Wehrmacht scrambled to react, and with the Anglo-Americans bogged down, the East was the priority. The month of February saw 1,675 new and repaired panzers sent to face the Soviets, with just sixty-seven going west.

8

Italy – Reaching the Top of the Boot

The Italian front; once the darling of the Allied war effort, now, after the fall of Rome and D-Day two days later – the poor relation of the second cousin twice removed in comparison to the campaign in France. With the arrival of autumn, the planners at SHAEF were advising Eisenhower that by the beginning of 1945 he would have ninety-one Allied divisions on the German border facing ninety German ones, while in Italy twenty-seven German divisions would be struggling with twenty-four Allied – in effect the Allies wouldn't have a decisive advantage in either theatre. Their recommendation was to strip one front to reinforce the other; the question was, which one? Harold Alexander – the Supreme Allied Commander Mediterranean – was never going to win that fight; the Alps would be an obstacle that could hold the Allies for months on end. That meant him losing the best of his formations and the lion's share of his supplies, something he vigorously opposed. A persuasive and charming man – Churchill preferred him to Montgomery – he managed to make a case that saw him lose just three divisions from Italy and another two from Greece. Two of the former were his Canadians, and although experienced units, Ottawa had made it clear it wanted all of its manpower concentrated in France under Harry Crerar, so they were going anyway. Having said that, the scales were balanced out somewhat by Berlin deciding to withdraw three of their own divisions and send them north. Alexander cast his eyes hither to find troops for the Italian front – any troops – and he alighted on a whole range of units. He 'did a de Gaulle' and put thousands of local Italian partisans into Allied uniform, he also got two brigades of recently captured Poles who had been press-ganged into the Wehrmacht, the provisional government in Rome was squeezed for five new non-fascist regiments, the British-sponsored Jewish Brigade was shipped in from the Middle East, and the almost twenty-six thousand-strong Brazilian Expeditionary Force

(*Força Expedicionária Brasileira* or *FEB*) came to his aid too. The multinational make-up of the Allied armies now in Italy didn't escape the attention of their erstwhile foes, one of whom was the Italian fascist soldier Antonio Cucciati: 'There were Poles, Indians, New Zealanders, but there was no feeling of hatred between us ... as long as there were no orders to fire we were the best of friends.'[1]

German forces in Italy were at the bottom of just about every list the Germans had, and they knew it. The vehicles rolling out of the Reich's factories that autumn were sent east and west and not south, forcing *landsers* in Italy to commandeer civilian cars, buses and trucks from the local populace – hardly a move designed to win over public support. Even that soon became moot, as when Romania's oil was lost, what little the Reich could squeeze out of the Hungarian and Austrian wells didn't cross the Alps. A handful of tiny wells in the foothills eked out around a thousand litres of gasoline a day – a drop in the ocean – so, instead, as many vehicles as possible were converted to burning wood or methane gas, and horses and oxen became the staple draught animals as Germany's troops reverted to quasi-medieval transport. Of the fifty-five new *Volks-Grenadier Divisionen* created that autumn, only one, *Generalleutnant* Alfred-Hermann Reinhardt's *98. VGD*, was sent to Italy. One of Reinhardt's men was Friedrich Büchner from Ludwigstadt. Having done well in training, he had been posted on a probationary officers course. 'It was a big surprise when I found out I was going to Italy, there were forty men on my course and only three of us went to Italy, the rest went to the Eastern and Western fronts.'[2]

Another *landser* surprised to be posted to Italy was *Unteroffizier* Franz Maasen. Wounded at Kursk back in the summer of '43, after his convalescence he got his marching orders to join *Generalleutnant* Harry Hoppe's *278. Infanterie-Division* down on the Gothic Line: 'I was recommended for a commission, but I was just a baker's son with no qualifications, so they made me an Unteroffizier and sent me to Italy.' Maasen's first commander was a former Luftwaffe fighter pilot transferred to the infantry with no training or any combat experience; he was killed in short order and Maasen took over. Introduced to the highly decorated Hoppe he was asked if he had a family, and replied that he had a wife and son, and then was asked,

'"What are you fighting for?"

I gave him the standard nonsense. 'For Führer and Fatherland!'

To which Hoppe shot back, "Rubbish! You are fighting for your home and your family... and when you've got no more ammunition then you jump at the Tommies' throats!"'[3]

Franz Maasen wasn't the only convalescent sent south. Numbers of survivors from the Stalingrad disaster were despatched to Italy once healed, including Andreas Engel, a *feldwebel* in the *29. ID (mot)*, shot in the thigh by a Russian *jabo* in December 1942, and *Leutnant* Joachim Feurich, flown out with shell splinters in his leg. Even overall command of the front wasn't a priority for Berlin. In October 'Smiling Albert' Kesselring was very badly injured in an accident when his blacked-out staff car was hit by a towed artillery piece. Rushed to hospital with a fractured skull, he would remain effectively *hors de combat* until January the following year, but still remained in command of all Axis forces in Italy.

As for the fighting itself, the *landser* Herbert Holewa testified as to its difficulties: 'The terrain was hard, and the Allied jabos were very effective. You couldn't walk on the road – even if you were on a bicycle they would come down and shoot at you! Even to this day I can't understand why they didn't achieve more at the time.'

Outgunned and often outnumbered, the weather came to the Germans' aid, with torrential rain and freezing cold often turning the roads to slush, and keeping Allied aircraft grounded – not that Franz Maasen was grateful, as he made plain in a letter to his wife, Liesel:

> Yesterday was really shit, I began to feel as if I was in a canoe. The water in our foxhole was up to our knees and we had to bail it out with our cooking pots; it was like liquid manure. These are the joys of the infantryman, and there I was dreaming about being at home in a nice warm sitting-room ... as I've been writing these lines I have had to throw myself down at least twenty times because Tommy is not a bad shot with his artillery.

A few days later, to add to their misery, Maasen and his men began to suffer from diarrhoea. 'It's suicide to leave the foxholes during the day because of the artillery fire and jabos, so we shit in a tin can and throw it out of the foxhole... Tommy keeps drumming. We crawl as far as we can into our foxhole, hugging our legs close to our bodies, our knees tightly together... The force of the impacts throw our bodies against the wall with a thump ... our steel helmets knock together.'[4]

Finally scheduled for relief a few days later, Maasen watched his men withdraw as he stayed behind and covered them with a machine-gun. When he was sure they were clear he grabbed the gun, slung it over his shoulder and began to make his way to the rear. Following the path, he entered a narrow gully on a small hill, and found horror: 'I saw all my men and many more besides ...shells had landed amongst them... That evening we buried them, my good comrades.' Not one had survived.[5]

Incredibly, the *landsers* continued to fight, as Friedrich Büchner made clear: 'The war wasn't over yet, there was still a job to be done.' Herbert Holewa was of much the same opinion. 'We still had a very good fighting force. A lot of veterans were still around, and the youngsters looked up to them.'

That resistance was costing the Allies dear. General Mark Clark's four American divisions in Fifth Army lost a combined total of almost twenty-six thousand men in September and October '44; over half their strength. The 88th Infantry Division was especially badly hit – from a bayonet strength of 9,250, it lost 9,167 men – almost a one hundred per cent casualty rate in its frontline companies. Replacements would arrive from depots only to be killed or wounded before their new comrades had gotten to know their names. One Allied soldier wrote in despair: 'Knowing the Germans' remarkable capacity to recover from catastrophic defeats, some of us felt that the war might even go on for another year.'

Nevertheless, Alexander had somehow managed to find just about enough troops to continue the advance northwards in an attempt to comprehensively defeat the Wehrmacht in Italy. With the Allies pushing north, Italian partisans, many of them communists from the far-left heartlands of northern Italy's industrial cities and towns, significantly stepped up their attacks on the Germans. In the period 21 July to 25 September they killed 624 Germans and wounded another 993. An additional 872 were listed as 'missing', and since the partisans had no way of keeping prisoners it was safe to assume that these men were killed soon after capture. The Waffen-SS grenadier Rudi Schreiber expressed the views of many of his comrades about the partisans: 'We were furious that these civilians were getting involved in the war ... but the thing that really got to us was the brutality they showed towards prisoners. We were permanently in danger.' Franz Maasen was more blunt: 'I hated the partisans. I wasn't personally involved in any of the round-ups, but I wouldn't have minded if I was.'

Those 'round-ups' were brutal – even by Nazi standards – and have been a source of bitterness for Italians ever since. One unit heavily involved in fighting the partisans – and in the reprisals – was Max Simon's *16. SS-Panzergrenadier-Division 'Reichsführer SS'*. The communist *Brigata Stella Rossa* (Red Star Brigade), operating out of the Monte Sole area south of Bologna, was particularly active in disrupting the flow of supplies and reinforcements to the front. Simon sent Walter Reder's reconnaisance battalion to deal with the problem, as *SS-Hauptsturmführer* Wilfried Segebrecht described: 'The battles were made more difficult due to the malicious methods used by the partisans, such as shooting from ambush positions, from holes in cellars, haystacks, dugouts and caves. Some of these places were partly occupied by women and civilians, even by children, in order to trick us into believing they were harmless.' Reder and his men responded with barbarity. On arrival, the majority of partisans disappeared to their hiding places, leaving the SS troopers grasping at air, finding only unarmed civilians. Their reaction was to go on a murder spree, shooting whole families and burning down villages and hamlets. In total, some 770 civilians were slaughtered. As far as Segebrecht was concerned though, it worked. 'The Stella Rossa had been destroyed, and once again supplies and reinforcements could reach us.'

The destruction of the partisan threat couldn't hide the fact that the German front in Italy was breaking down as 1945 began. Supply trains from the north – running at thirty-eight a day the previous autumn – were now down to just eight per day, with Allied bombing wrecking the transport infrastructure just as it had done in France prior to D-Day. The *landsers* were shivering in their winter quarters as coal imports more or less ceased, and food was becoming scarce. The former Rhodes scholar and now Corps commander, Fridolin von Senger und Etterlin, wrote in his diary: 'Each further day would make the war more meaningless than it already was, claiming the blood of thousands of people, of fathers, and of adolescent sons.' His own son had just lost an arm in the fighting – his eighth wound of the war. Karl Wolff, the senior SS officer in Italy, was of much the same opinion as Senger: 'It was at the end of January that I realised the rottenness of our position.' Almost unbelievably for a Nazi general – particularly one from the SS – Wolff resolved to do something about it, and secretly contacted Allen Dulles – a senior officer in the American Office of Strategic Services (OSS, the forerunner of the CIA) – to begin negotiations for a German surrender in Italy. Even more unbelievable was that Wolff then saw Hitler in person and argued the case for capitulation. In reply, the dictator told Wolff that the Allies would fall out with each other soon and the Reich would be saved. Wolff responded by confessing all: 'I told the Führer everything ... that before that happens we shall be dead or beaten to the ground, and that must not happen – we must do something first.' Amazingly, Wolff was neither arrested nor relieved of command, and was able to return to Italy – stopping off in Switzerland for further talks with Dulles.

By the beginning of April the Allies had massed one and a half million men to face under six hundred thousand Germans and fascist Italians (439,224 of the former and 160,180 of the latter). With the talks going nowhere fast, the Allies decided to force the issue and crush the German army in Italy.

Just after midday on 9 April, a fleet of 825 American Liberators and Flying Fortresses appeared in the skies over the frontline. The droning of thousands of engines was blotted out as their bomb-bays opened and released a cascade of high-explosives on the German defenders, leaving them shattered and stunned, as Friedrich Büchner recalled: 'It was absolutely terrifying ... the noise of the exploding bombs was completely deafening.' Successive waves of medium bombers and *jabos* followed on, and when they finally disappeared, fifteen hundred guns opened up. 'That was day one ... we packed up and started to move back... We were under fire nearly all the time.' What was left of the German line crumpled, and in two days they suffered over three thousand casualties. Wolff tried once more to persuade Hitler to throw in the towel, travelling to see the dictator for the last time in Berlin on 18 April. Hitler refused, and told Wolff that he and Germany would fight on. Crestfallen, the urbane SS general headed back to Italy and met with Heinrich von Vietinghoff – the Wehrmacht's military commander in the country – who had just returned from a stint leading *Heeresgruppe Kurland*. Vietinghoff told Wolff his view in no uncertain terms: 'Hundreds of thousands of German soldiers are waiting for the words from me that will save their lives – time is running out.' One of those soldiers was Friedrich Büchner. Reaching the banks of the River Po, he and his men were desperate to cross to safety: 'We'd been retreating daily for twelve days, there wasn't any feeling left … we couldn't cross by day because of the jabos.' Senger und Etterlin found himself in the same situation as his erstwhile subordinate, as he attempted to get over the river:

> My headquarters staff was dissolved into separate groups. At dawn on the 23rd we found a ferry at Bergantino. Of the thirty-six ferries in the 14. Armee zone only four were still serviceable. Because of the incessant jabo attacks it was useless to try and cross in daylight… Many officers and men were able to swim across. The access road at Revere was blocked by columns of burning vehicles. I had to leave my car behind. In the twilight we crossed the river and together with my operations staff we marched the twenty-five kilometres to Legnano. We were unable to establish any communications. Generalmajor Friedrich von Schellwitz – who after General Pfeiffer's death had assumed command of the remnants of 65 and 305. IDs – was captured south of the river.

By now, organised resistance was beginning to crumble. Regardless, Senger carried on, attempting to set up a defensive line between the shores of Lake Garda and the Pasubio pass. 'The roads to the north were filled with an unending stream of stragglers.' Every man capable of carrying a weapon was dragooned into service, including the cadets from a *fallschirmjäger* officers' school, the staff and instructors from the Waffen-SS mountain warfare training school at Neustift, and the ski school at San Martino di Castrozza. Lacking heavy weapons, they were unable to hold the Allies, who liberated Verona and cut the German forces in two. Genoa was liberated by partisans the same day. *Generalleutnant* Graf von Schwerin – having survived his earlier attempt to surrender Aachen against Hitler's express orders, decided enough was enough for him and surrendered – with, according to James Holland in *Italy's Sorrow,* the remnants of his champagne – to the 27th Lancers. Holland refers to the wreckage on the river bank, where a thousand pieces of artillery, eighty panzers, and a huge number of carts and wagons pressed into service were abandoned – and fourteen thousand prisoners in the V Corps cages – as evidence that von Schwerin was right.

Not among the prisoners was the former Italian fascist dictator, Benito Mussolini. Captured with a handful of his entourage by communist partisans, he was shot, and his corpse hung up by his feet at a gas station in Milan for the crowds to jeer at. His young mistress, Clara Pettaci, begged the partisan commander to spare her life. He replied, 'I execute the will of the Italian people' and gunned her down. She was strung up next to her lover.

The para officer, Joseph 'Jupp' Klein, remembered an Italian civilian dancing towards him shouting, 'Hitler's dead! It came through on the radio!'

'Nonsense!'

'It's true, it's true!'

'I thought, what will become of us? I had in mind only the Russians, I thought that would be it for Germany, the Russians will come and we will cease to exist.'

Klein and his men surrendered to the Americans the following day. Friedrich Büchner wasn't as lucky as Klein. He and his men were taken prisoner by partisans near the town of Belluno on 1 May, and they feared for their lives. 'The communist leader turned up and they pulled out three of our soldiers who were Russians – Hiwis – they'd been with us since Russia and had served throughout the campaign in Italy.' The partisan commander then shot all three, but didn't kill them. 'He didn't do it properly, the Russians were lying on the ground screaming ... it was terrible, absolutely terrible.' After ten minutes writhing on the ground in agony, the three men were finally given the *coup de grâce* with a bullet in the head.[6]

The following day, German forces in Italy formally surrendered and hostilities ceased after a campaign that had lasted six hundred brutal days. German casualties topped a third of a million men, about twenty thousand more than Allied losses, while the Italians themselves suffered terribly; forty thousand Italian soldiers were killed or reported missing before the country switched sides, whereupon another thirty-five thousand died fighting *for* Mussolini, while the same number were killed fighting *against* him. Caught in the middle, over one hundred and fifty thousand civilians died from bombing, shelling or German reprisals.

9

Remagen and the Rhine

Having shot its bolt in the Ardennes and Alsace, the *Westheer* could do little else except huddle in its foxholes and await spring and the next Allied offensive. Despite this, the English brigadier, Hubert Essame, continued to be astonished at the Wehrmacht's martial ability: 'During the winter battles many of their formations displayed much of the skill, drive, flexibility and endurance which had taken their armies to the gates of Moscow.'

Generalmajor Gerhard Franz of the *256. VGD* may not have agreed with Essame's assessment. Shivering in the Dutch flatlands, he posted a notice around his division which contained these revealing lines:

It cannot be tolerated that a commander should get drunk, then wander around the woods all night shouting and firing his pistol at the sentry ... a unit shows little esprit de corps if a soldier can declare that owing to difficulty in walking he can no longer serve with the artillery since he couldn't escape quickly enough if Tommy arrived... During the last eight days no less than eleven desertions have been reported, seven of whom went over to enemy lines.

Not that Franz's unit was the only formation with problems. His fellow divisional commander, Günther Hoffmann-Schönborn of *18. VGD,* also put up a notice to his men after six of them had deserted to the Americans: 'These bastards have given away important military secrets ... rest assured the Division will see that they never see home and loved ones again.'

Those loved ones were increasingly sick of the war, as Erwin Bartmann discovered when walking to his local train station in Berlin to begin his journey back to his unit after some leave: 'A stone cracked against the wall a few metres in front of me, another struck even closer... I clasped my loaded pistol inside my uniform jacket ready to fire into the air. To feel the wrath of my fellow citizens was a harrowing experience.'

The Wehrmacht was in a death-spiral, and it was crystal clear that Germany was heading inexorably for total defeat. As Bartmann boarded his train, his comrades in the Luftwaffe and Kriegsmarine were feeling the full force of Allied military might. The Luftwaffe had been gutted by the *Bodenplatte* calamity, and its fuel situation was utterly desperate, as Norbert Hannig discovered after being ordered to report to his commander after scrambling:

'Hannig, you took off with your Rotte (wingman) without an official order or any authorisation being given and are therefore in breach of the regulations concerning the unnecessary wastage of fuel. I have had to report the matter to the judge advocate in Windau (modern-day Ventspils in Latvia). He will be here in two hours.'

'But I don't understand Herr Hauptmann, I heard the whistle and saw the green flare signalling an emergency scramble?'

'You should have looked more carefully at the flare's trajectory – it didn't come from us – somebody out at 6 Staffel's dispersal fired it.'

Hannig escaped with a warning, but the point was clear – every drop of aviation fuel was precious. At least Hannig survived his scramble. On the morning of 14 January 1945, the P-51 Mustangs of the American 357th Fighter Group took off from their base at Leiston on the south Suffolk coast and headed east to Germany on a bomber escort mission. They were joined by their fellow pilots of the 353rd and 20th Groups, and together they went hunting the *Jagdwaffe*. *Jagdgeschwader 300* and *301* scrambled to meet them, desperately climbing as quickly as possible to gain precious altitude. The two forces met some 26,000 feet up in the clear sky, twisting and turning as each pilot sought to gain the advantage over his opponent.

For the *jagdflieger* it was a disaster. With so many poorly trained pilots the Germans were swept from the sky; *JG 300* lost twenty-seven pilots killed and another six wounded, while *JG 301* had twenty-two killed and eight wounded. In all, 161 German aircraft were shot down that day – sixty by the 357th, a United States Air Force record that still stands to this day. The scores claimed were so high that Eighth Air Force ordered a recount, but the figures held. In contrast, the Americans only lost thirteen Mustangs and three P-47 Thunderbolts – a drop in the ocean considering the Allies now had fourteen thousand aircraft available in theatre.

The Reich's sailors weren't faring well either. By the end of 1944, almost thirty per cent of the Navy's manpower had been transferred to the Army – and that number was climbing – with even élite U-boat crewmen being sent to the frontline. Those left behind in the dark-blue ranks were increasingly inactive; back in 1942 of every one hundred days, the average U-boat crew spent sixty at sea, of which forty were directly on operations. By the beginning of 1945, only thirty-seven days were spent at sea, with a miserly nine of those on operations. Under serious threat from Allied air and naval forces, Germany's submariners found themselves spending less and less time hunting enemy vessels, and more and more ferrying supplies to the beleaguered German garrisons still holding out in ports along the French coast. *U-772* and *U-773* went on one such mission, transporting anti-tank weapons, ammunition and medical supplies to St Nazaire. However, even with eight of their torpedoes unloaded, they could still only take around thirty to forty tons of cargo each – not enough to keep the fight going for long. As it was, the Soviet's Vistula offensive in January brought the Red Army to within thirty kilometres of the U-boat and Naval Staff Headquarters at *Lager Koralle* (Camp Koralle), forcing its abandonment. The building programme for the new generation of U-boats continued, but the German war economy was struggling to cope. The new submarines needed sophisticated electrical components, such as radar search receivers and underwater listening apparatus, and this demand curtailed the production of parts for power stations and locomotives – both desperately needed by the Reich. The U-boats also needed high-grade steel plate for their hulls, as did Germany's panzers for their armour protection. This was the worst bottleneck in the entire German steel industry, with demand for top-quality plate three and a half times total production. Inevitably, these problems slowed construction. With the new boats still being built, Dönitz had no option but to send out the old types. By now, fuel was in such short supply that it had to be siphoned out of some of the remaining surface fleet – the *Admiral Scheer* and *Lützow* were two such fuel donors – to enable the U-boats to sail. But sail they did; thirty-six patrolled out in February, with thirty-eight in March and forty in April. Despite this, Allied control of the shipping lanes was now absolute. Antwerp was finally in operation, and Eisenhower's logistical problems – while not solved – had at least eased.

At the same time, both services were seeing their ranks plundered to fill gaps in the Army. That Army – still by far Nazi Germany's dominant service arm – was fighting on three fronts and haemorrhaging manpower; more than 450,000 men were killed in January, and a further 295,000 would suffer the same fate in February. It had lost access to most of its ethnic German recruiting grounds now those populations had been overrun by the Soviets, and its training depots in the Reich were increasingly empty. The Wehrmacht was so desperate for manpower now that it even took in many of the monsters guarding the concentration camps, as one inmate, Agnes Erdős, saw with her own weary eyes: 'Our guards were now two new SS girls – our male guards had been sent to the front, and girls were put in their place.' Unbelievably, after all the

Germans had subjected her to, Agnes was still capable of compassion towards these new gaolers:

> I asked one of the new guards why she looked so sad ... she looked completely surprised, and then started to cry uncontrollably ... she said she didn't know where her mother, her sisters, and her son – who was around two – were. She knew the Russians had captured her home province near the Polish border and had had no news of them... I comforted her, saying we were both innocent victims of this war.

Werner Block – still driving his Tiger – knew the end was near: 'We'd occasionally get sent a replacement – a new guy – but it was rare. What could we do, we had to carry on, even though we all knew it was useless.' Gustav Palm saw the same:

> New volunteers arrived. They'd signed up for the Kriegsmarine, but after training were told their ships no longer existed, so they could choose either to go home or join the Waffen-SS. All except one chose the Waffen-SS – the one who opted to go home ended up in a concentration camp ... one of the newcomers was an eighteen-year-old who had been arrested for stealing ration cards, and given the choice of prison or the Kriegsmarine, and was now with us.

Palm himself only just managed to escape the Red Army at the Oder River by securing a valuable place on a motorboat crossing the waterway.

> I realised I had to get across the river. The Russians were firing at all the bridges... I was introduced by the doctors [Palm had a bullet wound in the leg at the time] to a man in civilian clothing ... he had a motorboat waiting to cross the river to Stettin. As well as me there were six other wounded soldiers in the boat. We crept down to the beach and sat in the boat. It took a long time to cross the river, but no one shot at us. When we got ashore on the Stettin side, the five of us who could walk took a streetcar to the hospital.

The Third Reich was still standing though. In the East, entire German regions were now under Soviet control, but in the west, the Anglo-Americans had still not crossed the Rhine, and in the south the Allies were stuck on the Italian side of the Brenner Pass. The Anglo-Americans had suffered during the winter as well, with losses in the frontier battles stubbornly high. From the liberation of Brussels to the launch of the *Westheer*'s Ardennes offensive, the three northern American armies had suffered over ninety-two thousand battle casualties, and a staggering 113,000 non-combat casualties – mainly from trench foot and combat fatigue.[1] However, the training depots Stateside continued to churn out replacements and new units, with two-thirds of the Allies 3.7 million men in theatre in January now being Americans, with an additional nine divisions on the way. As for the British, they were at full stretch, with thirty-six divisions now facing the *Westheer* – from this point on the British Army could only get smaller.[2]

The *Westheer* now relied on the Rhine to hold back its Anglo-American foe. The River Rhine. One of Europe's great waterways, akin to the Danube, the Don and the Seine. The 'natural' western border of Germany, in truth Germans had lived in large numbers on its far bank for centuries. Long considered too wide and fast-flowing to be bridgeable, Julius Caesar had awed Germanic barbarian tribes by doing just that in 55BC, and again in 53BC. Now, Berlin hoped the Rhine would keep the Anglo-Americans *out*, and not the Germans *in*. The river was the Wehrmacht's last real defensive line in the West, and everyone knew it. Behind it lay a dozen other rivers, but nothing even remotely resembling the power of the mighty Rhine. The river must be held at all costs. But how? The forces available for the task were woeful. The Third Reich's best remaining formations had been sent southeast to Hungary and left behind were a patchwork of almost immobile infantry and *Volkssturm* units, supported by scatterings of artillery, engineer, Luftwaffe and Kriegsmarine flotsam. This was no massed river guard, rather a crust waiting to crumble.

The responsibility for piercing that crust and crossing the Rhine into Nazi Germany's heartland was handed to Montgomery. Ever the king of set-piece operations, the British field marshal devised *Operation Plunder*, a three-army assault, utilising Miles Dempsey's British Second Army and William H. Simpson's American Ninth Army, as well as the paratroopers of First Allied Airborne Army, who would land on the river's eastern bank and establish a bridgehead for the infantry to cross into. Over five thousand guns would fire in an Allied force comprised of 1.3 million men, who would be supported from the sky by the full might of Anglo-American airpower. Thousands of tons of supplies were carefully brought forward and stockpiled, and huge amounts of bridging equipment and trackway were also trucked to storage sites near the embarkation points, ready for the engineers to start construction as soon as the far bank was secure. To help prepare the ground, *Operation Grenade* was launched in February by Simpson's Ninth Army, and Crerar's Canadians. Advancing from the Roer River, the two Allied forces met up at Duisburg on the Rhine, as Hodges' US First Army reached Cologne and Euskirchen. The Germans were thrown back, losing almost ninety thousand men, of whom half became POWs.

To the south – again to unbalance the Germans and keep them guessing as to where the main crossing would occur – de Lattre de

Tassigny's French troops finally crushed the Colmar pocket, suffering twenty thousand casualties into the bargain – about the same number as their foes. The stage was set for Montgomery's grand plan to unfold; then, on 7 March – a full two weeks before Montgomery could unleash his meticulously planned operation – lead elements of the American 9th Armoured Division approached the Rhine at the town of Remagen, some ninety miles south of Monty's planned landing zone at Wesel. To their astonishment the 326-metre long span of the Ludendorff bridge stood intact before them. Originally built in the First World War as a military bridge for the purpose of transporting troops and supplies to the front in France, there were barracks built into it to hold two whole battalions of troops for local security. However, on 7 March, forty-one-year-old *Hauptmann* Willi Bratge had just thirty-six men – all convalescents – to guard it. His fellow *hauptmann*, Karl Fiesenhahn, had an engineer company of 125 men who had wired the bridge for demolition, and there were a miscellany of other units in and around the town; just under two hundred Hitler Youth youngsters, a Luftwaffe anti-aircraft battery, five hundred local *Volkssturm* militia, and even some one hundred and twenty Hiwis. This was no-one's definition of a significant defence force. Brushing aside weak resistance, and knowing the bridge would be wired for demolition, American infantrymen bravely surged onto the bridge and across it, even as the Germans detonated the charges. Amidst a deafening explosion the huge span lifted into the air – and then settled. As the smoke cleared, it was obvious the demolition had failed; the Ludendorff bridge was still standing. Bratge turned to a subordinate and ordered him to contact headquarters: 'Inform them that the demolition of the bridge was unsuccessful, and that the Americans have crossed.'

Bratge and Fiesenhahn surrendered in the railway tunnel on the eastern bank, along with a number of civilians and their few remaining men. At a 1962 veterans reunion of those who fought at Remagen, Bratge tried to explain why he thought the demolition hadn't worked:

> I asked for six hundred kilos of high-grade military explosives; I received instead three hundred kilos of far weaker commercial explosives. They were to be exploded electrically; we activated the detonator, and only one charge went off blowing a crater in front of the bridge... The main charge didn't go off; a tank round must have hit the pipe carrying the cable to the explosives.

Anton Klute, an Army telephone operator at the bridge more or less agreed with his former commander: 'An American grenade hit the cable.' However, Jacob Kleebach, a *feldwebel* in the bridge security force that day, didn't agree with his former *kameraden*: 'All those stories are not true. Nobody knows. It just didn't explode.' Karen Loef, a Remagen resident and one of those in the railway tunnel who surrendered with Bratge, agreed with Kleebach: 'Nobody really knows. There was too much confusion.' Whatever the truth, the bridge stood, and the Americans pushed troops across it as fast as they could. For their part, the Germans desperately tried to bring it down.

First up were the Luftwaffe, as the Junkers Ju-88 airman Heinz Phillip recounted:

> Some volunteers were wanted and I took part, my pilot was always keen to volunteer for almost everything, but I wasn't exactly filled with enthusiasm, but I had to go with him. A five-hundredweight bomb was attached below each of the wings – left and right, and we were meant to drop them on the bridge at Remagen. Four or five planes in all went on this mission, which took place at night. But, of course, the Amis had put everything they had at the Rhine crossing ... it was quite some firework display ... for us it wasn't good at all because we had drawn number three – we were going to be the third plane to attack. Each plane was given a time to attack, and so we knew when the first one was going in, and then there was a fireball and he no longer existed. Then the second plane went in – another fireball, except that one was a little lower down, and then it was our turn. You can imagine what our feelings were. It wasn't great, but we made it – we didn't hit the bridge, our bombs fell either side of it, but we got out in one piece. I'll never forget it though – when we landed, we found eighty-eight bullet and shell holes in the aircraft.[3]

Phillip and his crew were indeed lucky to survive. To protect the bridge the Americans assembled the largest concentration of anti-aircraft guns in the war. Over the next ten days over 350 aircraft – including Phillip's – attacked, with almost a third shot out of the sky. A week into the bombardment, Hitler ordered V-2s to be fired at it – the only time they were employed against a pin-point target – but the eleven missiles launched failed to hit it, with the nearest only getting to within a quarter of a mile. Even Kriegsmarine frogmen were utilised, swimming downriver guiding large floating mines as they had done at Nijmegen – this time round they were unsuccessful, with all seven divers being killed or captured.[4]

Needless to say, Hitler reacted badly to the capture of the Ludendorff bridge. Rundstedt, as *OB West*, was sacked for the third time in the war, this time permanently, with the dictator simply saying, 'I thank you for your loyalty.' His replacement was Albert Kesselring, who announced his arrival to his staff on 11 March by jokingly declaring, 'Well gentlemen, I am the new V-3.' Siegfried Westphal, as Chief of Staff, briefed his new boss on the situation: 'When I pointed out to him the dangerously depleted state of our forces he answered that "the Führer had told him something different". I requested my immediate dismissal ... this he rejected out of hand.'

Ever the optimist, Kesselring then met with Model as commander of *Heeresgruppe B,* and tried to relay to him what Keitel and Jodl had told him back in Berlin regarding the position in the West, to which Model snarled, 'From them I want to hear nothing!' The monocled Prussian field marshal had every reason to dismiss Hitler's lackeys. At the same time as the two officers were meeting, Meinrad von Lauchert's *2. Panzerdivision* – one of Model's best formations and the unit that had advanced furthest west during the Ardennes offensive – had been shoved back to the Rhine without being able to reach a secure crossing-point. Hemmed in from three sides, and without the strength to break out, Lauchert divided his command into small groups and ordered them to make their own way east to the German lines. Lauchert himself ended up swimming the Rhine with a few of his staff. On reaching the far bank, the thoroughly disillusioned panzer general made an extraordinary decision, and instead of finding the nearest German forces and reporting for duty, he began to walk home to Bamberg in northern Bavaria.

A number of other German generals were kicking their heels that spring, one of whom, Kurt *Panzermeyer*, spoke for many: 'We followed the fighting in our country with heavy hearts,' although he had more reason that most to be thankful. Following his surrender to Belgian partisans back in September, he had been robbed of his medals, his watch and his wedding ring, but his life was spared – unlike many of his compatriots. Passing himself off as an *Oberst* in the *2. Panzer* of all units, his true identity was only revealed after the discovery in an Allied POW camp of his SS blood group tattoo. Even then he almost got away with it, insisting to his captors: 'You are mistaken. Although the Waffen-SS introduced the blood group markings, the army panzer troops started using it as well ... after it had proved so useful ... all students at the panzer schools were sent back to their units with the tattoo.' Sent to a camp for senior officers near Windermere in the British Lake District, his commander there was none other than *Oberst* Gerhard Wilck, captured at Aachen.

Down at Trent Park, the coterie of senior detainees oscillated between defiance and despair at Germany's position. Ferdinand Heim, arrested after his failure at Stalingrad, then belatedly reprieved and installed as the commander of *Festung* Boulogne, had led a somewhat half-hearted defence of the port, surrendering over nine thousand of the ten-thousand-strong garrison after refusing to burn the city to the ground as ordered: 'I merely put a big red circle on my map to show that the demolitions had been theoretically carried out.' Whilst being recorded during the winter of 1944/45 he had said, 'The only thing is to fight to the last, even if everything is destroyed. Fighting until the last moment gives a people the moral strength to rise again, a people that throws in the towel is finished for all time. That is proved by history.' When the Ludendorff bridge was captured, he changed his tune: 'It has to end, it's simply insanity.' His fellow panzer general, Heinrich Eberbach, probably best expressed this duality in sentiment among the generals:

> One man thinks – 'the moment has come when we must capitulate …
> in order to preserve the essential being of the German race.' The other
> thinks, 'Things are now so desperate that the best thing is to fight to
> the bitter end … so that the German race may at some future date rise
> again.'[5]

Whatever the generals thought, the fact remained that the Anglo-Americans were now across the last great natural barrier in the west before Berlin. At this moment of crisis, Berlin's eyes were fixed firmly on the East – and Hungary; again.

10

West and East

Budapest had fallen on 13 February 1945, after a lengthy fifty-day siege that devastated the Hungarian capital. With it had gone some seventy thousand Hungarian-German troops in the city itself, and around thirty-eight thousand Hungarian civilians killed in the fighting. The Soviet victory wasn't the end of the city's agony; thousands more of its inhabitants were arrested by the Soviets after the battle, classified as 'combatants' and forcibly sent to labour camps in the East as collective punishment. The Red Army had paid the blood price for its victory; over one hundred thousand casualties, but more importantly for them they had captured a great European capital, and were now less than one hundred and fifty miles from Vienna.

The Nazis weren't finished quite yet though. Berlin still commanded considerable military forces, and – unbelievably – ammunition and equipment were still being produced and sent to the various fronts. The fabric of the Wehrmacht was fraying and tearing, but was still holding good; orders were issued, and soldiers looked to obey – despite the growing sense of despair. One such order was the call-up of some of the last teenage boys in the Reich; fifty-eight thousand of them duly reported for duty and were pretty much sent directly to the front – sometimes without weapons. *SS-Untersturmführer* Oswald Van Ooteghem was selected to be one of the boys' new officers:

I was posted into the 1st Battalion of SS-Freiwillige Grenadier Regiment 68 – known as the 'Hitler Youth' Battalion because it was composed almost entirely – around seventy-five per cent – of young volunteers from the Flemish youth organisation, the NSJV, that I'd been a member of before the war. I was given a platoon of forty young volunteers, they were all youngsters of fifteen to seventeen-years – most had been working in the Junkers aircraft factories – and they were convinced they would win the war. My battalion commander was Oluf von Krabbe, a former Danish Army officer... Goebbels's propaganda still spoke of the secret weapons that were being developed that would settle the war in our favour, but we knew the war was lost. Nevertheless, they sent us to fight the Red Army on the Oder River... I was ordered to guard a supply depot, containing weapons and ammunition. It was also a communications site. I only took twenty-one of my youngsters; the older ones of sixteen and seventeen, those aged just fifteen I left behind in the barracks, as we didn't have enough weapons for all of them anyway. We had been told 'make sure the young soldiers won't be sacrificed anymore. Ensure that they are withdrawn in time.' But we were overtaken by the Russians and our losses were huge. We didn't blame Hitler though. At that time there was no thought of political considerations. The survival instinct was all we had. We had to turn around and fight ... but we had no panzers, no food, not enough ammunition. It was impossible. Many youngsters were killed there... After a while we were all alone and were surrounded by the Russians. We escaped into a nearby wood but were soon surrounded again. That night I managed to lead a break-out with a few of the young lads, and we headed west as fast as we could. We went west on a compass bearing passing lakes, forests trying to hide from Russian tanks and troops. We only moved at night to avoid the Russians and Allied aircraft, and on the journey many other soldiers joined my group. I had almost a whole company, and because they could not pronounce my name, we called ourselves 'Kampfgruppe Oswald'. We still had to engage in some short fire-fights, but we made it.

Two other European Waffen-SS volunteers; Jan Munk and Theo D'Oosterlinck, were on their officer training course at the Bad Tölz academy when it received the order to halt all instruction and form the instructors and cadets into a new Waffen-SS division – the last one that would ever be established – the *38. SS-Panzergrenadier-Division 'Nibelungen'*.

D'Oosterlinck: 'We were sent to the Black Forest to form the Nibelungen Division. We were sent on buses; they were the buses from the local public school in the town. We were given Hitler Youth lads to lead; they were just boys, some were only fourteen or fifteen-years-old. We weren't even issued enough weapons for them all. We were always pulling back and trying to get out unscathed, trying not to lose anybody, you understand?'

Jan Munk: 'I was given a company of Volkssturm and Hitler Youth – boys and old men. We had no equipment, morale was poor, and the desertion rate was very high. We were employed as guards

on the roads, and we saw quite a few troops who were just trying
to escape south to Italy to surrender to the Americans or the British.
After a few days we sent everyone home... We were then issued with
orders to find our way back to our old divisions. Mine was still the
Wiking of course, which I was told was in Hungary, so that's where
I decided I would go.'

Munk packed his kit, slung it over his shoulder and headed off east
in the general direction of Hungary. En route he had an encounter with
some former Italian allies.

> I have no idea how long I was marching for and I really wanted to
> find some transport, and then I met two high-ranking Italian officers
> who had a very new looking lady's bike with them. I really wanted that
> bike. My opinion of the Italians as soldiers was not very high, as we
> had fought next to an Italian unit back in Russia and they were more
> trouble than they were worth. I told these officers I wanted the bike and
> they just handed it over without protest.

Youthful call-ups and 'new' SS divisions weren't the only ways the
Third Reich decided it was going to continue the fight that spring.
Having been on the receiving end of national resistance movements
since it had started the war, Nazi Germany decided to create one of its
own – the *Werwolf*. First mooted in senior Nazi circles the previous
autumn, the original concept was for a locally based fifth column of
ideologically sound Nazi operatives operating in conjunction with
the regular armed forces against the Anglo-Americans and Soviets in
areas 'temporarily' occupied by the enemy. On 19 September 1944,
Himmler appointed *SS-Obergruppenführer* Hans-Adolf Prützmann as
Nazi Germany's first *Generalinspekteur für Spezialabwehr* (General
Inspector for Special Defence), in reality, Head of *Werwolf*. Prützmann
had spent much of his war so far murdering Jews across Ukraine
and Latvia and was, as his fellow senior SS contemporary Ernst
Kaltenbrunner described him: 'Lazy, liked to travel around, never good
for serious, consistent work'. Prützmann was not at all enthused about
his new post, realising that it would significantly raise his profile with
the Allies at a time when he was keen to look at ways of disappearing
into the woodwork.

Nevertheless, orders were orders, and the SS general set about
recruiting volunteers and organising training. Fred Borth – a sixteen-
year-old Viennese Hitler Youth leader – volunteered, and was sent to a
camp in Passau for training under the tutelage of an *SS-Sturmbannführer*
nicknamed the 'Bishop', because he had apparently been ordained before
the war as an Eastern Orthodox priest.

The Bishop's idea of training was to get his charges to lie on railway ties and let trains pass over them, or to show his students how to commit suicide by folding back their own tongues over their throats. The highlight of the training schedule was a wild run through an obstacle course that started with the Bishop tightening a noose around the necks of the participants, so that they were choked nearly to the point of unconsciousness and then had to navigate the course in that state. To add to the 'sport', live ammunition was fired at the trainees, and grenades were tossed behind them to keep them moving.[1]

Another recruit remembered his instruction:

> Orders were to be carried out by any means. We were warned not to trust anybody, not even our own comrades, and we were to watch over each other. If a sabotage assignment was allotted to one man, he was to be covered by three others with snipers' rifles, who were to shoot anyone who interfered. Members of the organisation were told that in case of disobedience they would be killed by their own comrades.[2]

The object of such bizarre training was set out in a *Werwolf* pamphlet, distributed to Hitler Youth youngsters at the beginning of March 1945: 'The enemy will be obliged to deprive his front lines of troops which instead must be employed for the security of his rear areas. The enemy will lose vital material and cannot employ it against our soldiers... Everything that handicaps the enemy helps our soldiers!'

Strange as it may seem today, but there were still those in Germany who believed in the final victory of Nazism – even were it to be delayed until some point in the future, as one captured junior officer explained to his captors. 'A master race born to govern cannot be held down eternally.' Not that this was the prevailing view among the majority of Germans, as the baker's daughter, Hildegard Trutz, heard from the lips of her own SS trooper husband, Ernst:

> Fighting the Russians was all he could talk about until I got him alone, then he sat on the bed and buried his face in his hands and told me the war was lost. He told me he wasn't in his office job anymore but in the Waffen-SS... His job was to form a group of Werewolves and continue the struggle behind enemy lines. He said the *Werwolf* personnel were hardly more than a crowd of inexperienced HJ boys and the whole thing was pointless.[3]

As preparations for resistance in the German borderlands was stepped up, Hitler was still fixated on the Nagykanizsa oilfields southwest of Hungary's Lake Balaton. Unable, and unwilling, to accept the end game had been reached in his war, the Nazi dictator continued to rail about the need to safeguard the Wehrmacht's access to its last reserves of gasoline. That access was now seriously threatened by the Red Army, which had continued its advance west from Budapest. Hitler's answer was yet another 'surprise' offensive. This time the plan was to advance from north of Balaton not only to retake Budapest but also encircle and destroy at least two Soviet armies to the south. The main forces to accomplish this miraculous feat were to be none other than Sepp Dietrich's 6. *Panzerarmee,* hurriedly withdrawn from the Ardennes. On arriving in the assembly area, one of Dietrich's own senior staff officers was un impressed by what he found: 'In the constricted area between Lakes Balaton and Valencei the mud became alarming ... the land was underwater – impassable for all kinds of vehicles ... a panzer attack in open terrain under these conditions is out of the question.'[4]

Codenamed *Unternehmen Frühlingserwachen* (Operation Spring Awakening), the Wehrmacht's last major offensive of the war got underway on 6 March 1945. Spearheaded by the panzers and grenadiers of the *Leibstandarte* and *Hitlerjugend,* the attack went well at first, the Soviets taking heavy casualties and thrown back in some confusion, before resistance stiffened as a panzer crewman recalled: 'When we reached the Russian trench system we found a long row of dug-in flamethrowers which could be fired electrically ... our panzer-grenadiers ran into a wall of flame.' The spring thaw then intervened and effectively killed the offensive off in the mud, as Otto Holst saw for himself: 'The frozen ground turned bottomless. Of the seven operational jagdpanzers, six quickly became hopelessly stuck, they sank up to their track guards ... the infantry companies continued without our support.' Dieter Kuhlmann was right in the middle of it all:

The roads were deep and mushy and there were large puddles in the fields. Dead Red Army soldiers and pieces of equipment lay all around. Suddenly we heard a roaring overhead and all hell broke loose as we were caught in a barrage ... there were screams and curses and then a breathless stillness ... we laid the wounded down in a barn, Herbert called faintly for me, on each side of his chest he had a hole the size of a pigeons egg, a thin stream of blood ran out of the corner of his mouth, he closed his eyes.[5]

The German attack stalled, and in the pause the Red Army launched its own counter-offensive. The *Hohenstaufen's* commander, Sylvester Stadler, described it thus:

The Russians attacked all day long in battalion and regimental strength ... scarcely was one attack repulsed when they appeared in another place. The Division ...was able to hold off all the attacks and make them extremely costly for the enemy. Unfortunately, our own losses were equally high.[6]

The SS NCO, Martin Glade, remembered it vividly: 'We were at the end of our physical strength, at each orientation stop comrades dropped to the ground where they stood.' Ordered to set up defences on a hill, Glade and his company began to dig in, but fatigue overcame him. 'When I woke up, I was hardly able to get to my feet.' Then the Russians shelled them and attacked. 'The effect of the enemy fire was devastating ... to the left and right of me men were lying motionless, silent, strangely curled-up ... last night we'd been forty-eight.'[7] Wolfgang Lincke, an officer cadet in the *Hitlerjugend,* was caught up in the same fighting:

Suddenly, around noon, a signal flare climbed into the sky from the forest. Right away a concentrated rocket fire was directed at our positions ... at the same time hordes of Russian infantry stormed out of the forest ... next to me a shell exploded, when I regained consciousness it was clear to me that I was wounded – I had to get help, anything but fall into the hands of the Russians!

Lincke somehow made his way to the battalion command post and was evacuated. The *Ostheer* still continued to make life difficult for its Soviet foe though, as the Danish volunteer Erik Brörup described:

It was St Patrick's Day, 17 March 1945, near Szekesfehervar in Hungary. I was Adjutant – with the rank of SS-Obersturmführer – to SS-Sturmbannführer Fritz Vogt, holder of the Knight's Cross. I had established a command post in a small house and set up communications with a switchboard and radio while shells fell around us. SS-Obergruppenführer Gille telephoned to congratulate Vogt on his birthday and to tell him he had just been awarded the Oakleaves to his Knight's Cross. His face lit up and he said: 'This calls for a drink!' We hoisted a few, then the Supply officers showed up bearing some bottles of beer, and all the other officers found time to show up for a quick drink. All the while the war was going on around us. One company commander was having some trouble with the enemy, so I suggested to Vogt that I go and try to straighten things out. Vogt laughed and said: 'What's the matter with you, do you feel like a hero today?' I answered that he had just got himself a new medal and should let others have a chance to win one. He replied: 'Okay but watch what you are doing!' By that time of course we had all had a good drink and were in excellent spirits!

I got an SdKfz 250/9 [an armoured personnel carrier with a mounted 20mm cannon] and went into battle. We were firing high-explosive shells and it seemed easy, like shooting fish in a barrel. Then the Russians brought up an anti-tank rifle and shot up my vehicle, forcing us to bail out. We ended up in hand-to-hand combat with them. I had a panzerfaust but it wouldn't fire. I therefore used it like a club and cracked one Russian's head with it. I was in trouble though. However, Fritz Vogt then appeared with a few more armoured personnel carriers and got me out. He told me to take a couple of hours off, and later he and I went off alone on a reconnaissance behind the enemy lines. I got the Iron Cross First Class for all this.[8]

Regardless of Brörup's semi-inebriated success, the German position in Hungary was untenable, and by the end of March the country had been abandoned as the Wehrmacht retreated into Austria; often hounded by Anglo-American equipment shipped to the Red Army, as one Waffen-SS officer saw first-hand: 'More and more often we faced Shermans, Churchills and Cromwell tanks, which had been thrown into action without even having their English markings removed.'

The Wehrmacht would now have to make do with the fuel it had, even as new equipment and reinforcements turned up:

3. Kompanie was refitted with ten new Panzer IVs and their assigned crews from Linz. Subsequently the Kompanie received a Panther platoon from an Army division and a kompanie of gebirgsjäger ... the atmosphere was truly hopeless, the issue of orders sluggish, inconsistent and lacked conviction. I had the impression we were facing our last battle and that we could only delay the impending collapse.

With grim humour, Sepp Dietrich agreed. He told the Austrian capital's *Gauleiter*, Baldur von Schirach: 'Do you know why we're called 6. Panzerarmee? Because we only have six panzers left!'

All along the Eastern front, the *Ostheer* was beginning to crumble. *Hauptmann* Curt Vogt of the *344. ID* was in Rasselwitz (modern-day Polish *Racławiczki)* trying to escape west before being encircled:

All night long soldiers, mixed in with civilians, many of them women with young children, pushed themselves through the 'hole' which had been opened ... they would have risked jumping through the flames ... anything but fall into the hands of the Red Army!... hits from shells had a dreadful effect. Bodies were hurled aside, lying shattered on the ground. Those who had been hit writhed in their own blood, giving the death rattle, groaning or crying for help. Sometimes you could see women bending over the bodies of children ... they lifted them up, shaking them, calling them by name but getting no answer.

To the north of Vogt and the Rasselwitz tragedy – up in Gotenhafen (modern-day Gdynia) on the Baltic coast – Bruno Friesen and seven of his comrades were standing around near their *jagdpanzers* when there was a violet explosion:

> I found myself flat on the ground... I could hear, I could see, I could speak. I could feel I was wounded, I could smell the explosion, and my own blood ... the diagnosis was multiple shell fragments; my right shoulder, my right arm above the elbow, right buttock and left shin – all hit... My guess was that a mortar shell got us. Three of our group were dead. Unteroffizier Fehler looked dead – he was – the rest were wounded, some very badly and worse than me.

Evacuated to Denmark by boat, he boarded a hospital train back to Germany with a number of other wounded men: 'A diverse bunch on the train ... one man I recall lamented the loss of his penis, intermittently consoling himself by remembering that he was already the father of two children – the Russians had hit his fly with a small-calibre bullet.'[9]

Feldwebel Willibald Casper of the Army's élite *Panzergrenadier-Division 'Grossdeutschland'* was caught with the remnants of his unit hard up against the Baltic coast: 'The Russians attacked Heiligenbeil, I remember the day well as it was my thirtieth birthday – I had a party in hell.' Reduced to just four thousand men from its original twenty thousand-plus establishment, many grenadiers tried to escape across the sea to a neighbouring peninsula: 'Many threw together rafts made from planks and watertight containers but most were flimsy, and at night we heard the cries of the drowning.' Hendrik Verton had been on an NCOs course in Pomerania, when he and his fellow cadets were instead pressed into *SS-Regiment Besslein* and sent to help defend Silesia's capital, Breslau. Verton – a native of Schouwen-Duiveland in the Netherlands – would spend the next eighty-two days fighting for the city. In March,

> We were about to take over new quarters in the Zimpel district. The responsible Nazi Party district officer accompanied us to garages that had corrugated iron doors. In attempting to open one, he hit the door with the butt of a fully-loaded machine-pistol without its safety catch on. It exploded. Our Hauptschar received the full burst in his intestines and was killed on the spot. We pounded on the man, shouting and cursing him ... our Hauptschar's death was very bitter for us, he

had gone through all of Russia without a scratch... One day three 'unarmed' Russians wearing Red Cross armbands carried a stretcher to within yards of us. We honoured the code of stopping firing whilst they recovered their dead and wounded – that was sacred to us. When they got near us though, they threw grenades at us that had been hidden under a blanket on the stretcher. Before we could react they had disappeared to the other side of the street.[10]

Alongside Verton in the besieged city was Lucie Lefever, a Flemish nurse serving in the German Red Cross:

I felt it was my duty to stay. We felt protected. Afterwards we found out that this was not the case when we had to surrender. The Russians came closer and closer to the Oder ... we used a castle about a kilometre behind the river as a dressing station. The wounded kept on being brought to us from the fighting, it went on day and night. We had no proper ambulances. Our wounded soldiers were brought in on trucks, on wagons pulled by horses, on anything that could be found – we were terribly short of medicines, and only had paper for bandages; so many young men died who would have lived if we'd had proper equipment ... then we had to leave the castle as the Russians were too close, and we set up a new dressing station in Frankfurter Strasse, near the Gandau aerodrome. The Russians bombed us for two whole days ... we were obliged to flee into the *Jahrhunderthalle* – a large modern building for exhibitions.[11]

Unlike Remagen on the Rhine, there was no easy crossing point on the Oder River for the Soviets, as the *Ostheer* put every man into the line it could find to try and hold them. Although by now the Wehrmacht's manpower shortfalls were stark, as the sniper Sepp Allerberger saw for himself with the arrival of some supposed reinforcements, 'The troop consisted entirely of young boys of about sixteen years old, who had been called-up only a few weeks earlier. After a two-week training course they had been sent to the front. A young *SS-Untersturmführer* was in charge of the forty-odd youngsters and clearly didn't care about their lives.'

There were also some rather bizarre replacements, as the Romanian ethnic German Frank Bereznyak remembered: 'After the intense fighting in Pomerania and the retreat towards Altdamm – where we suffered heavy losses – we sought rest in a forest near the Oder. Among the reinforcements that joined us were five Englishmen – former POWs – who had volunteered.'[12]

Even now, Nazi propaganda sought to offer some sort of hope of final victory, although *landsers* like Günter Korschorrek weren't fooled: 'Some people still believe in the top secret "Wunderwaffen" everyone is still talking about. I am sceptical – very sceptical – because in the past so much has been promised and not delivered.'[13] The reality at the front was one that Herbert Maeger – an ethnic German from Belgium serving as a medic – knew only too well:

> The last weeks on the Oder front live in my memory as a chaos of blood, defeat and despair... the rows of stretchers in front of the operating theatre lengthened, men suffering from shock, loss of blood ... we simply couldn't handle the numbers of wounded ... everybody could see that the end was near, and ever present was the fear of falling into the hands of the Russians... I spoke to a friend of mine Hans Bender, and said 'if we are going to get out of this mess we need more than a miracle, our only reserves exist in our imagination.'[14]

Morale in the Wehrmacht – so long its backbone – was beginning to fracture, as Erwin Bartmann noticed as he and some hastily assembled replacements were packed off to the east: 'Around midday ... a convoy of trucks arrived and we hurriedly packed our machine-guns and ammo onto them. "I think it's the Oder front for us!" I said, a deathly silence had fallen over the recruits, their faces were as grey as potter's clay.'

In Courland, Norbert Hannig and his comrades were reduced to trawling the canal for eels, using old Soviet bombs to blow fish out of the water, and stealing rabbits from their meteorological service brethren, so as not to go hungry in the besieged pocket. When asked by a comrade what they should do when the war ended, he replied, 'We stick by our men whatever happens.'

'Good. That's all I wanted to hear you say.'

11

It's All Over!

Short, with a dark complexion and beak nose that marked him out, fifty-year-old *General der Fallschirmtruppe* Alfred Schlemm had taken over command from Kurt Student on the German-Netherlands border, and now faced the Anglo-Canadians with his back to the Rhine. Desperately short of troops, Rundstedt had nevertheless told the Russian front veteran that he 'mustn't yield an inch of ground without my authorization'. Also under the *Führer* order not to allow a bridge over the Rhine to fall intact into Allied hands, Schlemm said, 'Since I had nine bridges in my sector I could see my hopes of a long life rapidly dwindle.' The diminutive para general could still count on some veteran units though, such as von der Heydte's *FJR.6*, once again being rebuilt, with its hard-bitten commander exhorting its replacements:

> From the moment a man volunteers … and joins my regiment, he enters into a new order of humanity. He is ruled by one law only – that of our unit. He must give up personal weaknesses and ambitions and realise that our battle is for the existence of the whole German nation … he must believe in this victory even when reason tells him it cannot be.

Then, on 23 March, Montgomery finally launched his showpiece crossing of the River Rhine, *Operation Plunder*. In his last major offensive of the war, the British field marshal combined heavy bombing, massed artillery, and the final Allied airborne assault of the Second World War, to overwhelm the defences of Model's *Heeresgruppe B*.

The day before Montgomery's assault, Patton crossed the Rhine at Oppenheim, just south of Mainz. *Obergefreiter* Henry Metelmann had spent more than three years fighting on the Russian front as a panzer driver, before being wounded for the third time and sent west to recuperate. Dragooned into a scratch *kampfgruppe* from his convalescence, he was not impressed with his situation: 'I was issued with a rifle with a 1917 stamp on it and a broken sight. I was also issued with a panzerfaust which was heavy and awkward to carry.'

The *Westheer* the Anglo-Americans now faced had an Order of Battle listing no less than sixty divisions – only three fewer than were present back on D-Day. Despite the transfer east of Dietrich's *6. Panzerarmee,* Berlin could still count three army groups in the West; Ernst Busch's *Heeresgruppe H* in the Netherlands with von Zangen's *15. Armee* and Student's *1. Fallschirm-Armee,* Paul Hausser (the only Waffen-SS officer to reach the dizzying heights of army group command) and his *Heeresgruppe G* with the *1.* and *19. Armees* in southern Germany, and sandwiched in the middle Walter Model's *Heeresgruppe B.* On the giant wall maps of various senior Wehrmacht headquarters, this was an impressive array. It wouldn't win the war, but it could hold its own against the Anglo-Americans; except it was all an illusion. Half of those sixty divisions were reduced to *kampfgruppe* strength – about one-third of their proper divisional establishment – and the majority of the rest were shards. Kurt Wagener, Model's Chief of Staff, said of his command, 'We had only a confused army of stragglers who, when gathered up, only slipped away again.' Wagener was right, but it wasn't just his own army group that was dying, it was the Wehrmacht as a whole. *Landsers* had been joking with grim humour for months that the Luftwaffe was nowhere to be seen in a sky dominated by the Anglo-Americans, and now it really was true. Aircraft rolling off the production lines had no aviation fuel to get them into the air, and the flight schools had more or less stopped functioning, cutting off the supply of new pilots. The collapse of the Luftwaffe didn't go unnoticed by their opponents. The American 56th Fighter Group – officially the most successful Allied fighter unit in the European Theatre of Operations (ETO) – claimed just twenty-three Bf 109s in the last four months of the war; there just weren't any Germans left to shoot down.

Regardless, the slaughter went on. In March, 284,000 members of the Wehrmacht were killed. The dreaded death notices sent to relatives stated '*Gefallen für Führer, Volk und Vaterland*' (Fallen for Führer, People and Fatherland'). Some civilians in Germany's western provinces were now openly calling on their soldiers to end the fighting and stop the slaughter, as Henry Metelmann saw for himself: 'I was stopped by a group of women … they begged me not to be silly and start fighting with the Amis in the streets as it would only end in death and destruction. Deep down I agreed with them, but I was still a German soldier.'

Two days after Montgomery crossed the Rhine, on the evening of 25 March Dr Franz Oppenhoff, a lawyer and the American-appointed *Oberbürgermeister* (Mayor) of Aachen, was out for an evening with his wife when he was called home by his housekeeper Elisabeth Gillessen, ostensibly to deal with three downed Luftwaffe aircrew asking for passes to allow them to get through American Army checkpoints. Arriving at his back door he was instead confronted by two men, one armed with a silencer-equipped Walther pistol. The gunman hesitated, whereupon the second, a hulking man with blond hair, grabbed the gun and without saying a word, shot him once in the head. Oppenhoff was killed instantly. The assassins ran off into the darkness. The *Werwolf* had just claimed its most high-profile target of the war so far.[1]

With the Rhine crossed in the north and south, the Anglo-Americans had the opportunity to do something they had so far failed to achieve in the whole European war; encircle and destroy an entire German field army. With Busch and Hausser's army groups so weak, and Model's virtually immobilised due to lack of gasoline, a vast pincer movement was in the offing. This was the operation Eisenhower had dreamt of since being named as Supreme Commander – his very own Cannae. The cauldron at Falaise had been the closest he had come, but large numbers of Germans had escaped that debacle, and a Wehrmacht collapse had been averted – would it now? Did the Germans have something up their sleeve?

The Allied plan was ambitious. Montgomery's Anglo-Canadian force would form the northern pincer, and Omar Bradley's Americans the southern. The two jaws of the trap would meet in the area of Lippstadt, some eighty miles east of the Rhine. Within the sack would be the Ruhr, at the time the world's largest single industrial complex, dotted with the smoke-stack cities of Essen, Dortmund, Duisburg and Hamm. Those same cities were built on top of the second largest coalfield on earth and produced two-thirds of Germany's steel – it was the very heart of the Reich's war economy. Allied intelligence reported that if it were lost then Germany would be unable to continue the war, and that the pocket could contain as many as eighty thousand Germans – they were correct about the former, and woefully under-cooked on the latter.

Model requested permission from Hitler to at least try and withdraw east out of danger, but predictably, the *Führer* refused; *Festung Ruhr* would hold out to the last man and the last bullet, tying down vast Allied forces, buying time for new weapons and new formations to go over to the offensive and turn the tide – or so Berlin said. The reality on the ground was a world away from what was becoming a bloody fantasy. 'Survival was what mattered to us. To lose a war was terrible – we all felt that. We spent a good deal of time speculating about what we might have to face, imprisonment, that sort of thing. How can life go on, what will happen – our towns were in ruins.'[2]

Not all *landsers* agreed with Otto Henning; Robert Vogt had been wounded in Normandy and was now back fighting in the Ruhr: 'We were soldiers and had taken the oath to the Führer. I didn't believe that our panzerfausts could win the war, but to desert, well, that never crossed my mind.' Another *landser* agreed: 'I don't think any men from Germany proper would desert, only Austrians and all those volksdeustche.'[3] To help stiffen the sinews of Wehrmacht personnel, the Nazis instituted a draconian punishment regime, with squads of SS and *feldgendarmerie* (field police) empowered to check the papers of every man they found, and summarily execute anyone they suspected of dereliction of duty. Joseph Goebbels had a proclamation read out on state radio:

> Any man found not doing his duty will be hanged from a lamp post after a summary judgment. Moreover, placards will be attached to the corpses stating: 'I have been hanged here because I am too cowardly to defend the capital of the Reich. I have been hanged because I did not believe in the Führer. I am a deserter and for this reason I shall not see this turning point in history.'

More often than not, the executioners didn't bother with such a long-winded explanation and the wooden board hung round the poor unfortunate's neck simply read, '*Ich bin feige*' (I am a coward). One German civilian remembered that 'boys who were found hiding were hanged as traitors by the SS as a warning that, 'He who was not brave enough to fight had to die.' When trees were not available, people were strung up on lamp posts. They were hanging everywhere, military and civilian, men and women, ordinary citizens who had been executed by a small group of fanatics.'

Civilians were too afraid of retribution to cut the bodies down. For Robert Vogt the choice was stark: 'A fanatical officer might have shot us, so we'd fight as long as we had weapons and some kind of command.' Not everyone agreed, even among the so-called élite of the armed SS, as one imprisoned ex-*SS-Frundsberg* member stated: 'I shall probably be sentenced to death, but it's better to be alive under sentence of death for desertion than to be lying dead on the battlefield.' German resolve was breaking, as an internal SS report on the mood of the populace at large made plain: 'Until the last few days people retained a remnant of belief in a miracle, which has been so skilfully and purposefully nurtured by the propaganda, about the new weapons.'

No new miracle weapons were forthcoming, and then it happened. On 26 March the British Second Army, advancing east, produced the following astonishing assessment: 'This is the collapse. The enemy no longer has a coherent system of defence between the Rhine and the Elbe. It is difficult to see what there is to stop us now.'

A few days later, on April Fools' Day 1945, the British and American spearheads met up in Lippstadt – just one week after the crossing of the Rhine at Wesel. All of *Heeresgruppe B* was now trapped in a huge pocket of some four thousand square miles. The initial Allied assessment of eighty thousand German troops encircled was first upgraded to 125,000, and then increased again to 150,000. Even this was a massive underestimate – there were actually 323,000, including twenty-five generals, one admiral and a field-marshal.[4] Gerda Ehrhardt, now a staff assistant at *Heeresgruppe B*'s headquarters, saw that lone field-marshal:

> Model was striding up and down like a tiger in a cage. He didn't know what to do … it was over for him… I didn't care anymore. I lay flat out in an apple orchard and the Ami shells screamed over me, one after another. I saw Model's cartographer. 'I'm walking to Munich, come with me,' I'd had enough, it was time to go home.[5]

Ehrhardt wasn't alone, Robert Vogt was trying to defend an *autobahn* when the Americans attacked:

> It was pointless. We were gambling with our lives for a lost cause. It became clear – even to us – that the war was lost. So we threw our weapons into a stream and waving a white pocket handkerchief, moved towards the autobahn.

As the rest of the Allied armies headed to the Elbe River, some eighteen American divisions were left behind to smash the pocket. Rolf Munninger – one of Model's staff officers remembered: 'We were hunted, really hunted. There was no longer a proper headquarters, we just parked our vehicles where we could and always in a wood, then at least we had some cover.' An order arrived from Hitler instructing them all to break out, Munninger ignored it as irrelevant, but Model found out and exploded: 'I ought to have you executed on the spot!' Munninger wasn't overly concerned. 'It would have been difficult to have me shot – we didn't have any guns or ammunition left.'

In desperation, Model requested that Berlin supply his forces by air – clearly an impossible ask given that the Luftwaffe had almost ceased to exist – and he was duly turned down. By now, only some twenty per cent of his men even had weapons with which to fight. The situation was hopeless, and Model finally acknowledged it. On 15 April he discharged all sixteen- and seventeen-year-olds from the Army and did the same for those aged forty and over. Two days later he dissolved *Heeresgruppe B* rather than surrender it – his men were free to lay down their arms and try and make it home. He then gathered his headquarters staff together: 'Has everything been done to justify our actions in the light of history? What can there be left for a commander in defeat? In antiquity they took poison.'

Rolf Munninger recalled: 'Model said to us, "Gentlemen, it's over, there is nothing more we can do. It is up to you what you do from here." That was it – the end. There were no more orders, just six of us left, still in uniform.'

The response from Berlin was emphatic. Goebbels took to the air waves and branded them the *'verrätische Ruhrarmee'* – the 'treacherous

Ruhr army'. Model – for so long Hitler's 'fireman', the general who had followed his *Führer*'s orders without question – turned to his remaining three companions: 'I sincerely believe that I have served a criminal. I led my soldiers in good conscience ... but for a criminal government.' There's a strong argument that it took Walter Model far, far too long to recognise that basic fact. Perhaps his sudden damascene moment was spurred by the news that he had been indicted by the Soviet government for war crimes, specifically his part in the forced mass deportations from the East – not that there was evidence of his direct involvement, or that he even knew about it, but hundreds of thousands of civilians had been sent to their deaths on his watch.

Three days later, on 21 April, with the Americans closing in, Model had his sole remaining aide drive him to a wood northeast of Düsseldorf. He pointed down a logging road, and the staff car turned off and carried on into the trees. Telling his aide to stop, they both got out. Model put his wedding ring and a letter to his wife inside an envelope and gave it to his subordinate: 'A Feldmarschall does not surrender. Such a thing is not possible.' Walking to an old oak tree, he pointed at the ground next to it and said, 'You will bury me here.' Then he took out his Walther pistol and blew his brains out.[6]

The end of *Heeresgruppe B* spelt the end of the *Westheer*. With no natural defensive barriers to build a line upon, and no major formations left to block the Anglo-American advance, it was now only a matter of time before the very heart of Germany was overrun. From now on, resistance was fitful and disjointed, but it still existed, as the agony continued. Over ten thousand Americans were killed in the April fighting – 10,677 to be exact – that's almost as many as were lost in the month after D-Day. They would be joined by a staggering 281,000 Germans; although the majority of those fell in the east of the country facing the Soviets.

The demarcation line agreed between the Anglo-Americans and the Soviets was the wide and meandering Elbe River. The German experience east and west of that line would be markedly different, to say the least. The position in the west was aptly described by a report from Charles Hunter Gerhardt's American 29th Infantry Division: 'We're advancing as fast as the looting will permit.' In the east, the soldiers of the Red Army were exhorted to exact revenge on the nation that had so brutalised their own. Mass rape and destruction were the norm. As one Red Army officer said, 'Our men shoot the parents who try to save their children.'[7] The reaction of the remaining *landsers* mirrored the threat. A *Leibstandarte* officer candidate who had fought in the Ardennes was in a *kampfgruppe* south of Munich: 'We were ... trying to delay the progress of the Amis, but we didn't try too hard ... for the first time, the officers were allowing people to desert, and by the time we got to Bad Reichenhall we were down to about four hundred men.'[8] Felix Steiner's *SS-Panzer-*

Armeeoberkommando 11 (also known as the 11th SS-Panzer Army) was a bellwether for the Wehrmacht's attitude in those final months. Newly formed in early February with enough units to form a corps, it was named an army because 'panzer army has a better ring to it' and immediately deployed for an offensive – *Unternehmen Sonnenwende* (*Operation Solstice*) – to hit the Soviets in their exposed flank in Pomerania. Crashing forward, the Army reached the besieged town of Arnswalde (modern-day Choszczno), rescuing its garrison of two thousand and enabling the civilian population to evacuate. Up against the Red Army it fought hard, as one of its members – the Swedish volunteer Erik Wallin – recounted:

> I got the machine-gun going and fired for all I was worth … our weapons spat fire and death… I saw a Bolshevik working his way through a depression towards us… He aimed a burst from his submachine-gun at me… I got hold of an assault rifle and waited for him… Finally the Russian made a mistake… I squeezed the trigger and before he could react he had a hole between his eyes.

Wallin was then involved in another attack: 'With wild roars of "hurrah!" we pushed on through thickets and bushes, firing madly … we recaptured the whole wooded sector in a matter of minutes… The whole field was covered with fallen enemy soldiers.' The price paid was high. Wallin's number two on the machine-gun, Gebauer, 'a nineteen-year-old German farmer's son from Romania … suddenly jerked backwards and sank to one side… He was hit under the left eye, the bullet passing through his neck. He was still alive … he embraced me … "write to my mother." The embrace slackened, the arms sank… I was alone.' With Arnswalde relieved, and the Soviets bringing up fresh troops, the offensive petered out, and the 11th was transferred south into the care of *General der Artillerie* Walther Lucht. Its Chief of Staff – *Oberst* Fritz Estor – described it as 'not having a single complete unit with any real fighting power, no artillery worth mentioning, no reserves, and no air support'. Shorn of pretty much all its combat divisions, left as they were in the north to face the Red Army – it could do little except retreat in front of the Americans towards the Harz Mountains. Alfred Sturm's *'Division Sturm'* was typical of its composition now; from a miserly complement of two thousand, enough stragglers were scooped up in just over a week to build it to a strength of seven thousand by 10 April, but with desertion rife a fortnight later Sturm could muster just thirty men, almost all of them on his own staff, as the rest simply abandoned their weapons and headed home. Three such ex-soldiers marched up to an American tank parked by the side of a road, snapped to attention, raised their hands in the air and surrendered to the bemused sergeant sitting on top of the turret. 'Get the hell outta here! We ain't about to feed ya!'

For the senior NCO, Karl Jauss, the biggest moment was when 'for the first time we saw white flags on the houses.' Two young officers, Walter Fröbe and Paul Senghas, remembered the end of their war. Fröbe:

> We dug in at the entrance to a village ... all of a sudden we saw Ami tanks ... they'd seen us too. In the same instant there was a crash next to us, the Amis had sent over a couple of high-explosive rounds – that was the moment it got all of us – then everything was quiet. Sepp was mortally wounded next to me. I got it in the leg and thigh. I wasn't capable of walking. I lost consciousness as the result of losing so much blood and didn't come round until later in a cellar of a farmhouse where my comrades had hidden me. Then I went to a military hospital and two years in captivity.

Paul Senghas:

> We requisitioned a civilian car... I rode with three other men, I was sitting on the left front bumper ... there were already white flags hanging out of windows ... then we were hit by an Ami armoured car... I fell into the roadside ditch, badly wounded. I had a bullet embedded in my thigh, another in my left foot, and a ricochet through my lower left arm, grazing the artery and damaging the nerves... After a short while we were taken prisoner by Ami soldiers.

There was still resistance in the west, but more often than not it was half-hearted, as Jan Munk testified:

> We were with this Standartenführer in April and it was a marvellous time. He told us he wanted to collect as many pistols, machine-guns, mortars and panzerfausts as we could get hold of, and so we stopped military convoys, took what we wanted, loaded it into a truck and took it to a hiding place on a farm. I believe it was all connected to the Werwolf organisation who were meant to be SS men who had vowed to undertake guerrilla fighting and never surrender. In reality nothing like that happened... We were then split up and I was once again given command of a company of Hitler Youth and Labour Service boys – most of them were sixteen but some were just fifteen. We were in Eggenfeld north-east of Munich ... my orders were to take up a defensive position, where a road entered a wood, and stop any enemy tanks getting through. I put my boys to digging foxholes and told them to keep under cover at all costs. They were all extremely keen and determined to do their bit for the war. A few hours later ten or twelve American tanks appeared with no infantry. The road was very narrow and built high above the surrounding fields, which meant the tanks were forced to drive in convoy, one after the other, making our

job easier. I fired first and crippled the lead tank and then the Americans fired all their ammunition, blasting the wood until I think they ran out of shells. I watched as the crew of the stricken tank were taken on board another one, and then they all reversed back the way they had come. None of my boys had been injured, which was all well and good, but the situation was hopeless. I told my boys we had to move out before the nearest enemy aircraft came and bombed us. Back in the safety of a nearby village I told the boys that was it and they had to go back to their homes. Some of them were bitterly disappointed and cried. This was my only encounter with the Americans.

Munk and his youngsters were lucky. With victory, peace and home so close, many Allied soldiers weren't prepared to take any risks and were outraged at any lingering signs of German resistance, as Sergeant Ellis of Britain's Royal Tank Regiment made abundantly clear:

We hadn't come all this way to be knocked about in the last weeks of the war or be buggered about by those kids … their tactics were hopeless … they tried street fighting using methods that only work in open country. For example, they'd throw a grenade and run into a house. We'd open fire on the house with our main armament and a couple of shots would bring it tumbling down … whenever we fired our main gun they didn't scatter but bunched together, it was pathetic really.[9]

Ellis couldn't be blamed for his approach, after all the Wehrmacht – and its *Werwolf* arm – were still killing Allied soldiers. As late as 21 April, Major John Poston, one of Montgomery's favourite liaison officers, was ambushed in his jeep and killed in a gun battle with suspected *Werwolf* guerrillas. Allied reaction was swift and final, as one soldier from the American 5th Infantry Division remembered:

One day I heard a commotion outside the building I was in. Looking out of the window I saw a GI shoving a civilian along – the GI was crying and loudly accusing the civilian of killing his friend. The civilian was terrified and trying to move away from the GI. Shortly I heard a shot. Those of us in the room I was in looked at each other, and then we went back to whatever we were doing.[10]

Capitulation was now the norm though, as a wounded Richard von Rosen explained: 'In April a large town or city fell every day. It was entirely obvious that the end was near and not even a miracle could stave off our total defeat. On 20 April, the Führer's birthday, Goebbels made a speech of praise which ended – as did all those made over those years – with the sentence, "May he remain what he is to us and always was: our Hitler!"'

Obergefreiter Henry Metelmann and his comrades found themselves surrounded by the Americans while hiding in a cellar.

> I said to my comrades: 'Right, that's it, we're going to surrender.' No-one objected... I fixed a dirty white towel to a broomstick ... and, followed by my friends, I climbed up the cellar steps, opened the door and stepped out into the street ... a group of women on the opposite pavement looked at us and one of them mockingly said, 'There's Hitler's last hope.'

This was categorically not the situation in the east, where Nazi Germany's *landsers* fought on. Why? What did they hope to achieve? Victory was a long-forgotten dream, and the idea of allying with the Anglo-Americans to fight the Soviets had been shown to be the forlorn hope it always was, as Kurt Meyer and his fellow officers in the far-away British Lake District were at last beginning to understand.

> We somehow believed in the peoples of Europe changing their minds and preventing the military occupation of eastern and central Germany by the Red Army, but we were mistaken. Destiny took its course and let the Asiatics up to the Elbe and into the heart of Europe. The complete collapse of Germany shook us to the core. We had been waiting for it to happen for weeks, but it still hit us deeply ... we had had no news from our families in months, none of us could say for certain where our families were, or whether they were even alive.[11]

The Soviet Union may have invaded Poland in the autumn of 1939 along with the Wehrmacht, and Stalin may have refused to allow Allied aircraft to land on Soviet airfields after dropping supplies to the Polish Home Army during the Warsaw Uprising, but the grand alliance wasn't about to fall apart – even though it had a few cracks in it. After all, the French had put up with Britain's Royal Navy killing thirteen hundred of their sailors at Mers-el-Kébir in July 1940, and then the Americans killing another fourteen hundred French soldiers when they landed in French North Africa back in November 1942; not to mention the almost seventy thousand French men, women and children lost to Allied bombing. The partnership constructed with so much skill and care by Britain's Prime Minister Winston Churchill was close to final victory and wasn't going to fall apart now. So, the *landsers* had forsworn glossy illusion for the practicalities of painful reality – and in the spring of 1945 that meant keeping as many German civilians and members of the *Ostheer* as possible out of the hands of the Soviets. That meant *landsers* tenaciously fighting for every inch of German soil to allow civilians and their comrades to head west – but it also meant a last hurrah for the Wehrmacht's Cinderella service; the Kriegsmarine, and its ordinary *Matrosen* (naval version of the *landser*).

Utilising just about anything that could float, Karl Dönitz instigated and organised probably the largest maritime rescue operation in history – *Unternehmen Hannibal (Operation Hannibal)* and, moreover, he did it without Hitler intervening to stop it. Between 21 January and 9 May 1945, the Kriegsmarine transported over two million German soldiers and civilians to the west from Courland, East Prussia, Pomerania and the German Baltic coast. Over one thousand vessels were involved, from major capital ships such as the battle cruiser *Admiral Hipper*, to tramp steamers and pleasure craft. Regardless of whether the ships were ferrying soldiers or civilians – and on many there was no distinction between the two – the Soviet navy and air force viewed all as legitimate targets and hit them hard. Some 206 ships were sunk, including the former cruise ship the *Wilhelm Gustloff*. Setting off from Danzig on 30 January, crammed to the gunnels with almost eleven thousand soldiers and civilians. She was spotted by Alexander Marinesko's S-13 submarine. After stalking her for several hours, Marinesko fired four torpedoes at her; one jammed in its tube, but the other three all hit home – the *Wilhelm Gustloff* was doomed. With the winches frozen in the icy weather, hardly any lifeboats could be lowered – there weren't nearly enough anyway – and when the ship sank below the waves the freezing cold water killed most of the passengers in minutes. About a thousand survived – rescued by other German ships in the area – but 10,600 people, including five thousand children, drowned. By comparison, fifteen hundred people died on the *Titanic*. The sinking of the *Wilhelm Gustloff* was – and thankfully still is – the greatest maritime loss of life in history.

It wasn't the only mass tragedy in the Baltic that spring; just eleven days later, Marinesko sank the passenger liner the *General von Steuben*, sending another four thousand people to the bottom of the sea. Much has been said, and written, since the war about the Soviet navy's actions during the evacuation, with terms such as 'war crimes' bandied about. The fact is that both the Germans and the Soviets were abiding by the rules of war at the time; the Germans didn't alert the Soviets the *Wilhelm Gustloff* was a hospital ship or one only carrying civilians, because it wasn't either of those things – there were wounded on board, around one hundred and seventy, and they were part of the sixteen hundred or so service personnel on the ship (of whom three hundred and seventy-three were female auxiliaries). The ship had anti-aircraft guns fitted too, and as such was fair game. The German writer Günter Grass said of it, 'They said the tragedy of *Wilhelm Gustloff* was a war crime. It wasn't. It was terrible, but it was a result of war, a terrible result of war.'[12] Perhaps a more fitting comment on the Soviet navy's actions was that since the Nazi invasion of its homeland in the summer of 1941, its contribution to the war effort could charitably be described as wholly negligible, and now, when the war was already won, it made its presence felt by sinking ships teeming with helpless civilians.

The evacuation turned out to be the Kriegsmarine's final act. On 30 April instructions were issued to scuttle the remaining ships of the fleet on receipt of the codeword *Regenbogen*. In their harbours and anchorages all around the Baltic and the Norwegian coastline, Nazi Germany's sailors sat and waited to hear the signal that would send Hitler's navy to the sea floor.

Unlike the Kriegsmarine, the Luftwaffe could do very little to assist the soldiers and civilians fleeing west. Their service branch was now nothing more than a pale shadow. On aerodromes and dispersal airfields scattered over the shrinking Reich, hundreds of German aircraft lay becalmed; unable to move for want of fuel, spare parts or a pilot – or all three. Norbert Hannig, like so many of his peers, still tried to get up in the air and at least try and help his comrades on the ground. He took off on 6 April with his wingman and went hunting.

I looked up to my right out to sea and there they were; twenty Il-2s in tight formation slipping in and out of sight as they hugged the uneven cloud base for protection. It was a smart move, as it meant they were safe from attack from above. 'Amor 1 from Blaufuchs 1, I have contact, am attacking.'... I closed in on the leading machine. We knew from experience that the formation leader was usually the only pilot who would have been briefed on the target. If he could be taken out the remainder were more often than not at a complete loss as to what to do. From a range of just fifty metres I put a short burst of cannon fire into his radiator... A gout of flame erupted from the enemy's belly... The Ilyushin tipped forward and went down into the water blazing like a torch... The rest of the formation scattered... A green shape emerged not far away. I attacked again and he caught fire. I watched as the Il-2 plummeted down to join his leader at the bottom of the Baltic – it was my forty-second and final kill of the war.

Thirteen days later, the only Bf 109 *geschwader* left in the west, *JG 53* – the '*Pik As*' – claimed their last American P-47 Thunderbolt kill of the war. From then on, the skies really did belong to the Allies. In fact, so much so that on 25 April the American Eighth Air Force flew its last raid – the Fifteenth's was on the following day – there were simply no more targets left to hit. When the Luftwaffe did get into the air, its efforts were appreciated by its earth-bound brethren, as Hans von Luck testified:

We had been promised we would receive support from the famous fighter-bombers of our most highly decorated soldier, Oberst Rudel. His speciality was to use his Ju-87 dive-bombers, equipped with anti-tank guns, to swoop down on Russian armoured units and destroy their tanks with direct hits... After so long it was a great feeling for us old hands to no longer be exposed without cover to the enemy air force. Much more important however, was the effect on the morale of our youngsters who were seeing action for the first time.

Rudel, Hannig and their fellow surviving *jagdfliegers* were doing the best they could for their Wehrmacht comrades, but it was on the ground where the main fighting was still taking place as the *landsers* tried to hold the Soviets. Herman Van Gyseghem – a radio operator cum machine-gunner cum loader in a *Hetzer jagdpanzer* – was in eastern Germany in the path of the advancing Red Army:

It was chaos. The Russians were everywhere, and all heading in the direction of Berlin. On a map you could see it very clearly. All the roads fanned out from Berlin and out to the east, and from February 1945 onwards they were all loaded with Russian tanks. For us this was an advantage. We didn't have to hunt them out – they were all there – and there were so many of them you just couldn't miss. We were about sixty kilometres from Berlin, laid up in a tiny village called Alt Wriezen, waiting for the Russians... My crew in Hetzer 322 were two other Flemings; Gustaaf Segers the driver, Michel Parmentier the gunner, and our Austrian commander, *SS-Oberscharführer* Wiesener. It was Wednesday 18 April, and spring was finally arriving. It wasn't warm yet, but neither was it cold, we'd moved into blocking positions and camouflaged our jagdpanzers, our guns pointing east towards the village of Wriezen – over a kilometre away on the Old Oder... We didn't have to wait long. We heard tank engines, and minutes later a convoy of seven Red Army T-34s, carrying bunches of infantrymen on their hulls, turrets and engine decks, came driving towards us. Wiesener gave his commands through his throat microphone. Parmentier knew exactly what to do and sighted the cannon on the approaching targets. It was all routine, but even so in the close confines of the hull we found themselves bathed in sweat, our faces streaked with lines of black powder. The adrenaline was pumping, all was silence, we all held our breath, and then Wiesener shouted: 'Fire!' A fraction of a second later a 7.5cm tank shell flew out of the long barrel with an enormous bang. We shot the first Russian T-34 tank in the convoy – direct hit! It came to an immediate stop and caught fire. A few Russian infantrymen were burning too and there were cries of pain as a few of the Russian crew members from the T-34 tried to climb out of the tank just as the turret exploded. The narrow street was now blocked, and the Russian convoy was at a standstill. All the Russians could do was reverse back the way they had come, but we didn't let that happen.

Van Gyseghem quickly reloaded the cannon with a fresh armour-piercing round, and Parmentier fired again. The Russians didn't get any time to react.

> We shot the last Russian tank next. That blocked them all in... Then we shot the ones in between. The Russians thought the roads were completely open to Berlin and that we had all run away, and the next thing they knew we were hitting them, and they were trapped. We were so euphoric as we destroyed all seven in a matter of minutes and we watched all these tanks burning. At one point it was so easy, and even almost funny, that we forgot our own safety and ignored all the rules we had learnt, and the next thing we knew the tables had turned, the Russians started to bring their guns to bear on us and it was our turn to take punishment.

Elated by their success, Wiesener climbed out of his *Hetzer* to go and speak to the commander of a neighbouring vehicle. At that point another Soviet tank suddenly appeared and opened fire. Wiesener took the full force of the shell in his chest, which blew him apart as it exited from his back and sped on. Van Gyseghem then jumped out and ran towards his stricken commander. Reaching the shattered corpse, all he could do was break Wiesener's identification tag in two, take half with him, and try to get back to his own *Hetzer*. Without a commander, the remaining crew hesitated for a moment, and that hesitation proved disastrous. The Soviet tank fired again, and this time hit *Hetzer 322* full on – in seconds it was on fire and burning. Gustaaf Segers was badly wounded, but somehow managed to climb out. Parmentier and Van Gyseghem were pulled out by some SS paratroopers caught up in the fighting. The impact of the Soviet tank round had left Van Gyseghem unconscious, but otherwise unwounded. Parmentier was not so lucky. Badly wounded by shrapnel and with severe burns, he was taken to the neighbouring village of Bliesdorf, a couple of kilometres to the southwest, where a field hospital had been set up. Segers was sent there too. For Parmentier, one shoulder and part of his back were stripped of flesh, and the bones were showing through. Medic and fellow Fleming, Stan Scheltjes, helped to treat the wounded gunner and tried to comfort him: 'It's not so bad Michel my friend, you'll be alright.' It wouldn't be alright. Scheltjes said that Parmentier was crying, partly from the pain, but also because he knew his death would leave his younger brother – who had joined the Waffen-SS a few weeks earlier despite Michel's objections – all alone at the front.

As darkness began to fall, the aid station had to be abandoned for fear of being overrun by the Soviets. The staff and wounded had no option but to find cover in the woods to the west. In the chaos, Scheltjes lost contact with Parmentier. Another wounded Fleming, Alexander Colen, was the last man to see the young gunner alive. Officially listed as 'Missing in Action', neither his body, nor that of his commander, Wiesener, was ever found. Van Gyseghem soon recovered and fought on, while Gustaaf Segers's injuries were so severe that even though he survived the war he was disabled for life. Van Gyseghem's company destroyed sixteen Soviet T-34 tanks that day, with seven claimed by *Hetzer 322*. For this action all the crew were awarded the Iron Cross 2nd Class.

> We fought hard, but our losses were so large. Near to Berlin we were running out of everything; panzers, guns, no Luftwaffe, no ammunition, and always more and more Russians. Many of us were killed or wounded. After the Oder we lost control of the battle and were just fighting to try and stay alive. Everyone was fleeing west. But we were Waffen-SS, we had committed ourselves, and even though we knew the war was lost, we still fought on, we just had to.

The Soviets were reducing the hold-out ports on the Baltic coast, and were fighting around Vienna, but their main focus was on reaching and conquering Berlin. Stalin had no political concerns to manage with the Red Army, and so no need for a 'broad front' strategy as did Eisenhower – indeed he was more a proponent of encouraging rivalry between his top commanders, and had told Ian Koniev and Georgy Zhukov that the honour of capturing Berlin would go to the commander who reached it first. As the two marshals gathered their forces for the assault, the Wehrmacht massed what troops it could on the Seelow Heights; the last piece of defendable ground between the Red Army and Berlin. Although, as one SS grenadier said, those sent forward sometimes weren't up to much: 'We couldn't believe our own eyes. Some of these poor devils had a pronounced limp, one was deaf, another couldn't see very well, and one was a hunchback!... One of my comrades joked we'd have to put two of them on sentry together; one who can see the enemy and another who could hear him coming!' One *landser* at the front who still did have all his faculties was Erwin Bartmann, in charge of a heavy machine-gun section, who watched the Soviets opening barrage on the Heights:

> I stopped to watch the clouds above the horizon pulse as it lit from within by violent lightning... At 0230hrs on the morning of 20 April, the Russians made an all-out attack on us and suffered heavy casualties. Then, at, 0530hrs they attacked again after a heavy artillery bombardment. This time we couldn't hold our positions – our machine-gun barrels had become so over-heated with constant firing that they were unusable...we were in a bad situation; no-one was in charge, our officers had left us, and our company commander was an eighteen- or nineteen-year-old youngster with no combat experience ... my platoon commander, an officer cadet, told me our regimental commander – *SS-Obersturmbannführer* Rosenbusch – had shot himself.

For Bartmann, the worst thing was seeing Soviet tanks rolling towards Berlin carrying human cargo: 'The tanks had German women and girls, even children, tied to their gun barrels as they drove past us – we couldn't do anything, let alone fire at them.' Amazingly, the Luftwaffe were still fighting in the skies over Berlin, although Johannes Kaufmann recognised it was a lost cause: 'We carried out armed reconnaissance and *freie Jagd* ('free hunting') sweeps over the city, during the course of which I managed to claim three more enemy aircraft – all Soviet Yak-3 fighters ... the war was clearly in its death throes.'

By 22 April the capital of the Thousand-Year Reich was all-but surrounded and cut off. One of the one and three-quarter million civilians (one and a half million had already fled) trapped in the city wrote in her diary, 'The street is now under fire. Men come stomping along; broad backs, leather jackets, high leather boots.'

Hildegard Trutz asked her SS husband what would happen now: 'I asked him about the *Volkssturm*, and he said they were worse than useless. The men had no guts and weren't even National Socialists, but what the hell, it would all be over soon.' Ernst Trutz may not have believed in final victory anymore, but there were still some Germans who believed in Hitler and his ability to save the Reich. One such was Fritz Mühlebach; wounded in the fighting in East Prussia, he had been evacuated to Berlin for treatment: 'A relief army under General von Wenck was advancing towards the city. It was said that the Western Allies were joining with us against the Russians and that the Führer had a terrible wonder weapon at his disposal which he was only prepared to use if all else failed.'[13]

All three of these suppositions were illusory; Hitler had no secret weapons waiting to be deployed, the Anglo-Americans weren't joining with the Wehrmacht, and Wenck's *12. Armee* had been stopped outside Potsdam by the Soviets. Desperate to open a corridor out of the doomed city for trapped soldiers and civilians alike, *General der Panzertruppe* Walther Wenck exhorted his men to one last effort: 'Comrades, you've got to go in once more... It's not about Berlin anymore, it's not about the Reich anymore, it's about the people of Berlin.' On the afternoon of 22 April – in a scene famously dramatized in the German 2004 film *Downfall* – Hitler was told of the failure of the relief attempt, and in an emotionally charged rant the Nazi dictator vented his spleen on everyone but himself, for what he finally acknowledged was a lost cause. That admission did not, however, lead him – or anyone around him – to take the logical step and bring the agony to a close. In an act of nihilism typical of his personality, he retreated to his private rooms and let the slaughter continue in the city above him; a city that, according to Johannes Kaufmann flying over it, was now 'a smoking ruin ... nothing but a vast expanse of rubble, a scene of utter destruction with few recognizable landmarks'.

A motley collection of units and nationalities defended Berlin; alongside native Germans in Wehrmacht and SS units, were Frenchmen, Latvians, Norwegians, Danes and Swedes. Erik Wallin was one of the latter:

> All that was left of my Kompanie were in action some streets south of Hermann Platz ... we saw depressing signs of disorganisation on our way into the city centre – numerous Wehrmacht soldiers standing, weapon-less, in doorways and other soldiers who were helplessly drunk, staggering around in the streets, without caring about the howling shells or bombs.

Henri Fenet – a French Waffen-SS officer – had been wounded in the leg and brought to his divisional command post for treatment. Attempting to leave to return to his men, Gustav Krukenberg – his commander – demanded, 'Where are you going?'

'Back to the battalion.'

'Do not move from here, you can't stand up; get your orders carried by messenger and stay here at headquarters.'

The bespectacled Fenet protested, to no avail. As the fighting raged street-to-street, the French SS in particular were successful in holding up Soviet attacks with panzerfausts, and two of their number, François Appolot and Eugène Vaulot, won the Knight's Cross for their exploits – although both awards were unconfirmed due to the ensuing chaos.[14] Wilhelm Weber, a German officer serving with the French battalion, showed a comrade a hole in a wall overlooking Wilhelmstrasse. 'Look! Isn't it beautiful!' He was pointing at a T-34 he had just knocked-out. Wallin's battle came to an end shortly after:

> I was on my way down to see Lindenau (a comrade) when suddenly an entire house gable collapsed over us... There had been an explosion close behind, right among the vehicles... Our half-tracks looked like scrap! They were burning and our crews lay spread here and there. The entire platoon of about twenty men had been annihilated... My uniform was torn to shreds, my nice soft officers' boots that I'd been so happy about, were completely ripped... l touched my left leg with my hand. It got quite wet – it was blood, I was wounded. There was a large hole in my thigh. 'I'm wounded!' I cried... Then I fainted.

Waltraudt Williams was a civilian sheltering in a Berlin cellar, praying for the end to come.

> By 26 April – my birthday – the end was getting nearer and nearer ... it was only a matter of time. Little bands of German soldiers and SS were trying to join together to continue the fight... I remember a German

Army lorry standing right outside where we lived. An elderly lady who was one of the tenants rushed into the house shouting 'Meat! Meat!! They've brought us meat!' I've seen it in the lorry outside!' Some of us went out to look and saw her 'meat', the lorry was full of dead soldiers and what she thought was meat was the blood dripping through the lorry's floorboards.

Waltraudt was disgusted at the depths the Nazi authorities stooped to in the fighting: 'They tried to turn all sorts of people into soldiers – they gave Belgian rifles to men aged seventy and over, and they issued children with panzerfausts. That's a terrible weapon for a child to carry on his shoulder, and then be told to go and destroy enemy tanks.'

On the afternoon of 30 April, Adolf Hitler and his new wife Eva Braun committed suicide. After years of extolling the virtue of a glorious death in battle for millions of members of the Wehrmacht, the Nazi dictator decided not to follow his own maxim, and instead chose to shoot himself – it was the last in a very long line of betrayals.

In accordance with his last will and testament, Karl Dönitz now became the head of the Nazi state as *Reichspräsident,* with Joseph Goebbels as Chancellor. Goering and Himmler had written themselves out of the succession by virtue of their cack-handed attempts to assume power in the case of the former and negotiate a peace for the latter. Goebbels and his wife Magda then proceeded to murder their own six children with cyanide and morphine, before taking their own lives – so Dönitz was now in sole charge.

News of Hitler's death was met with mixed feelings by the *landsers.* Hendrik Verton, fighting on in Breslau, was 'simply stunned by the news... I realised that this was the fall of the Third Reich ... for me it meant all that I had given, all I had sacrificed, was now null and void. There was no saving Germany anymore. We had lost.' A wounded Gustav Palm was making his way on foot to a hospital in Schwerin with two Dutch comrades when he heard the news: 'A rumour flew from soldier to soldier – "Hitler is dead!" We were shocked, but above all we didn't want to end up in Russian captivity.' Günter Korschorrek, writing in his diary, spoke for the feelings of many: 'Three days ago we heard about the suicide of Adolf Hitler and Eva Braun. We were shocked that the proud leader had decided to shirk his responsibilities in this cowardly way. But within a couple of hours he is forgotten – we have our own problems.'[15] Richard von Rosen saw it in much the same way, although he realised that the war wasn't quite over yet: 'On 1 May the Special Bulletin came reporting Hitler's death, kept back from us for twelve hours, and that he had reportedly "fallen in battle for the Reich capital". Finally ... it's over and we can put an end to this pointless butchery. Make it quick, for better an end with horror than a horror without end.'

It's All Over!

Karl Dönitz was now ensconced in a headquarters in Flensburg, next to the Danish border, and, being a naval man through and through, immediately made two naval decisions; the fleet evacuation of soldiers and civilians from the east would continue until decreed otherwise, and *Regenbogen* would be rescinded – there would be no mass scuttling. However, many of his own U-boat commanders were beyond orders now, and in a show of defiance some two hundred and eighteen submarines were sent to the bottom by their crews.

Fighting continued, but in the west at least it was the dying embers of a heath fire, briefly sparking to life before flaring out – although still capable of causing damage, as the Waffen-SS officer, Karl Nicolussi-Leck described:

> A U-boat crew that wanted to fight joined us, as well as a battery of self-propelled guns. At Hanomag we were even able to get our hands on seven new Jagdpanthers. When the Americans advanced from Hildesheim towards Hanover we were able to knock out sixty armoured and other vehicles with the help of the Jagdpanthers. A few days after that Hanover was surrendered to the Amis without our knowledge ... we then had to blow up the Jagdpanthers in the Gifhorn area, since we no longer had any ammunition. I wound up in Ami captivity there along with my adjutant.

The *Werwolf* was still active on a very small scale, with individual acts of resistance, although nothing happened of any real significance except for those involved. Fifteen-year-old Hugo Stehmkämper was arrested for *Werwolf* activity. 'I was interrogated by an Ami officer who spoke very good German. A soldier sat behind me ... whether it was part of the interrogation, or he just got excited, I don't know, but the soldier jumped up, put his pistol to my head and screamed "You Werewolf!" I believed it was all over for me... Then I was put in with other POWs.'[16] Another *Werwolf* in Fulda was arrested by the local American garrison and on being led to the jail, offered his guards a drink – they refused – whereupon the youngster took a swig himself and promptly collapsed – the drink had been poisoned. Poison was used again by a former Wehrmacht soldier-turned-*Werwolf,* who was arrested trying to sell brandy laced with cyanide to an American soldier. During his interview he was candid about the reasons for his actions:

> I've been fighting for five years. I come home and find my family's house gone – Ami bombing. I find my girl living with an Ami officer for the food he can give her. I can't get a job because I'm on the Nazi blacklist of the Ami military government. You'll have a hard time making me love you. And if we ever get a chance to pay you back, we will.[17]

In the east, there was little talk of giving up just because Hitler was dead. After all, the Wehrmacht had defended Berlin to the bitter end, costing the Soviets a third of a million men, including eighty thousand killed, when they lacked just about every military asset needed to make a stand. But even in the east, the *landsers* knew it was all coming to an end, as Richard von Rosen admitted: 'No more war, not yet quite peace, but no air raids, no shootings, no deaths and no new mutilations. Now we had the prospect of life without fighting, without danger, and perhaps one day peace would really come.' For the remaining members of the Wehrmacht – and there were millions of them – it was now another chapter dominated by whom they were facing at the time. The men in the west, more often than not, threw away their weapons and surrendered to the first Allied soldiers they could find.

In the east it was altogether different. The race was on to escape the clutches of the Red Army and head west – cross the Elbe – and throw themselves on the mercy of the Anglo-Americans. Herbert Maeger was one of them: 'Ever present was the fear of falling into the hands of the Russians. Everybody took off in the space of a minute… I crammed my most important belongings into my field-pack, and, without giving it much thought I strode towards the West… I had no idea in mind except to get away from the Russians as quickly as possible, and the threat of damnation in Siberia.' The Red Army wasn't the only threat, as a member of the *SS-Horst Wessel* discovered:

> I joined the Division as a clerk … the German-speaking enlisted men were Hungarian … I heard that they had laid down their weapons. In any event, the entire battalion had to form up, and the divisional judge appeared with SS-Pionier Scherzel. The judge had him shot in front of us for cowardice in the face of the enemy… After that the unit's morale was dreadful. The enlisted men only spoke to each other now in Hungarian.

Retreating through Czech lands, the SS clerk realised that the once-docile locals were now anything but: 'The drivers set their vehicles on fire and we destroyed our SS badges … that saved us from a painful death at the hands of the Czechs … they searched among the prisoners for SS, and those they found were worked over with sabres and the like, before being shot in a clay pit.' *SS-Unterscharführer* Franz Wunsch was also retreating through Czech territory towards Austria:

> The entire country seemed to be in revolt, everything was decorated with Czech banners and flags … we overtook a steady stream of units from other divisions; some on horseback, some walking, all moving in the same direction over the Bohemian roads … signs of

disintegration in the Wehrmacht were visible everywhere. Only a few units maintained discipline in the situation. The roads were clogged and progress was slow.

Wunsch's fellow SS grenadier – sixteen-year-old Hermann Melcher – was part of a force trying to safeguard German civilians fleeing Prague:

> I had a bullet wound in my right calf and it wasn't healed, but the medic said 'the wound looks good' and that was that, I was passed fit for duty and sent to Prague... We made first contact with the enemy ... suddenly it seemed as if there was fire coming from every corner ... we worked our way forward, then the shooting stopped as quickly as it had begun. The silence was downright eerie as we advanced towards the first houses ... the partisans began shooting again and our troop leader – SS-Obersturmführer Ertl – ordered, 'Prepare to attack!' Pistol drawn, he dashed out into the road, a shot rang out and he collapsed groaning. SS-Junker Dürrwitz dragged him back behind the wall and paid for it with a through-and-through wound in the back. Chalk-white in the face and foaming at the mouth – Ertl; blood-smeared, spitting out teeth – Dürrwitz.

Heinz Knoke was driving north from Prague when the car was 'rocked by an explosion. The steering is broken and we crash out of control into the parapet of a bridge. Beside me, Günter Gerhard is thrown through the windshield and breaks a leg... My left knee is shattered, and so is my right pelvis ... splinters are embedded in my legs and blood is oozing out of my boots ... it's sabotage, mines were laid on the road by Czech terrorists.' It was the end of the war for Knoke.

The end for everyone else – when it came – was one of bureaucracy, egos and farce; as these things tend to be. On the main western front, it was to Montgomery that the Germans turned. *Generaladmiral* Hans-Georg von Friedeburg – Dönitz's successor as commander of the Kriegsmarine – was the man chosen to appear at the British headquarters at the old Wehrmacht training ground on the Lüneberg Heath. Greeted by the beret-wearing field marshal with a typically caustic 'Who are you? I've never heard of you. What do you want?' Friedeburg attempted to negotiate, only to be immediately shot down by the British commander – it was unconditional surrender or nothing. In the early evening of 4 May, he signed the former – and with it a million men of the Wehrmacht became POWs. The next day, Johannes Blaskowitz surrendered the Netherlands and all of his troops in a hotel room in Wageningen, just west of the ruins of Oosterbeek. Albert Kesselring – still *OB West* – was unearthed by two American reporters on a five-car train parked in a siding on the Austrian border. Wrongly assuming that they were in fact emissaries from Eisenhower, he invited them to have lunch with him; ham, cabbage, potatoes and beer. On discovering his mistake, 'Smiling' Albert sat back, chuckled, and said, 'Well, bugger me.'

Dönitz was now shamelessly playing for time; every hour of delay allowed more German soldiers and civilians to get west and escape the Soviets, and so, on 6 May he broadcast to the German people: 'By virtue of the truce which has been put into effect, I ask all German men and women to abstain from any underground fighting activity in the Werwolf or any other organisations in the enemy-occupied western territories, since such activity can only be to the detriment of our people.'

This announcement effectively ended the *Werwolf* threat. Not that it was ever seen as a viable one by the Wehrmacht anyway. As Siegfried Westphal said of it and its four to five thousand recruits, 'As if what the Wehrmacht had failed to do could be accomplished by a rabble of boy scouts.' The announcement also, pointedly, didn't refer to the ongoing fighting in the east – there was still time. Although not for all. On 6 May, after eighty-two days of siege, *General der Infanterie* Hermann Niehoff surrendered *Festung Breslau* to the Red Army. Almost thirty thousand German soldiers had been killed or wounded in its defence, with the Soviets losing twice that number. Hendrik Verton left his bunker to watch the entry of a Red Army he and his comrades had fought so long to keep out:

> I was enveloped straight away with an uncomfortable, bitter feeling. I saw the enemy I had fought for so many years, so close by, and for the first time I was unarmed. The scene was similar to a colourful, wailing caravan, moving through the rubble-covered streets ... the trigger-happy drunken Reds were firing everything into the air... A single Russian soldier tottered down the cellar steps. He was a little man, short and stocky ... he grasped me to his breast and kissed me on both cheeks, declaring, 'Hitler kaput!'

The Dutchman had his wristwatch stolen by his new-found friend: 'All of my comrades lost their watches too, adding them to those already decorating his arms, up to his elbows, one on top of another.' He swapped his SS uniform for an Army one and 'with a heavy heart burned my *Soldbuch* with all the entries of my military service in it, including all the details of my close-combat days.' Verton realised though, that while he was out of immediate danger, the same could not be said for females in the city: 'All the women and girls were "fair game" for the Russians, like prey running wild in the woods. Even when a decent Russian officer could and did deter acts of rape, there were hundreds who didn't.' One victim was the Flemish nurse, Lucie Lefever: 'After the surrender we tried to escape west. Me and some others were stopped by a Russian commissar. I had my Red

Cross pass, and I showed it to him and asked him to let us carry on. He just took it from me and ripped it up in front of my eyes – and that was that.' Lefever was violently raped.

Dönitz could delay no longer. On his behalf, Alfred Jodl signed the formal document of surrender in the French city of Reims, whereupon Eisenhower cabled Washington: 'The mission of this Allied force was fulfilled at 0241, local time, May 7, 1945, Eisenhower.' It was D+335.

On hearing of the ceremony, an outraged Stalin immediately demanded a delay until Soviet representatives were present – despite the fact that it had already gone ahead. Not to be outdone in the drama queen stakes, de Gaulle then complained that there was no French flag there either. Solemnity was replaced by farce. To accommodate these demands, and smooth ruffled feathers, the official surrender date was set at Tuesday 8 May 1945 – Victory in Europe Day.

That same day, Richard von Rosen went home. 'It was an indescribable feeling, this returning home, after everything... I recognised my mother from afar and she came towards me. How tired she looked. Then she recognised me... "Son, I can't believe you're back home! Erich, Richard is home!" And papa – I can still see this clearly – jumped up and came down to me, unable to speak... How thankful I was to be back home.'[18] Rosen had lost an uncle, three cousins and a brother-in-law killed in the fighting. After his tearful welcome, he went to his old bedroom and couldn't find any trousers that would fit his half-starved frame – he put on a pair of shorts from his youth.

The general surrender came into force at 0001hrs 9 May 1945, and Dönitz sent out his last report to the Wehrmacht:

> Since midnight arms have been laid down on all fronts ... the German forces have ceased a struggle that had become hopeless. With this, a battle that has lasted almost six years has come to an end. It has brought us great victories, but also heavy defeats. The German forces have, finally, honourably succumbed to crushing superiority. The German soldier has remained true to his oath and has ... won victories that will forever go down in history... Even our enemies cannot hide their respect for the achievements of German soldiers on land, on the sea and in the air. Every soldier can now lay down his arms, and in this saddest hour in our history, proudly return to his work for the future life of the German people.

For the victors there was immense cause for celebration, and then time to reflect. The Wehrmacht believed it had been defeated by an Anglo-American *Materialschlacht* (a war of *matériel* and attrition) – after all, it pointed out, from D-Day until VE-Day the Americans alone fired twenty-three million artillery shells in the ETO, and five hundred million machine-gun rounds. How could it compete? There was also the belief among many German veterans that Allied tactics were slow and cumbersome, as the bespectacled *Hauptmann* Walter Schäfer-Kehnert mused: 'It took the Allies a ridiculously long time to get into Germany. If they had used our tactics they could have been in Berlin in weeks.' This was only part of the story though. Allied logistics and firepower may have seemed overwhelming, but men take ground, and the western Allies had paid the price of victory; three-quarters of a million casualties, two-thirds of those being American, with 151,000 American, British and Canadian dead in all.

For the now ex-members of the Wehrmacht, the position was of course desperate and still fraught with danger. Some were luckier than others. Günter Korschorrek was lying injured in hospital in the Sudetenland when peace was declared. Taken prisoner by the Americans, he was slated for handover to the Red Army, so infected his own wound to avoid that fate, and was discharged home. Franz Wunsch had managed to escape the clutches of vengeful Czech partisans and reach Austria: 'We learned of the end of the war and the Wehrmacht surrender – my spirits were lower than they had ever been before... A mood of defeatism surrounded us, we tossed weapons, ammunition and equipment onto a large fire in a clearing and with sunken shoulders each of us spent a while lost in his own thoughts.' Erwin Bartmann and a few remaining comrades from his unit made it to the River Elbe, found a boat and rowed it across to the American-held bank. 'We landed in an Ami artillery position on the other bank. There were no sentries to be seen – everyone was asleep. We bypassed the position and set off.' Arrested a few weeks later, Bartmann would serve almost four years in a British POW camp before being released. He stayed in the United Kingdom and was naturalised in 1955. As was Werner Block, who ended up serving his time as a prisoner on a farm in Hampshire. Jan Munk served a prison term in the Netherlands, then married an English nurse and emigrated to rural Devon, where he became a civil engineer. Gustav Palm surrendered to the first American soldiers he met in the city of Schwerin: 'They didn't hesitate to take watches, valuables and other souvenirs from German soldiers ... they took everything of value we had, however I was able to keep my old pocket watch, probably because the Amis considered it worthless.' In a most extraordinary twist, Palm would later meet the Jewish Hungarian concentration camp inmate Agnes Erdös, and the two would fall in love, marry, and emigrate to Sweden. Kurt 'Panzermeyer' was eventually outed as the notorious Waffen-SS general, and tried by the Canadians for war crimes relating to his time in Normandy. Found guilty and condemned to death, his sentence was commuted to life imprisonment. Released in September 1954, he became a leading member of the *HIAG* (*Hilfsgemeinschaft auf Gegenseitigkeit der Angehörigen der ehemaligen*

Waffen-SS, literally 'Mutual aid association of former Waffen-SS members'), the main welfare and apologist group for ex-armed SS men. He died in December 1961 from a heart attack, aged fifty-one, having suffered several years of very poor health. Helmut Schreiber, the eighteen-year-old cavalryman captured in Budapest, spent nine years in the Soviet gulag system as a forced labourer before being released back to Germany in 1954. Hildegard Trutz, the baker's daughter married to an SS man, lost her youngest child in the freezing cold of the trek west, and left husband Ernst in disgust. As she had feared, she was repeatedly raped by Red Army soldiers before – as she put it – 'adjusting', and then sleeping with them for food and other favours. She then became the girlfriend of an African-American soldier for a while, and then finally that of a black-marketeer who was one of the few surviving Polish Jews; the irony – if you can call it that – of her previous racism and marriage to an SS man didn't seem to trouble her. Herbert Maeger, desperately trying to reach the Elbe River and safety, was captured by Red Army soldiers and imprisoned. Somehow convincing the camp authorities he was too sick to work, he was released in August and sent home. On his way back to Belgium he decided to remain in Germany, thinking – rightly – he would not be welcome in his homeland. Oswald Van Ooteghem thought the same:

> When the war ended I thought of committing suicide, but instead I got rid of my uniform, changed into some civilian clothes and decided to stay in Germany rather than risk going back to Belgium. I knew I had to hide and deny I had served in the Waffen-SS, that's when I had some photos taken of me in German Army uniform, so I could show them to anyone who asked. The shoulder boards and collar tabs were all made of paper and stuck onto the uniform, but they looked real enough to fool anyone. I had to do it, they were looking for SS men, and there were signs everywhere saying that if someone offered shelter to an SS soldier they would get twenty years in prison. So, I made my way to the French sector of Germany and called myself Hans Richter, pretended I was a German, and married a German woman because I just didn't trust the Belgian authorities. I became an architectural draughtsman down in the Black Forest.

A few years later, Van Ooteghem, contemplating emigrating to South America, was persuaded by his mother to return home to Flanders. On arrival he was arrested, tried, found guilty of collaboration, and imprisoned alongside his father and several hundred other Flemish nationalists. Years later he would be elected as a Senator to the Belgian parliament. Joining a Flemish Waffen-SS veterans' group, the *Sneyssens*, he met up with his wartime comrades Herman Van Gyseghem, Dries Coolens and Theo D'Oosterlinck.

Erik Wallin managed to survive the fall of Berlin. Hidden in a cellar, he recovered enough to make it out of the city a few weeks after the war ended. Along with another Swedish SS comrade he walked to the Elbe River and got across to the Anglo-American side. The Danish officer, Erik Brörup, ended up emigrating to Canada after the war, where he joined the Army and eventually became a pilot for the flying doctor service. Bjørn Lindstad deserted the day before the war ended and then served a prison term back in Norway before being released. Norbert Hannig was training on the Me 262 jet-fighter when the war ended. He went home, was arrested by the Soviets, imprisoned and then released. Bruno Friesen was even luckier: 'I was never a POW, I was never interrogated, I never even attended de-Nazification lectures.' He stayed in Germany after the war, then travelled to the United States in 1950 and from there back to his native Canada. Hans-Adolf Prützmann – first and only leader of the *Werwolf* – was captured by the Allies and committed suicide in custody on 21 May, before he could be tried for war crimes. Two days later, Hans-Georg von Friedeburg did the same when arrested by the British for being a member of the Flensburg government. Albert Kesselring was remanded to Luxembourg for suspected war crimes, and, under interrogation, said of his former warlord, 'Hitler was the most remarkable historical character I ever knew.'

Two other Wehrmacht members who agreed with that judgement were the *fallschirmjäger Oberst* Martin Vetter, and the *jagdflieger* Anton Wöffen, as they were secretly recorded in captivity at the war's end.

Vetter: 'Whatever you think of National Socialism, Adolf Hitler as our Führer has given the German people a very great deal up till now, at last we were able to be proud of our nation once again – one should never forget that.'

Wöffen: 'Nothing can ever take that away.'

Vetter: 'Despite the fact that I'm convinced he will become the grave-digger of the German people.'

Wöffen: 'Yes, her gravedigger.'

Vetter: 'He's that all right, undoubtedly.'[19]

Appendix

Waffen-SS, German Army and Comparable British Army Ranks

Waffen-SS	German Army	British Army
SS-Schütze	Schütze/Grenadier	Private
SS-Oberschütze	Oberschütze	Private
SS-Sturmmann	Gefreiter	Lance corporal
SS-Rottenführer	Obergefreiter	Corporal
SS-Unterscharführer	Unteroffizier	Lance Sergeant (only used in the British Brigade of Guards)
SS-Scharführer	Unterfeldwebel	Sergeant
SS-Oberscharführer	Feldwebel	Colour/staff Sergeant
SS-Hauptscharführer	Oberfeldwebel	Sergeant-Major - Warrant Officer Class 2
SS-Sturmscharführer	auptfeldwebel	Sergeant-Major - Warrant Officer Class 1
SS-Untersturmführer	Leutnant	Second-Lieutenant
SS-Obersturmführer	Oberleutnant	Lieutenant
SS-Hauptsturmführer	Hauptmann	Captain
SS-Sturmbannführer	Major	Major
SS-Obersturmbannführer	Oberstleutnant	Lieutenant-Colonel
SS-Standartenführer	Oberst	Colonel
SS-Brigadeführer	Generalmajor	Brigadier
SS-Gruppenführer	Generalleutnant	Major-General
SS-Obergruppenführer	General	Lieutenant-General
SS-Oberstgruppenführer	Generaloberst	General
	Generalfeldmarschall	Field-Marshal

Notes

Introduction

1. SHAEF Weekly Intelligence Summary No. 24, 02.09.1944.

Chapter One: Summer 1944: the German Defeat

1. Neitzel, Sönke and Welzer, Harald, *Soldaten*, p146, recording of *Leutnant* Meyer.
2. Neitzel, Sönke and Welzer, Harald, *Soldaten*, p145, recording of SS-man Blaas of the *16. SS-Panzergrenadier-Division 'Reichsführer SS'*.
3. Neitzel, Sönke and Welzer, Harald, *Soldaten*, p85, recording of two *fallschirmjäger* talking about the allied advance in the summer of 1944. The second speaker, Heuer, is probably a 'plant' placed in the cell by the British to 'steer' the conversation.
4. Von Thoma to fellow POW Ludwig Crüwell, recorded/translated by British captors, 22 March 1943. 'I saw it once with Feldmarschall Brauchitsch, there is a special ground near Kunersdorf [sic] ... they've got these huge things which they've brought up here. ... They've always said they would go 15 km into the stratosphere and then. ... You only aim at an area. ... If one was to ... every few days ... frightful. ... The major there was full of hope – he said: 'Wait until next year and the fun will start!'
5. Hagen, Louis, *Ein Volk, Ein Reich,* p111 – interview with Hermann Voss.
6. Kershaw, Robert J., *It Never Snows in September*, p20.
7. Knoke, Heinz, *I Flew for the Führer*, p170.
8. Carruthers, Bob (ed), *The U-Boat War in the Atlantic Volume III: 1944-1945*, p218.
9. The Kriegsmarine lost a total of 250 ships in 1944, all but eight of them U-boats. Nazi Germany began the war with 57 U-boats, and built an additional 1,153 during the conflict, of which 830 took part in three thousand operations, sinking in excess of 3,500 merchant ships – although British records dispute this figure and put it at 2,500 – with two-thirds of those losses occurring in the Atlantic. Some 175 warships

and auxiliaries were also sunk. A total of 636 U-boats were lost to enemy action, and a further eighty-five to collisions and other non-combat events. Approximately forty-thousand sailors served in U-boats – about the same number as in three German infantry divisions – with around twenty-eight thousand being killed – a horrifically high casualty rate. On the cessation of hostilities, 154 U-boats surfaced, raised the black flag of capitulation and sailed to their designated surrender ports. The vast majority – some 121 – were then scuttled in deep water off Lisahally, Northern Ireland, or Loch Ryan, Scotland, in late 1945 and early 1946.

10. Von Rosen, Richard *Freiherr, Panzer Ace,* p276.
11. Beevor, Antony, *Arnhem,* p10.
12. Knoke, Heinz, *I Flew for the Führer,* p176.
13. Author interview with Julien Hertenweg.
14. Author interview with Jan Munk, *5. SS-Panzerdivision 'Wiking'.*
15. Williams, Andrew, *D-Day to Berlin,* p219.
16. Meyer, Kurt, *Grenadiers,* p308.
17. Perret, Bryan, *Knights of the Black Cross,* p192.
18. Author interview with Werner Block, *5. SS-Panzerdivision 'Wiking'.*
19. Klapdor, Ewald, *Viking Panzers,* p364.
20. Holland, James, *Italy's Sorrow: A Year of War, 1944-1945,* p352.
21. Holmes, Richard, *World at War,* p434.
22. Atkinson, Rick, *The Guns at Last Light,* p358.
23. For context; the United States produced 600m tonnes of oil during the war, against Romania's 25m tonnes – total Hungarian wartime production was just 3.1m tonnes, but after the loss of Romania's oil, Hungary was producing 80 per cent of the Reich's gasoline.
24. Kershaw, Robert J., *It Never Snows in September,* p20.

Chapter Two: Flight Turns to Fight!

1. Neitzel, Sönke and Welzer, Harald, *Soldaten,* p205.
2. Kershaw, Robert J., *It Never Snows in September,* p53.
3. The Royal Navy would end the war with 553 warships on its roster.
4. Hastings, Max, *Armageddon,* p177.
5. Bradley graduated from West Point military academy in 1915 alongside Dwight D. Eisenhower as part of the so-called 'class the stars fell on.' During the First World War he guarded copper mines in Montana, before becoming commander of the United States Army Infantry School in 1941. He only received his first front-line command in 1942 during *Operation Torch*, and then served under Patton in North Africa. He commanded the First Army in Normandy, and after the breakout took command of the Twelfth Army Group, which ultimately comprised forty-three divisions and 1.3 million men, the largest body of American soldiers ever to serve under a single field commander.
6. Hastings, Max, *Armageddon,* p25.

7. Theft and black-marketeering became so endemic that by the end of September 1944 half of those self-same twenty-two million jerrycans had 'disappeared'.

8. Figures are disputed on the convoy system; Atkinson gives a daily tonnage of five thousand, while Beevor gives ten, and others go as high as twelve thousand – this is to be expected in the controlled chaos of what was an extraordinary logistical effort.

9. Atkinson, Rick, *The Guns at Last Light*, p241.

10. In 1943, Ramcke published his memoir, *From Cabin Boy to Paratroop General*. The Nazi Minister of Propaganda, Joseph Goebbels, ordered all German mayors to purchase a copy, and a total of 400,000 copies were eventually sold. This made Ramcke a lot of money, as well as enriching Hitler, who personally owned a large share of the publishing house.

11. Kershaw, Robert J., *It Never Snows in September*, p24.

12. The *59, 70, 245, 331, 334, 346, 711, 712 IDs* and the *17. Luftwaffe-Feld-Division*.

13. Exact figures are disputed; Atkinson quotes six hundred guns, five thousand vehicles and four thousand horses, while Hastings says it was 225 guns, a thousand horses and 750 trucks. Atkinson's numbers look high, especially on artillery and vehicles, so I have gone for lower numbers.

14. Atkinson, Rick, *The Guns at Last Light*, p301.

15. Author interview with Rudolf von Ribbentrop, *12. SS-Panzerdivision 'Hitlerjugend'*.

16. Kershaw, Robert J., *It Never Snows in September*, p47.

17. *World at War* interview with Siegfried Westphal, p159.

18. *SS-Wachbataillon 3* was, as the Dutch historian Lou de Jong described, 'an irregular lawless mess'. Standards of admission were very low, with many of the men filling the ranks totally unsuited to the physicality of soldiering. In its first battle with the advancing British it lost two hundred men killed and another two hundred who simply ran away. Within a few days the battalion had lost two-thirds of its original twelve hundred men.

19. Michael Lippert accompanied his boss, Theodor Eicke, to Stadelheim Prison on the 'Night of the Long Knives' back in 1934, where the two men executed the former head of the SA, Ernst Röhm, on Hitler's orders. Lippert would go on to command a Dutch SS division before the end of the war.

20. The 'Blitz train' system was the name given to the process whereby the German rail system was put to immediate use if a crisis at the front occurred. It allowed railway officials to cancel existing timetables and move all non-essential traffic off priority routes, while trains were commandeered to take reinforcements to the crisis point.

21. Kershaw, Robert J., *It Never Snows in September*, p39.

22. Ibid, p22.

23. Griesser, Volker, *Lions of Carentan*, p164.

24. Kershaw, Robert J., *It Never Snows in September*, p26.

25. Neitzel, Sönke and Welzer, Harald, *Soldaten*, p315.

26. Ibid, p272.

27. British XXX Corps intelligence assessment.

28. American 82nd Airborne Division intelligence assessment.

29. Beevor, Antony, *Ardennes,* p5. Allied casualty figures for the three-month period September to end November were a total of 209,672, with 36,976 killed. The majority of these casualties – some 140,000 – would be American.

Chapter Three: Arnhem and the German Miracle

1. Bosquet famously said those words after watching the Charge of the Light Brigade during the Crimean War.
2. Adams himself was an officer in the 250th (Airborne) Light Company of the Royal Army Service Corps and drew on the exploits of the company at Arnhem as his inspiration for *Watership Down.*
3. Beevor, Antony, Arnhem, p370.
4. Kershaw, Robert, *It Never Snows in September,* p41.
5. Ibid, p69. Krafft was the commanding officer of the *SS-Panzer-Grenadier-Ausbildungs und Ersatz-Bataillon 16 (16th SS-Panzer-grenadier Training & Replacement Battalion).*
6. Ibid, p52.
7. Ibid, p50.
8. Ibid, p62.
9. Ibid, p68.
10. Griesser, Volker, *Lions of Carentan,* p169.
11. Kershaw, Robert, *It Never Snows in September,* p36, the twenty-year-old Rolf Lindemann.
12. The local Arnhem area commander *Generalmajor* Friedrich Kussin had been ambushed in his staff car earlier in the day by British paras and killed.
13. Kershaw, Robert, *It Never Snows in September,* p108.
14. Ibid, p79.
15. Griesser, Volker, *Lions of Carentan,* p173.
16. The *Deutsche Reichsbahn* was, and is, Germany's state railway system.
17. Kaufmann, Johannes, *An Eagle's Odyssey,* p209.
18. Atkinson, Rick, *The Guns at Last Light,* p274.
19. Kershaw, Robert, *It Never Snows in September, p130.*
20. Ibid, p168. Nineteen-year-old *SS-Rottenführer* Paul Müller of the 9. *SS-Panzerdivision 'Hohenstaufen.'*
21. Ibid, p127.
22. Ibid, p127.
23. Ibid, p177.
24. Ibid, p172.
25. Ibid, p209.
26. Ibid, p91.
27. Ibid, p205.
28. Atkinson, Rick, *The Guns at Last Light,* p280.
29. Kershaw, Robert, *It Never Snows in September, p183.*
30. Author interview with Ivar Corneliussen, *5. SS-Panzerdivision 'Wiking'.*

31. Reynolds, Michael, *Sons of the Reich*, p181.

32. Nazi Germany also produced 3,617 tank destroyers and 1,246 self-propelled artillery guns in 1944.

33. Ever prone to unnecessary experimentation, the Germans also produced the *Jagdtiger*, a behemoth weighing over seventy tons and with frontal armour 250mm thick. Its main armament was a huge 128mm gun. The whole project was a distraction, and only some forty-seven were ever built.

34. Hooton, E.R., *Eagle in Flames*, p325. In 1944 Germany produced a total of 39,788 aircraft, including over three thousand bombers. Of the 3,103 single-seat fighters built in September 1944, 1,874 were Bf 109G's and 1,002 were FW 190's.

35. Spink, Mike, *Aces of the Reich*, p171.

36. Holmes, Richard, *World at War*, p304.

37. Hagen, Louis, *Ein Volk, Ein Reich*, p56, interview with Dr Franz Wertheim.

38. Hastings, Max, *Armageddon*, p305.

39. Neitzel, Sönke and Welzer, Harald, *Soldaten*, p187.

40. Bartmann, Erwin, *Für Volk und Führer*, p160.

41. The German population in 1933 was officially 66 million; the annexation of Austria, the Sudetenland, Alsace-Lorraine and the incorporation of several million ethnic Germans or '*volksdeutsche*' increased this number to 80 million by 1940.

42. Hagen, Louis, *Ein Volk, Ein Reich*, p38.

43. Evans, Richard J., *The Third Reich at War*, p671.

44. Ibid, p673.

45. Interview with *Unteroffizier* Arthur Krüger, and secondly quote from Hastings, Max, *Armageddon*, p193.

46. Evans, Richard J., *The Third Reich at War*, p595.

47. Hagen, Louis, *Ein Volk, Ein Reich*, p38.

48. A standard American infantry division was equipped with sixty-six artillery guns, mostly of bigger calibre and greater range than their German counterparts, including no fewer than twelve 155mm *Long Toms*. All American units also had access to multiple other artillery units at Corps or Army level if required.

49. Nash, Douglas E., *Victory was beyond their Grasp*, p40.

50. Author interview with Herman Van Gyseghem.

51. Author interview with Andreas Fleischer.

Chapter Four: The Battle of the Border

1. Rogers, Duncan & Williams, Sarah (ed), *On the Bloody Road to Berlin*, p92.

2. As commander of *Panzer-Grenadier-Regiment 192* on D-Day, Rauch had led his men to counter-attack the Anglo-Canadian beaches, and to the astonishment of some of the landing troops actually reached the Channel, where he waited in vain for reinforcements before being ordered by his incompetent divisional commander – Edgar Feuchtinger – to retreat. The third regimental commander in the division, Hermann von Oppeln-Bronikowski led the formations panzer regiment. The author isn't sure where he was at this point in time, but as he took

over command of the *20. Panzerdivision* on 20 November he may well have been on the relevant divisional commanders' course.

3. Rogers, Duncan & Williams, Sarah (ed), *On the Bloody Road to Berlin*, p92.

4. Von Luck, Hans, *Panzer Commander*, p216.

5. Beevor, Antony, *Ardennes*, p24.

6. After medical treatment, Kittel was held at Trent Park along with other senior German officers. Secretly recorded, Kittel admitted witnessing Nazi atrocities while serving in Latvia: 'They seized three-year-old children by the hair, held them up and shot them with a pistol and then threw them in (to a death pit). I saw that for myself. One could watch it; the SD had roped the area off and the people were standing watching from about 300 metres away. The Latvians and German soldiers were just standing there, looking on.' In another postscript to the battle, Hitler ordered that a special armband be created and worn by the surviving defenders – despite having given express orders that there should be no survivors as they were all to fight to the death.

7. Holmes, Richard, *World at War*, p518.

8. Beevor, Antony, *Ardennes*, p31.

9. Neitzel, Sönke and Welzer, Harald, *Soldaten*, p271, recording of *Major* Heimann.

10. The name *Limes* was adopted as a cover for the building work; the name referred to the Roman Empire's eastern Germanic border – hence the story was that it was an archaeological exercise. In truth, the Romans almost certainly didn't refer to the border as the *limes* anyway.

11. Von Luck, Hans, *Panzer Commander*, p222.

12. Reynolds, Michael, *Men of Steel*, p33.

13. Atkinson, Rick, *The Guns at Last Light*, p251.

14. Williams, Andrew, *D-Day to Berlin*, p265.

15. Neitzel, Sönke and Welzer, Harald, *Soldaten*, p301, recording of *SS-Obersturmführer* Otto Wölcky.

16. Hastings, Max, *Armageddon*, p410.

17. Evans, Richard J., *The Third Reich at War*, p545.

18. Beevor, Antony, *Arnhem*, p11.

19. Ibid, p41 – a paratrooper from *FJR. 16*.

20. Palm, Hakan, O., *Surviving Hitler*, p86.

21. Author interview with Ivar Corneliussen, *5. SS-Panzerdivision 'Wiking'*.

22. Eriksson, Patrick G., *Alarmstart South and Final Defeat*, p186.

23. Atkinson, Rick, *The Guns at Last Light*, p350.

24. Von Rosen, Richard Freiherr, *Panzer Ace*, p348.

25. Nash, Douglas E., *Victory was Beyond their Grasp*, p41, *Unteroffizier* Helmut Braun.

26. Atkinson, Rick, *The Guns at Last Light*, p321.

27. Ibid, p324.

28. Nash, Douglas E., *Victory was Beyond their Grasp*, p93, *Unteroffizier* Hans Wegener.

29. Ibid, Zacharuk was born in Czernowitz in modern-day Poland.

30. Mitcham, Samuel W. Jr, *The Siegfried Line,* p132.
31. Griesser, Volker, *Lions of Carentan,* p205.
32. Nash, Douglas E., *Victory was Beyond their Grasp,* p150, Kurt Klein.
33. Ibid, p186. Karl Bolzmann of *VGR. 980* would have the tragic distinction of being the last officer from his division to be killed in the war, falling in action on 11 April 1945.
34. Ibid, p207.
35. Atkinson, Rick, *The Guns at Last Light,* p301.
36. Following their capture, both Eberding and the bespectacled Daser would be transferred to the prison camp for senior officers at Trent Park in England.
37. Griesser, Volker, *Lions of Carentan,* p185.
38. Ibid, p204.
39. In total 4,248 V-1s and 1,712 V-2s were fired at Antwerp.
40. Hastings, Max, *Armageddon,* p169.
41. Beevor, Antony, *Ardennes,* p41.

Chapter Five: *Wacht am Rhein* – Germany's Battle of the Bulge

1. Atkinson, Rick, *The Guns at Last Light,* p390.
2. Landau, Sigmund Heinz, *Goodbye Transylvania,* p84.
3. Inveterately barbaric, the Nazi response to the Warsaw Uprising was a low-water mark even for them. Utilising a number of units whose members were either convicted criminals or ethnic Ukrainians and Russian Cossacks with long-standing grievances against the Poles, the Nazis carried out mass atrocities that saw tens of thousands of men, women and children slaughtered. The SS authorities in charge were so concerned that details of what they had done would leak out they had the commander of one of the main formations involved – the turncoat Russian Bronislav Kaminski of the *Kaminski Brigade* – executed to try and hush it up.
4. Author interview with Stål Munkeberg, *SS-Skijägers.*
5. The Courland Pocket (in German *Kurland-Kessel*) refers to the Red Army's isolation of Axis forces on the Courland Peninsula from July 1944 to May 1945. The pocket was created during the Red Army's Baltic Strategic Offensive Operation, when forces of the 1st Baltic Front reached the Baltic Sea near Memel. The Soviet commander was General Ivan Bagramyan (later Marshal). This action isolated German Army Group North (*Heeresgruppe Nord*) from the rest of the German forces between Tukums and Libau in Latvia. Renamed Army Group Courland (*Heeresgruppe Kurland*) on 25 January 1945, the Army Group remained isolated until its surrender at the end of the war.
6. Stalin's Organ was the German nickname for the multi-barrel Soviet Katyusha rocket launcher, due to the fact it looked like an organ array before it was fired, and the noise of the motors when fired was extremely unnerving.
7. Author interview with Bjørn Lindstad, *11. SS-Panzergrenadier-Division 'Nordland.'*

8. After successful exploration by the American corporation *Eurogasco*, the Hungarian-American Oil Inc. was formed. Nagykanizsa became the centre of the Hungarian oil industry. During the Anglo-American Oil bombing Campaign from 1943 onwards, Nagykanizsa was bombed and so were the Hungarian refineries at Almásfüzitő, Budapest and Szöny.

9. Von Rosen, Richard Freiherr, *Panzer Ace*, p281.

10. Ibid, p308.

11. Ibid, p313.

12. Umbrich, Friedrich, (translated by Anna M. Wittmann), *Balkan Nightmare*, p173.

13. Ibid, p175.

14. Hagen, Louis, *Ein Volk, Ein Reich*, p211.

15. Williams, Andrew, *D-Day to Berlin*, p265.

16. The leaflet was attributed to the Soviet publicist and writer, Ilya Ehrenburg, but after the war he hotly denied being its author.

17. Grund, Helmut, (ed Stephen R. Pastore), *The Confession of Helmut Grund*, p35.

18. One of Frederick the Great's most famous victories, the Battle of Leuthen was fought on 5 December 1757 and saw Frederick's Prussians beat a far larger Austrian force.

19. Williamson, Gordon, *Loyalty is my Honour*, interview with Heinrich Springer.

20. Jodl, Alfred, *Kriegtagesbuch 19/08/1944*.

21. Holmes, Richard, *World at War*, p519, interview with *General der Kavallerie* Siegfried Westphal.

22. Ibid, p522.

23. Ibid, p520, interview with *General der Panzertruppe* Hasso Freiherr von Manteuffel.

24. *Guards* status was awarded to Soviet units and formations that distinguished themselves during the Second World War by the order of People's Commissar for Defence of USSR No.303, instituted on the 18 September 1941, with accredited units considered to have élite status.

25. Author interview with Andreas Fleischer, *3. SS-Panzerdivision 'Totenkopf'*.

26. Holmes, Richard, *World at War*, p524, interview with *SS-Standartenführer* Wilhelm Osterholz.

27. The fuel capacity of a Panther was 160 gallons, enough to cover 200 kilometres on road, and 100 kilometres cross-country – both without any fighting.

28. Williams, Andrew, *D-Day to Berlin*, p266.

29. Meyer, Kurt, *Grenadiere*, p308.

30. Ibid, p334.

31. Hastings, Max, *Armageddon*, p268. The *Hohenstaufen* officer was writing to his old comrade, Otto Skorzeny.

32. Griesser, Volker, *The Lions of Carentan*, p217. Heydte later claimed that 'Never in my entire career had I been in command of a unit with less fighting spirit.' This extremely negative judgement contrasted with some of his statements at the time.

33. Atkinson, Rick, *The Guns at Last Light*, p443.

34. Forty, George, *The Reich's Last Gamble*, p119.

35. Beevor, Antony, *Ardennes*, p109.

36. Hagen, Louis, *Ein Volk, Ein Reich*, p39.

37. Eriksson, Patrick G., *Alarmstart South and Final Defeat*, p210.

38. Whiting, Charles, '*44*, p181.

39. Villani, Gerry, *Voices of the Waffen-SS*, p112.

40. Neitzel, Sönke and Welzer, Harald, *Soldaten*, p275, recording of *Major* Frank, *FJR. 16.*

41. Hastings, Max, *Armageddon*, p94, interview with *Hauptmann* Walter Schäfer-Kehnert, *9. Panzerdivision.*

42. Reynolds, Michael, *The Devil's Adjutant*, p99.

43. Reynolds, Michael, *Men of Steel*, p68

44. Ibid, p63.

45. Meyer, Kurt, *Grenadiere*, p335.

46. Beevor, Antony, *Ardennes*, p167.

47. Ibid, p184, interview with *SS-Rottenführer* Straub of *LSSAH's* reconnaissance battalion.

48. Holmes, Richard, *World at War*, p300, interview with German Red Cross nurse, Frau Chantrain.

49. Beevor, Antony, *Ardennes*, p251.

50. Williams, Andrew, *D-Day to Berlin*, p281.

51. Villani, Gerry, *Voices of the Waffen-SS*, p240, interview with an officer candidate in the *LSSAH.*

52. Atkinson, Rick, *The Guns at Last Light*, p464.

53. Villani, Gerry, *Voices of the Waffen-SS*, p112, interview with Heinrich, an NCO in the *Hohenstaufen.*

54. Holmes, Tony (editor), *Dogfight*, p266.

55. Ibid, p246.

56. Ibid, p123.

57. *Der Grosse Schlag* was meant to consist of JGs 1, 4, 7, 11, 16, 17, 76, 300 and 301, leaving 2, 26, 27 and 53 in the West, and 5, 51, 52 and 54 in the East.

58. Reynolds, Michael, *The Devil's Adjutant*, p120.

59. Reynolds, Michael, *Men of Steel*, p105.

60. Reynolds, Michael, *The Devil's Adjutant*, p149.

61. Ibid, p163. The building marked with the Red Cross was the former abbey and it was indeed being used as a hospital, hospice and orphanage, however a part of it was not being used by any of those functions, and it was from there that the Americans were firing. Pfeifer and his men can be forgiven for being unable to distinguish the difference in the heat of battle.

62. Reynolds, Michael, *The Devil's Adjutant*, p216, interview with Erich Makamul.

63. One of Peiper's Tiger IIs – number 213 – still stands in La Gleize, off the high street, just outside the museum dedicated to the battle.

64. Reynolds, Michael, *Sons of the Reich*, p224.

65. Ibid, p235.
66. Reynolds, Michael, *Men of Steel*, p165.
67. Williamson, Gordon, *Loyalty is my Honour*, p139.
68. Williams, Andrew, *D-Day to Berlin*, p287.
69. Landau, Sigmund Heinz, *Goodbye Transylvania*, p89.
70. Villani, Gerry, *Voices of the Waffen-SS*, p112, interview with Heinrich, an NCO in the *Hohenstaufen*.
71. Williams, Andrew, *D-Day to Berlin*, p289.
72. Hastings, Max, *Armageddon*, p97.

Chapter Six: Last Gasps in the West

1. Hastings, Max, *Armageddon*, p189, *Leutnant* Rolf-Helmut Schröder of *18. VGD*.
2. Williams, Andrew, *D-Day to Berlin*, p297, SS-Hauptsturmführer Hans Bernhard.
3. Interview with Johann-Adolf Graf von Kielmansegg.
4. Eriksson, Patrick G., *Alarmstart South and Final Defeat*, p215.
5. Accurate figures for both Allied and German losses for *Bodenplatte* are disputed; some estimates are as high as over 350 Allied aircraft destroyed, whereas Antony Beevor puts it as low as 167 destroyed and 111 damaged – a number Michael Reynolds also uses. Mike Spick is at the two hundred mark.
6. This was in actual fact the 827th Tank Destroyer Battalion. Plagued by inadequate training and equipment, the battalion suffered from discipline problems from its inception. While some of its members fought creditably that January, there were cases of drunkenness, and one officer was shot after shooting one of his own men.
7. Scho-Ka-Kola was – and is – a popular German brand of bitter-sweet dark chocolate containing caffeine and kola nuts.

Chapter Seven: Avalanche in the East

1. Wacker, Albrecht, *Sniper on the Eastern Front*, p143.
2. Neitzel, Sönke and Welzer, Harald, *Soldaten*, p5, recording of POW Müller.
3. Blosfelds, Lisa (ed), *Stormtrooper on the Eastern Front*, p157.
4. Pencz, Rudolf, *For the Homeland!* p10.
5. Gunter, Georg, *Last Laurels*, p255.
6. Ibid, p76.
7. Carruthers, Bob (ed), *The U-Boat War in the Atlantic*, p198.
8. Guderian, Heinz, *Panzer Leader*, p382.
9. Friesen, Bruno, *Panzer Gunner*, p148. Friesen was born in Kitchener, Ontario to German parents who sent him to the Reich before the war in 1939 to learn about his native land. Called up in late 1942, he was awarded the Iron Cross 2nd Class and the *Panzerkampfabzeichen* (Panzer Combat Badge) in Silver while fighting in Lithuania in September 1944. Despite the title of his book he was initially trained as a driver and not a gunner.

10. Author interview with André Bayle. Bayle joined the Waffen-SS in 1943 as a sixteen-year-old volunteer.
11. Friesen, Bruno, *Panzer Gunner*, p174.
12. Korschorrek, Günter, *Blood Red Snow*, p290.
13. Author interview with Julien Hertenweg.
14. Williams, Andrew, *D-Day to Berlin*, p298.
15. Hagen, Louis, *Ein Volk, Ein Reich*, p113 – interview with Hermann Voss.
16. Gunter, Georg, *Last Laurels*, p106.
17. Ibid, p66.
18. Ibid, p242.
19. Ibid, p139.
20. Guderian, Heinz, *Panzer Leader*, p417.
21. Reynolds, Michael, *Men of Steel*, p210.
22. Meyer, Kurt, *Grenadiers*, p337.
23. Williamson, Gordon, *Loyalty is my Honour*, p101, interview with Hans-Gerhard Starck.
24. As ever with Soviet casualties in the Russo-German war, it is incredibly difficult to get accurate figures given Moscow's desire to downplay them. Atkinson quotes a figure of four hundred thousand killed, wounded and missing, while Hastings opts for two hundred thousand – I have plumped for the middle ground.

Chapter Eight: Italy – Reaching the Top of the Boot

1. Holland, James, *Italy's Sorrow*, p500.
2. Ibid, p498.
3. Ibid, p367.
4. Ibid, p394.
5. Ibid, p410.
6. Ibid, p526.

Chapter Nine: Remagen and the Rhine

1. Hastings, Max, *Armageddon*, p213.
2. Atkinson, Rick, *Guns at Last Light*, p491. The ongoing struggle to man the British Army wasn't helped by its perception in the minds of potential recruits. A perception the historian Jeremy Crang described in his book *The British Army and the People's War, 1939-1945*, as '...the British Army being the least popular service compared to the Royal Navy and RAF, a higher proportion of Army recruits were said to be dull and backwards.' There were also the equivalent of eight full British infantry divisions fighting in the Far East at the time in Bill Slim's 'Forgotten' Fourteenth Army, as well as the British Eighth Army in Italy, and the 80-90,000 strong British expeditionary force in Greece.
3. Carruthers, Bob, *Voices from the Luftwaffe*, p123.

4. The Kriegsmarine divers were so-called '*K-Männer*', members of the all-volunteer '*Klein Kampf Verbände*' – or 'Small Battle Units' – modelled on the Italian Prince Borghese's *Decima Flottiglia MAS (Decima Flottiglia Motoscafi Armati Siluranti*, also known as *La Decima* or *X MAS*, '10th Assault Vehicle Flotilla) that utilised human torpedoes, speed boats and midget submarines against enemy shipping. *K-Männer* were used against the D-Day landings and Allied shipping in the Scheldt estuary with mixed results; one attack in the Scheldt on New Years' Eve 1944 saw only two *Seehund* midget submarines return from the original eighteen. A frogmen attack with mines succeeded in putting the lock gates at Antwerp harbour out of action for several weeks sometime later, and most famously the Nijmegen railway bridge was attacked during the night of Friday 29 September. Twelve frogmen – one an ex-Olympic swimmer – strapped sixteen-foot long explosive tubes to the bridge piers before struggling ashore, exhausted, where ten were captured. Sergeant Max Hearst of the 5th East Yorkshires was present at the time: 'We dug in both sides and held the position for a number of days. Frogmen came up the river to blow the bridge, but they were spotted in time and shot in the water.' Despite Hearst's vigilance, at 6.30am the next morning the mines went off, destroying the central span of the railway bridge and ripping an eighty-foot hole in the road bridge.

5. Neitzel, Sönke and Welzer, Harald, *Soldaten*, p254, recording of *General der Panzertruppe* Heinrich Eberbach.

Chapter Ten: West & East

1. Biddiscombe, Perry, *The Last Nazis*, p175.
2. Ibid, p63.
3. Hagen, Louis, *Ein Volk, Ein Reich*, p212 – interview with Hildegard Trutz.
4. Reynolds, Michael, *Sons of the Reich*, p259.
5. Reynolds, Michael, *Men of Steel*, p206.
6. Reynolds, Michael, *Sons of the Reich*, p270.
7. Reynolds, Michael, *Men of Steel*, p239.
8. Author interview with Erik Brörup.
9. Friesen, Bruno, *Panzer Gunner*, p178.
10. Verton, Hendrik, *In the Fire of the Eastern Front*, p161.
11. Author interview with Lucie Lefever.
12. As many as forty members of the so-called 'British Free Corps' were sent to reinforce the Waffen-SS *Nordland* Division, with most of the first batch allocated to a platoon whose members were mainly Swedes. Not many of these British turncoats were enthusiastic about actually fighting, and most tried to get out of it. One of them – Kenneth Edward Berry – deserted and was later taken prisoner by the Soviets. Berry, an ex-merchant seaman, had been captured by the Germans back in 1940 at the tender age of fourteen, when his ship had been sunk by a German raider.
13. Korschorrek, Günter, *Blood Red Snow*, p300.

14. Maeger, Herbert, *Lost Honour, Betrayed Loyalty*, p194. Maeger was just eighteen years old when he enlisted in the *SS-Leibstandarte*. Having served on the Russian front, he was overheard making a defeatist remark and sent as punishment to the notorious *SS-Dirlewanger Division*.

Chapter Eleven: It's All Over

1. The assassin who pulled the trigger – *SS-Unterscharführer* Josef 'Sepp' Leitgeb, a thirty-year-old Austrian veteran of the Russian front – tried to make it back to German lines only to step on a landmine – he was killed instantly.
2. Williams, Andrew, *D-Day to Berlin*, p314 – *Feldwebel* Otto Henning of the *Panzer-Lehr-Division*.
3. Neitzel, Sönke and Welzer, Harald, *Soldaten*, p271.
4. As always it is difficult to get wholly accurate figures, particularly in the chaos of the last few months of the war. This is also true of the number of general officers, with Rick Atkinson stating the number to be twenty-four, and Andrew Williams says twenty-five – others go as high as twenty-nine – although all agree it was only one admiral. I have plumped for Williams's figure.
5. Williams, Andrew, *D-Day to Berlin*, p316.
6. Atkinson, Rick, *The Guns at Last Light*, p584. The aide in question refused to divulge the grave location when interrogated by the Allies. Ten years after the war he took Model's son Hansgeorg there, whereupon his son had the body disinterred and re-buried in the military cemetery at Vossenack.
7. Ibid, p513.
8. Villani, Gerry, *Voices of the Waffen-SS*, p240.
9. Lucas, James, *Kommando*, p211.
10. Biddiscombe, Perry, *The Last Nazis*, p234.
11. Meyer, Kurt, *Grenadiers*, p347.
12. Grass – a Nobel Laureate - knew what he was talking about. Long the doyen of left-wing post-war German literature, he outed himself as a wartime member of the Waffen-SS in 2006, explaining he had unsuccessfully volunteered to serve in U-boats, before becoming a panzer gunner in *10. SS-Panzerdivision 'Frundsberg'*.
13. Hagen, Louis, *Ein Volk, Ein Reich*, p40.
14. Eugène Vaulot was killed in action in Berlin. François Appolot – in one of the insane twists somehow so common in the war – was at the time a card-carrying member of the *Parti Communiste Français*.
15. Korschorrek, Günter, *Blood Red Snow*, p311.
16. Biddiscombe, Perry, *The Last Nazis*, p238.
17. Ibid, p88.
18. Von Rosen, Richard Freiherr, *Panzer Ace*, p357.
19. Neitzel, Sönke and Welzer, Harald, *Soldaten*, p209. Recording of Martin Vetter and Anton Wöffen.

Select Bibliography

I would especially like to thank the following for the interviews they have given me over the years or for answering my innumerable questions:

Rudolf von Ribbentrop, Oswald Van Ooteghem, Dries Coolens, Werner Block, Jan Munk, Ivar Corneliussen, Julien Hertenweg, Bjørn Østring, Bjørn Lindstad, Stal Munkeberg, Asbjørn Narmo, Hermann van Gyseghem, Albert Olbrechts, André Bayle, Robert Soulat, Theo D'Oosterlinck, Lucie Lefever, Karin Matre, Elizabeth Kvaal, Andreas Fleischer, Magnus Møller, Vagner Kristiansen, Bjarne Dramstad, thank you.

Arthur, Max, *Forgotten Voices of the Second World War*, Ebury 2004

Atkinson, Rick, *The Guns at Last Light, The War in Western Europe, 1944-1945*, Abacus 2013

Bacyk, Norbert (translated by Tim Dinan), *The Tank Battle at Praga July-September 1944*, Leandoer & Ekholm 2006

Bartmann, Erwin (translated by Derik Hammond), *Für Volk and Führer*, Helion 2013

Beevor, Antony, *Arnhem*, Viking 2018

Beevor, Antony, *Berlin: The Downfall 1945*, Penguin 2002

Beevor, Antony, *Ardennes 1944; Hitler's Last Gamble*, Viking 2015

Biddiscombe, Perry, *The Last Nazis – SS Werewolf Guerilla Resistance in Europe 1944-1947*, Tempus 2004

Bishop, Chris, *SS: Hell on the Western Front*, Spellmount 2003

Blosfelds, Mintauts (edited by Lisa Blosfelds), *Stormtrooper on the Eastern Front – Fighting with Hitler's Latvian SS*, Pen & Sword 2008

Carruthers, Bob, *Voices from the Luftwaffe*, Pen & Sword 2012

Coolens, Dries, *My time with the Legion Flanders and the Division Langemarck (Flemish Nr. 1)*, self-published 2018

Cooper, Matthew & Lucas, James, *Panzer – The armoured force of the Third Reich*, Book Club 1979

Cornish, Nik, *Armageddon Ost: The German Defeat on the Eastern Front 1944-5*, Ian Allan 2006

Darman, Peter (editor), *Victory in Europe: Day by Day*, Brown Bear 2013

Davies, Norman, *Europe At War 1939-1945: No Simple Victory*, Macmillan 2006

De Zayas, Alfred-Maurice, *A terrible revenge: The ethnic cleansing of the East European Germans*, Palgrave Macmillan 2006

Eriksson, Patrick G., *Alarmstart South and Final Defeat: The German Fighter Pilot's Experience in the Mediterranean Theatre, 1941–1944 and over Normandy, Germany and Norway, 1944–1945*, Amberley 2019

Evans, Richard, J., *The Third Reich At War*, Allen Lane 2008

Fischer, Wolfgang (edited & translated by John Weal), *Luftwaffe Fighter Pilot – Defending the Reich*, Grub 2010

Fitzgerald, Michael, *Hitler's Secret Weapons of Mass Destruction*, Arcturus 2018

Forbes, Robert, *Pour L'Europe*, self-published 2000

Forty, George, *The Reich's Last Gamble: The Ardennes Offensive, December 1944, Cassell 2000*

Friesen, Bruno, *Panzer Gunner*, Helion 2008

Fürbringer, Herbert, *La Hohenstaufen: 9. SS Panzer Division 1944: Normandy, Tarnapol-Arnhem*, Heimdal 2002

Galland, Adolf, *The First and the Last*, Blurb 2018

Griesser, Volker (translated by Mara Taylor), *The Lions of Carentan: Fallschirmjäger Regiment 6, 1943-1945*, Casemate 2011

Grund, Helmut (edited by Stephen R. Pastore), *The Confession of Helmut Grund: Waffen-SS Cavalry*, American Bibliographical Press, 2017

Guderian, Heinz (translated by Constantine Fitzgibbon), *Panzer Leader*, Michael Joseph 1952

Gunter, Georg (translated by C.F. Colton, MA), *Last Laurels: The German Defence of Upper Silesia January-May 1945*, Helion 2002

Hagen, Louis, *Ein Volk, Ein Reich – Nine Lives Under the Nazis*, Spellmount 2011

Hessler, Günther (edited by Bob Carruthers), *The U-Boat War in the Atlantic volume III: 1944-1945*, Pen & Sword 2013

Hillblad, Thorolf (editor), *Twilight of the Gods: A Swedish Waffen-SS Volunteer's Experiences with the 11th SS-Panzergrenadier Division 'Nordland' Eastern Front 1944-45*, Helion 2004

Holmes, Richard, *The World at War*, Ebury 2007

Holmes, Richard, *Battlefields of the Second World War*, BBC 2003

Holmes, Tony (editor), *Dogfight – the greatest air duels of World War II*, Osprey 2011

Hooton, E.R., *Eagle in Flames – The Fall of the Luftwaffe*, Arms & Armour 1997

Kaufmann, Johannes (translated by John Weal), *An Eagle's Odyssey; My Decade as a pilot in Hitler's Luftwaffe*, Greenhill 2019

Kershaw, Robert J., *It Never Snows in September*, Crowood Press 1994

King, Martin, *The Battle of the Bulge: Hitler's Final Gamble in Western Europe*, Arcturus 2019

Klapdor, Ewald, *Viking Panzers: The German 5th SS Tank Regiment in the East in World War II*, Stackpole 2011

Knoke, Heinz (translated by John Ewing), *I Flew for the Führer; The Story of a German Airman*, Evans Brothers 1953

Korschorrek, Günter K. (translated by Olav R. Crome-Aamot), *Blood Red Snow, The Memoirs of a German soldier on the Eastern Front*, Greenhill 2011

Kurowski, Franz (translated by Fred Steinhardt), *Bridgehead Kurland: The Six Epic Battles of Heeresgruppe Kurland*, J. J. Fedorowicz 2002

Landau, Sigmund Heinz, *Goodbye Transylvania – A Romanian Waffen-SS Solider in WWII*, Stackpole 2015

Lindstad, Bjørn, *Den Frivillige – en frontkjemper forteller sin historie*, Kagge 2010

Lowe, Keith, *Savage Continent*, Viking 2012

Lucas, James, *Storming Eagles – German airborne forces in World War II*, Cassell 1988

Lucas, James, *Kommando – German special forces in World War II*, Cassell 1985

Lucas, James, *Das Reich*, Cassell, 1991

Luck, Hans von, *Panzer Commander: The memoirs of Colonel Hans von Luck*, Cassell 1989

Maeger, Herbert (translated by Geoffrey Brooks), *Lost Honour, Betrayed Loyalty – The memoir of a Waffen-SS soldier on the Eastern Front*, Frontline 2015

McNab, Chris, *The Luftwaffe 1933-45, Hitler's Eagles*, Osprey 2012

Metelmann, Henry, *Through Hell for Hitler*, Spellmount 1990

Meyer, Kurt (translated by Michael Mendé and Robert J. Edwards), *Grenadiers*, J.J. Fedorowicz 2001

Michaelis, Rolf, *Cavalry Divisions of the Waffen-SS*, Schiffer 2010

Michaelis, Rolf, *Panzergrenadier Divisions of the Waffen-SS*, Schiffer 2010

Mitcham, Samuel W. Jr, *Eagles of the Third Reich*, Stackpole 1988

Mitcham, Samuel W., *Hitler's Legions: German Army Order of Battle World War II*, Leo Cooper 1985

Mitcham, Samuel W. Jr, *The Siegfried Line*, Stackpole 2009

Møller, Magnus Johannes, *I krig for Danmark*, self-published 2008

Munk, Jan, *I was a Dutch Volunteer*, self-published 2010

Munoz, Antonio, *Iron Fist: A Combat history of the 17th SS Panzergrenadier Götz von Berlichingen*, Axis Europa 1999

Murray, Williamson, *Strategy for Defeat – The Luftwaffe – 1933-1945*, Chartwell 1986

Nash, Douglas E., *Victory was beyond their grasp – with the 272nd Volks-Grenadier Division from the Hürtgen Forest to the Heart of the Reich*, Casemate 2015

Neitzel, Sönke and Welzer, Harald, *Soldaten*, Simon & Schuster 2012

Newton, John (editor, et al), *The Third Reich – Descent into Nightmare*, Time Life 1992

Olsen, Jack, *Silence on Monte Sole*, Pan 1969

Palm, Hakan, O., *Surviving Hitler: The Unlikely Story True Story of an SS Soldier and a Jewish Woman*, Deseret, 2014

Parker, Danny S., (editor), *Hitler's Ardennes Offensive - The German view of the Battle of the Bulge*, Frontline 2016

Pencz, Rudolf (translated by C. F. Colton), *For the Homeland! – the history of the 31st Waffen-Volunteer Grenadier Division*, Helion 2002

Perrett, Bryan, *Knights of the Black Cross*, Robert Hale 1986

Poller, Herbert, Mansson, Martin, Westberg, Lennart (translated by Tim Dinan), *Armoured Reconnaissance with the Waffen-SS on the Eastern Front and the Swedish SS-Platoon in the Baltic states, Pomerania and Berlin, 1943-1945*, Leandoer & Ekholm 2010

Rawson, Andrew, *Battle of the Bulge 1944-45*, Spellmount 2011

Reynolds, Michael, *Sons of the Reich: II SS Panzer Corps*, Spellmount 2002

Reynolds, Michael, *Men of Steel: I SS Panzer Corps - The Ardennes and Eastern Front 1944-45*, Spellmount 1999

Reynolds, Michael, *The Devil's Adjutant – Jochen Peiper, Panzer Leader*, Spellmount 1995

Ribbentrop, Rudolf von, *My father Joachim von Ribbentrop*, self-published 2015

Ritgen, Helmut (translated by Joseph G. Welsh), *The Western Front, 1944: Memoirs of a Panzer Lehr Officer*, J. J. Fedorowicz 1996

Rogers, Duncan and Sarah Williams, *On the Bloody Road to Berlin: Frontline Accounts from North-West Europe and the Eastern Front, 1944-45*, Helion 2005

Roland, Paul, *The Nazis: The rise and fall of history's most evil empire*, Arcturus 2019

Rosen, Richard Freiherr von (translated by Geoffrey Brooks), *Panzer Ace: The Memoirs of a Panzer Commander*, Greenhill 2018

Snyder, Timothy, *Blood Lands; Europe Between Hitler and Stalin*, Vintage 2010

Taylor, Brian, *Barbarossa to Berlin Volume Two: The Defeat of Germany, 19 November 1942 to 15 May 1945*, Spellmount 2004

Thorn, Manfred, *Von der Leibstandarte zum Sündenbock und Prügelknaben*, Nation & Wissen Verlag 2016

Umbrich, Friedrich, (translated by Anna M. Wittmann), *Balkan Nightmare*, Columbia University Press, 2000

Ungvary, Kristian, *Battle for Budapest: 100 Days in World War II*, I. B. Tauris 2005

Verton, Hendrik C., (translated by Hazel Toon-Thon), *In the fire of the Eastern Front – The experiences of a Dutch Waffen-SS volunteer on the Eastern Front 1941-45*, Helion 2007

Villani, Gerry, *Voices of the Waffen-SS*, self-published 2015

Voss, Johann, *Black Edelweiss – A memoir of combat and conscience by a soldier of the Waffen-SS*, Aberjona 2002

Wacker, Albrecht, *Sniper on the Eastern Front – The Memoirs of Sepp Allerberger*, Pen & Sword 2005

Werner, Herbert, *Iron Coffins*, Da Capo Press 2002

Whiting, Charles, *'44 – In Combat on the Western Front from Normandy to the Ardennes*, Century Publishing 1984

Whiting, Charles, *Siegfried – The Nazis' Last Stand,* Leo Cooper 1983

Whiting, Charles, *Werewolf – The Nazi Resistance Movement 1944-1945*, Pan 2002

Williamson, Gordon, *Loyalty is my Honor*, Motorbooks 1997

Other books by the author:

Hitler's Gauls – The History of the French Waffen-SS
Hitler's Flemish Lions – The History of the Flemish Waffen-SS
Hitler's Jihadis – The History of the Muslim Waffen-SS
Hitler's Vikings – The History of the Scandinavian Waffen-SS
Hastings 1066
Death on the Don: The Destruction of Germany's Allies on the Eastern Front 1941-44 (nominated for the Pushkin Prize for Russian history)
The Defeat of the Luftwaffe – The Eastern Front 1941-45; Strategy for Disaster
Voices of the Flemish Waffen-SS: The Last Testament of the Oostfronters
Voices of the Scandinavian Waffen-SS: The Last Testament of Hitler's Vikings
D-Day Through German Eyes: How the Wehrmacht Lost France

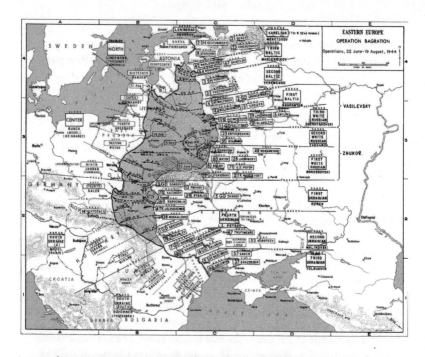

EASTERN EUROPE
OPERATION BAGRATION

Operations, 22 June–19 August, 1944

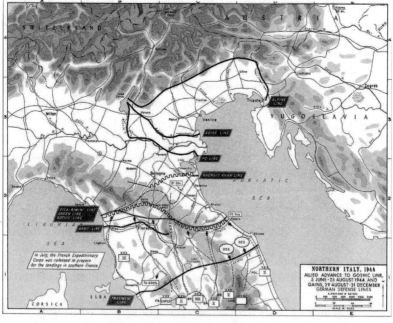

In July, the French Expeditionary Corps was released to prepare for the landings in southern France.

NORTHERN ITALY, 1944
ALLIED ADVANCE TO GOTHIC LINE
5 JUNE–25 AUGUST 1944 AND
GAINS, 29 AUGUST–31 DECEMBER
GERMAN DEFENSE LINES

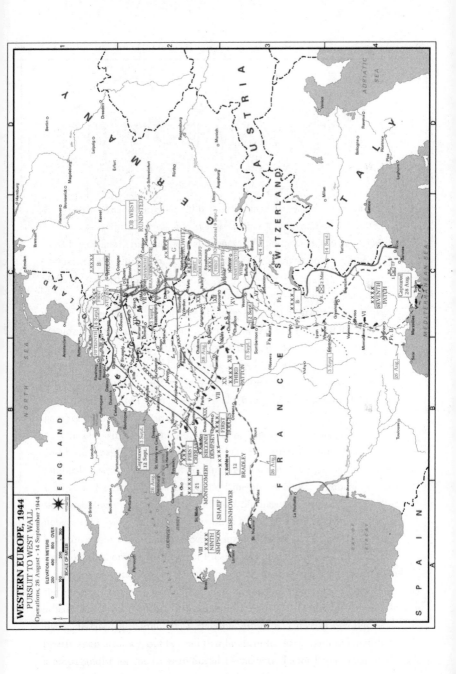

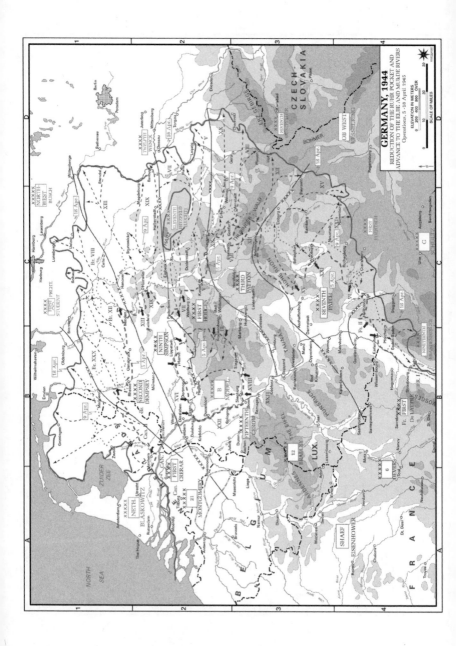

GERMANY, 1944
REDUCTION OF THE RUHR POCKET AND
ADVANCE TO THE ELBE AND MULDE RIVERS
Operations, 5–18 April 1945

ELEVATION IN METERS
0   200 400 600 OVER

0   10   20   30
SCALE OF MILES

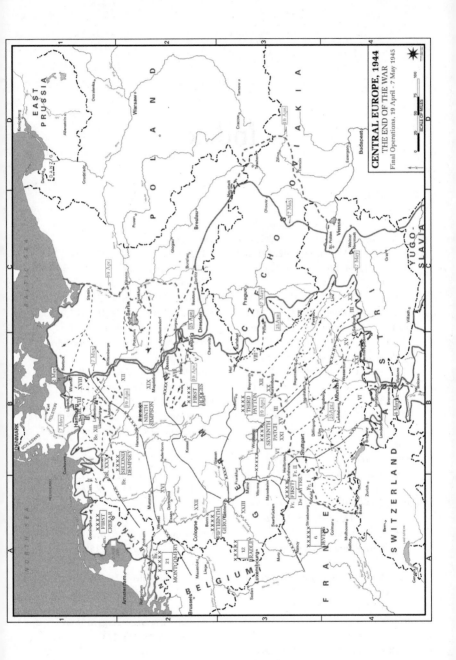

CENTRAL EUROPE, 1944
THE END OF THE WAR
Final Operations, 19 April - 7 May 1945

SCALE OF MILES
0   25   50   75   100

Index